THE HARP THAT ONCE—

PORTRAIT OF MOORE BY SIR THOMAS LAWRENCE

THE
HARP THAT ONCE–

A Chronicle of the Life of Thomas Moore

HOWARD MUMFORD JONES

Posterity sees less or sees more. A few points stand forth in distinct
rigidity; there is no idea of the countless accumulation, the collision of
action, the web of human feeling, with which, in the day of their life,
they were encompassed.

—Walter Bagehot

NEW YORK / RUSSELL & RUSSELL

COPYRIGHT, 1937, BY HENRY HOLT AND COMPANY, INC.
COPYRIGHT RENEWED, 1965, BY HOWARD MUMFORD JONES
REISSUED, 1970, BY RUSSELL & RUSSELL
A DIVISION OF ATHENEUM PUBLISHERS, INC.
BY ARRANGEMENT WITH HOWARD MUMFORD JONES
L. C. CATALOG CARD NO: 75-102508
PRINTED IN THE UNITED STATES OF AMERICA

The harp that once through Tara's halls
  The soul of music shed
Now hangs as mute on Tara's walls,
  As if that soul were fled.

Preface

THE chief source of information about the life of Tom Moore is the *Memoirs, Journal, and Correspondence of Thomas Moore*, edited by Lord John Russell in eight volumes (1853-1856). Lord John was both a busy statesman and a careless editor. Motives of prudence led him to suppress or change a great many passages in the original manuscript, and Moore's habit of not dating his letters, or dating them only by days of the week, did not make the noble editor's task any easier. Now that those who are mentioned in the diary and the correspondence have passed from the scene, it would be possible to supply the omissions, were it not for the fact that, according to information furnished me by Mr. W. A. Kelk of the firm of Longmans, the originals were destroyed at some time close to the opening of the present century. One is therefore forced back upon the eight volumes for good or ill. In addition, Moore himself furnished autobiographical prefaces to the ten-volume edition of his *Poetical Works*, nine volumes of which appeared by 1841. There is some slight bibliographical mystery about the tenth volume, my copy being dated 1848. Some of this autobiographical material reappears in the "Memoirs of Myself" with which the first volume of Lord John Russell's monumental series opens, and which John Wilson Croker, in his celebrated article in the *Quarterly Review* (Vol. XCIII, pp. 239-310) found so unreliable. On the whole, however, both the "Memoirs of Myself" and the prefaces check fairly well with what external evidence can be brought to bear upon them;

at any rate, they are the chief source of information for the poet's early years.

In addition to these printed sources, two other publications have special value. These are *Prose and Verse Humorous, Satirical, and Sentimental by Thomas Moore, with suppressed passages from the Memoirs of Lord Byron, chiefly from the Author's Manuscript, and all hitherto inedited and uncollected,* London, 1878; and *Notes from the Letters of Thomas Moore to his Music Publisher, James Power, (the publication of which were suppressed in London.) With an Introductory Letter from Thomas Crofton Croker, Esq.,* etc., etc., New York [1854]. The first was edited by Richard Herne Shepherd, and contains a number of Moore's compositions not included in the *Poetical Works.* The "suppressed passages from the Memoirs of Lord Byron" are not from the memoirs of Byron at all, but are simply unused notes left over from Moore's biography. This volume also contains a fragment of an unpublished prose tale, and several letters, chiefly to Leigh Hunt, which are not in Russell. The second volume is in fact an American reprint of a sales catalogue of Moore's letters (1853), a copy of which is in the British Museum; it is prefaced by a letter of Thomas Crofton Croker, who was aggrieved because he was not appointed to write the official biography of Moore, and who thought that Lord John Russell and Bessy Moore, the poet's wife, had treated the heirs of James Power, the music publisher, shabbily.

In addition, *A Bibliographical Hand-List of the First Editions of Thomas Moore,* by M. J. MacManus, Dublin, 1934, has great value. This first appeared serially in *The Dublin Magazine* for July and September, 1933, and is the first attempt at a scientific bibliography of the poet's writings. Although I have differed from Mr. MacManus's conclusions once or twice, his list is invaluable to the biographer of the poet; and I have also to thank him for many personal courtesies. Other printed source material will appear during the course of this biography, but I cannot conclude this paragraph without expressing my obligation to the life of Moore by Stephen Gwynn in the English Men of Letters series. Widely as I differ from Mr. Gwynn in a number of my conclusions, this little book has been a guide through the mass of materials I have consulted, without which my labors would have been doubled.

Moore's letters and manuscripts are widely dispersed, the least valuable portion of them being, oddly enough, in Ireland. I have not, however, been able to consult the Trinity College, Dublin, collection, but the Moore material in the National Library and in the Royal Irish Academy is not of first importance, with the notable exception that the Royal Irish Academy houses a great portion of the poet's library, and from Moore's annotations on the margins of his books it is sometimes possible to learn of his habits of work and of the sources of his prose and poetry. For the rest, the manuscript material is scattered among the major libraries of the English-speaking world, and I cannot pretend to have seen all of it. Collections of special importance are those in the Henry E. Huntington Library, the Pierpont Morgan Library, and the British Museum. In addition, the William L. Clements Library of American History houses the John Wilson Croker papers and the correspondence of John Gibson Lockhart; and among the Croker papers is a long correspondence between John Wilson Croker and Thomas Crofton Croker, in which the latter supplied the former with information which John Wilson Croker partly used in his review of Lord John Russell. The unpublished portion of this correspondence has been of first importance for the light it throws, scanty and dim though it be, on the Dyke family. The Lord John Russell papers in the Public Records Office are also useful, especially for Moore's closing years and those of his wife.

Almost every prominent person in the first fifty years of the last century said something about Moore either as a personality or as a poet. For example, there are innumerable references to Moore in the collected edition of Hazlitt edited by Mr. P. P. Howe. To have attempted to include all such material, supposing I could find it, in the present volume would have swelled the book immeasurably. I have therefore contented myself with such extracts from contemporary opinion as throw light upon Moore's reputation in his life, but I have not attempted an exhaustive study of his literary fame.

I am under obligations to so many persons that I despair of enumerating them. I must, however, record my indebtedness to Mrs. Guy Maier of Ann Arbor; to Professor John P. Dawson of the University of Michigan; to Senator Oliver St. John Gogarty of Dublin; to Walter Connelly, Esq., of the American University Union, London; to the Rev. E. R. P. Devereux of Kegworth; to the Rev. Arthur E. G. Peters of Bremhill; to Alfred Sutro, Esq., of San Francisco; to Professor Campbell Bonner of the University of Michigan; to Henry Wadsworth Longfellow Dana, Esq., of Cambridge, Massachusetts; to Lord Ilchester; to Professor Stanley Williams of Yale; to Christopher Cheney, Esq., now of the University of Manchester, for procuring me copies of Moore materials in the Rylands Library; to Miss E. Jones-Bateman, for permitting me to inspect the Bowles-Moore correspondence; to Lord Lansdowne, for giving me generous access to the Moore materials at Bowood; to Bertrand Russell, Esq., for his kindness in uncovering letters by Moore, Bessy, and Thomas Longman in the possession of the Russell family; to Sir John Murray, for giving me access to the Moore correspondence in his office; to W. A. Kelk of Longmans for searching the records of that famous publishing house for me, discovering, among other things, Moore's suppressed book; to Thomas Conolly, Esq., of Chicago, for a copy of Moore's school certificate; to Senator Miss Kathleen A. Browne of Wexford, for invaluable assistance with the Wexford records of the Codd family; to Cyril J. Palmer, Esq., of Plymouth, for finding the birth certificate of Bessy Dyke; and to M. H.

Spielmann, Esq., of Uplands, Folkestone, Kent, for a rare portrait of Moore. Where so many persons have shown unwearying kindness, it is invidious to single out any, but I must record my gratitude for the patient interest of C. H. Collins Baker, Esq., now of the Henry E. Huntington Library, for many kindnesses in England; and to James Montgomery, Esq., of Wellington Lodge, Booterstown, County Dublin, for so frequently answering my inquiries about Irish life that without his aid I should have committed many an error. It is my great regret that some of the persons in this list are no longer living to see this acknowledgment of their aid.

I am also under a debt of gratitude to the John Simon Guggenheim Memorial Foundation and to the Research Fund of the University of Michigan for subsidies which made this book possible; and to the officers and staffs of the National Library of Ireland, the Royal Irish Academy, the Henry E. Huntington Library, the University of Michigan Library, the British Museum, the New York Public Library, the Virginia Historical Society, the Valentine Museum, the Bermuda Historical Society, the William L. Clements Library of American History, the Pierpont Morgan Library, the Bodleian Library, the Public Records Office, and the Widener Library for much helpful aid and for permitting me in many cases to reproduce material in their possession.

Most phrases expressive of one's sense of obligation have an unfortunately shopworn air. There is of course the celebrated (and apocryphal) story of the author who dedicated his book to his wife, in spite of whom it was written. The present page, however, must record an indebtedness of an opposite sort to "my poor Bessy," whose patient hand has gone to the shaping of every chapter, and without whose penitential reading in the files of innumerable magazines this book would have lost half its substance and much of its interest.

HOWARD MUMFORD JONES.

Harvard University
March 17, 1937

Illustrations

THE HARP THAT ONCE—

Chapter 1

O N SATURDAY, May 29, 1779, the *Dublin Evening Post* informed the nobility and gentry that the lady of Michael Sweeny, Esq., in Aungier-Street was delivered of a son, and that the Rt. Hon. Lady Anne Talbot in Mount-Talbot had also blessed her lord with an heir. Readers learned that General Burgoyne's conduct was to be looked into, that Timothy Tracy had read a public recantation from the errors of Rome in the parish church of Monktown, and that Eliza Vipon, Milliner, had removed to No. 8 Castle-Street where, with due "Sentiments of Gratitude" to the public, she proposed to exhibit the "same Care, Attention, and Dispatch" to the trade as she had shown at No. 41. "Hibernicus" spiritedly advised the Earl of Shelburne not to be lukewarm in the cause of Ireland. The *Post*, however, overlooked the most important news of Dublin, which was that Mrs. John Moore of No. 12 Aungier-Street had on May 28 given birth to a boy. This child was christened Thomas, and was to write the *Irish Melodies*. If the *Post* was thus unprophetically negligent, neither *Faulkner's Dublin Journal* nor *The Register, or, Freeman's Journal* did any better.[1] The Moores were people of small importance who lived above a shop which John Moore, grocer and vintner, had come from Kerry to manage, and it was not to be expected that their domestic chronicles would interest the newspapers of the day.

The child was born into the last decades of that comfortable eighteenth-century world which knew no reason why it

3

should ever change. The old dynasties still ruled. A lonely, shrunken, bright-eyed old man of sixty-seven, his dogs his dearest friends, Frederick the Great found time to inform the Prussian Royal Academy in 1778 that he had searched seventeen centuries to find a man of talents equal to Voltaire, and listlessly manoeuvered through a war against Austria, fighting no battles and signing in May, 1779, a treaty which assured the Bavarian succession. Maria Theresa, now sixty-two, accepted defeat, gazed about at her diminished empire, and prepared to die in favor of the well-meaning Joseph II, who, as Frederick said, always took the second step before he took the first. In St. Petersburg the Serbian Adonis, Zoritch, temporarily replacing the eccentric Potemkin, divided the attentions of the great Catherine, now fifty, with her grandchild, the future Czar Alexander, whose education was to be philosophic in the eighteenth-century sense. The petty Italian states slumbered in various modes of picturesque decay; the vain and amiable Pius VI occupied the papal chair; in Portugal the half-mad Maria, married to her uncle, ascended the throne and presently dismissed Pombal, the most intelligent man in her dominions; in Spain Charles III at sixty-three was about to embark on one more international adventure, the Spanish forces beginning their interminable siege of Gibraltar in July. A lank-haired Corsican, age ten, had sulkily entered the military school at Brienne, and Arthur Wesley, also age ten, was playing the violin in London.

The American War had sunk into a queer mixture of apathy and pillage. General Clinton was in New York, where, after sending General Matthews to raid the Virginia towns by way of demonstrating the blessings of royal government, he was contemplating a dash on King's Ferry below West Point. Martha Washington left camp in May because her husband's campaign was about to open, but there was no campaign, the British having thoughtfully flooded the country with counterfeit American currency so that patriot wages sank to unattractive levels. Amid the dissipations of

Philadelphia Benedict Arnold, recently married to Peggy Shippen, was meditating the profitableness of treason; and in harbor at Martinique, D'Estaing, having as usual arrived too late to intercept Admiral Byron's British frigates, was wondering what to do next. George III patiently appealed once more to the better nature of Lord North not to resign from a government he did not believe in; Lord Cornwallis was explaining to the Commons that America was a country of ambuscades at every few yards; Lord George Germaine, who had been courtmartialed at Minden, sat "thoughtfully organizing defeat in the war office," and Lord Sandwich, whose mistress had just been killed by a disappointed lover, was demonstrating his total incompetence to manage the navy. A French fleet held the Channel, to the deep gratification of Vergennes; and around the rising star of Louis XVI a little group of energetic French officials was doing what neither the Grand Monarque nor Napoleon could do—humiliating the British on land and sea. The Whigs were almost as gloomy as the Tories.

The effect in Ireland of British defeat abroad was a series of paradoxes such as only that illogical country could produce. Torn between the Privy Council and the Irish Parliament, a succession of Lords Lieutenant—the Earl of Buckinghamshire occupied the Castle at the moment—struggled irritably to play with dignity the part of Mr. Facing-Both-Ways. The British ministry had denuded the country of troops; and the Earl was puzzled to know what to do with the Volunteers, who, orderly, disciplined, and in strict point of law illegal, were sworn to fight off American privateersmen and French invaders. Invaders, however, were lacking; and their leaders were considering what could be done about that perennial topic, the woes of Erin. The Volunteers were Protestants, who decorated the statue of King William in Dame Street, but inasmuch as they also hauled a couple of cannon to stand beside the idol of the Orangemen, their procedure was, from the Tory point of view, not without inconsistency. The Presbyterians in the north were enthusiastic supporters of the American rebels; the Catholics everywhere else were loyal to the King, but the government, though it winked at occasional Catholic enlistments, continued to insist upon the virtues of the Protestant ascendancy. A Parliament more corruptly managed than that at Westminster was virtuously showing signs of patriotism, and, a minority of a minority, had won the approbation of a majority it did not represent. Having relaxed the Catholic disability laws, Lord North almost in the same breath denied freedom to Irish trade; blind to the lessons of the Boston Tea Party, he seemed perplexed when Irishmen emigrated to join Washington, while in Dublin, as in other cities, Hibernian merchants formed non-importation associations. Nowhere in Europe was there such poverty; but Arthur Young found the upper classes all "gaiety and pleasure, luxury, and extravagance."

The second city in the empire, a strange mixture of appalling wretchedness and social splendor, Dublin basked in the golden afternoon which preceded the twilight of the Union.[2] Architecturally the town was beginning to take on form. The Custom House, with its statues representing "the friendly union of Britannia and Hibernia, with the good consequences resulting to Ireland," had not yet, it is true, arisen beside the Liffey, and the Four Courts were incomplete, but elsewhere Italianate versions of classical architecture adorned the twisting streets. Looking across Essex Bridge up the short new length of Parliament Street, one saw the shining Corinthian columns of the Royal Exchange, which had opened in January; and from the Corinthian portico of Parliament House the figures of Justice, Liberty, and Fortitude stared stonily at the equally Corinthian front of Trinity College. Across the river, Charlemont House adorned Rutland Square; and in Merrion Square (newly fashionable), around St. Stephen's Green, in Harcourt Street, Ely Place, and adjacent areas, stately Georgian mansions lifted their four storeys to the rainy skies. Their exteriors were gracious with "classical" door-ways; the long, oblong windows of the second floor opened here and there on graceful iron balconies; and within, under high ceilings designed by Italian artists or their Irish suc-cessors, gentlemen in white wigs and small-clothes waited by candlelight for the soft tread of beauty down the perfectly proportioned stairs.

When the weather was fine, under the trees along the low wall which fenced in the stone horse of George II, the nobil-ity and gentry sauntered of an evening along the gravel walks of St. Stephen's Green, or else repaired, three times a week in summer, to the gardens behind the Lying-In Hospital to listen to music. Arthur Young found the streets unattractive, "the dirt and wretchedness of the canaille" making walking "a most uneasy and disgusting exercise"; but those who did not own coaches or who did not ride, might hire the Irish ver-sion of chaises (known as noddeys) or even a hackney-coach. The full tide of fashion rose during the sitting of Parlia-ment, when one might hear Grattan or Flood, and the degree of social splendor also depended upon the predilections of the Lord Lieutenant for display, but one might always drive to see fine collections of pictures and curios at Charlemont House, Robert Fitzgerald's home, or the residence of Lord Moira; and one might attend the play in Smock Alley, where the theater was supposed to be "one of the most elegant and commodious in the two kingdoms," its curtain representing a frigate with the legend, "All's well that ends well." There were concerts and oratorios during the season, for Dublin prided itself on its music; and there was always conversation, Richard Twiss gallantly describing the Irish ladies as "ex-tremely well educated and engaging." Perhaps that helped to explain the duels in Phoenix Park of a dewy morning. If the coffee houses numbered only seven or eight, it did not matter, for Irish hospitality expressed itself in lavish dinners and in balls or parties where, as Arthur Young gloomily observed, "the polite circle meet, not to enjoy but to sweat each other." In his opinion there were but four or five houses large enough to "receive a company commodiously," but as he found lodgings dear and not overly clean, it is possible he viewed Dublin with a jaundiced eye.

South of the Liffey and west of the fashionable district lay the dark purlieus of the "Liberties," where, as in the Alsatia of Old London, the Lord Mayor had no authority. In 1798 the Rev. James Whitelaw heroically undertook a census of the city, from which one catches lurid glimpses of the filth and wretchedness in that portion of Dublin.[3] Thirty-two contiguous houses in Plunket Street were found to contain 917 inhabitants, rooms not fifteen feet square housing from ten to sixteen persons of all ages and sexes, stretched "on a wad of filthy straw, swarming with vermin, and without any covering, save the wretched rags that constitute their wearing apparel." A single house in Braithwaite Street contained at one time 108 "souls." Trying to enumerate the inhabitants of a ruinous dwelling near Castle Market, Whitelaw was interrupted by an inundation of putrid blood alive with maggots, which had burst in the back door and filled the lower hall to a depth of several inches; in the garret he found "the entire family of a poor working shoe-maker, seven in number, lying in fever, without a human being to administer to their wants," and the landlord, failing to receive his rent for their "apartment," had ordered them out. In Schoolhouse Lane the entire side of a four-storey house fell in, but some thirty of the wretched occupiers clung to the open ruin, and the landlord claimed, and received, the usual rent. Slaughterhouses, soap factories, distilleries, cow-yards, and dairies indiscriminately mingled with these tenements; and hundreds of alehouses helped the wretched to forget their woes. Sewage was flung into the back yards or dumped openly in the streets, though there was an attempt to drain the town into the Liffey; and in the outskirts Richard Twiss noted the "hovels of dried mud" which sheltered another variety of poverty. The statues of Justice and Fortitude over the entrance to Upper Castle Yard (the English were tactless in the matter of allegory) had much to contemplate; and the dirt, disease, and drunkenness of the poorer parts of Dublin were in odd contrast to the vice-regal presence chamber, its "throne and canopy . . . covered with crimson velvet, richly ornamented with gold lace, and carved-work gilt," its ornate stucco ceiling, and its glass luster (added later) costing two hundred and seventy pounds.

II

The poet's ancestry is veiled in an Irish mist which the labors of genealogists have not dissipated. Moore himself says he never heard his parents speak of their families, though, he adds, "when I came indeed to be somewhat known, there turned up into light a numerous shoal of Kerry cousins . . . who were eager to advance their claims to relationship with me." An uncle, one Garrett Moore, emerges into history long enough to be named, and vanishes. Investigating old Kerry records, a Mr. Hickson of Tralee surmised in 1882 that the Moores were either Anglo-Irish of Elizabethan origin or descendants of the old Irish Moores or O'Moores, who, always intransigent, were pushed gradually westward before the slow spread of English authority.[4] But though Mr. Hickson established a line of Protestant Moores, he did not succeed in connecting them with John Moore, the poet's father. The Rev. H. L. L. Denny vainly sought in 1913 to prove that Thomas Moore was distantly related to a Sir Barry Denny of Tralee.[5] In 1931 Jeremiah King, author of *County Kerry Past and Present*, counted some fifty-three Moore families in that interesting region,[6] but the number only increases uncertainty. In the glamorous sense of the word Tom Moore had no "ancestors."

The neglected burial ground of St. Kevin's Church, Dublin,

gives the inquirer something to work on. For there, among
the tottering gravestones, rises the Moore family monument,
on which he may read:

Sacred to the Memory of John Moore, Esq:
formerly Barrack Master of Island Bridge
in the County of Dublin
Who departed this Life December 17th 1825
aged 84 years
Here is also interred Anastasia Moore,
alias Codd his beloved Wife
Who departed this life May 8th 1832
aged 68 years
Also six of their Children who died young
and their beloved Daughter Ellen
who died February 14th, 1846
Deeply mourned by her brother Thomas Moore
the bard of his much beloved Country, Ireland

This last line is not self-advertisement; it is simply the un-
official title of the author of the *Irish Melodies.*

If the inscription be correct, John Moore must have been
born about 1741 and was therefore thirty-eight or thirty-
nine in 1779, whereas Anastasia Jane Codd Moore must have
been born about 1764 and would have been only fifteen or
sixteen when her son arrived.   That the poet believed his
mother was very young is evident from his own statement.
"It was," Tom writes,

some time in the year 1778, that Anastasia, the eldest daughter of
this Thomas Codd, became the wife of my father, John Moore,
and in the following year I came into the world.   My mother
could not have been much more than eighteen (if so old) at the
time of her marriage, and my father was considerably her senior.
Indeed, I have frequently heard her say to him in her laughing
moods, "You know, Jack, you were an old bachelor when I married you."   At this period, as I always understood, my father kept
a small wine store in Johnson's Court, Grafton Street, Dublin;
the same court, by the way, where I afterwards went to school.
On his marriage, however, having received I rather think some
little money with my mother, he set up business in Aungier

MOORE'S BIRTHPLACE, DUBLIN

Street, No. 12, at the corner of Little Longford Street; and in that house, on the 28th of May, 1779, I was born.[7]

But though there seems little reason to doubt the age of John Moore, the poet was utterly mistaken about his mother's age, as will presently appear.

John Moore was, in the old sense of the word, a respectable man. Cregan's painting of him in the National Portrait Gallery, Dublin, shows very clearly what he was—quiet, dignified, and aware of his own importance. The curly hair just touched with gray, the light, bright eyes under overhanging brows, the full lips, the black neckcloth, dark coat, and plaid waistcoat adorned with a gold watch chain, seal, and key—all bespeak the rising citizen. S. C. Hall, who met him first in 1821 when the elder Moore was eighty, thought him homely; but Bessy Moore, annotating Hall's proofs in 1864, loyally denied the impeachment.[8] John Moore, she says, was "handsome, full of fun, and with good manners." His son tells us that he had a "sanguine nature and quiet humour." He seems likewise to have been "close"—he thought one good suit a year sufficient for any boy, so that Anastasia had to get around him by buying two identical suits. He seems to have shared the rationalism prevalent in eighteenth-century Dublin, for there are traces of a mild anti-clericalism in what we learn of him. He was also a sincere, if unaggressive, patriot.

One's total impression is of a man having good sense, warm natural affections, and some native ability. During Tom's boyhood the grocery shop apparently flourished, for we hear of two clerks being employed; of the purchase of a piano; of a pony for the boy to ride; and of long summers for the children at Sandy Mount. Later (in 1806) it was necessary for the son to solicit from Lord Moira an appointment for his father as barrack-master. Obviously there were affection and sympathy between parent and child. "Surely," John Moore wrote, in the only letter of his which seems to have survived, "no parents had ever such happiness in a child"; [9] and the precocious lad wrote from London in 1799 to the "dearest, best of fathers," much as the man of letters testified at the Dublin public dinner of 1818 that "one-half of the honours heaped upon me" were due to his father for "the education he struggled hard to give me."

Tom was, however, emphatically his mother's boy and in a fair way to be spoiled. He thought, as we have seen, that she was not much older than Juliet at his coming into the world; but her birth certificate (kindly secured by Senator Miss Kathleen A. Browne) shatters the legend, for it shows that she was born and baptized August 27, 1749. She was therefore almost thirty years old when her son was born; and one may reasonably conjecture, in the light of what one knows about eighteenth-century ideas of youth and middle age, that the wild affection she lavished on the boy may be due to the fact that like Samuel he had come when it appeared the Lord had forgotten his handmaid. Certainly her emotional tone was that of Hannah: "My heart rejoiceth in the Lord, mine horn is exalted in the Lord: my mouth is enlarged over mine enemies; because I rejoice in thy salvation." She came from Wexford, where, as the poet remembered, his gouty grandfather, Thomas Codd, lived in the Cornmarket and engaged in the provision trade. More likely, he was a butcher. Thomas Crofton Croker, who exchanged a series of gossipy letters with John Wilson Croker after the poet's death, thought he had discovered that Moore's "father and maternal grandfather were in the Smuggling line—'Free Traders' in short"; [10] but even if true, this casts no reflection on the family, since smuggling was an occupation without dishonor in eighteenth-century Ireland. Apparently the Codds were fairly prosperous, for Anastasia brought some money with her as a dowry, and her interests and ambitions bespeak a woman of considerable pretensions to culture. Moreover, though the Codd genealogy is inextricably confused, the recurrence of the family name in Wexford history indicates that the clan possessed considerable status. As for the Joyce family (Mrs. Moore's mother was a Catherine Joyce), an Aunt Joyce hovers uncertainly over some of Moore's correspondence long enough to be roundly cursed as a trouble-maker—we owe the references to T. C. Croker—but beyond that, little appears. Anastasia, however, had all the charm which the mother of a sentimental poet should possess. When she died, the *Evening Freeman* spoke of her "happy facility of expression" and said her intellect was "of the highest order." "It was impossible to know Mrs. Moore even slightly," according to a writer in the *Dublin University Magazine* the year of Tom Moore's death, "without being pleased with her urbanity, kindness, humour . . . and her intelligent conversation," [11] and all other testimony is to the same effect. A painting of her, exhibited at the Moore Centenary Celebration in Dublin, is not now traceable, but we learn that in person she was small and finely formed, her features resembling (one must get over this as best one can) those of Mrs. Trollope. S. C. Hall, who knew her, speaks of her retiring manner, her "gentle yet sparkling eyes," her "flexible and smiling mouth," and her kindliness. Tom resembled her more than he did his father and for half a century was devoted to her.

Proud of her first-born, Anastasia Moore determined to record the epochal event.[12] As soon as she could, she secured a Spanish milled dollar of 1772, had the coat of arms erased from the obverse, and in the blank thus created caused to be engraved:

Tho:̧ Moore
born
28 May 1779

—

Jane Codd

This she kept by her until a year before her death in 1832, when she gave it to the poet.

Loving gaiety, and socially ambitious for her children, Mrs. Moore flooded the little rooms in Aungier Street under the

gray shadow of St. Patrick's with laughter, music, and conversation. It was a small edition of the great world around
St. Stephen's Green. Struggling artists, amateur musicians—
and all Dublin was musical—half-pay actors, friends and acquaintances likely to help her children came to her supper
parties where the curly-headed infant held (perhaps too
often) the center of the stage. The writer in the *Dublin
University Magazine* already quoted thought that, though
Tom was then "nervous and sensitive to a degree," this in-
fantile social training removed all trace of shyness from the
boy. James D. Herbert, a bohemian artist-actor of twenty,
whose amusing *Irish Varieties* reflects this life, remembers
Tom at three as "an entertaining little fellow" who used to
climb upon his knees.[13] When he was four, Mrs. Moore, who
loved "recitation," and who was intensely patriotic, taught
him a verse satire against Grattan, that statesman having just
accepted a grant of £50,000 from Parliament. He was, said
Moore of himself, "a sort of *show* child," who abandoned
his toys to hear Herbert declaim Shakespeare. At five the
urchin had learned Hamlet's soliloquy on his mother's marriage, which, with droll gravity, he once recited to astonished
guests at one of Herbert's parties. There were those who
thought he would be a second infant Roscius.

III

The baby grew into boyhood surrounded by an atmosphere of music, love, poetry, and patriotism.[14] Dublin could
not forget that, disgusted with British hostility, Handel had
first produced the *Messiah* in Neal's Music Hall, Fishamble
Street, when *Faulkner's Journal* had exclaimed: "Words are
wanting to express the exquisite Delight it afforded to the
admiring crowded Audience." (At Oxford Thomas Hearne
had written bitterly in his diary of Handel "and his lousy
crew.") Gentlemen in wigs and small swords, ladies in
patches and hoops were still chaired to the Capel Street
Theatre to hear Giordani and Lini, to the house in Crow

RECORD OF MOORE'S BIRTH

Street for Michael Kelly in *Cymon,* or to the Rotunda for
the music of Bach and Handel. Lord Mornington, father of
the Duke of Wellington, supported his own orchestra and
wrote compositions for it. Dublin was, said Kelly, the mecca
of foreign musicians in the summer months, having, as he
thought, "much musical excellence" to boast of. It was perhaps the most musical city in the empire.

Taste, however, was changing. The nobility and gentry
still supported the formal masterpieces of the eighteenth century, but "Politics, Gaming, and every species of Dissipation
have so blunted the finer feelings of their Souls," lamented
Walker, "that their warm Devotion has at length degenerated
into cold Neglect." It was not altogether neglect; a consciousness of nationalism made for change. In 1788 Kelly
had popularized a song to Martini's air; later, when he and
Miss Cranch began the duo in Arne's *Artaxerxes,* "Fair
Aurora, prithee stay," a voice cried out with a yawn, "Ah,
then, will ye give us, 'Oh, thou wert born to plaze me,' instead." The populace was making known its desires. Bands
played incessantly the lively and characteristic "Volunteer's
March." Stevenson, the coryphaeus of the new movement,
lately free from his labors in the Trinity Church choir, was
already flooding the ten music publishers of Dublin with his
facile songs, catches, and glees, or incorporating Irish melody
into O'Keefe's ballad opera, *Dead Alive.* This was in 1780;
two years later O'Keefe's *Son-in-Law* included some of Carolan's airs in the score, and next year *The Poor Soldier* had
more of them. When Robert Owenson (the father of Lady
Morgan) opened his National Theatre in 1783, the overture
was composed entirely of Irish music. Inevitably, of course,
the influence of Handel, Haydn, and Mozart "polished" the
native airs out of resemblance to their original forms, but the
thrill of patriotism compensated for the loss in authenticity.

The flood of universal melody engulfed the little rooms in
Aungier Street. Music, said Moore, was "the only art for
which in my own opinion, I was born with a real natural

love; my poetry, such as it is, having sprung out of my deep feeling for music," a statement which is a clue to his success and failure as a poet. One of the earliest evidences of this passion is Moore's picture of himself as a very small boy sitting under the table at Miss Dodd's tea party, a small barrel-organ anxiously clasped in his lap, waiting to astonish the company with mysterious harmonies. An old harpsichord which his father had taken on a debt succeeded the barrel-organ; with the aid of the piano-tuner's boy, Tom learned to pick out simple melodies with his right hand. Afterwards, when the harpsichord, at Mrs. Moore's insistence, was exchanged for a piano, Tom and his sister Catherine were given lessons by William Warren. It was early discovered that the lad possessed "an agreeable voice," and he began as a child that long career of singing in company which makes him unique among British poets. He learned easily. Still a child, he sang the duets in a children's production of *The Poor Soldier* with a little girl named Fanny Ryan, with whom he fancied himself in love. The small drawingrooms over the shop, "distended to their utmost capacity" on social occasions, overflowed with rollicking Irishmen—Wesley Doyle of the "sweet and touching voice"; his boon companion, Joe Kelly, brother of the great Michael Kelly; James Herbert; Paulet Carey, editor of the *Sentimental and Masonic Magazine*, who wanted to publish a picture of the lad; [15] Matthew Dowling, a clever, drunken attorney, later involved in the Fitzgerald tragedy. Mrs. Moore sang with them, lifting her clear, soft voice in "How sweet in the woodlands," and Master Tommy warbled songs out of Dibdin's collection. Did he, one wonders, lend his small efforts to

> Crown me Bacchus, mighty god,
>   The victory is thine,—
> Cupid's bow yields to thy rod,
>   And love submits to wine;

and to

Lovely woman, pride of nature,
   Good, and sweet, and kind, and fair,
Than man a higher stile of creature,
   Perfect as celestials are?

The sentimental eroticism of Moore's poetry cannot be understood except against the background of these songs. And as the boy's talents expanded, he was adroitly pushed into higher social circles where he became a universal favorite.

IV

Ambitious for her son, Anastasia realized the necessity for his thorough education. "On more than one occasion," writes Moore, "when having been kept out too late at some evening party to be able to examine me in my task for next day, she has come to my bedside on her return home, and waked me (sometimes as late as one or two o'clock in the morning), and I have cheerfully sat up in my bed and repeated over all my lessons to her." Extraordinary mother and extraordinary son! He first attended a "Classical English School" near by, kept by an eccentric genius named Malone, who spent most of his nights in the public houses and then whipped the boys all round next day for waking him at noon—whippings which Tom, through maternal diplomacy, escaped. Remaining long enough to win a silver medal [16] for reading history (at the age of six!), he was presently removed to the English Grammar School at 75 Grafton Street, kept by Samuel Whyte, who was to have a profound influence on the poet.

Whyte was one of the celebrities of Dublin. Born in 1733, he was the natural son of Captain Solomon Whyte, deputy governor of the Tower of London. He soon developed a genius for pedagogy. The mother of Richard Brinsley Sheridan (the dramatist was a pupil of Whyte's) told him that Nature had cut him out for his profession. When Whyte tried to collect money he had lent the Sheridans, that lady put him off in letters of a masterly and Micawberesque indirection, so that the compliment rings a little hollow, but there can be no doubt of Whyte's extraordinary success. In person he was of medium height; he had a high forehead, eyes set wide apart, the right eye a little drooping, a prominent nose, and the large, sensitive lips of an overgrown cherub set above a round, dimpled chin. He early formed his theories of education. A suppressed essay on the *Art of Reading and Speaking in Public* laments the neglect of English grammar and elocution in the schools and calls upon teachers to speak with purity and grace, to teach proper pronunciation and accent, to regulate the tones and modulation of the pupil's voice, and to adjust gestures, eyes, and countenance to what is said. In view of Moore's subsequent career, the following passage is even more significant:

We are told, and we seem to take it for orthodox too, that our language is unfit for music; but upon what authority? We annually cram the pockets of certain Italian emigrants of low education and mean parts, except in their vocation, whose performances we extravagantly affect; we entertain them as teachers, and that doctrine they propagate wherever they gain access . . . our countryman Purcel, and some other modern masters, have afforded us pleasing proofs that English is not quite destitute of musical expression. . . . There is a national music, as well as national language, both, probably, deducing their character and peculiar properties from the cast and genius of the people. . . . Had the characters of poet and musician been united, as when they flourished in the golden days of old, matters would have taken a different turn. . . .[17]

Such was Whyte's doctrine in 1761; twenty-five years of teaching had not dulled his enthusiasm for poetry, music, and the stage. He acted; he encouraged his pupils to act. He wrote verse, and his pupils wrote verse. He discussed *The Art of Speaking*, declaring in a profusion of italics that

a judicious speaker is master of such a *variety* of decent and natural *motion* . . . that he will not be long enough in *one posture* to *offend* the eye of the spectator.

He published in 1772 *The Shamrock; or, Hibernian Cresses,* a collection of poems in which young Tom read such amatoria as:

> WHEN first thy soft lip I but civilly press'd,
> ELIZA, how great was my Bliss!
> The fatal Contagion ran quick to my Breast;
> I lost my poor Heart with a Kiss.
>
> And now, when supremely thus blest with your Sight,
> I scarce can my Transports restrain;
> I wish, and I pant, to repeat the Delight;
> And kiss you again, and again.
>
> In Raptures I wish to enjoy all those Charms;
> Still stealing from Favour to Favour—
> Now, now, O ye Gods! let me fly to your Arms,
> And kiss you for ever and ever.

An amazing man! Hand in glove with Tom's extraordinary mother, who, when all the tall boys in the reading class on one occasion ranged themselves ahead of her small son at a public exhibition, called aloud to the teacher from the gallery that Tommy was entitled to be the head of the class!

For Tom was a pupil after Whyte's own heart. He was always being called upon to declaim or recite. "I obtained the honour," he writes, "of being singled out by him on days of public examination, as one of his most successful and popular exhibitors . . . as I looked particularly infantine for my age, the wonder was, of course, still more wonderful." Once he recited "Alexander's Feast" before Miss Campion, the actress; and when she subsequently bowed to him in public, it was as if Corinne had saluted him in the Capitol. At eleven he spoke an original epilogue for a performance of *Jane Shore* at Lady Borrowe's private theater, being kept up beyond his bedtime and almost falling asleep. He dreamed of playing harlequin, and jumped assiduously over his bed to perfect himself in the head-foremost leap of that hero.

But in fairness it should be said that Whyte and his staff—

including the Latin usher, Donovan, "uncouth, honest, hard-headed, kind-hearted," and an ardent patriot—did not neglect the substance of education.   There exists testimony to the effect that "Master Thomas Moore Having distinguished himself in an extraordinary and most honourable manner duely supporting his rank and character at a private examination held Oct 30th 1790—in Latin speech obtained THIS Certificate in testimony of his diligence and good behaviour," with the additional information: "Rank 1st boy in his class." [18] He was thoroughly grounded in Latin and Greek.   Three months later he was presented with an abridgment of Richardson's novels [19] for "having acquitted himself in a very distinguished manner in Castalia's Dialogues."   And finally, Whyte wrote to John Moore:

Dear Sir: I most heartily congratulate you on the success of your incomparable Boy for in the Course of thirty one years experience; I have not met one that has done equal Business in the time.   I beg my Compts to Mrs Moore. . . .

Tom thirsted after fame.   In January, 1793, one Richard Edward Mercier founded the *Anthologia Hibernica,* a monthly magazine "illustrated with beautiful engravings," designed to forward Dublin literature.   Among the subscribers listed in the second volume is "Master Thomas Moore," who had the deep gratification of seeing his first printed poem in the October issue—"To Zelia, on her charging the Author with writing too much on Love."   Zelia was a Miss Hannah Byrne, much older than Tom, with whom, in the character of Romeo, he kept up a poetical correspondence. "A Pastoral Ballad" follows the Zelia effusion, a lyric which the mature author found not unmusical, and later issues contain other products of his aspiring pen.   The poems are neither better nor worse than others in the magazine.   "To Zelia" will serve as a sample:

'Tis true my Muse to love inclines,
And wreaths of Cypria's myrtle twines;

Quits all aspiring, lofty views,
And chaunts what Nature's gifts infuse;
Timid to try the * mountain's height,
Beneath she strays, retir'd from sight,
Careless, culling amorous flowers;
Or quaffing mirth in Bacchus' bowers.
When first she rais'd her simplest lays
In Cupid's never-ceasing praise,
The God a faithful promise gave—
That never should she feel love's stings,
Never to burning passion be a slave,
But feel the purer joy thy friendship brings.

* Parnassus

One notes the false rhetoric, the affectation of ennui.

For Tom was merely echoing the age. The decade was drowned in elegance and sentimentalism. Curran could never read *The Sorrows of Werther* without weeping, and Grattan shed tears when Miss O'Neill played Ophelia. It was, moreover, impossible to say anything simply; polysyllabic periphrasis wiped out the substance of what was meant. If one consults the poetical department of the *Anthologia Hibernica*, one will find such effusions as an "Epistle to EMMA, on her saying she preferred Friendship to Love," containing lines like:

When age with chilling fingers tears
The cheek's carnation from its bed.

Another poem refers to "the thund'ring tube, which lays the field in gore." The editor reprinted with approbation Henry Baker's "Invocation to Health," containing such odd personifications as "Palsy" and "Moist Diabetes," "each an urinal incessant using." Mrs. Charlotte Smith in another poem addressed her daughters as "dear objects of my anxious care"; and an anonymous address to Erasmus Darwin describes the embryo which

Sips with rude mouth the salutary waves;
Seeks round its cell the sanguine streams that pass,
And drinks with crimson gills the vital gas.

And always eroticism was varnished with sensibility, as in
Thomas Dermody's "Beauty":

> Fix'd on the splendours of thy face,
> Oh! let me taste the seraph's bliss,
> Now, sinking wooe the free embrace,
> Rave o'er the bosom's snowey grace,
> And now, more ardent, steal the incense-breathing kiss.

Small wonder that the precocious boy translated Anacreon
and wrote *The Poems of Thomas Little.* Sensibility, eroticism, music, and poetry surrounded him; he fell in love ex-
perimentally with a pretty cousin, Mary Doyle, whom he
visited in Wexford, and who came to Dublin to live.[20]   For
her he scribbled verses, all of the same false style, the same
sentimental rhetoric.[21]   And yet the influence of the *Anthologia Hibernica* was not wholly bad: years afterward, Moore
remembered having read Rogers' *Pleasures of Memory* in its
pages, which also contained poems by Burns, Bowles, Sir
William Jones, and various Gaelic effusions.

Chapter II

T HAT the curly-haired darling of Mrs. Moore's drawingroom ever came into contact with Irish poverty does not appear. That (if one excepts boyish visits to Wexford) he ever set foot in Ireland beyond the purlieus of the capital is not recorded. His sense of nationalism was formed when he was young and impressionable; it was sincere, but it was of another strain than the fanaticism of the men of '98. He not only failed to adhere to the wild enterprise of Lord Edward Fitzgerald, but he suffered himself to be led gently out of danger by—of all people—Robert Emmet. Because one's whole understanding of Moore depends upon one's understanding of these boyish years, it is important to realize that Moore's nationalism—the nationalism which endeared him to the nineteenth century and lost him the allegiance of the twentieth—is a faithful reflection of the dominant sentiment of Dublin at a particular decade of Irish development.

In the eighties and early nineties the patriotism of the capital was the patriotism of Flood, Grattan, and Charlemont, thoroughly respectable, thoroughly middle-class, and thoroughly Whig.[1] England had graciously granted legislative independence to the sister kingdom in 1782; and though Flood and Grattan might differ as to the extent of the parliamentary surrender, they agreed that legislative independence meant government by the respectable classes. In Lecky's words, "the memory of ancient Athens with its democracy of 30,000 free citizens rising above a vast population of unrepresented slaves was probably present to many minds,"

23

especially of those who desired "a democracy planted in an aristocracy." When, for example, in 1784 a corps of the Volunteers enlisted "about two hundred of the lowest class" from the Dublin liberties, Grattan denounced "the alarming measure of drilling" the dregs of the populace; and, as the uneducated poured into the ranks, it is significant that Charlemont, that "Whig of Whigs" increasingly relinquished control. In the eighties, however, partisan feeling had not risen into bitterness, Irish patriots declared their sincere adherence to the House of Hanover, and innumerable Catholic addresses protested an unalterable attachment to the Protestant supremacy.

Throughout Europe the eighteenth century was enjoying a brief, deceptive golden age. On the far-off Turkish borders, it was true, a war was going on, and a Swedish king performed extraordinary gyrations in the Baltic, but when had the eighteenth century been without its war? The eternal Polish question was discussed by diplomats from London to St. Petersburg, and Pitt avoided trouble over Belgium largely because the successor of the great Frederick did not know his own mind; but these were mere ripples on the universal calm. On the whole, the friends of man could be pardoned a slight feeling of pride. Benevolence and reason were everywhere the watchwords of enlightened despotism. In France a succession of philosophic ministers had all the outward seeming of reform, in America a new republic was founded, in Great Britain the Whigs, conscious of rectitude, had infected the Tories with the spirit of progress. There was even a commercial treaty with Ireland in prospect—damaged, to be sure, by the enlightened self-interest of British mercantilism. But the intention was everything. Mankind was on the mend.

Because the golden glow of the enlightenment held the religious life of Europe in its spell, the age seemed to feel with Chesterfield that the only sensible religion was the religion of all sensible men. The Pope had suppressed the Jesuits.

Catholic bishops in France, turning from the uncertainties of the next world to the certainties of this, engaged in social reform; Franciscans and Benedictines joined the Freemasons; and when a scandalized Gallic bishop complained, his ecclesiastical superior dismissed the protest with a smile. Anglican sees were notorious political plums; and as for the country parsons, the historians of the Establishment dryly remark that "the professional duties of the clergy did not press very heavily upon them." Nor was Ireland, or at any rate Dublin, immune from the universal disintegration. Burke, whose wife was a Catholic, wrote Sir Hercules Langrishe that "in the general decadence of theology" the Catholics would probably be converted to Protestantism "through political reasons." Presbyterian dissenters presented an address to that extraordinary clergyman, the Bishop of Derry, expressive of "their perfect approbation of the liberality of his Lordship's religious sentiments," to which his lordship replied that his "liberality of sentiment" flowed "from the rare consistency of a Protestant bishop." Grattan paid Father O'Leary, the most brilliant writer among the Catholics, this singular compliment: "if I did not know him to be a Christian clergyman, I should suppose him by his writings to be a philosopher of the Augustan age." The most persuasive preacher in the city was Kirwan, educated by the Jesuits at St. Omer; and Kirwan, after being professor of natural and moral philosophy at Louvain, conformed to the Establishment in 1787, and wrote, before preaching his first Protestant sermon, that he would still seek "the same object—to improve the human heart; to enlarge and enlighten the understanding of men; banish religious prejudices, and diffuse through society the great blessings of peace, order, and mutual affection." Testifying before the committee of the House of Commons in 1798, Thomas Addis Emmet said that "as the human mind grows *philosophical*, it will, I think, wish for the destruction of all religious establishments, and therefore, in proportion as the catholic mind becomes *philosophic*, it will of course entertain the same wishes." Dublin Catholicism verged perilously close to Christian deism.[2]

If the Whig version of Irish nationalism must be kept in mind for an understanding of Moore's impressionable years, the special quality of Dublin Catholicism is equally important to a comprehension of his curious religious life. The family attended mass in a friary in Great Stephen Street; and the earliest priest mentioned by Moore is one Father Ennis, his Italian preceptor, of whom he says: "it would be difficult . . . to find a priest less meddling or less troublesome." The boy went first to confession when he was twelve or thirteen, but though he liked Father O'Halloran (who reappears in the *Travels of an Irish Gentleman*), he did not like "the necessity of raking up all my boyish peccadilloes," a practice he calls "both painful and humiliating," and, after entering college, he refused to go. His mother, "after a slight remonstrance, sensibly acceded to my wish." The priest made no recorded comment. It was seriously debated whether, before entering Trinity, the lad should not turn Protestant, and John Moore, at any rate, raised no objections, though Anastasia, who, says her son, "gave in to some of the old superstitions connected" with Catholicism, would not have it; and Tom, ever obedient, did not then or later formally lapse. He ever described himself as a Catholic and attended mass when he could. But he also attended Protestant services with apparent impartiality, married a Protestant wife, brought up his children as Protestants, and was buried in a Protestant churchyard by a Protestant clergyman. Religious practices, it is true, were lax, and Moore was undoubtedly sincere, but it is obvious that Catholicism was as much a political matter with him as it was a question of spiritual conviction.[3]

In this mellow atmosphere Tom discovered that life was full of pleasant occupations. He hung his diminutive bedroom with poetical compositions "in the manner, as I flattered

myself," he says, "of Shenstone's at the Leasowes"; he wrote
a few political squibs; he participated in the joyous foolery
of the mock kingdom of Dalkey—the Dublin equivalent of
the Feast of Unreason; and he managed to read a good deal.
He likewise organized his father's clerks (two in number)
into a weekly debating society with himself as president.
Although the principal business of each meeting seems to
have been the production of "an original enigma, or rebus,
in verse," Irish politics were discussed, Ennis, the elder clerk,
being both patriotic and literary. Tom also grew intimate
with the son of Beresford Burston, a lawyer of some emi-
nence; and, as he naïvely tells us, "my acquaintance with this
family was one of those steps in the scale of respectable
society which it delighted my dear mother to see me attain
and preserve." The younger Burston was a fellow pupil at
Whyte's; they entered Trinity together; the elder Burston
put down both their names for admission to the Middle
Temple, London, on November 19, 1795; and they both got
their degrees from Trinity in 1799. The Burstons owned a
country villa near Blackrock where Tom went in the summer
to read Mrs. Radcliffe and listen to the Burston girls play
Haydn on the harpsichord. Happy summer! "The most
happy and the most *poetical*" of all his industrious life!

It had not been necessary to abandon the errors of Rome.
The waves of the enlightenment had washed even against the
gray walls of Trinity, where, after 1793, Roman Catholics
might legally proceed to a degree. It was resolved to make
a collegian out of Tom, and, at the age of fifteen, he passed
entrance examinations which did credit to Whyte's Latin
usher. His name was solemnly entered upon the Trinity
College books June 2, 1794—"Thomas Moore, P. Prot.," that
is to say, *pensionarius*, Protestant, though he did not change
his religion. Apparently he did not begin his college course
until 1795. Whyte was so proud of him that, thriftily combining literature and publicity, he included in his next volume
a set of Tom's verses addressed to Whyte, which begin

Hail! heaven-born votary of the laurel'd Nine;

and, unabashed at printing

> If e'er from Genius' torch *one little spark*
> *Glow'd in my soul,* thy breath increas'd the flame,

appended the incredible note that the author "entered college at a very early age, with distinguished honour to himself as well as to his able and worthy preceptor."

II

Trinity was still the brilliant and worldly college which had graduated Sheridan and Burke. John Hely Hutchinson's administration had been a long scandal that ended in 1795 when the amiable Richard Murray became provost; but Hutchinson (though Lord North said of him that if the King gave him England and Ireland, he would ask for the Isle of Man as a potato garden), had known what he wanted. He aimed to attract the nobility and gentry, and instituted instruction in riding, fencing, and the modern languages as parts of a genteel education. The curriculum had been revised in 1793 and was, as a matter of fact, an advance over Oxford and Cambridge. As a "Junior Freshman" Tom might look forward to Murray's *Logic,* equal parts of Virgil, Homer, and Horace, the first three books of Euclid, and portions of Livy and Herodotus. Education was of course classical, but the curriculum included some astronomy and physics, a touch of political science, Conybeare's *Defence of Revealed Religion,* and "Locke on Government." Trinity was not a mere college for future curates. Moore's first tutor, the Rev. Robert Burrowes, though he wrote for the *Transactions of the Royal Irish Academy* and rose to be Dean of Cork, was chiefly famous for having written a "flash" song beginning "The night before Larry was stretched" (*anglicé,* "hanged"), in which, when the parson calls to administer consolation to the condemned,

TRINITY COLLEGE, DUBLIN

Larry tipped him an elegant look,
And pitch'd his big wig to the devil.

If the undergraduates had abandoned the pleasing habit of hanging up the town butchers on their own meathooks, the tutors had not gone in for piety: the Rev. Mr. Burrowes, after an exchange of rhymed incivilities with Theophilus Swift, who had lampooned his wife, went to jail for a fortnight, where Tom visited him.

The future translator of Anacreon paid only a decent amount of respect to his lessons. During his first year he won a "premium" mainly to please his mother; and during his third year he contested a classical prize with one Ferral, failing of the award because of his curious inability to write Latin hexameters. He also once tried for the empty honor of a scholarship which, on account of his religion, he could never have held. But for the most part he went his own gait, and fortunately, there were men at Trinity who appreciated English letters. What interested Tom was literature rather than learning; and poetry and politics received, one suspects, more of his attention than did Conybeare and Locke. He did, it is true, pick up a goodly amount of miscellaneous erudition. He continued to write verses, and also a masque, for which he pillaged one song from Haydn and drew on William Warren for another—the opus being produced in the front drawingroom at Aungier Street. And he likewise ventured into such literary society as Dublin afforded.

The amusing "Memoirs of Myself," which, fragmentary as they are, make one wish that Moore had written more prose of this order, give a vivid glimpse into this shabby-genteel Bohemia. A widow, Mrs. Battier, lived up two pair of stairs in Fade Street in a single room with her two daughters; and thither, because Mrs. Battier wrote satires in the manner of Churchill and kept a diminutive salon, the young collegian was accustomed to climb. Long afterwards he could still recall one of these gatherings:

There had lately come over from some part of England one of
those speculators upon Irish hospitality and ignorance which at
that period of Dublin civilisation were not unfrequent,—a Mrs.
Jane Moore, who had come upon the double speculation of publishing her poems, and promulgating a new plan for the dyeing
of nankeens. . . . I rather think that poor Mrs. Battier was reduced to a single room by the state of her circumstances, for
I remember well that it was in the bed-room we drank tea, and
that my seat was on the bed, where, enthroned as proudly as
possible, with these old poetesses (the new arrival being of the
largest and most vulgar Wapping mould), I sate listening while
Mrs. Jane Moore read aloud her poems, making havoc with the
v's and *w*'s still as she went, while all the politeness of our hostess
could with difficulty keep her keen satirical eyes from betraying
what she really thought of the nankeen muse.

On another occasion Tom was introduced to an English
lecturer, who, when the literary undergraduate asked him if
he knew Shenstone's *Schoolmistress*, replied, "Yes, but ha'n't
seen her of some time."

III

Outside the walls of Trinity the peace of the Augustans
had dissolved to nothingness as the eighteenth century sank
into the murky twilight of 1793. The Terror was abroad
in France, and a milder form of terror was loose in England.
Waking from his easy indifference, Pitt undertook the fatal
recall of Fitzwilliam just as Catholic Emancipation seemed on
the point of being granted; and when in March, 1795, the
last popular Lord Lieutenant of the century departed, weeping Dublin merchants shut up shop, draped their doorways
in mourning, and drew the vice-regal coach to the quay.
Thereafter, in Grattan's phrase, disaffection overspread the
land "like the mist at the heels of the countryman," and Ireland set foot on the long road that led to the rebellion of '98.
There was a riot in the capital when Camden, Fitzwilliam's
successor, arrived; violence and assassination overran half the
kingdom, indiscriminately attributed to the Defenders, the

Peep o' Day Boys, the Orangemen, or "Captain Stout," as exuberant fancy might dictate. The United Irishmen opened treasonable correspondence with France, and the English government paid Leonard MacNally to betray the United Irishmen. And daily on the streets of Dublin came and went Lord Clare, Major Sirr, James O'Brien the informer, Francis Higgins the Sham Squire, and others destined to play their sinister roles in the tragedy to come.

Neither Tom nor the college was immune. The future melodist, who had sat as a boy on the knee of Napper Tandy, and who had waved his laurel branch at Grattan from the paternal window, joined in 1796 a small debating society, the chief ornament of which was a modest and brilliant youth whose saturnine features, preternaturally long nose, and resolute jaw gave no hint, except when his face lighted with the fervor of eloquence, of the smoldering passions in his soul. This was Robert Emmet, half conscious of his doom, an elder student by a year than Moore, one who exercised over the poet an extraordinary fascination. Presently both entered the Historical Society, that club founded in 1745 by Burke which, at one time or another, counted almost every brilliant young man in Ireland among its members. Then as now, university authorities were fearful of political discussions; but, debating the history of Rome or some abstract proposition, Emmet indicted the existing government by indirection more powerful than assault. The age was declamatory, but the impression made by the young genius on his contemporaries was deep and permanent. "So gifted a creature," said the Rev. Archibald Douglas, "does not appear in a thousand years." "The power of Emmet's eloquence," Moore wrote almost four decades later, "was wonderful; and I feel at this moment as if his language were still sounding in my ears."

According to Moore's account, his chief contribution to the society was a burlesque "Ode upon Nothing," for which he was solemnly voted a medal, and for which he formally apologized. But the spell of Emmet's enthusiasm drove him forward to steps which he omitted to describe in his "Memoirs." He seems to have acquired something of a reputation as a speaker; at least a writer in the *Irish Quarterly Review* for 1854 remembered that "young Moore, in his first speech, made an impression on the auditors that engaged their attention, and struck deeper at every successive debate." [4] And in 1853 Thomas Crofton Croker reported to John Wilson Croker that he had received from Ireland two bits of information about Moore. Upon the arrival of Lord Camden as viceroy, the provost, fellows, and scholars of Trinity proceeded in a body to the Castle to present a complimentary address. "On their arrival," so runs Croker's account, "the Scholars suddenly wheeled about and retired to Hyde's Coffee house where Thomas Moore since distinguished as a Poet being called to the Chair, and W. H. Ellis being appointed Secretary an address was voted to the R^t Honble Henry Grattan expressive of their approbation of his conduct and principles during the late popular administration [of Lord Fitzwilliam]." [5] The episode seems incredible, since college freshmen do not usually serve as chairmen of political meetings, but it is confirmed by Grattan's *Memoirs*,[6] though the name of the secretary is different. Here is the address:

SIR,—We, the students of the University of Dublin, entering with the warmest sympathy into the universal feeling and interest of our countrymen, beg leave to unite our voice with theirs in declaring our admiration of your great and uncommon talents, and a reliance on your steady patriotism and unshaken integrity. We have with sorrow beheld the removal of a beloved Viceroy, *whose arrival we regarded as the promise of public reform, and his presence the pledge of general tranquillity.*

If this event should be accompanied (as we have reason to apprehend) by your removal from His Majesty's councils in this nation, our regret will have received the last additional circumstance of aggravation, and our despondency will be complete. Relying, however, on the wisdom and benignity of His Majesty, we yet entertain a hope that the nation will not be deprived of the salutary measures flowing from your councils and advice, and *that the harmony and strength of Ireland will be founded on the*

solid basis of Catholic Emancipation, and the reform of those
grievances which have inflamed public indignation.

We therefore entreat you to persevere in exerting the full
energy of your splendid talents for the attainment of those objects which the present alarming posture of affairs, and the consenting wishes of the nation so loudly demand.

THOMAS MOORE, Chairman.

N. WILLIS, Secretary.

Croker further states that Moore made a speech, of which
he has a copy, concluding with

One boon I ask of Heaven—for myself, may death arrest me ere
I see the day a Union takes place; for Ireland may the Atlantic
close and bury it for ever in an immeasurable gulph!

This speech was delivered in the Francis Street Chapel on
April 9, 1795, at a Catholic meeting, but whether it preceded
or followed the meeting at Hyde's Coffee House that same
day is not clear; and Croker's account is not otherwise confirmed.

There was founded in 1797 an organ of the United Irishmen called the *Press,* a tri-weekly, which chiefly existed to
annoy the government. Greatly daring, Tom romantically
slipped by night into the letter-box of this paper an imitation
of Ossian; and, when this was printed, followed it by a letter
to the students of Trinity College, which was also published.
The letter was read at home, the secret leaked out, and Tom
promised his alarmed mother to write no more—at least, such
is his story. The facts, however, are somewhat different.
The imitation of Ossian was printed in the sixty-second
number of the *Press,* February 20, 1798, whereas the letter
appeared in the twenty-ninth number, December 2, 1797; [7]
so that, if Tom promised to write no more for this publication after his letter was detected, he did not keep his promise.

Both are schoolboy productions. The Ossianic fragment
strikes the note of literary emotionalism which Irish patriots
have too often mistaken for a plan of campaign:

Sad is the sleep of Erin, and her dreams are troubled and gloomy. Her enemy has come—he has come in the hour of her slumber, and his hand has stolen the *emerald* from her brow; but Erin has not awakened—no! she still sleeps.

Bloody is the field where she lies, and her garments are weeping with blood—for the wounds of her sons are streaming around her, and the ghosts of her heroes are moaning for vengeance! but Erin has not awakened—no! she still sleeps.

A sigh comes on the night breeze—'tis the spirit of *Orr* that complains! pensive he leans from his cloud, and weeps over the slumber of Erin—He touches the lyre of song; the Heavenly harp of Union—and the orisons of freedom tremble over the chords— 'twas a strain he loved, for he *"died singing it."* Has Erin heard the voice of her hero? has Erin awakened? No! she still sleeps.

The "Letter to the Students of Trinity College," signed "A SOPHister," is, in the words of Moore's parents, "very bold," that is to say, highly declamatory. The "SOPHister" urges the students to catch fire from the pages of Demosthenes, denounces "the sombrous frown of some monkish despot," suggests that the undergraduates will raise Ireland "to that rank in the climax of nations, from which she is fallen," provided the adolescent heart is not "hardened by ministerial frost," and roundly denounces "those mercenary prefects, sent hither as to a province devoted to rapine and desolation." We catch the echo of Emmet's rolling periods in such a passage as this:

Alas! our afflicted country! how long will her green plains be dyed with the gore of butchery, and obscured with the ashes of conflagrations! When will she profit by the lessons so brilliantly exhibited to her eyes, and which she has been so slow, so very slow in learning? Oh, when will 'the Nemean Lion' rouse from his trance, and shake off the vermin that engender on his crest?

The riper judgment of the author repudiated this "turgid Johnsonian sort of style," due rather to the influence of the oratory of Emmet. That precocious youth, hinting that to write like a brass band was perhaps not the best method of concealing conspiracy, flatly told Moore that, tied as Tommy was to his mother's apron strings, he had better steer clear of the United Irishmen—advice which the poet's second tutor unwittingly abetted when he advised John and Anastasia to keep their darling out of Emmet's company. It is a mark of the power which the orator exercised over the poet that Moore seems not to have resented the slur on his manly independence.

Meanwhile, the incredible drama of Irish history continued to unfold. Wolfe Tone, finding Philadelphia an unsatisfactory base from which to overthrow the Lord Lieutenant, sailed for France, where, through the aid of James Monroe, he intrigued with the French Directory; and the romantic Lord Edward Fitzgerald, confiding his purpose "with the habitual frankness of his nature" to a mistress of one of Pitt's colleagues *en route*, journeyed to Hamburg via London to set up an Irish republic. The French, who had fourteen armies in the field, agreed to throw a fifteenth into Ireland under Hoche; and as they were under the impression that half the British sailors were Irishmen, they thought the task would be relatively simple. Wolfe Tone commented bitterly on their ignorance. Disaffection being strongest in the north, the French selected Bantry Bay in the south for a landing; and, sailing in perfect weather at the close of 1796, sank their best ship on a rock in their own harbor, mislaid the commanding general, and, arriving piecemeal on the Irish coast, did nothing until a storm swept them out to sea. The Catholics rallied to resist the infidel French invasion, and a grateful government repressed papistical meetings to demand parliamentary rights. When a second invasion by the Dutch was threatened in the spring of 1797 and the British fleet had mutinied, the inspired executive made the wife of the solicitor-general a baroness and created a profusion of earls, viscounts, and smaller fry. William Orr, who opposed assassination, had been hanged in October for being a United Irishman (after a judicious admission of whiskey bottles into the jury room); and with all Ireland honeycombed by conspiracy, the government forced the resignation of Abercromby, commander-in-chief of His Majesty's forces, because he had suppressed military outrages and had issued an order which stated that the troops were "formidable to everyone but the enemy." And in April, 1798, Lord Clare, Vice-Chancellor of Trinity, hatchet-faced and terrible, descended on the college, accompanied by Dr. Duigenan, representing the Protestant archbishop of Dublin, to suppress sedition among the undergraduates.

Moore's account (written thirty-five years later) is the classic description of the event.[8]   On the first day three episodes struck terror into the timid. When the names of Robert Emmet and certain others were called, there was a dead silence that "proclaimed how deep had been their share in the transactions of the United Irishmen." Dacre Hamilton, an intimate friend of Emmet's, early examined, refused to answer questions which might incriminate himself and his friends, and was as a consequence dismissed from Trinity and from all opportunity to enter the learned professions. And Whitley Stokes, a tutor, thought to have been a member of the United Irishmen, when asked if he knew of secret societies in the college, electrified the court of inquiry by answering, "Yes," and blandly amplified his response by testifying that "the only societies of that description which I am aware of are Orange societies, and I know some members of them," a piece of effrontery which drew Lord Clare to his feet in a "spasm of anger."   Other students were more pliable, and Moore witnessed "the degrading spectacle" of those who gave evidence against Emmet and his friends, "persons," he says, "who had themselves, of course, been implicated in the plot, and now came forward, either as volunteer informers, or else were driven by the fear of consequences to secure their own safety at the expense of their associates and friends." He paid them back on the morrow.

There was gloom in the Moore household that evening, but it was resolved that, come what might, if Thomas were so questioned that his answers might incriminate others, he was to follow Hamilton's example and refuse to speak. The next day he was called and offered the oath, which he at first declined to take. "I have no fear, my lord," he said, "that anything I might say would criminate myself, but it might tend to affect others; and I must say that I despise that person's character who could be led under any circumstances to criminate his associates." After some parleying, he took the oath with the reservation that he might refuse to answer; but as he had not joined the United Irishmen, his testimony was valueless for the government's purposes. He was again asked why he had refused the oath. Reiterating his former reasons, he now said that "it was the first oath I ever took, and it was, I think, a very natural hesitation," a reply which, with its indirect hit at the inquisitorial methods of the government, drew from Stokes the audible comment that it was the best answer that had yet been given. So many others followed Moore's contumacious example that it proved impossible to dismiss so large a portion of the student body; and the result was that less than a score were expelled. The excitement proved too much for Tom, who fell ill, a fact which perhaps prevented him from participating in the bloody events of May. On the nineteenth Napoleon sailed for Egypt, having persuaded the Directory that the East was more vulnerable than the British Isles; and on the same day Lord Edward Fitzgerald was surprised, wounded, and jailed, dying in prison June 4. Moore long remembered his feelings of awe as the street lamps of Dublin, one after another, went out towards midnight on May 23, amid hopes and fears that the rebels might attack the city.

The emotional shock of this whole experience is of first importance in understanding Moore, for it helps one to see why, after this brief dip into the dark whirlpools of rebellion, he retreated for the rest of his life into the safe Whig view which holds that progress comes, not from revolution, but from reform.

IV

Life at Trinity, however, was by no means confined to the ambiguous pleasures of conspiracy, and Thomas had not forgotten that he was born for music. In all Ireland an interest in traditional song was becoming entangled with patriotic fervor, perhaps on the theory that what could not be said could be played. The results were, as usual, inconsistent. *The Beggar's Opera*, filled with Irish tunes and forbidden for political reasons, was revived about 1793, when the engaging Kelly wheedled permission from the grim Lord Clare to produce it, and was thereafter regularly performed. Half the bands in the British army were in charge of Irish musicians; and detachments of the hated Sassenach were marched through the streets of Dublin to the tune of "The Girl I Left Behind Me," first published in 1794. Even the Earl of Camden, however harsh he might be to Irish patriots, knighted William Parsons, Master of the King's Band of Music, in 1795; and while the Castle strove to stem the tide of nationalism, it permitted the music publishers to fan patriotic emotions. In Belfast the influence of the French Revolution took the odd form of a patriotic meeting to revive traditional music; and there in 1792 a popular and somewhat dissipated young music master named Edward Bunting (not yet twenty) feverishly took down the melodies of the harpers, thence departing at his own expense to search Ulster, Munster, and Connaught for more tunes. J. C. Walker had published in 1786 his epochal *Historical Memoirs of the Irish Bards;* memories of Carolan, last of the traditional harpers, were revived; and from 1790 to 1796 various important collections of Irish airs appeared—Jackson's *Celebrated Irish Tunes*, J. Brysson's *Curious Selection of Favorite Tunes*, the anonymous *Hibernian Muse* (a "Collection of Irish Airs"), J. M'Fayden's *Repository of Scots and Irish Airs*, and, most important of all, Bunting's classic *General Collection of the*

Ancient Irish Music (1796), originally published in London but promptly pirated in Dublin. A Celtic revival was sweeping over the British Isles, part of the musical rhetoric of the romantic movement, and Dublin, the musical capital of the empire, was one of the foci of the excitement.

The sensibilities of the young poet were troubled by this music, at once martial and melancholy. He, too, attempted to grasp the inner spirit of the folk, trying for a time to learn the guitar that he might play these airs, and then reverting to the pianoforte, at that period a novel and exciting instrument. Moore had a friend, Edward Hudson, "a remarkably fine and handsome young man," member of a family that has done much for Irish music; and Hudson, "now talking with indignant feeling" of the wrongs of Ireland, and now playing on his flute these airs, passionate and mournful, aroused in Moore an equal ardor. Hudson himself knew many of the traditional melodies, and when Bunting's collection appeared, the two pored over it with delight. Hudson alone was admitted to the secret of Moore's contributions to the *Press;* indeed, an incautious query of his betrayed the young author to his parents. The Emmet family were also adepts, Thomas Addis Emmet solacing himself with a copy of Bunting in Kilmainham jail. Once when Moore was strumming an inspiriting Irish tune,[9] Robert Emmet started up and exclaimed: "Oh, that I were at the head of twenty thousand men marching to that air!" When in March, 1798, Hudson was arrested at the fateful meeting of the United Irishmen at Oliver Bond's house, when Emmet was jailed for three years only to conspire again and be executed, the seal of sacrifice and death was placed upon these memories.

v

Meanwhile literature was not forgotten. Trinity was in advance of the British universities in its appreciation of modern letters, and a number of the fellows and tutors wrote prose and verse, indulging a taste for donnish waggery which, though heavy-handed, had at least the merit of treating subjects more recent than the wars of Alexander. Besides Latin and Greek, young Moore had learned to read French and Italian; and it would appear that writers as miscellaneous as Bayle, Ronsard, Petrarch, Raynal, Voiture, and Johannes Secundus stimulated his poetic aspirations. Once, called upon to write a theme in Latin prose, Moore delivered a set of English verses to John Walker, the examining fellow, for which, after due academic hesitation, he was awarded a copy of the *Travels of Anacharsis*, "the first gain," he wrote, "I ever made by that pen which, such as it is, has been my sole support ever since." He astonished William Magee, the future archbishop, by rendering Lucian into fluent English prose at six o'clock in the morning; and his translation of Horace before Dr. Kearney in competition for a scholarship seems to have been notable for literary tact, whatever its prosodic deficiencies. How many of Moore's miscellaneous juvenilia date from his university days it is now impossible to say, but *The Poems of Thomas Little* includes at least two. These "Fragments of College Exercises" are of no value except for the fluency of the versification and for the nationalistic note of one of them:

> Is there no call, no consecrating cause,
> Approv'd by Heav'n, ordain'd by Nature's laws,
> Where Justice flies the herald of our way,
> And Truth's pure beams upon the banners play?
> .   .   .   .
> Oh! 'tis our country's voice, whose claim should meet
> An echo in the soul's most deep retreat.

Whatever his other defects, Tom had mainly rid himself of the heavy circumlocutions through the aid of which late eighteenth-century versifiers sought to attain dignity by standing on stilts.

During his college years he likewise began making a collection of poems by Irish patriots—Grattan, Curran, Sir Hercules Langrishe, and lesser lights—which, amounting to some

3700 lines, he later sold to Power for £100, but which was never published. A copy of a preface, written a quarter of a century later, survives in some letters of Thomas Crofton Croker, who himself brought out such a collection in the nineteenth century. Moore wrote:

From a feeling of reverence for some of those great names which adorned the brief and bright era of Irish History from 1782 to 1798, I was induced near thirty years since to set about collecting the various political trifles with which some of the most distinguished ornaments of that period . . . were known occasionally to have amused their leisure hours.

But he went on to doubt

whether I should be acting fairly towards the memory of my great Countrymen, in inviting attention to compositions, which, had they been published at the period when they were written, might have doubtless secured for themselves a prescriptive right to fame. . . .[10]

The young collegian seems to have written a good deal of miscellaneous prose. One such bit [11] appears in *Walker's Hibernian Magazine* for February, 1799, and is a "puff" for Herbert, the actor friend of the family, who had returned to the stage the previous month in the character of Osmond in *The Castle Spectre*. The droll affectation of infinite age by our twenty-year-old is seen in the concluding paragraph:

He has since appeared in *Oronooko*, and *Beverly*, in The Gamester; and we cannot help saying, that his performance of these characters, are as highly superior to his personation of *Osmond*, as the classical beauties of both are to the quaintness and *extravaganza* of The Castle Spectre.

But the chief literary occupation of Moore's college years was his translation of Anacreon, an interest in which dates at least from 1794, when he published a version of the fifth ode in the *Anthologia Hibernica*. As an undergraduate Tom fell into the habit of frequenting Marsh's Library, that dusty home of extinct learning, haunted by the shade of Swift, which the Protestant Archbishop Marsh founded near St. Patrick's in 1707. Passing through the tall gateway under the primate's arms, the diminutive scholar spent endless hours among the tall, dark bookcases, the deep windows, the carved wooden mitres, and the reading desks of oak. Admitted through his friendship with the son of the librarian, Thomas Cradock, the poet might read with faint irony an inscription, dated October, 1750, to the effect that

A considerable number of books having been, from time to time, stolen from the library, by persons under the denomination of Gentlemen, claiming a privilege to read in it, according to the statutes, To guard against the thefts of such *infamous villains* in future, no person will be admitted unless he produce a well attested certificate to the librarian, of his being a scholar and a gentleman. An honest porter is appointed to watch and search every person leaving the library.

Here, where time stood still and the noises of rebellion faded away, Tom dreamed over Greek and Latin folios, church fathers, and forgotten tomes of futile erudition from which he picked up that "odd, out-of-the-way reading" which clutters too much of his printed work. And here in the dusty quiet he apparently polished his versions of those Greek lyrics which proclaim

> That still as death approaches nearer,
> The joys of life are sweeter, dearer;
> And had I but an hour to live,
> That little hour to bliss I'd give!

Can one doubt that the lush sensibility of these poems owes something to the contrast between their themes and the hoary antiquity of the good primate's immemorial volumes?

Selecting twenty of the Anacreon odes, Moore submitted them to Dr. Kearney, the provost next in succession to Murray (who died in 1799), in the hope that "should they appear to him worthy of a classical premium, he should lay them before the Board of the University." Dr. Kearney was im-

pressed: he lent the young translator his own copy of Spaletti's edition of Anacreon; and—one warms to the man—he
advised Thomas to publish the poems because "the young
people will like it." But he had his academic doubts whether
a work "so amatory and convivial" could properly be recognized by as solemn a body as the governing board.

Publication, however, was not an immediate possibility,
and, taking his degree in the spring of 1799,[12] young Tom
was presently on the road to England and the Middle Temple,
a supply of guineas "carefully sewed up by my mother in the
waistband of my pantaloons," and (unknown to him) a scap-
ular, blessed by a priest and sewed into some remoter portion
of his clothing. This was in April. To London Beresford
Burston presently followed him.

Chapter III

IN DUBLIN the eighteenth century still ruled, but when Thomas Moore landed at Holyhead in 1799, he set foot for the first time in a country where the last vestiges of the Augustan order were dissolving like a dream. The ruling classes could make nothing of the world. There had always been a king whose relation to the constitution it was the business of the Tories to defend and of the Whigs to attack; there had always been a landed gentry and a due proportion of lower classes; there had always been a metaphysical something known as the rights of Englishmen and a metaphysical something else called Providence, which saw to it that British armies (except for the annoying Americans) should never know defeat. But now George III, who had once been determined to rule, was a pathetic invalid of sixty-one, trembling on the verge of madness; and in succession to him stood his heir, a profligate prince of thirty-seven who, having secretly married an English Catholic in 1785 only to deny her, married a German Protestant in 1795 only to detest her. If there were still liberals at Holland House, the Whigs in the Commons had dwindled to an ineffectual group of fifty, so that the two-party system had in truth disappeared. In Ireland the stench of corruption rose to heaven as the English government bribed its way to the Union; and in England the rising bourgeoisie jostled the old aristocracy while the agricultural population slowly drained into the mushroom cities of the north. As for the rights of Englishmen, the Habeas Corpus

Act remained suspended, the Treasonable Practices Act forbade people to speak or write except what the government permitted, and the Seditious Meetings Act denied their right to assemble when the magistrates disapproved. English judges, driven by pressure and fear, presided over extraordinary trials: the staff of the London *Courier* was, for example, indicted for libeling a friendly monarch because the paper suggested that Russian tariffs were hard on British trade, and the London Corresponding Society was legally suppressed under a regulation which reduced unlicensed debating clubs to the status of brothels.

In fact, wherever one turned, there was, from the point of view of right reason, universal chaos. Pitt was wearily attempting to direct events and strove like his father to wield the thunderbolts of diplomacy and war in three continents. But the classical tactics of a continental balance of power seemed not to apply to the French Republic, and, though Wellesley was winning brilliant victories in India, the filching of sugar islands had no effect on Europe. Dundas was in the War Office, of whom it was said that "he knew as much of war as a monthly nurse," and Dundas planned campaigns which, theoretically justified by the strategy of the Seven Years' War, succeeded only in wasting British man power. Nelson had destroyed the French fleet in Aboukir Bay, and Sir Sidney Smith had driven Napoleon from Acre, but Napoleon had slipped into Paris, and Nelson, in silken dalliance led by Lady Hamilton, was wasting his genius and the fleet on the Neapolitans. By autumn the Consulate was established; in 1800 Napoleon won Marengo; in 1801 the Second Coalition was a wreck. It was no time for political reform; in Sydney Smith's famous sentence, it was rather "an awful time for those who had the misfortune to entertain liberal opinions."

All this must be kept in mind to understand the disappearance from the letters and writings of our young Irishman in the next few years of any reference to the nationalist

cause. None of his extant papers speaks of Emmet; and none
refers even distantly to the visitation at Trinity or to the rebellion of '98. One would not, of course, expect any allusion
in the *Odes of Anacreon*, but *The Poems of Thomas Little*,
which, being mainly original compositions, might conceivably
contain a patriotic reference, are equally barren except for
the two fragments of a college exercise already quoted.
Collected in the 1840-41 *Poetical Works* are "Juvenile Poems"
which date in the main from his first sojourn in England or
from his American tour; yet even these exhibit none of those
veiled allusions through which Celtic poets have spoken
secretly to Irish patriots. The emotional shock had been too
great; and doubtless his parents and his friends cautioned
him to be silent. Moore seemed to close his mind for a
while to Irish woe.

> Come, take thy harp—'tis vain to muse
> Upon the gathering ills we see,

he wrote during these years, and though the Epicurean pose
is boyish, there is something conscious and determined in this
turning away from the patriotic theme.

The one poem which does reflect an interest in contemporary affairs is "Peace and Glory," collected in *Epistles, Odes,
and Other Poems*. An earlier version, printed in the *Gentleman's Magazine* for July, 1804, and thence reprinted in
Dennie's *Port Folio* November 17, 1804, is ironically entitled
"Ode for his Majesty's Birth-day, June 4, 1803, written ex-
tempore by Thomas Moore, Esquire, Poet Laureat for *Ireland*
pro tempore," and is chiefly notable for stanzas which
prudence or maturity omitted when the verses appeared in
book form:

> Sacred chain, from heaven descended,
>   Chain, that Britain calls her own,
> Which, by FETTERS, PURE AND SPLENDID,
> BIND'ST A PEOPLE TO THE THRONE.

Blest, we hail the morn, that shining,
    Fair and welcome from above,
To the ties so softly winning,
    Adds another link of love.

Brightly may the chain be lengthen'd,
    Through the lapse of future hours,
When the links, by glory strengthen'd,
    Peace again shall deck with flowers!

Was this sarcasm? At any rate, he left out these twelve lines.

II

The diminutive scholar, "after a most tedious and sicken-
ing crossing" late in March, arrived at Holyhead at night,
and secured passage in the Chester coach next morning only
by impersonating another passenger who wished to resign
his seat.[1] His other initial experiences of English life were
equally odd. "Alone, and as sooty as a sweep," he wandered
the streets of Chester, compelled to wait a day for the mail
coach. While he was breakfasting next morning, an escaped
lunatic entered the room, boasted that he had killed a woman
and a child the night before, and proposed that he and Moore
walk the streets together. Escaped from this danger, Tom
next found that the only other passenger on the London
coach was a sharper, who, taking Moore for a mere boy, suggested himself as a cicerone and stuck to the lad up to the
very door of his friends, the Mastersons, in Manchester Street,
London. Moore also left his portmanteau at an inn, from
which it was fortunately recovered; and, thoroughly home-
sick, passed to his lodging at 44 George Street, Portman
Square (a region inhabited by French refugees). Thence,
from the second floor of a washerwoman's house, he began
his conquest of London.

Though he was enrolled in the Middle Temple (where,
because he knew nobody—what had become of Burston?—he
had some trouble in giving an obligatory dinner), that conquest seems to have been his main business in England, since

of his legal studies there remains scarcely a trace. His triumph, immediate and amazing, was due in part to his friends and in part to himself. During his last year at Trinity he had apparently much extended his list of admirers. Dr. Kearney seems to have taken a fancy to him; and Moore also commenced an acquaintance with John Wilson Croker (Trinity College, 1800) which was to have some pleasant, and some sorrowful, consequences. But of all this group the most immediately useful proved to be Joseph Atkinson (1750-1818), a captain in the army, and at the time secretary to the Irish Ordnance Board.[2] Atkinson, "the Maecenas and Halifax of our city," had written a comedy, *The Mutual Deception* (1785), produced at the Haymarket by Colman as *Tit for Tat;* an opera, *A Match for a Widow* (1786); and was on the verge of producing another, *Love in a Blaze* (1800), the music by Stevenson. Brilliant and engaging, he knew everybody, he went everywhere, and he was "charmed by the singular freedom and simplicity" of the poet. When Atkinson died, Moore published in the *Morning Chronicle* for October 22, 1818, some elegiac verses which paint this happy spirit:

> If ever lot was prosperously cast,
>   If ever life was like the lengthen'd flow
> Of some sweet music, sweetness to the last,
>   'Twas his who, mourn'd by many, sleeps below.
>
> The sunny temper, bright where all is strife,
>   The simple heart that mocks at worldly wiles;
> Light wit that plays along the calm of life,
>   And stirs its languid surface into smiles;
>
>   .   .   .   .   .
>
> The happy grateful spirit, that improves
>   And brightens every gift by fortune given;
> That, wander where it will with those it loves,
>   Makes every place a home, and home a heaven:
>
> All these were his. . . .

Atkinson not only encouraged Moore with praise and letters of introduction; one may also reasonably attribute to his influence Moore's excursions into the field of commercial opera.

Atkinson, or somebody else, had instructed Dr. Thomas Hume, another Trinity graduate, to interest himself in the young bard; and presently we find this worthy busy in London about the publication of Moore's "trifling poems" (presumably the Anacreon volume) and consulting the learned Dr. F. Lawrence about the merits of Moore's translations from the Greek. And Atkinson introduced the young law student to a much more important individual, who was profoundly to affect the poet's future. This was the Earl of Moira, under whom Atkinson had served in America, an enormously tall, horse-faced military peer, one of the ugliest men in London, whose career at the moment was becalmed between his ambiguous success as Lord Rawdon in South Carolina and his extraordinary triumphs in India as the Marquis of Hastings some years later. Just now Moira was uncertainly taking up Irish politics as a diversion. A member of the English House of Lords, he had two years before denounced British oppression in that unhappy island as "the most absurd as well as the most disgusting tyranny that any nation ever groaned under," and in March, 1799, he spoke against the Union, only to vote for it in 1800. Lady Holland, who had few illusions, wrote in her journal that Moira's politics were conducted "so that he may be in power with either side—a shabby mode of proceeding," and even the grave pages of the *Dictionary of National Biography* dryly observe that political consistency was not one of his virtues. This trait was to have its effect on Moore, but at the turn of the century Moira was all affable condescension, and, as chief adviser to the Prince of Wales, he saw to it that the First Gentleman in Europe accepted the dedication of *Anacreon* and flattered the translator. He invited Moore in December to visit his enormous country house, Donington Park, rebuilt at vast expense in 1793, where "his company usually withdraw from the dining-room, to the library: and the evening is then given either to conversation . . . or, perhaps, by every dif-

ferent person, to private study." [3]   Moore draws a pleasant
picture of the six-foot soldier lighting his tiny guest up
the curving stone staircase and "stalking on before me
through the long lighted gallery, bearing in his hand my
bed-candle, which he delivered to me at the door of my
apartment." "I thought it," he continues with engaging can-
dor, "all exceedingly fine and grand, but at the same time
most uncomfortable"; in a few months, however, he was to
be thoroughly at home in the vast park, the enormous library,
and the innumerable rooms of this extravagant estate.

Neither Atkinson nor Moira would have been long interested in Moore had there not been something frank and
engaging in the poet himself. For he was a lovable youth.
His small stature gave him an "uplook," as though "it was
actually necessary to keep his range of vision *au courant* of
his neighbours," which was irresistible, and which his nose, a
little tilted upwards, further emphasized. [4]   The dark brown
curly hair contrasted with the brightness of the face, and
echoed the dark eyes. His face was alive with a mobility
which no painter could ever catch, and already the restless-
ness of his movements corresponded to the vivacity of his
moods. In society, he scarcely sat down, and when he composed, he was in perpetual motion. Remembering that in
1799 he was an ingenuous youth of twenty, gifted with a
sweet, clear, ringing voice said to be especially liquid when
he sang, that his speech was Dublin English, that is to say,
the most musical English in the empire, and adding to these
traits his talents for music, poetry, mimicry, and humor, one
understands his conquest of everybody from his landlady to
the Prince of Wales.

A return to Dublin that summer to still the pangs of homesickness was the sole interruption of this campaign of triumph.
Moore seems to have shifted his lodgings once or twice as his
social engagements increased, but the main business of this
first year in London was the preparation of *Anacreon* for the
press, and that "reading and scribbling"—one may add music—

DONINGTON HALL

concerning which he wrote apologetically to his father in May. His affectionate letters home enable us to follow his movements among the great and the near great: how "I sat near an hour with Lord Moira this morning"; or how "I am to be at a large party on Wednesday at Mrs. Campbell's, and on Friday at Lady Rich's, and am perfectly stout again." But mingling with the social register and with his anxiety about "my best black coat, the only one I have been able to wear," which is "quite shabby" (he is getting his shoes shined at two shillings a month, he records with relief), there are glimpses of Moore hard at work, especially at music. When he arrived, "Mr. Masterson lent me a piano." Sally Masterson "has a very nice harp." In May he received some music by Mozart, and frequented a Mrs. Cologan, "one of the first private performers on the harp." In December he dined with a Mr. and Mrs. Biggin: "she is the most exquisite performer I ever heard on the piano; and he has a beautiful organ, which she plays in the grandest cathedral style." The Biggins also imported all "the newest music from the continent." Moore was likewise in correspondence with William Warren and John Stevenson in Dublin, and was composing (probably with their aid and advice) his earliest songs: at least we read in a letter of December 14, 1799, that Johnson [Johnstone] of the Covent Garden Opera "sings some of my songs in company." In January he was studying thorough bass.

His first meeting with Stevenson [5] was too characteristic to be overlooked. This seems to have occurred either during Moore's last year at Trinity or during the summer visit to Dublin. At the opening of the century Stevenson was a man of middle height and slender figure, thirty-eight years old, whose hatred of corpulency subjected him to endless practical jokes. Though pompous in speech and punctilious in dress, he was at heart a simple soul who resigned himself to a subordinate role in the associations that were to follow. They were introduced by Cradock, the custodian of Marsh's

Library, apparently at the house of Mr. Ferns, the verger of St. Patrick's. Moore had his *Anacreon* translations under his arm and told Stevenson he wanted to recite the odes to him. "With all my heart, my dear boy," the musician replied, "but it must come after dinner. So, if you and Ferns will dine with me, you shall spout your verses." Stevenson afterwards composed a series of glees from the *Anacreon* poems, for one of which ("Give me the harp of epic song") he was knighted by Lord Hardwicke when that viceroy dined with the Irish Harmonic Society in 1803. Gifted with natural taste, which he had subjected to some professional training, Moore was yet, in the better sense, only a musical amateur; consequently, the combination of good nature and technical skill which Stevenson brought to their subsequent collaboration was invaluable. Music poured out of Sir John as rapidly as verses came from Tommy; and until the quarrel of the Power brothers broke up this famous partnership, their long association (Stevenson died in 1833) was in the main unruffled, despite Stevenson's social eccentricities and his inability to catch a stagecoach or keep an engagement.

Tom's immediate anxiety was *Anacreon*, for which he and his friends were obtaining subscriptions. Unfortunately he fell seriously ill of a complaint which had troubled him in Ireland, of which he almost died in London, and which was to recur at intervals during the rest of his life. One learns very little about the nature of the trouble, except that a large abscess formed on his side, and that this malady was now accompanied by ophthalmia. He was delirious for two weeks, but by Thursday, March 20, 1800, he was able to write cheerfully to his mother during a "lucid interval of ease" of the calomel with which the rude medical science of the times had dosed him, and of the kindness of "Dr. Baillie, the first physician here," and of "Woolriche, the surgeon," both of whom had been in constant attendance. There are also traces of pretty ladies eager to nurse so interesting an invalid—he remembered long afterwards how the beautiful Duchess of

St. Albans had come to his lodgings during those two dreadful months to take care of him, climbing the stairs to his Bury Street rooms (whither he had moved) to see that the brave little Irishman did not die of neglect.

But he gallantly concealed the danger from his family and scarcely allowed his confinement to interrupt the prodigious business of bringing out his translations. Stockdale had agreed to publish the book, and Moore was all enthusiasm. "Dr. Lawrence has read my Anacreon," he wrote, "paid wonderful attention to it; and has written a Greek ode himself, which he allows me to publish.[6] I have got Mrs. Fitzherbert's name, and Mrs. Biggin promises me the Duke of Bedford's." By February, 1800, there were fifty subscribers, and "I find the retouching and finishing my Anacreon to be an increasing and almost endless labour." Even the failure of "the scoundrelly monks of Trinity" to subscribe did not dampen this ardor, for "I have got the Prince's name, and his permission that I should *dedicate* Anacreon to him. Hurra! hurra!" It was a dedication he was to regret. In July the book was out, and the first copy went to Anastasia: "How did you look at it? What did you feel? Oh! I know what you felt, and I know how you looked! My heart is with you, though I am so delayed from meeting."

III

The instantaneous success of the *Odes of Anacreon* is among the minor wonders of literature—a success which historians of the romantic movement have ungratefully overlooked. In the absence of any important reviewing medium, the book had to make its way by word of mouth, and doubtless the social brilliance of the "List of Subscribers," opening with "His Royal Highness THE PRINCE OF WALES" and including two dukes, sixteen earls, eight or nine viscounts, and a variety of other nobility, insinuated the volume into drawingrooms where it would not otherwise have gone. As a result, the poet was long known as "Anacreon" Moore.

Yet, despite the skillful and easy versification—perhaps because of it—the book leaves on the modern reader an impression of lush monotony.

In 1800, however, the romantic movement was yet young.
The *Lyrical Ballads* were two years old, but they lacked an
Earl of Moira and a Dr. Hume to publicize them. Wordsworth's "An Evening Walk" and "Descriptive Sketches"
(both in 1793) were in the prevailing Georgian mode, and
Coleridge's *Poems on Various Subjects* (1796) scarcely
prophesied "The Ancient Mariner." Southey had published
nothing in the new manner; Blake was unknown; Burns was
Scotch; Byron, a boy of twelve, was sulkily fighting off his
mother at Newstead; Shelley, a lad of eight, was frightening
his sisters with amateur chemical experiments at Field Place;
and Keats was an infant of five. The most impressive poet
before the public was Crabbe, but Crabbe had been silent
fifteen years. Surveying with desperate optimism the state
of poetry in the last half of 1800, the editors of the *British
Critic* could point only to Mr. Cottle's *Alfred*, Mr. Hayley's
Essay on Sculpture, the "elegant volume" of the Earl of Carlisle (Byron was to refer disrespectfully to his "paralytic
puling"), Thompson's *Pictures of Poetry*, Mr. Bidlake's *The
Summer Eve*, Hoole's Metastasio, and kindred forgotten volumes. Poetry was stagnating in a Sargasso Sea of weedy
rhetoric.

Moore's historic mission was to restore music to English
verse as the romantics understood verbal music. Opening the
volume at random, one finds the liquid movement of the lines
admirable in their kind, even when the passage does not rise
above the dead level of lusciousness. Here, for example, is
an excerpt from Ode LVII describing Venus on the waters:

> And stealing on, she gently pillows
> Her bosom on the amorous billows.
> Her bosom, like the humid rose,
> Her neck, like dewy-sparkling snows,

Illumine the liquid path she traces,
And burn within the stream's embraces!

There had been nothing like this since the seventeenth century. Readers found it strange, intoxicating, and sweet. Granted that to our taste this is vicious writing—vicious because the sense is drowned in the sound—it has yet that "luxury" in which Keats was to delight. Indeed, it is curious how *Anacreon* anticipates the styles of greater men. Byron, of course, went to school to Moore in his handling of octosyllables, but it is startling to find the movement of Shelley's "Lines Written Among the Euganean Hills" foretold in Moore:

Listen to the Muse's Lyre,
Master of the pencil's fire!
Sketch'd in painting's bold display,
Many a city first portray;
Many a city, revelling free,
Warm with loose festivity.
                    (Ode III)

A famous passage in "Kubla Khan" is foreshadowed in Ode XLIII:

A youth the while, with loosen'd hair
Floating on the listless air,
Sings, to the wild-harp's tender tone,
A tale of woes, alas! his own—
And then, what nectar in his sigh,
As o'er his lip the murmurs die!

Moore could not of course wholly shake off the baneful rhetoric of Georgian poetry, so that the *Anacreon* contains periphrases as cumbrous as any in the *Anthologia Hibernica:*

Taught the unnumber'd scaly throng
To trace their liquid path along;
While for the umbrage of the grove,
She plum'd the warbling world of love.
                    (Ode XXIV)

But he could also be succinct:

Swift as the wheels that kindling roll,
Our life is hurrying to the goal:
A scanty dust, to feed the wind,
Is all the trace 'twill leave behind.
(Ode XXXII)

And Carew or Herrick might have signed such a passage as:

I wish I were the zone, that lies
Warm to thy breast, and feels its sighs;
Or like those envious pearls that show
So faintly round that neck of snow,
Yes—I would be a happy gem,
Like them to hang, to fade like them;
What more would thy Anacreon be?
Oh! any thing that touches thee.
(Ode XXII)

Presumably the fashionable world of readers cared little for this astonishing revival of Cavalier beauty, but it certainly warmed to the delicate artifice of Moore's fusion of eroticism, wine, roses, and elegance:

Vulcan! hear your glorious task,
I do not from your labours ask
In gorgeous panoply to shine—
For war was ne'er a sport of mine.

.   .   .   .   .

But oh! let vines luxuriant roll
Their blushing tendrils round the bowl.
While many a rose-lip'd bacchant maid
Is culling clusters in their shade.
Let sylvan gods, in antic shapes,
Wildly press the gushing grapes;
And flights of loves, in wanton ringlets,
Flit around on golden winglets;
While Venus, to her mystic bower,
Beckons the rosy vintage-power.
(Ode IV)

Few poets upon their first entrance into English literature have sounded so fresh and individual a note.

Moreover, the volume displayed a gentlemanly scholarship, flattering the noble graduates of Eton and Oxford with casual references to an erudition most of them never possessed. "There is very little known with certainty of the life of Anacreon," the preface begins. "Chamæleon Heracleotes, who wrote upon the subject, has been lost in the general wreck of ancient literature"; and our brilliant collegian touches lightly upon "Monsieur Gaçon (le poëte sans fard,)", Bayle, Madame Dacier, Solinus, Scaliger, and "the Danish Poets collected by Rostgaard." The notes likewise display a profusion of superfluous learning. Yet, though Moore had access to Spaletti's facsimile edition of the Palatine manuscript containing the odes, which dates from the tenth century A.D., he did not suspect that the poems were not the work of Anacreon, who lived in the sixth century B.C. "The soul of Anacreon," he writes, "speaks so unequivocally through his odes, that we may consult them as the faithful mirrors of his heart"; wherefore Moore paints a charming picture of an "elegant voluptuary" who never existed. He even refers to the poems as "the most polished remains of antiquity," though the Greek, dating from Roman and even Byzantine times, is far from impeccable.[7]   But it is unfair to blame him; the error was shared by almost all Grecians, including the next translator of the poems, the Rev. Hercules Young, whose version,[8] posthumously published in 1802, excessively ignores that of Moore.

But more important than the showy learning is the impulse that the *Odes of Anacreon* helped to give to the literary revival of Hellenism which forms an important living element in the romantic movement. For the Augustan age antiquity had been Roman or, when it was Greek, Greek in the fashion of Johnson's *Irene.* Now antiquity was becoming warm, colorful, and Hellenistic. *The Antiquities of Athens* by Stuart and Revett, first published in 1762, began in 1787 a series of new editions. The Society of the Dilettanti brought back exciting reports of Greece under the rule

of the Turks, and the Elgin Marbles were about to be trans-
planted from the blue sky of Hellas to the smoke of London.
"Classical" architecture, which had begun by adopting Roman
motives, ended by turning Greek, passing from austerity to
gracility in the process, as Doric temples commenced to
sprout on English lawns and the Greek fret or "anthemion"
ran in long friezes over the heads of diners in the houses of
noblemen. In the entrance hall of Carlton House the Discob-
olus, Antinoüs, and two of the muses stared with plaster eyes
at a stove of "new and elegant" construction garnished with
a Greek bas-relief, and the Trinity Brethren met in their new
house amid a profusion of Ionic pilasters to license poor sea-
men to row on the Thames. The new mode had invaded
painting, to the disgust of Horace Walpole, who referred
unclassically to Barry's Venus "standing stark naked in front
and dragging herself up to Heaven by a pyramid of her own
red hair"; but despite the petulance of the builder of Straw-
berry Hill, Barry, Fuseli, Flaxman, and others were to find
flowing line and poetic coloring appropriate to the gods
of Hellas. In literature the gap which separates Pope's
Homer from Byron's *Childe Harold* had still to be bridged;
Shelley's *Hellas* and Keats' *Lamia* must be prepared for; and
there can be little doubt that the warmth, the eroticism, the
lyricality of Moore's *Anacreon* led the way. Nor was its
vogue transient; if one judges by the critical notices, laudatory verse, and biographical accounts evoked by the poet's
growing celebrity, the translation continued to be extensively
read three or four decades after it first appeared.

IV

He was "Anacreon" Moore, and vibrated between the ex-
citements of town and the rural pleasures of Donington Hall,
where he did most of his composing. Town included the
affability of that hope of the Whigs, George, Prince of Wales
("He is beyond doubt a man of very fascinating manners,"
who "was happy to know a *man of my abilities!*"), and sing-

ing in his fresh young voice at an endless succession of evening parties. Moore's performances at the piano were unique. Sir Jonah Barrington remembered him "now throwing up his ecstatic eyes to heaven, as if to invoke refinement—then casting them softly sideways, and breathing out his cromatics [*sic*]." William Jerdan describes him, in a spate of luxuriant adjectives, seated at the piano and chanting his own melodies "with all the sentiment and expression of the poet."

Though almost recitative and without strong powers of voice, he was then in his glory, his small figure magnified into an Apollo, and his round countenance beaming, or perhaps the more accurately descriptive word would be sparkling with intelligence and pleasure, whilst Beauty crowded enamoured around him and hung with infectious enthusiasm upon his every note. . . . I have seen instances of extraordinary excitement produced by his musical fascinations,

> Trembling, fainting,
> Possessed beyond the Muse's painting,

young female feeling almost overcome in decorum; yet, sometimes, the playful dominating, so that it was not out of place to hear, as I once did, a witty old Scotch lady perpetrate a bad pun, and tell him that he made a paradise like the Greek Hesperides by his Peri-days.

Edmund Griffin long remembered his "bright smile and the brilliant eye-beam" which accompanied the flashes of his wit. "I cannot," he writes,

describe his singing; it is perfectly unique. The combination of music, and of poetic sentiment, emanating from one mind, and glowing in the very countenance, and speaking in the very voice which that same mind illuminates and directs, produces an effect upon the eye, the taste, the feeling, the whole man in short, such as no mere professional excellence can at all aspire to equal. His head is cast backward, and his eyes upward, with the true inspiration of an ancient bard. His voice, though of little compass, is inexpressibly sweet. He realized to me, in many respects, my conceptions of the poet of love and wine; the refined and elegant, though voluptuous Anacreon.[9]

And how Moore reveled in his success! He was introduced to Lord Lansdowne; he had a "splendid déjeuner" at Sir John Coghill's "with charming music. I sang several things with Lord Dudley and Miss Cramer" [why should not a lord sing as well as a commoner?]; he "dined with the Bishop of Meath on Friday last, and went to a party at Mrs. Crewe's in the evening." And "what do you think, young Lord Forbes and another young nobleman dine *with me* tomorrow!" Happy world, with such goodly creatures in it, prepared to notice an impecunious Irish boy! "My songs have taken such a rage! even surpassing what they did in Dublin." All this and more he poured out in letters to "sweetest, dearest mama," who cherished every glittering name.

But there were anxious intervals at Donington Hall. He could not live indefinitely on the sale of *Anacreon* and of the songs Carpenter published, and he did not want to be a drain on the little shop in Aungier Street. At "Mrs. Crouch's cottage in the King's Road" Joseph Kelly introduced him to his famous brother, Michael. Why not write a light opera together—something like *Adelmorn the Outlaw*, which Kelly and "Monk" Lewis had just produced at Drury Lane? So Moore and Kelly went to work with somewhat indifferent success, Moore finding Kelly no composer; and *The Gypsy Prince* [10] was accordingly brought out at the Haymarket July 24, 1801, with Kelly as the principal gypsy. Although the airs were "uniformly encored" the first night, and though Kelly found the poetry "pretty," the piece had no run, the *Morning Post* observing next day that "the reputed author of the dialogue had not been very studious of originality." Meanwhile, Moore was working on another dramatic piece (possibly *M. P.*),[11] which, however, proved "too expensive for Colman's theatre." But in 1801 Moore also published the commercially profitable *Poems of Thomas Little*, which paid off certain of his debts. Yet money seemed somehow to slip through his fingers, though he wrote home indomitably that "I'll make you as rich as a nabob."

He held sober consultations by mail with "Monk" Lewis, who, like everyone else, was charmed with him, but who was cannily "not conscious of possessing '*personal influence*' with any one person," and declined hunting Moore a job. He held conversations with the stately Lord Moira, who was just then under the pleasing illusion that he was to be called to office by his gracious sovereign. His gracious sovereign, however, merely made that nobleman commander-in-chief for Scotland, where, in 1803, he could not even get himself elected Lord Rector of Glasgow. Politics had its ironies; it was planned to create an Irish laureateship, which Atkinson and Moira contrived to keep in view for Tommy; but Moore's patriotic family apparently objected to hymning the House of Hanover, and after the experimental "Ode for the Birthday" already cited, he resigned the "paltry and degrading stipend," or the prospects of it, explaining that he had accepted only under the "*urging* apprehension that my dears at home wanted it." We hear something of a "very promising *periodical work* to commence in about a month or two," [12] expected to "*double* the *income* of the laureateship to me," which remains persistently anonymous. Meanwhile, Uncle Joyce Codd was not worried about the money he had lent; Carpenter continued to make advances; and Moore, with affectionate imprudence, shipped a new piano to Dublin for Kate to play. Then the government suddenly offered to place any friend of Lord Moira's as registrar of a naval prize court in Bermuda; and at midnight one August Sunday Moore sat down to explain the thing to his mother without revealing his destination—a deception for which his father rebuked him nine days later. So he wrote soothingly in September that Bermuda is "a place where physicians order their patients when no other will keep them alive"; and having made the acquaintance of the newly wedded Mr. and Mrs. Anthony

Merry, who were going to Washington, Moore set sail from Portsmouth, late in September, 1803, into the unknown. Unfortunately, he left *Thomas Little* behind him.

v

The Poems of Thomas Little proved to be a mistake. The transparent subterfuge of attributing the book to a young poet dead at twenty-one, who had given "much of his time to the study of the amatory writers," deceived nobody, especially since a second edition contained a dedicatory preface to Atkinson signed "T. M." Moreover, the disingenuous plea that "their author, as unambitious as indolent, scarce ever looked beyond the moment of composition" was both false and an invitation to a crushing critical rejoinder. The contents of the volume were negligible. Moore recovered the light precision of Prior in such a stanza as

> Still the question I must parry,
>   Still a wayward truant prove;
> Where I love, I must not marry,
>   Where I marry, cannot love;

and, as always, his handling of anapaests was exquisite:

> "Come, tell me," says Rosa, as kissing and kist,
>   One day she reclin'd on my breast;
> "Come tell me the number, repeat me the list
>   "Of the nymphs you have lov'd and carest."
> Oh Rosa! 'twas only my fancy that rov'd,
>   My heart at the moment was free;
> But I'll tell you, my girl, how many I've lov'd,
>   And the number shall finish with thee!

But the attempt of Tommy to present himself to the world as a desperate rake was merely funny, the one or two poems which attempt the blood-pudding melodrama of "Monk" Lewis merely imitative. The "note" of the collection is amatory and Epicurean. Moore offended the strait-laced in certain pieces unduly "warm," in which his imagination threatens to hover on the edge of prurience, and he frightened the godly by seeming to be indifferent to all ethical codes:

> I find the doctors and the sages
> Have differ'd in all climes and ages,
> And two in fifty scarce agree
> On what is pure morality!
> 'Tis like the rainbow's shifting zone,
> And every vision makes its own.

Even though "Morality" utters conventional praise of

> The plain, good man, whose actions teach
> More virtue than a sect can preach,

Moore's association with the circle of the Prince Regent led many to believe that he was preaching sexual licence and religious indifference. Though he subsequently suppressed some of the objectionable pieces, he had furnished the Tories with a handle against him which they never failed to use; and the result was to give Thomas Little a notoriety (helped by a rapid succession of editions) out of all proportion to his artistic importance in the life of Thomas Moore.

The verses written by Moore in this period (the *Thomas Little* poems being distributed among them) occupy almost a volume of the *Poetical Works* and deserve more attention than they have received. These poems fall into several categories. Some are songs to music, for Moore was already in Carpenter's hands and was publishing in this vein. Moore's ability in this genre is unsurpassed, but unfortunately the verses, detached from the accompaniment, lose half their force. Occasionally, however, even among these early poems, the words mount to lyric emotion:

> Take back the sigh, thy lips of art
>   In passion's moment breath'd to me;
> Yet, no—it must not, will not part,
> 'Tis now the life-breath of my heart,
>   And has become too pure for thee.

Take back the kiss, that faithless sigh
    With all the warmth of truth imprest
Yet, no—the fatal kiss may lie
Upon *thy* lip its sweets would die,
    Or bloom to make a rival blest.

Take back the vows that, night and day,
    My heart receiv'd, I thought, from thine;
Yet, no—allow them still to stay,
They might some other heart betray,
    As sweetly as they've ruin'd mine.

Before one complains that this has all the lyric virtues except intensity, one should remember that intensity has no place in songs of this order, as greater lyric poets have failed to discover.

A second group is composed of those poems of occasion and compliment which such a social being was expected to write. Two may be singled out for comment. A poem addressed to Mrs. Henry Tighe, the authoress (she deserves the feminine ending) of *Psyche,* admired by Keats, is illuminating, first, because it perfectly expresses Moore's delight in the light, sensuous Hellenism he was popularizing, and second, because Mrs. Tighe of the "rich, flowing, dark-brown hair, a few tendrils of which stray upon her smooth, intellectual forehead," the large, pellucid, deep-blue eyes, and the face "sweet, innocent, and lofty, but tinged with a look of inexpressible sadness," [13] exactly embodied his feminine ideal. The second of these poems, "To the Invisible Girl" [14] (a sister of William Beckford), achieved a mild celebrity and sets forth that neo-Platonic sexuality which was to charm so many of the romantics:

Then, come and be near me, for ever be mine,
We shall hold in the air a communion divine,
As sweet as, of old, was imagin'd to dwell
In the grotto of Numa, or Socrates' cell.
And oft, at those lingering moments of night,
When the heart's busy thoughts have put slumber to flight,

You shall come to my pillow and tell me of love,
Such as angel to angel might whisper above.

If one remembers Shelley's expressed admiration for Moore's
poems, it is not too cruel to recall that this seraphic formula
for amatory communion precedes by some twenty years the
cave and island to which the too imperfect Emilia Viviani was
adjured to send her soul:

Seraph of Heaven! too gentle to be human,
Veiling beneath that radiant form of Woman
All that is insupportable in thee
Of light, and love, and immortality!

. . . at the noontide hour, arrive
Where some old cavern hoar seems yet to keep
The moonlight of the expired night asleep,
Through which the awakened day can never peep;
A veil for our seclusions. . . .

A third group is directly Hellenistic in origin or theme.
Among these are the fragments of a longer poem (which
eventually became *Alciphron* and, after that, *The Epicurean*,
Moore's solitary novel), a handful of translations, two or
three irregular odes, and one or two poems on Greek philosophy. Here the important thing is Moore's endeavor to express a sincere, if shallow, neo-Platonic mysticism in verse
possessing the sensuous grace of an antique intaglio; and in
these poems Moore ever and again attains that sweet, silver
rhetoric which was his peculiar contribution to the Greek
revival, as in

Who is the maid, with golden hair,
With eye of fire, and foot of air,
Whose harp around my altar swells?

or

Who that has cull'd a fresh-blown rose
Will ask it why it breathes and glows,
Unmindful of the blushing ray,
In which it shines its soul away;

Unmindful of the scented sigh,
With which it dies and loves to die.

His endeavor in two or three of these pieces to trace

        the soul's untraceable descent
From that high fount of spirit, through the grades
Of intellectual being, till it mix
With atoms vague, corruptible and dark,

whatever it may lack in intellectual rigor, is of importance to
his philosophical outlook.

Finally, a discussion of these juvenilia cannot close without
quoting that gem of elvish humor in which Moore pokes fun
at himself:

Good reader! if you e'er have seen,
  When Phœbus hastens to his pillow,
The mermaids, with their tresses green,
  Dancing upon the western billow:
If you have seen, at twilight dim,
When the lone spirit's vesper hymn
  Floats wild along the winding shore,
If you have seen, through mist of eve,
The fairy train their ringlets weave,
Glancing along the spangled green:—
  If you have seen all this, and more,
God bless me, what a deal you've seen!

Chapter IV

THE change was startling. One month the center
of attention in London drawingrooms or among the liveried
servants of Donington Hall, Moore was the next month a
voyager—a lonely, dandiacal little figure pacing the deck of
the *Phaeton* frigate as it loitered under George Cockburn's
command southward through the Atlantic. The ship sailed
from Spithead September 25, 1803, having on board Mr.
Anthony Merry and his bride, a rich widow who was bringing a large retinue of servants and a well-developed sense of
punctilio to the conquest of barbarous Washington. Mr.
Merry had given up the pleasures of diplomacy in France
for the doubtful honor of being British minister to the United
States. "I thought you the first day you came aboard," the
first lieutenant told Moore, "the damnedest conceited little
fellow I ever saw, with your glass cocked up to your eye."
But the conquest of the quarter-deck, like the conquest of
the ministerial family, was complete. Long afterwards, Captain Sir James Scott, then a midshipman on the *Phaeton*, remembered how Moore "appeared the life and soul of the
company," and how "the loss of his fascinating society was
frequently and loudly lamented by the officers" when he
quitted the vessel.

In Dublin meanwhile the plausible MacNally was efficiently betraying his client's secrets to the same government
which had appointed Moore registrar; Robert Emmet, eloquent in the dock, mournfully demanded that no man write
his epitaph; and Sarah Curran was lying prostrate with grief.

Moore could know nothing of these things, though his father
had cannily remarked on the "special interference of Providence" in getting Tom "so honourable a situation at this very
critical time" in Ireland. The author of "She is far from the
land where her young hero sleeps" was unprophetically contemplating life in the Azores, where, he remarks in a characteristic note, the inhabitants "are much addicted to gallantry."
The first leg of the voyage had been accomplished in "almost
continuous calms," or, more poetically,

> The sea is like a silvery lake,
>   And, o'er its calm the vessel glides
> Gently, as if it fear'd to wake
>   The slumber of the silent tides,

as he wrote in his rhymed epistle to Lord Strangford, the
noble translator of Camoëns. This slow progress gave Moore
plenty of time to think over his situation; and his first letters
home are full of anxious injunctions to Stevenson and Carpenter about the forthcoming *Songs and Glees,* published in
London in 1804. For these seven songs Moore apparently
chose the airs and Stevenson composed the accompaniments
and "symphonies." "The table we sit down to every day is
splendid," he wrote home at the same time; "and we drink
Madeira and claret in common. There is every hope, every
prospect of happiness for all of us."

The vessel woke the silent tides during the rest of the
voyage, however, which was "rather boisterous upon the
whole," and Moore landed in Norfolk in November a little
shaken by his experience. Cockburn gave him a seal from
his watch for remembrance and put to sea again, leaving
Moore and the Merrys to the care of Colonel John Hamilton,[1] the Irish loyalist, a "short, stout, red-faced man, well-
bred and well fed," "the very crest of Tory organization in
the South" during the Revolution, whom a thoughtful government had made British consul with a view to ingratiating
itself with the Virginians. As Lord Dunmore and the patriots

had between them burned Norfolk in 1776, the British were not popular; not being allowed to engage in business, Colonel Hamilton had transferred his ships to his nephew, Thomas Hamilton, a ruse which deceived nobody and added to the general unpleasantness; and, according to the Duc de la Rochefoucault-Liancourt, who thought Norfolk "one of the ugliest, most irregular, and most filthy towns that can anywhere be found," the consular staff spoke of the Americans "with aversion and contempt." Hamilton had served under Moira, whose views he seems to have shared; but the consul's acts of kindness during the bitter partisan warfare in the South probably saved his life during the excitement over the *Leopard-Chesapeake* affair, when an angry mob stormed through the streets of the city.

Mrs. Merry was fairly eaten up by mosquitoes and got a fever, but the ministerial train eventually withdrew to the mud of Washington, leaving Tom to contemplate republican institutions. Ever susceptible to surrounding opinion, he promptly adopted the Federalist view of the democratic experiment, the consulate being the center of the disgruntled Federalist merchants. "Nothing to be seen in the streets," he wrote home, "but dogs and Negroes, and the few ladies that *pass for whites* are to be sure the most unlovely pieces of crockery I ever set eyes upon." He seems not to have realized that yellow fever had recently swept the place. However, the Hamiltons were kind; there was a harpsichord in the drawingroom, "which looked like civilisation"; and Miss Mathews, daughter of a Federalist statesman, "played and sung very tolerably," though "music here is like whistling to a wilderness." The wild Americans were sophisticated enough to reprint some of the Anacreon odes and Little's poems in their papers, with eulogies of the author couched "in the most flattering terms." Hamilton took him to see the Dismal Swamp and told him of a young man who, driven insane by the death of his sweetheart, had perished in searching the swamp for her; and, returning to the consulate, Tom wrote a dismal ballad on the theme, which that sentimental epoch greatly admired.² But he could not find a vessel for Bermuda; and he learned that the revenues of a registrarship in the island were extremely problematical unless a Spanish war broke out. Finally, on December 10, Captain Compton of the *Driver*, a vessel built in Bermuda of cedarwood, agreed to take him to St. George's.

II

The *Driver* lingered a week in port amid the severest winter Virginia had recently known, setting sail only to encounter "most tremendous weather" for a week. But Moore had become a good sailor, ate beefsteaks and onions, and composed "ridiculous verses" amid the howling gale. After a terrible passage the little vessel dropped anchor in the turquoise water of St. George's Harbor.³ It was like entering another world.

> The morn was lovely, every wave was still,
> When the first perfume of a cedar-hill
> Sweetly awak'd us, and with smiling charms,
> The fairy harbour woo'd us to its arms.
> Gently we stole, before the languid wind,
> Through plaintain shades, that like an awning twin'd
> And kiss'd on either side the wanton sails,
> Breathing our welcome to these vernal vales;
> While, far reflected o'er the wave serene
> Each wooded island shed so soft a green,
> That the enamour'd keel, with whispering play,
> Through liquid herbage seem'd to steal its way!
> Never did weary bark more sweetly glide,
> Or rest its anchor in a lovelier tide!
> Along the margin, many a brilliant dome,
> White as the palace of a Lapland gnome,
> Brighten'd the wave; in every myrtle grove
> Secluded bashful, like a shrine of love,
> Some elfin mansion sparkled through the shade;
> And, while the foliage interposing play'd,

Wreathing the structure into various grace,
Fancy would love, in many a form, to trace
The flowery capital, the shaft, the porch,
And dream of temples, till her kindling torch
Lighted me back to all the glorious days
Of Attic genius; and I seem'd to gaze
On marble, from the rich Pentelic mount,
Gracing the umbrage of some Naiad's fount.

Thus he wrote in the epistle to Lady Donegal, but the Hellenic vision was soon shattered. Securing lodgings on the hilltop, apparently near Cumberland Lane, he wrote his mother of the "fairy enchantment" of Bermuda, but added that the nymphs were not beautiful and the "few miserable Negroes" were not proper inhabitants of this Greek paradise. So many prize courts had been established that the income of his post was not worth staying for; and (not knowing that the ministry would attack the Spanish treasure fleet in October), he had no sooner landed than he commenced planning his return.

Although he transacted some of the business of his post, he was soon caught up in a round of entertainment: "there never was such a *furor* for dissipation in the town of St. George's before." An uncollected letter to a naval friend gives a brief glimpse into Moore's Bermuda life:

After dancing till two o'clock at the ball on Friday I had myself roused up at *six* yesterday in order to be time enough in St. George's to attend you, and I refused a most pressing invitation to dine at the speaker's, which otherwise I should have accepted, as an opportunity of seeing the *natives*—after these efforts, which I take no merit from, as it was in my old pursuit (fun), when I came to the cursed ferry, they could not pass our horses, we waited and waited till it was quite hopeless, and we were forced to cross without them and walk home. . . .[4]

In truth, social gatherings were about all the amusement the quaint little place could offer him. He dined regularly with the commanding admiral, Sir Andrew Mitchell; he sang and he played, even though the pianofortes emitted an insupportable jingle due to the dampness; he went to dances; he ate turtle and drank Madeira; and he visited Walsingham House on Walsingham Bay, the residence of Samuel Trott, near which grows the calabash tree supposed to be celebrated in the dancing lines of Moore's epistle to Atkinson:

> 'Twas thus, by the shade of a calabash-tree,
> With a few, who could feel and remember like me,
> The charm, that to sweeten my goblet I threw,
> Was a sigh to the past and a blessing on you!

Obsessed by his dream of Greek perfection, he could find no better comparison for the "miniature heaven" of Bermuda

"NEA" (HESTER LOUISA TUCKER)

than the mountains of Sicily where Daphnis was nursed by the nymphs. And, like everyone else who visits that enchanted island, he rode over the winding lanes "through a thick shaded alley of orange trees and cedars, which opened now and then upon the loveliest coloured sea you can imagine, studded with little woody islands, and all in animation with sail-boats." Bermuda has had few authors who have more enthusiastically described her charms.

If tradition and his verses are to be believed, Tom also fell once or twice in love—at least as rhyming sensibility interpreted the tender passion.[5] A Miss Hinson, who is said to have locked a mouse in her workbox, whence it jumped out at Moore, appears uncertainly in the light of history long enough to receive a lyrical trifle beginning: "When I lov'd you, I can't but allow," included in the *Epistles, Odes, and Other Poems* of 1806. More dangerous was the "Nea" of that same volume. This enchanting creature was named Hester Louisa Tucker and was born August 20, 1786. In June, 1803, she married her cousin, William Tucker, who lived in Cumberland Lane, where she died in 1817. For her, or about her, Moore wrote thirteen "odes," in which, with a profusion of Greek allusions, he hinted that he had loved her in a previous incarnation, or, in the present one, begged her to

> roam no more
> Along that wild and lonely shore,
> Where late we thoughtless stray'd.

Since he also pictured himself and Nea bending over a Greek gem of two lovers kissing, or sending a dove to lead him to her while she slept, or reproaching him at a dance

> When passion broke the bonds of shame,
> And love grew madness in your sight,

it is easy to understand why William Tucker would not permit Moore's books to enter his house. It was all probably innocent enough; and yet, underneath the sentimental rhetoric, one detects a note of more human passion than had yet appeared in Moore's verses:

> Heedless of all, I wildly turn'd,
> My soul forgot—nor oh! condemn,
> That when such eyes before me burn'd,
> My soul forgot all eyes but them!

I dar'd to speak in sobs of bliss,
Rapture of every thought bereft me,
I would have clasp'd you—oh, even this!—
But, with a bound, you blushing left me.

Forget, forget that night's offence,
Forgive it, if alas! you can;
'Twas love, 'twas passion—soul and sense—
'Twas all the best and worst of man!

In view of Mr. Tucker's anger, it was amusingly inconsistent
of the family to name two of Hester's great-granddaughters
Nea!

III

Tom was bored, and possibly a little frightened. He
thought of visiting the West Indies, but "Monk" Lewis wrote
alluringly of founding a coterie which should be "the rally-
ing point of beauty, genius, and worth" in London, and
Moore's family did not write at all, or rather, he received no
letter from them until the middle of March, by which time
he had resolved to leave. Appointing a deputy,[6] he secured
passage to New York in the frigate *Boston*, Captain John
Douglas, which left Bermuda April 25, 1804.[7] He so cap-
tured that officer's regard that ten years later, when Douglas
had risen to be an admiral in command at Jamaica, he offered
to make Moore his secretary, though they had scarcely met
in the interval.

The *Boston* lay for a week in New York harbor, where
"Madam Jerome Bonaparte, and . . . a slight shock of an
earthquake" were "the only things that particularly awakened
my attention"; and then sailed for Norfolk with Moore on
board. After all, Mrs. Hamilton had wept when he left her
in December! Their second meeting had, one gathers, its
tender moments, for Tommy paid that lady the singular compliment of printing in Dennie's *Port Folio* October 6, 1804,
the following extraordinary effusion:

STANZAS

Addressed to Mrs. H. . . . . . . at Norfolk, Virginia.

[Mrs. H. . . . . . . the lady of the British consul, is remarkable for the beauty and redundance of her flowing tresses. Our gallant poet complained that such hair should ever be restrained by the bandeau of Fashion, and requested that he might be gratified by seeing those auburn locks 'unbound and free.' The lady graciously granting this boon, the delighted and sensitive bard immediately wrote the ensuing impromptu.]

> I prithee bind that hair again,
> Oh! do not think that many men
>   Are blest with Joseph's coldness:
> Run not the risk our souls to damn,
> By signs, which (*pious* as I am)
>   Would tempt e'en *me* to boldness.
>
> I've often seen those locks of gold,
> In brightest, dearest tresses roll'd,
>   Yet sat quite cool beside you;
> Each ringlet, by the graces drest,
> The devil and you did all your best,
>   Yet still I have defied you.
>
> But oh! 'twould ruin saints to see
> Those tresses thus, unbound and free,
>   Adown your shoulders sweeping;
> They put *such thoughts* into one's head,
> Of dishabille, and night, and bed,
>   And—any thing but sleeping!

After his visit to Norfolk, Moore set out over the unspeakable Virginia roads for Richmond. Isaac Weld describes the taverns of the region as "most wretched" hostelries where "nothing was to be had but rancid fish, fat salt pork, and bread made of Indian corn." Mrs. Merry had written Moore of the sullen inhospitality of the innkeepers; and, judging by the venom of the poet's remarks on American social conditions, he experienced similar discomfort. In Richmond, however, he was warmly received by a Federalist circle of which his host, John Wickham, the future defender of Aaron Burr, and John Marshall, whose labors in Washington usually ended in March, were the principal luminaries. Wickham is described in the dazzling rhetoric of the age as distinguished

for a genius quick and fertile, a style pure and classic, a . . . beautiful elocution, an ingenuity which no difficulties can entangle . . . and a wit whose vivid and brilliant corruscation can guild and decorate the darkest subject.[8]

He likewise gave good dinners; and Moore, who could also "guild" and decorate, seems to have warmed to a kindred coruscator. Doubtless Wickham introduced him to the Barbecue Club, composed of the legal wits of Richmond, and doubtless the errors of Jeffersonianism were made clear. Departing for Fredericksburg, the poet left on his writing table a set of indifferent verses, whose only value lies in the fact that in them he praises something American:

Yes! I did say on the pine barren view,
　　As weary I journeyed the wild road along,
Virginia's rude soil I would glad bid adieu
　　And never remember Virginia in song.

I had passed through her towns and no converse had met,
　　Though in converse my heart knew its fondest delight.
And so firm in my breast had dear friendship been set,
　　That of friendship I thought I might challenge the right.

But soon was the change when to Richmond I came,
　　For the stranger here met with a heart like his own,
And he sighs that his verse will ne'er equal its fame,
　　And give it for friendship the highest renown.

In the house on the hill a free welcome he found,
　　The welcome that told him its friendship was true,
And long shall the praise of its master resound,
　　While gratitude claims from his heart the just due.

O woman, here too both in beauty and sense
　　Thou art blest with the boon which art can not improve,
Thy looks and thy smiles such sweet favours dispense
　　That the heart of the stranger is tempted to love.

Then, Richmond, accept a stranger's farewell!
If the tear of regret of his love be the proof,
Long, long in his heart shall thy memory dwell,
And in age be the theme of the days of his youth.⁹

From Richmond he set forth by way of Fredericksburg for Washington, pausing in Fredericksburg long enough to write out for a pretty girl a poem to a fire-fly which he later untactfully incorporated into his burlesque rhymed journal addressed to George Morgan, the vice-consul at Norfolk. "Such a road as I have come! and in such a conveyance!" he wrote home. "The mail takes twelve passengers, which generally consist of squalling children, stinking Negroes, and republicans smoking cigars!" An enormous Quaker and his daughter, the latter without a sound tooth in her head, disturbed him; and a talkative student added to his discomfort. He was appalled by the bridges with loose planks thrown over the supports, the vast mud-holes, the rivers "with names as barbarous as the inhabitants; every step I take not only *reconciles*, but *endears* to me, not only the excellencies but even the errors of Old England." He had forgotten the horrors of Irish civil war.

The Merrys, after innumerable difficulties by sea and land, had at length settled down in one of Colonel Peter's houses in Washington, that phantom

> metropolis, where Fancy sees
> Squares in morasses, obelisks in trees.

Mr. Jefferson occupied the White House, or at least as much of the White House as was completed. There, after crossing a canvas carpet painted green in the "hall of audience," set about with twenty-eight mahogany chairs, one or two settees, and eight fire-buckets, the minister of His Britannic Majesty had been formally introduced in a small corridor to the President of the United States. Since Jefferson was "actually standing in slippers down at the heels, and both pantaloons, coat, and underclothes indicative of utter slovenliness," as the

incensed minister informed his Foreign Office, Merry concluded that his master had been slyly insulted. Nevertheless,
he accepted an invitation to a state dinner December 2, 1803,
to which, with the iron-clad logic of republican simplicity,
the French representative, who hurried back from Baltimore
to rub it in, had also been asked. Jefferson had abolished
diplomatic precedence for what he called the "pele-mele"
system. Accounts of the ensuing catastrophe, which became
an international incident, are not unnaturally confused.
Merry wrote Lord Hawkesbury that

Mrs. Merry was placed by Mr. Madison below the Spanish minister, who sat next to Mrs. Madison. With respect to me, I was
proceeding to place myself, though without invitation, next to
the wife of the Spanish minister, when a member of the House
of Representatives passed quickly by me, and took the seat, without Mr. Jefferson's using any means to prevent it. . . .

Four nights later things happened again, and Jefferson poured
out his troubles in a letter to William Short:

Mrs. Merry, happening from the position where she was seated,
not to be foremost, Merry seised [*sic*] her hand, led her to the
head of the table, where Mrs. Gallatin, happening to be standing,
she politely offered her place to Mrs. Merry, who took it without prudence or apology.[10]

This social civil war was further complicated by the arrival
in Washington of Jerome Bonaparte and his wife, whom
Moore had seen in New York, and whom Jefferson found it
tactful to flatter. Mrs. Merry, who had a majestic sense of
her own importance, forbade her husband to accept any
further invitations from the White House, and opened her
drawingroom to the embittered Federalists, who informed
Merry that New England intended to secede—an idea which
he enthusiastically endorsed. When Moore arrived, his hosts
poured their wrongs into his too attentive ear; and when
Merry presented him to the President, and Jefferson gazed
down on him in silence, the little poet's distaste deepened

into ineradicable dislike. He took an unworthy revenge by perpetuating in his verse epistle to Thomas Hume the Federalist libel that Jefferson had a black mistress, and meanly added in a subsequent footnote that "the President's House, a very noble structure, is by no means suited to the philosophical humility of its present possessor, who inhabits but a corner of the mansion himself and abandons the rest to a state of uncleanly desolation, which those who are not philosophers cannot look at without regret." For the moment he was a hot British chauvinist; and a paragraph which he did not include in *Epistles, Odes, and Other Poems* shows how enthusiastically he adopted the ideas of the anti-Jeffersonians:

In the ferment which the French Revolution excited among the democrats of Ame[rica] and the licentious sympathy with which they shared in the wildest excesses of Jacobinism, we may find [?] one of the sources of that vulgarity of vice, that hostility to all the graces of life, which distinguishes the present demagogues of the United [States] and has become indeed too generally the characteristic of their countrymen. But there is another and more permanent cause of corruption which threatens the decay of all honest principles in America. Those fraudulent violations of Neutrality, to which they are indebted for the most [profitable?] part of their commerce, by which they have long infringed & contracted the maritime rights and advantages of this country . . . a system of collusion, imposture & perjury as cannot fail to spread rapid contamination. . . .[11]

Scarcely pausing in Baltimore, the poet wretchedly jerked through the night in another stagecoach to Philadelphia, whither Edward Hudson had gone after being imprisoned in Ireland and in Scotland. Hudson had just married Maria Byrne, daughter of a well-to-do bookseller, but had not yet embarked on his brilliant career in dentistry. He was still an unregenerate republican; but Moore, fresh from his experiences with the Merrys, was repelled by the Jacobin flavor of his old friend's conversation. "I feel awkward with Hudson now," he wrote his mother June 16, 1804; "he has perhaps

had reason to confirm him in his politics, and God knows I
see every reason to change mine." Moore ostensibly lashed
at the United States, but was he perhaps thinking of Irish
Jacobinism when he wrote:

> Oh! was a world so bright but born to grace
> Its own half-organiz'd, half-minded race
> Of weak barbarians, swarming o'er its breast,
> Like vermin, gender'd on the lion's crest?
>
> .   .   .   .
>
> Did heaven design thy lordly land to nurse
> The motley dregs of every distant clime,
> Each blast of anarchy and taint of crime,
> Which Europe shakes from her perturbed sphere,
> In full malignity to rankle here?

He could not too harshly condemn

> That Gallic garbage of philosophy,
> That nauseous slaver of these frantic times,
> With which false liberty dilutes her crimes!

And any dream he may have nursed of an Athenian republic
was shattered by the rude reality of

> christians, mohawks, democrats and all
> From the rude wig-wam to the congress-hall.

Tommy turned from Hudson to the more flattering attractions of the Tuesday Club, a society of Federalist wits,
littérateurs, and gourmets, who gathered about Joseph Dennie, the caustic editor of the *Port Folio,* then the leading
magazine of the republic. To himself Dennie was "a man of
weak habit of body, with a mind volatile and chagrined,
obliged to drudge in literature for a mere subsistance in this
miserable country," but to the literate public he was an odd
paradox—an editor who wrote with the brutality of Cobbett
(he found fault with the Declaration of Independence, called
Paine "a drunken atheist," and was under indictment for
libel), but who also reprinted portions of the *Lyrical Ballads*
with sympathetic comment. His ordinary style, with its

"frequent italics, quotations, and highflown language," was in the taste of the time. Because Moore's poems elegantly phrased the Epicurean philosophy of this circle, Dennie had already reprinted a number of the *Anacreon* odes with flattering introductions.

The diminutive lion purred audibly in Philadelphia.¹² He dined with Mr. and Mrs. William Meredith (the former a lawyer of taste and breeding, firm in his belief in a classical education and in the overthrow of Thomas Jefferson). He suggested to John E. Hall, the "Sedley" of the *Port Folio*, that a mock "Memoirs of Anacreon," illustrated with Moore's translations, would be a neat thing, and that dazzled young man obediently set to work to write them. He sang to Mr. and Mrs. Hopkinson: the husband was the author of "Hail Columbia"; the wife appears in Moore's poems draped in the usual amatory elegance as

> oh! woman! whose form and whose soul
> Are the spell and the light of each path we pursue;
> Whether sunn'd in the tropics or chill'd at the pole,
> If woman be there, there is happiness too!
>
> Nor did she her enamouring magic deny,
> That magic his heart had relinquish'd so long,
> Like eyes he had lov'd was *her* eloquent eye,
> Like them did it soften and weep at his song!

One wonders whether Mrs. Hamilton read this effusion. Moore also kept a canny eye on Edward Thornton, who had been British *chargé d'affaires* in Washington and who was to arrange to introduce Dennie to Mr. and Mrs. Merry. He admired the poetry of Samuel Ewing, whose "Reflections in Solitude" adorns an early volume of the *Port Folio* with metrical sensibility. And doubtless he also admired John Hall's mother, Sarah Ewing Hall, who as "Constantia" and "Florepha" contributed essays to the same magazine. Above all, he drank in the wine of Dennie's assiduous attention. That journalist became "my dearest Dennie," "my dear

fellow," "I only wish that I was *deserving* of such eulogies."
And he testified publicly to the delights of the Tuesday Club
in prose and verse:

In the society of Mr. Dennie and his friends, at Philadelphia, I
passed the only agreeable moments which my tour through the
States afforded me. Mr. Dennie has succeeded in diffusing
through this elegant little circle that love for good literature and
sound politics, which he feels so zealously himself, and which is
so very rarely the characteristic of his countrymen. They will
not, I trust, accuse me of illiberality for the picture which I have
given of the ignorance and corruption that surround them. If
I did not hate, as I ought, the rabble to which they are opposed,
I could not value, as I do, the spirit with which they defy it;
and in learning from them what Americans *can be*, I but see
with the more indignation what Americans *are*.

After ten days of this incense, he departed for New York,
where he entered upon some complicated negotiations with
Captain Douglas, who was to pick him up in the *Boston* at
Halifax, for England. A letter to that officer, written from
New York June 28, 1804, gives an amusing glimpse into his
state of mind:

After struggling with ye break-neck roads of Virginia and the
break-heart girls of Philadelphia, here I am, much—*much* later
than I ought to be, and if you scold me for loitering, I am afraid
I shall partly deserve it. . . . I dread the heat and the return
to-night. I had totally given up the idea of Canada from the
delays I was *forced* and *seduced* to make . . . notwithstanding
the Heat I should go down to the Hook to-day, if they had not
given me to understand that you had some idea of going on a
short cruise immediately. Can *I* be of any use to you or add
my great *weight of metal* to you in your engagement with these
damned French Poltrons? [*sic*] You might make a *powder-
monkey* of me—but I have got so much inflammable material in
me from my contact with the Philadelphia girls, that I am afraid
my interference might endanger the magazine. . . .

From New York he sent for Dennie to publish, and Mrs.
Hopkinson to read, the "Lines Written on Leaving Philadelphia," in which, like the local poets, he dutifully admired the

Schuylkill River. And from Halifax, by the by, on September 29, he sent Dennie "a couple of poems which my lines to the Invisible Girl gave rise to," adding in a postscript: "Do not say I sent you these poems; they are too full of flattery, tho' few people *hate* me more cordially than the person who wrote the English one." The other, in French, "is written by a son of Lord Trimlestone's, and is a tolerable imitation of the style of Bernard de Bernis." Which two poems Dennie dutifully published in the *Port Folio* January 19, 1805.

After a week in New York Moore ascended the Hudson to Saratoga, having paused in his journey to gaze upon two waterfalls—the Passaic and the Cohoes. The latter he admired because it permitted him to make appropriate remarks upon the transitoriness of human life; the former drew from him this interesting comment:

The Falls of the Passic delighted me extremely, and I feel quite indebted to Mr. Meredith for having urged me to visit them. Niagara (*which I have resumed my resolution to see*) must be almost too tremendous to produce sensations of pleasure. I know not whether it is that I feel the magnificence of nature to an excess almost painful, or that I have some kind of *kindred* affection for her miniature productions; but certainly I rather dread such grandeurs as those of Niagara, and turn with more pleasure to the 'Minora Sidera' of creation.

The country about Saratoga seemed to him "the very home of savages," where, appropriately, the barbarous Americans came to drink the waters, but he plunged courageously into the wilderness towards Niagara. The Oneida Indians received the little man courteously, and the valley of the Mohawk drew him to some genuine expressions of regard:

Never did I feel my heart in a better tone of sensibility than that which it derived from the scenery on this river. There is a holy magnificence in the immense bank of woods that overhang it, which does not permit the heart to rest merely in the admiration of *Nature*, but carries it to that something less *vague* than *Nature*, that satisfactory source of all these exquisite wonders, a Divinity!

Meanwhile, in numbers of the *Port Folio* that were to catch up with him in Halifax, members of the Tuesday Club were rapturously rhyming:

> Ye, who saw Genius like a meteor's gleam,
>   On glowing fancy's sportive pinion soar,
> When wak'd by rapture from the pleasing dream,
>   Will find the fleeting prodigy was Moore.

"Right witty, and dearly beloved," ran one comment; "some gentle god inspires thy clay," sang a second; "the celebrated MR. MOORE," wrote a third.   (In distant Westmoreland that year William Wordsworth was remembering daffodils, addressing Mr. Wilkinson's spade, and, as Tom struggled on to Niagara, solemnly writing Sir George Beaumont that Reynolds' *Discourses* were "truly admirable."   Coleridge was off to Malta, and Dorothy was trying to console her loneliness with her infant nephew, John.)

Arrived at the Canadian boundary July 22, 1804, Moore hastened to set foot beneath the Union Jack before viewing the sublimities of Niagara Falls.   The ampler ether of the British empire seems, in view of his earlier qualms, to have fortified him with appropriate emotions.   "Never shall I forget the impression I felt," he wrote in his journal,

at the first glimpse of them. . . . We were not near enough to be agitated by the terrific effects of the scene; but saw through the trees this mighty flow of waters descending with calm magnificence. . . . I felt as if approaching the very residence of the Deity; the tears started into my eyes; and I remained, for moments after we had lost sight of the scene, in that delicious absorption which pious enthusiasm alone can produce. . . . Oh! bring the atheist here, and he cannot return an atheist!

He descended by the "New Ladder" to gaze at the "awful sublimities" from the bottom of the gorge.   Sometime during these days (his movements about Niagara are a little difficult to follow) he visited Buffalo, where, if his poems are trustworthy, he sat down to meditate upon the American scene in another rhymed epistle, this time to the "Honourable W. R. Spencer," which bears the unflattering motto: "Nec venit ad duros musa vocata Getas." He could not but be struck by the contrast between the grandeur of the land and the meanness of the society he had traversed. The one was

> All that creation's varying mass assumes
> Of grand or lovely;

the other,

> one dull chaos, one unfertile strife.

Doubtless Moore's diatribes are neither profound nor brilliant, though he was not more violently anti-democratic than various other European travelers or even the Connecticut wits. The important fact is that if we except the superficial Epicureanism of his earlier books, his experience in this alien land forced him to think philosophically for the first time. Only after visiting the United States did Moore attempt those larger themes which appear in his later satires and in his prose.

It is also fair to state that he recanted his views. He made a half apology for them in the "Preface" to *Epistles, Odes, and Other Poems.* He told Richard Vaux in 1837: "Ah! those unfortunate American letters of mine must have left a bad impression of me. Would to God I had never written them, that I had never so acted." He wrote John E. Hall even earlier—in June, 1816:

. . . there are few of my errors I regret more sincerely than the rashness I was guilty of in publishing those crude and boyish tirades against the Americans. My sentiments both with respect to their National and individual character are much changed since then, and I should blush as a lover of Liberty, if I allowed the hasty prejudices of my youth to blind me now to the bright promise which America affords of a better and happier order of things than the World has perhaps ever yet witnessed.[13]

IV

Moore was detained at Niagara by contrary winds for
more than a week, during which time he fidgeted lest Douglas might sail from Halifax without him.   But the wind
changed; and on his way by boat down the St. Lawrence to
Montreal the *voyageurs* sang him that haunting air which the
poet made familiar as the "Canadian Boat-Song," one of his
most popular compositions.   The air, though he did not know
it, came originally from Poitou; [14] and it is a tribute to
Tommy's genius as a song writer that thousands of school
children who do not know where Poitou is and have not the
slightest notion of what is meant by "Utawas' tide," have
lifted their childish trebles in:

> Faintly as tolls the evening chime,
> Our voices keep tune and our oars keep time.
> Soon as the woods on shore look dim,
> We'll sing at St. Ann's our parting hymn.
> Row, brothers, row, the stream runs fast,
> The rapids are near and the day-light's past!

At Montreal the inevitable lady received the inevitable
rhymed effusion; and there Moore seems to have lingered
long enough to write the ninth of his epistles, addressing this
one to Lady Charlotte Rawdon, the sister of Lord Moira.
In this queer hodgepodge Moore passed in review the wild
scenery through which he had come, tried his hand at an
Indian poem in the best manner of Anacreon, and, after
dragging in the angel Dante saw from the base of the mountain of Purgatory, concluded with a welter of compliments
to Moira, Donington Hall, and the Prince of Wales.   Even
homesickness cannot excuse this unbelievable passage on the
First Gentleman of Europe:

> the bright future Star of England's Throne,
> With magic smile, hath o'er the banquet shone,
> Winning respect, nor claiming what he won,
> But tempering greatness, like an evening sun

Whose light the eye can tranquilly admire,
Glorious but mild, all softness yet all fire!

Quebec the poet oddly compared to "a hog in armour upon a bed of roses," but after a passage of thirteen days he left that porcine city behind him and arrived at Halifax a month later than the date on which Captain Douglas had promised to pick him up.[15] Luck, however, was with him, for the *Boston* was still refitting and would not sail for three weeks.   The interval was diversified by his serving as examiner at the "new university" in Windsor at the request of the governor of Nova Scotia, and by dining with the governor of Lower Canada, so that, despite "chill Nova-Scotia's unpromising strand," the time passed pleasantly; and he even managed a poem about a ghost ship off Dead-Man's Island in the Gulf of St. Lawrence, which, within the limitations of the romantic genre, is too good not to be quoted in full:

See you, beneath yon cloud so dark,
Fast gliding along, a gloomy Bark?
Her sails are full, though the wind is still,
And there blows not a breath her sails to fill!

Oh! what doth that vessel of darkness bear?
The silent calm of the grave is there,
Save now and again a death-knell rung,
And the flap of the sails, with night-fog hung!

There lieth a wreck on the dismal shore
Of cold and pitiless Labrador;
Where, under the moon, upon mounts of frost,
Full many a mariner's bones are tost!

Yon shadowy Bark hath been to that wreck,
And the dim blue fire, that lights her deck,
Doth play on as pale and livid a crew,
As ever yet drank the church-yard dew!

To Deadman's Isle, in the eye of the blast,
To Deadman's Isle she speeds her fast;
By skeleton shapes her sails are furl'd,
And the hand that steers is not of this world!

> Oh! hurry thee on—oh! hurry thee on
> Thou terrible Bark! ere the night be gone,
> Nor let morning look on so foul a sight
> As would blanch for ever her rosy light!

There are surprises in Moore for anyone who will read him, and this poem, utterly different from everything he had written hitherto, is one of them. One finds no evidence that he had seen "The Ancient Mariner" by 1804; and unless Dennie introduced him to the *Lyrical Ballads* in Philadelphia, one cannot suppose that this spectral ship and its ghastly crew were suggested by Coleridge; wherefore Moore's achievement is all the more noteworthy.

The *Boston* finally sailed in October for England, and the long voyage gave Moore opportunity to polish his manuscripts. A poem "To the Boston Frigate," written in anapaests, is a kind of coda to the experiences of the last nine months. In it he bade farewell to his Federalist friends, who, like him, had

> sigh'd that the powerful stream
> Of America's empire should pass, like a dream,
> Without leaving one fragment of genius, to say
> How sublime was the tide which had vanish'd away,

an interpretation which, in the light of history, seems slightly premature; and in it he assured Douglas that he would gladly sail anywhere with him, were it not that the west wind

> Takes me nearer the home where my heart is inshrin'd;
> Where the smile of a father shall meet me again,
> And the tears of a mother turn bliss into pain.

After twenty-eight days Moore landed at Plymouth November 12, 1804, writing at once to his "darling mother" of his joy at being again on English ground, and assuring her that "I am not at a loss for employment and that I have it within my power, in the course of two or three months, to draw the sponge over every pecuniary obligation I have contracted."

Chapter V

Despite Tom's eagerness to rejoin the family, he did not rush to Dublin. Instead, he went up to London, taking lodgings at 27 Bury Street, St. James's, where he labored over the manuscript of *Epistles, Odes, and Other Poems* (1806) for Carpenter, and where, it would appear, he also worked up various songs. He was almost penniless. The endless American journey had been possible only because his transportation over most of it had cost him little; now, back in London, the Epicurean bard must devise some way of making both ends meet. "I work as hard as a Scaliger all the mornings," he wrote home with a touch of pedantry, "and a dinner now and then with Lady Donegal or Mrs. Tighe is the utmost excess I allow myself to indulge in." Barbara, Lady Donegal, the third wife and, after 1799, the relict of the Marquess of Donegal, was one of the daughters of the Rev. Luke Godfrey, D.D., an Irish rector. Moore seems to have made the acquaintance of the "Godfrey girls" before sailing for Bermuda; and now, as the lively letters of the widowed peeress and her sister Mary show, the two women offered amusement, advice, and admiration to the struggling author. Mrs. Tighe, on the other hand, offered sensibility. Now an invalid, she had almost died in February, though she survived to publish *Psyche* privately during the year, and lingered on, an interesting consumptive (strange how the romantics warmed to tubercular beauty!) until 1810. Moore commemorated her death in the fourth of the *Irish Melodies* (1811):

I saw thy form in youthful prime,
  Nor thought that pale decay
Would steal before the steps of time,
  And waste its bloom away, Mary!
Yet still thy features wore that light
  Which fleets not with the breath;
And life ne'er look'd more truly bright
  Than in thy smile of death, Mary!

But his letter home was not quite candid. He took an occasional week-end off to visit Tunbridge, where Lady Donegal was staying. A letter from Samuel Rogers to his sister, dated October 13, 1805, written from that classic place, describes a house party given by the Donegals, the guests including Lady Heathcote, Lady Anne Hamilton, Susan Beckford and Thomas Hope (who made love to her), William Spencer (indolent and witty), Rogers, and Moore. "We have had music every evening; your friend Moore and Miss Susan Beckford have charmed us out of ourselves, and our mornings have passed away in curricles and sociables . . ."[1] Were there perhaps some tender moments between the Irish poet and Miss Beckford?

The demands of the publisher proved more exigent than Moore had anticipated, despite the fact that he must have sketched out most of the contents of the new collection before the autumn of 1805. He did not, in fact, leave London until late. For one thing, the facility of Moore's versification is deceptive; and an examination of the original drafts of a number of these poems, now in the Huntington Library, reveals how meticulously he worked over his materials.[2] Moreover, there were mottoes to be looked out, and footnotes to be got up, for the age of sensibility leaned heavily upon erudition at the bottom of the page to support emotion at the top; and there was also the question of the dedication, which, in September, Moira wrote affably from Edinburgh to accept. More troubling still was the problem of the general political drift of the epistles. The preface betrays

Moore's hesitation—he was obviously ill at ease lest he be mistaken for a Tory—and is almost a recantation of the text. "I am conscious," he wrote, "that, in venturing these few remarks, I have said just enough to offend, and by no means sufficient to convince." One's sense of Moore's uneasiness in that political age is strengthened by the foreword to the second volume of the *Poetical Works* of 1840-41, in which, discussing the American epistles, Moore says flatly that

it was the only period of my past life during which I have found myself at all sceptical as to the soundness of that Liberal creed of politics, in the profession and advocacy of which I may be almost literally said to have begun life, and shall most probably end it.

The original introduction made matters worse by pleading that the book was merely "a mass of unconnected trifles," and hinting that "the liberal offers of my bookseller" brought them forth in a time unfit "for the idle occupations of poetry" —an argument in extenuation which, if true, should never have been made. The volume was in fact a *pot-pourri*, as Moore afterwards acknowledged by reclassifying the poems, placing all but the Bermudian and American pieces in the category of *juvenilia*. Obviously he did not foresee the critical tempest which the book was to arouse.

While Tom struggled with proofs and poetry in the summer of 1805, the *Trident* brought Sir Arthur Wellesley from his Indian glories to a command in that futile expedition which, intended to recover Hanover, never left the German coast; Nelson died in the autumn at Trafalgar; Mack simultaneously surrendered at Ulm; and Napoleon celebrated the first anniversary of his coronation as the sun broke through the winter fogs of Austerlitz. The dying Pitt gave directions to roll up the map of Europe and expired January 23, 1806, and by February Grenville had summoned all the talents to a patchwork ministry which lasted but a year. Among the talents, somewhat to his stiff astonishment, Lord Moira figured as Master General of the Ordnance, and Tom, back

in London, wrote excitedly that "something bright, I hope,
will rise out of the chaos; and if a gleam or two of the
brightness should fall upon me, why, Heaven be praised for
it!" Heaven, however, deserved little gratitude. The noble
Earl was affable but vague: "we must not," he said, "banish
you to a foreign garrison," despite Moore's naïve eagerness
to "undertake any kind of business whatever." The duties
of office seem to have absorbed most of the time and energy
of the military minister; at any rate, even though Moore fell
ill (his old abscess which had troubled him in 1800), it was
not until May that Moira offered "a small appointment,"
which the bewildered poet refused "till something worthier
both of *his* generosity and *my* ambition should occur." The
reduction of Dublin to secondary rank consequent upon the
Union, and the general economic upset of the times had led
to a fall in the fortunes of the grocery shop in Aungier Street;
and Moore finally suggested, and Moira found, an appointment for John Moore as barrack-master of Island Bridge,
Dublin, in June. Meanwhile, there were vague promises of
an "Irish commissionership" for Anacreon in the air. But
with the usual irony attending all things Irish, the ministry
fell on a question of opening all commissions in the army and
navy to Roman Catholics, and the Portland cabinet of March,
1807, had no place for a Whiggish general.

II

When Tom published his first volume, critical book reviewing was still rudimentary, and the notices of Anacreon
were not only innocuous, they were empty. The *Monthly
Review*, after congratulating the poet, remarked that he had
not "trained his Pegasus to the true Anacreontic *allure* or
rate," but that "his winged courser becomes more fleet, the
farther he advances." The *British Critic* in 1802 found him
too luxuriant in expression but was otherwise flattering. Of
the *Little* poems the *Monthly Magazine* said that, though a
few pieces might show "inconsiderate levity," the style was

"uniformly splendid"; the *British Critic*, hinting that certain verses were "in a high degree, exceptionable," found the book full of spirit and elegance; and the *Monthly Review* discovered the fire of genius in the collection, even if some of the poems were not the kind of thing "rigid virtue would approve." [3]

Then on October 10, 1802, a group of embattled Scots launched the *Edinburgh Review*, the first number of which carried on its blue and buff cover the ominous motto: *Judex damnatur cum nocens absolvitur*, and by way of showing that no guilty writer was to escape, cut up a Tory pamphleteer named John Bowles, described by Sydney Smith as "hangman for these ten years to all the poor authors in England." In July, 1803, the *Edinburgh* got around to a judicial view of *Anacreon*, with some little attention to *The Poems of Thomas Little*. The magazine was shocked by both the unfaithfulness and the licence of the translations. "A style so wantonly voluptuous is at once effeminate and childish; and it is as unlike the original, as it is unmanly in itself," the article concluding that the *Anacreon* of the Rev. Mr. Younge "is well fitted for a pothouse; Moore's is much better calculated for a bagnio." It is not pleasant to be told that one's first book is fit for a brothel, but Moore, busy about his Bermuda business, did not see, or did not notice, the review.

But in July, 1806, Francis Jeffrey himself undertook an Olympian examination of *Epistles, Odes, and Other Poems*. Jeffrey, who had already goaded John Thelwall into an abusive pamphlet, and drawn from the irritated Southey the statement that in taste he was a mere child, proposed to correct both Moore and the aristocratic reading of the age. The fact that the poems had sweetness, melody, smoothness of diction, brilliant fancy, and some show of classical erudition but added to the offense of their existence. The author's celebrity "rests on licentiousness"; he is the "most poetical of those who, in our times, have devoted their talents to the propagation of immorality." Nothing, said Jeffrey, is more indefensible than a

cold-blooded attempt to corrupt the purity of an innocent heart; and we can scarcely conceive any being more truly despicable, than he who, without the apology of unruly passion or tumultuous desires, sits down to ransack the impure places of his memory for inflammatory images and expressions, and commits them laboriously to writing, for the purpose of insinuating pollution into the minds of unknown and unsuspecting readers.

Moore was a new Sedley, a second Rochester. And then Jeffrey really warmed to his work:

It seems to be his aim to impose corruption upon his readers, by concealing it under the mask of refinement; to reconcile them imperceptibly to the most vile and vulgar sensuality, by blending its language with that of exalted feeling and tender emotion; and to steal impurity into their hearts, by gently perverting the most simple and generous of their affections. In the execution of this unworthy task, he labours with a perseverance at once ludicrous and detestable. He may be seen in every page running round the paltry circle of his seductions with incredible zeal and anxiety, and stimulating his jaded fancy for new images of impurity, with as much melancholy industry as ever outcast of the Muses hunted for epithets or metre. . . . Mr. Moore . . . takes care to intimate to us, in every page, that the raptures which he celebrates do not spring from the excesses of an innocent love, or the extravagance of a romantic attachment; but are the unhallowed fruits of cheap and vulgar prostitution, the inspiration of casual amours, and the chorus of habitual debauchery.

With much more of the same order, including the curious argument that the dedication of many poems to persons of rank could only mean that corruption, having worked havoc among the nobility, would then filter down to the middle classes!

Moore, who had spent some part of July at Donington Park, had heard rumors of the impending castigation. "I wait but for the arrival of the *Edinburgh Review*," he wrote Mary Godfrey, "and then 'a long farewell to all my greatness.' " But the periodical did not arrive to trouble the rural peace of Donington, and he departed, vastly curious, to pay a promised visit to Lady Donegal at Worthing. It was in that seaside city "in my bed, one morning, at the inn" that he learned how depraved he was; yet, "though the contemptuous language applied to me . . . a good deal roused my Irish blood," he did nothing immediately for the reason that, supposing the critic to be in Scotland, Moore did not have money enough to traverse the kingdom from end to end and challenge him to mortal combat. He went up to London only to discover from Rogers, who had just dined with Jeffrey, that the reviewer was at hand. Failing to secure the cautious Woolriche for his second, Moore turned to the more sanguinary and Celtic Hume, who became the bearer of this formidable message to the diminutive Scot:

You are a liar; yes, sir, a liar; and I choose to adopt this harsh and vulgar mode of defiance, in order to prevent at once all equivocation between us, and to compel you to adopt for your own satisfaction, that alternative which you might otherwise have hesitated in affording to mine.

Jeffrey, as innocent of modes of scientific bloodshed as his challenger, secured the aid of the faithful Francis Horner, a fellow-reviewer, who, on withdrawing from the Edinburgh bar, had left Jeffrey by way of legacy a wig he could not wear.

Firearms proved a difficulty. Apparently Moore was to secure pistols and give them to Hume, who was to pass them on to Horner, who in turn was to discover whether they met Jeffrey's approval. Moore set about his task with great earnestness. Rogers did not own any pistols; the tall, grave-faced Hume had none; and as for the poet himself, "I had once nearly blown off my thumb by discharging an overloaded pistol," and naturally he did not keep firearms in stock. Finally William Spencer, who, as one having a poem addressed to him in the offending volume, took a delighted interest in the affair, loaned his pistols and then ran to inform a wide circle of acquaintances of the approaching combat. This was on Sunday night. Moore had previously purchased powder and bullets in Bond Street "in such large quantities . . . as would have done for a score of duels." Having secured the pistols about midnight, he set off in a hackney-coach with Hume for Hume's lodgings, apparently from some obscure idea that all London would prevent him from fighting if he went home; but was nevertheless compelled stealthily to enter his own apartment and take the sheets off his own bed because Hume, with true Irish improvidence, lacked a clean pair with which to accommodate a friend. Moore says that "he slept pretty well." It is not recorded how Jeffrey spent the night.

Monday morning, at the canonical hour for bloodshed, the two embattled Irishmen drove to the stately woods of Chalk Farm, where Regency gentlemen were accustomed to settle their little differences. They found Jeffrey and Horner already on the ground, accompanied by a small battalion of interested friends, apparently all Scotch, Jeffrey carrying the bag of pistols, and Horner "looking anxiously around." There had been, it seems, vague traces of low fellows lurking about in the bushes. Hume and Horner retired peaceably behind the trees to load the pistols, whither the muse of history should also have retired, notebook in hand, since upon their mysterious operations the consequences of this queer affair depended. Meanwhile, Jeffrey and Moore, two small figures among the ancient trees, strode amiably up and down while the poet related an Irish anecdote to which the Scotch reviewer lent an attentive ear. It was then announced that the lethal weapons were ready.

The subsequent proceedings were rapid and confused. Spencer, dining with Lord Fincastle on Sunday night, had told him of the duel, and Fincastle, growing uneasy, had informed the Bow Street police, who had sent an officer by the comic-opera name of Carpmeal and two assistants, Crocker and Wilkinson, to apprehend the belligerents. According to Moore's recollection, just as the pistols were raised on both sides, an officer rushed out from behind a hedge, struck Jeffrey's pistol with his staff, knocked it some distance into the field, and arrested the editor, while a second officer took possession of Moore. The contemporary account in the *Morning Post* of August 12 is, if confused in syntax, presumably more authentic. The officers

discovered the parties in a field to the right of Chalk Farm; and as they were about to enter the field, the seconds had withdrawn, the parties had taken their sights, and they were just in the act of pulling the triggers, and had one of them been discharged, *Carpmeal* must have been shot, as he was exactly in the direction. Young *Crocker* seeing the danger of his brother officer, jumped over a hedge, ran behind the Gentleman, and knocked the pistol out of his hand. *Carpmeal*, at the same time, desired them to desist, shewed his staff, and said they were Bow-street officers. Having taken the pistols from the parties, they secured them and their seconds.

The belligerents, the surgeon (whom Hume had brought along), the seconds, the officers, and the spectators set off in carriages to Bow Street, where they were examined by the magistrate, J. Read, Esq., and admitted to bail to keep the peace—as Moore wrote Miss Godfrey, "for God knows how long." Bail for the principals was fixed at four hundred pounds apiece; for the unlucky seconds, at two hundred. Moore sent for William Spencer, who was shocked, not at the sum but at the earliness of the hour, since, as he plaintively told Rogers, "he could not well go out, for it was *already twelve o'clock,* and he had to be dressed *by four!*" The lean sardonic Rogers accordingly rescued Moore from the police (it does not appear who bailed out Jeffrey), and, as there was some talk of postponing the affair to the more lenient confines of Hamburg, hastily consulted General Fitzpatrick. That man of blood giving it "as his decided opinion that 'Mr. Jeffrey was not called upon to accept a second challenge,' " Rogers suppressed the insinuation that Moore might deliver another ultimatum and carried Moore off with him.

In the meantime, however, the pistols had been forgotten; and when Moore returned to Bow Street to pick them up, the officer refused to deliver them, "saying," wrote Moore, "in a manner not very civil, that it appeared to the magistrate there was something unfair intended; as, on examining the pistol taken from me, there was found in it a bullet, while there had been no bullet found in that of Mr. Jeffrey." Hume had departed for the country. In this embarrassing predicament Moore hurried off to Horner, who honorably assured him that Hume had put bullets into both pistols, and who returned to Bow Street with him. In all probability, of course, the bullet in Jeffrey's pistol had been knocked out by the blow of the police officer's staff at Chalk Farm. The officials accepted Horner's explanation and returned both weapons and the one bullet to Moore.

Unfortunately there was no stopping the newspapers. The *Times* next morning, either through an unlucky accident or, as Moore suggests, by way of humor, changed "bullet" to "pellet," making its account read: "On the parties being discharged, the pistols were examined, when it appeared that no dire mischief could possibly have ensued from the combat. The pistol of Mr. Jefferies [*sic*] was not loaded with ball, and that of Mr. Moore had nothing more than a pellet of paper. So that if the police had not appeared, this alarming duel would have turned out to be a game at pop-guns." The *Morning Post* contained the same error, and, what was worse, printed on Wednesday, August 13, a doggerel poem entitled: "The Paper Pellet Duel; or, Papyro-Pelleto-Machia. An Heroic Ballad," which, though it is no masterpiece, is irresistibly comic:

> "The pistols draw," the Justice cried,
>   "Produce the balls of death;
> "And prove how these dire men of pride
>   "Would stop each other's breath."

They search'd each pistol, some afraid,
　　But glad were they to tell it,
They found, instead of deadly lead,
　　Naught but a paper pellet!

Now God preserve our noble King,
　　And eke his Royal spouse,
And all the branches that do spring
　　From their illustrious house:

And God preserve all writing blades,
　　Who fain would cut a caper;
Yet nothing at each other's heads,
　　But pellets shoot—of paper.

It was in vain for Moore to send a dignified protest to the newspapers—printed, for example, in the *Morning Post* August 18. Hume refused to make any statement on the ridiculous ground that "he did not know who Mr. Horner was"—an attitude which for a time intermitted a friendship of years; and in spite of all Tommy could do, the Chalk Farm episode became a legend, for perpetuating which he later challenged Byron. Out of this *opéra bouffe* came only one perdurable result—the warm friendship of Jeffrey, for Rogers at one of his incomparable breakfasts managed to reconcile the Scotch and Irish Whigs.[4]

III

In truth, the new volume had not been a success. Following the lead of the *Edinburgh*, but with a fine show of editorial independence, other periodicals repeated the substance of Jeffrey's charges; and Moore could not fight all the editors in Great Britain. The *Monthly Review* said that Moore had substituted sensuality for refinement; the *Eclectic Magazine* called him "a literary pimp"; the *Annual Review and History of Literature* dubbed him "the pander of posterity"; the *Critical Review* admired a few passages written "in a lucid interval" but hinted that he was trying to initiate youth "into most impure mysteries"; the *Beau Monde* remarked that he had prostituted genius; the *Anti-Jacobin Review*, though it endorsed his interpretation of America, found in the poems "lust rather than affection"; *La Belle Assemblée* hoped his poetical gift might yet bloom; and the *British Critic* acidly announced that it would not, by noticing the volume, add to the publicity of the evil it engendered.[5] One and all, the editors dared him to coffee and pistols for two. Victorian prudery, it is evident, was not spontaneously invented in 1837; in 1806 the magazines were enjoying one of their seven-year fits of morality.

Though Lady Donegal and Miss Godfrey stood by him, though Moira condescended to write that he experienced "uncommon satisfaction" in the outcome of the duel, the chagrined poet, "neither happy nor comfortable," found it advisable to withdraw by way of Leicestershire to Dublin, where he remained until March, 1807. Almost immediately upon his arrival he was laid up for a week with his old complaint, but he was soon up and singing in various Irish drawingrooms, though he longed for Donington Park. Ireland he found distressingly altered, and, for the first time since his Trinity College days, Moore expressed in his letters some concern about British rule in that unhappy island. For the rest, he read a good deal in Marsh's Library; and he also wrote a prefatory life of Sallust for the translation of that historian by Arthur Murphy, which Carpenter was bringing out, and for which Carpenter paid him forty pounds.[6] This was hackwork, and he did not acknowledge the essay; and, moreover, it is probable that Murphy's Tory predilections led Moore to leave his preface anonymous. But the most important event of this domestic pilgrimage was the inception of the *Irish Melodies*.

IV

To understand the origins of this work, it is necessary to keep in mind not merely the musical taste of Dublin but that of London as well. Despite the lack of great composers, British musical taste in the Napoleonic era was rich and varied

—the admiration of Haydn, Mozart, Beethoven, and, at a later period, of Spohr and Weber. It was an age of great performers. "Instrumental music," wrote Jackson in 1791, "has been of late carried to so great perfection in London, by the consummate skill of the performers, that any attempt to beat time would be justly considered as entirely needless." Possibly the oddity of this judgment is paralleled by the oddity of a performance of the *Messiah*, heard by Haydn, given by a chorus of 1,068 singers, but despite these vagaries taste was generally sound. Salomon, the distinguished violinist, conducted an orchestra which played the symphonies of Haydn and Mozart; Ashley, a rival conductor, first produced Handel's *Creation* in England in 1800; Beethoven had been known for five years, and in 1813 his symphonies were being played by the Philharmonic Society orchestra. *Don Giovanni* had been performed the previous year with immense success.

While gentlemen in pantaloons escorted ladies in sleeveless dresses and high bodices (all supposed to be Greek) to the Italian opera, patriotism, archaeology, and the search for novelty contrived for a while to postpone the death of English popular song. E. T. Warren began in 1763 the publication of thirty-two volumes of glees, madrigals, canons, and catches, which did not reach an index volume until 1836; John Stafford Smith brought out his *Ancient Songs* in 1779 and his *Musica Antiqua* in 1812 (he wrote "To Anacreon in Heaven," which became "The Star-spangled Banner"); and Samuel Webbe published nine volumes of glees, including "Glorious Apollo," one of the most famous. There was a madrigal society, which began among workingmen in Spitalfields. The Noblemen's and Gentlemen's Catch Club grew red-faced singing "Would you know my Celia's charms"; the Glee Club gave concerts; and so did the Anacreontic Society until the presence of the Duchess of Devonshire at a performance put such a damper on their Rabelaisian spirits that the organization expired. In the taverns lusty commoners roared the naval songs of Dibdin, pensioned by a grateful government for his service in keeping the martial spirit alive; and in solitary chambers young gentlemen full of *Weltschmerz* breathed passion into a flute.[7]

In the drawingroom, however, Mozart was too difficult and Dibdin too ungenteel; and young ladies who sang, or who displayed their rounded arms over a harp (the pianoforte was still too expensive for general use) found songs to their liking in the ballad operas of the day or in compositions written for them by innumerable drawingroom composers. To the aid of musical sensibility, moreover, came the Celtic Revival.[8] For, while architecture went Greek, while the Della Cruscans warbled rhymed inanities and Gifford strove with cold fury to revive the style of Pope, this astonishing decade took up yet another artistic fashion. Sensibility had trembled to the morbid sweetness, the long, vague melancholy of Ossian, and shuddered before the bloody specters evoked by "Monk" Lewis, the Teutonic origins of which were obliterated as a mist of poetry, covering Ireland, the Scotch highlands, and the isles, floated over the North Sea to enfold the storied Rhine in a cloud of mysterious romance wherein bards, harpers, legend, folk-tale, and ancient music were alike enveloped. In 1788 the polite world had read in Collins' posthumous ode of gliding ghosts trooping over "wat'ry strath or quaggy moss"; in 1801 Scott offered for inspection the ghostly figure of Thomas the Rhymer, who, poet, prophet, and musician, spent seven years in fairyland:

> She mounted on her milk-white steed;
> She's ta'en true Thomas up behind;
> And aye, whene'er her bridle rung,
> The steed flew swifter than the wind.
>
> O they rade on, and farther on;
> The steed gaed swifter than the wind;
> Until they reach'd a desert wide,
> And living land was left behind.

The Minstrelsy of the Scottish Border appeared in 1802-3; Ellis' *Early English Metrical Romances* with its faint Celtic overtones was published in 1803; and, as poetry dissolved into northern cloud and dreamy wonder, Scott's minstrel, infirm and old, strode into London:

> His wither'd cheek, and tresses gray,
> Seem'd to have known a better day;
> The harp, his sole remaining joy,
> Was carried by an orphan boy.
> The last of all the Bards was he,
> Who sung of border chivalry.

The harps in the drawingrooms, the minstrels in poetic fancy —surely the fecund North could unite them; and George Thomson began in 1793 the publication of six volumes of *A Selected Collection of Original Scottish Airs for the Voice,* containing over one hundred songs and adaptations by Robert Burns. He was but following James Johnson's *Scots Musical Museum,* published in Edinburgh from 1787 to 1803 in five volumes, to which Burns had early contributed even a greater number of his adaptations.

Moore had been in touch with Thomson [9] (who, by the by, had sent him the fatal copy of the *Edinburgh Review*) but, despite the flattery of being asked to collaborate with Haydn, he had found the melodies given him flippant and uninteresting, and he had not taken up the challenge. In Dublin, meanwhile, two young music sellers, William and James Power, had seen their opportunity. The original idea seems to have been William's. If Thomson had been successful with Scottish songs, why should not Irish melodies be commercially profitable? Apparently William Power approached Moore and Sir John Stevenson during the poet's visit to Dublin in 1806. His first notion was that, though Stevenson was to be responsible for all the music, a group of poets were to furnish the words, as had been Thomson's practice. Moore, whose nationalist fervor had been rekindled by his visit to

Dublin, and who had already written the lyric: "Oh! breathe not his name," generally supposed to refer to Robert Emmet, seems to have immediately grasped the possibilities of the idea, as his letter to Stevenson, prefixed to Part One of the *Irish Melodies*, reveals:

I feel very anxious that a Work of this Kind should be under-taken. We have too long neglected the only Talent for which our English Neighbours ever deigned to allow us any Credit. Our National Music has never been properly collected; and, while the Composers of the Continent have enriched their Operas and Sonatas with Melodies borrowed from Ireland, very often without even the Honesty of Acknowledgment, we have left these Treasures in a great Degree unclaimed and fugitive. Thus our Airs, like too many of our Countrymen, for want of Protection at Home, have passed into the Service of Foreigners.[10]

Moore left Ireland late in February, 1807, for Donington Hall, where, except for a visit to Lady Donegal at Tunbridge, he remained until August, when he returned to Dublin, visit-ing that summer "the sweet vale of Ovoca" which his lyric has made classic ground. He did not return to England until late in the following year. During these months he was at work with Stevenson on the *Irish Melodies*, the first part or "Number" of which was issued simultaneously (or nearly so) by James Power, who had gone to London, and by William Power in Dublin, early in April, 1808. Part Two followed during the year. The success of these songs was so immediate that there was no further thought of securing any other poet to write the words; and presently Moore (though the details are not clear) was receiving an annuity of £500 from the brothers Power for his songs—mainly, of course, for the *Irish Melodies*. The facts of this agreement are obscured by a quarrel between James and William Power in 1816 and by later difficulties between James Power and Moore, but for the present it is sufficient to note that the success of the *Melo-dies* furnished Moore the first regular annual income he had ever enjoyed.[11]

Original issues of the *Irish Melodies* are now hard to come by; and it is a commentary on musical taste and Irish pride that they have not in recent years been reprinted. To examine them is to catch some glimpse of the reasons for their sweeping success. Take up the first number—a tall, thin folio almost fifteen inches high, so bound as to open for the pianofortes of the day; a border of shamrocks and willows running around the gray-green cover, the title a riot of type faces; a rude woodcut (said to have first appeared on a Dublin broadside commemorating Emmet) of the Muse of Ireland, chastely clad, pensively at ease under a willow tree, her right arm negligently resting on a Celtic harp—what a world of artifice and sincerity, of rococo grace and innocent simplicity rises as one picks up the book! One opens to the graciously engraved pages within and learns that "W. POWER takes the Liberty of announcing to the Public a WORK which has long been a *Desideratum* in this Country," and that, in his eagerness, the author had forgot to say "that the Public are indebted to MR. BUNTING for a very valuable Collection of Irish Music; and that the patriotic Genius of Miss OWEN-SON has been employed upon some of our finest Airs"—an apology that did not soothe the disgruntled Bunting. The elaborate title page, a perfect wilderness of scroll-work, is ornamented with a harp beside a blasted tree; the next page, an even more intricate flourish of scrolls, contains a dedication "To the Nobility and Gentry of Ireland," for this is folk music for the upper classes. Then the music begins—an "Introductory piece for two Performers on one Piano Forte," composed of "Carolans Concerto," "The Pleasant Rocks," "Planxty Drury," and "The Beardless Boy." Only then are we ready for the songs, arranged for solo voice, as duets, or for a quartet—"Go where Glory waits thee," "Remember the Glories of Brien the Brave," "Erin! the Tear and the Smile in thine Eyes." The fourth song is the tender lament for Emmet to the air of "The Brown Maid" ("An Cailín Donn"):

Oh! breathe not his name—let it sleep in the shade,
Where cold and unhonour'd his relics are laid!
Sad, silent, and dark, be the tears that we shed,
As the night-dew that falls on the grass o'er his head!

But the night-dew that falls, tho' in silence it weeps,
Shall brighten with verdure the grave where he sleeps;
And the tear that we shed, tho' in secret it rolls,
Shall long keep his memory green in our souls.

Number six is "The Harp that once, thro' Tara's Halls";
number twelve is—what Irishman even today does not know
it?—

There is not in this wide world a valley so sweet
As that vale in whose bosom the bright waters meet.
Oh! the last rays of feeling and life must depart
E'er the bloom of that valley shall fade from my heart!

One picks up the second volume—and two generations
before the Irish literary revival one finds Moore telling the
tale of Fionnuala the Swan:

Silent, oh Moyle! be the roar of thy water,
    Break not, ye breezes! your chain of repose,
While, murmuring mournfully, Lir's lonely daughter
    Tells to the night-star her tale of woes.
When shall the Swan, her death-note singing,
    Sleep with wings in darkness furl'd?
When will Heaven, its sweet bell ringing,
    Call my spirit from this stormy world?

—words exquisitely fitted to the melancholy air and, as poetry,
beautifully fingered. And at the end is that song which has
gone round the English-speaking world, that song, the beautiful falsity of which ridicule cannot kill nor parody quench,
because it has caught the sweet nostalgia of romanticized
love as no other English lyric of sentiment has ever done:

Believe me, if all those endearing young charms,
    Which I gaze on so fondly to-day,
Were to change by to-morrow, and fleet in my arms,
    Like fairy-gifts, fading away,—

PAGE FROM THE FIRST EDITION OF THE "IRISH MELODIES"

Thou wouldst still be ador'd as this moment thou art,
  Let thy loveliness fade as it will;
And around the dear ruin each wish of my heart
  Would entwine itself verdantly still!

It is not while beauty and youth are thine own,
  And thy cheeks unprofan'd by a tear,
That the fervour and faith of a soul can be known,
  To which time will but make thee more dear!
Oh! the heart, that has truly lov'd, never forgets,
  But as truly loves on to the close;
As the sun-flower turns on her god, when he sets,
  The same look which she turn'd when he rose!

It is useless for criticism to protest that Shakespeare and
Shelley can better this writing, useless to point out the laugh-
able ineptitude of "dear ruin," useless to speak of sentimen-
tality and hollow compliment.   The world has taken Tommy
to its bosom for this song, as it has for " 'Tis the last Rose
of Summer" and certain others, because these triumphs are in
their own genre absolutely and flawlessly *right*.

And it is equally useless for musical archaeology to protest
that Bunting's collection, which Moore plundered, is a truer
recording of Irish music; that Moore altered cadences, turned
gay tunes into sad ones, inserted grace notes and roulades,
and in general transformed Celtic folk tunes into something
that would please Regency dinner parties; useless likewise to
show that Stevenson's "symphonies" are frequently too much
like Haydn and too little like Ireland, his accompaniments
often commonplace and thin.[12]   What else were poet and
musician to do?   They had to work with the tools of their
time.   Neither pretended to be an antiquarian.   Moore, who
selected the airs and miraculously fitted words to them, went
to work much as Scott had done with the border ballads, that
is to say, in a fashion which modern scholarship abhors.   But
the *Irish Melodies* were never intended to be a work of
scholarship.   By one of those miraculous fusions of two
talents, poet and composer, amid their rain of little falsities,
their small musical and verbal prettinesses, somehow con-

trived to seize upon the essence of the material, somehow conveyed that mingling of mirth and melancholy, of sentiment and tragic undertone, of rollicking humor and plaintive nostalgia which, whether modern Irishmen like it or not, the world has agreed to recognize as characteristic.

Moreover, the ungrateful moderns have forgotten that, long before the Celtic twilight became a fad, the dapper little singer was preparing the way for Yeats and AE:

Through grief and through danger thy smile hath cheer'd my way,
Till hope seem'd to bud from each thorn that round me lay. . . .

. . . A Syren of old, who sung under the sea;
And who often at eve, thro' the bright waters rov'd,
To meet, on the green shore, a youth whom she lov'd. . . .

Avenging and bright fall the swift sword of Erin
On him who the brave sons of Usna betray'd! . . .

At the mid hour of night, when stars are weeping, I fly
To the lone vale we lov'd, when life shown warm in thine eye;
And I think oft, if spirits can steal from the regions of air,
To revisit past scenes of delight, thou wilt come to me there,
And tell me our love is remember'd, even in the sky. . . .

. . . some bright little isle of our own,
In a blue summer ocean, far off and alone,
Where a leaf never dies in the still blooming bowers,
And the bee banquets on through a whole year of flowers. . . .

The lifeless sky, the mournful sound
Of unseen waters falling round;
The dry leaves, quiv'ring o'er my head,
Like man, unquiet ev'n when dead! . . .

I saw from the beach, when the morning was shining,
A bark o'er the waters move gloriously on;
I came when the sun o'er that beach was declining,
The bark was still there, but the waters were gone.

Thus in successive numbers of the *Melodies* Moore ever and again caught the idiom of the Celt as no preceding English poet had done.   It is a nice critical task to sort out these passages from the Regency rhetoric in which they are too frequently embedded, but it is a rewarding one, for passages of Celtic lyricism exist in richer number than the contemporary neglect of Moore knows anything about.

Moore's position in the romantic movement is not quite that obscure niche to which the Wordsworthians and the Coleridgeans, the Shelley specialists and the Keats enthusiasts have rather blindly consigned him.   When he sang, calling forth laughter and tears, enthusiasm and sentiment, he embodied what no other poet of the age embodied—that mythical ideal of the romanticists, the national bard.   Composing his own songs to airs of his own choosing, singing the glories and misfortunes of his race, asking from great lords and ladies only the reward and recognition of his art, Moore presented in his small person the union of music and verse, of folk tradition and courtly accomplishment of which the age had read in Ossian, in Scott, in novel and historical romance.   In a sense Moore did not merely "belong" to the romantic movement; he incarnated it.   He sang at one and the same time the rights of the people and the glories of ancient kings, the pangs of romantic love and the sympathy of nature.   Hundreds who turned a deaf ear to Wordsworth listened, enraptured, to Moore; thousands to whom Shelley was a filthy atheist learned of tyranny and nationalism from the persuasive Irishman.   The curse of Cain might rest on Byron's marble brow, but Moore's insinuating presence inspired neither shudder nor regret.

If all this be admitted, what, it may be asked, of the enduring poetic values?   Granted that Moore was widely influential, does the fact make him a better poet?   It must be said that no special pleading can ever raise Moore to the stature of a great genius.   This fact, however, does not mean that he has received equitable critical appraisal in our time.   One of the peccant humors of literary judgments is to be afraid of popularity.   The faults of the *Irish Melodies* are patent: they

The harp that once through Tara's halls
  The soul of music shed,
Now hangs as mute on Tara's walls,
  As if that soul were fled,—
So sleeps the pride of former days,
  So glory's thrill is o'er,
And hearts, that once beat high for praise,
  Now feel that pulse no more.

13

ILLUSTRATION FOR THE "IRISH MELODIES"

are too facile, too shallow—to sum it up in a word—too commercial. Yet, though it is unfair to judge them apart from the music (this is, however, the only critical judgment they have ever had!), even as poems they are more various, more truly lyrical, more cunningly fingered, and more soundly built than careless reading knows. The brief quotations given offer to the trained ear a wealth of prosodic invention, a treasury of technical resource which neither Byron nor Wordsworth ever acquired, which as sheer craftsmanship must place Moore on a plane with Shelley and Coleridge and Keats in technique, and which, in the management of pause and metrical fingering within the line, sometimes go beyond anything that any other romanticist has to show. The better parts of the *Melodies* are rich in verbal music. The sensitive ear of Shelley was not deceived, when, in "Adonais," he pictured Moore:

> . . . from her wilds Ierne sent
> The sweetest lyrist of her saddest wrong,
> And Love taught Grief to fall like music from his tongue.

The author of "An Indian Serenade" may be said to know something about the requirements of lyric poetry, and he was not writing idle compliment when he placed Moore in the central group of romantic melodists. Even the acid Poe protested that "never was a grosser wrong done the fame of a true poet" than to belittle Moore—and he quoted the *Irish Melodies* in proof.

Chapter VI

O N APRIL 29, 1808, Moore wrote Lady Donegal from Dublin a letter announcing his visit to England, which contains one passage too significant to be overlooked:

I thought . . . that by republishing those last poems with my name, together with one or two more of the same nature which I have written, I *might* catch the eye of some of our patriotic politicians, and thus be enabled to serve both *myself* and the *principles* which I cherish; for to serve one at the expense of the other would be foolish in one way and dishonourable in the other. Though, however rash it would be to sacrifice myself to my cause, I would rather do it a thousand times than sacrifice my cause to myself.

He had left England an object of ridicule because of his duel, and of contempt (at least among the godly) because of the levity of his verse; he was determined to return in the more lofty character of a political writer with a cause. "Those last poems" refers, of course, to the political epistles already discussed; the "one or two more" are "Corruption" and "Intolerance" published in pamphlet form by Carpenter in 1808, and *The Sceptic*, "a philosophical satire," printed in 1809. If one adds the stately *Letter to the Roman Catholics of Dublin* (1810), the third number of the *Irish Melodies* (of which the *Hibernia Magazine* complained in May, 1810, that it contained more political literature than national harmony), and *M.P., or, The Blue Stocking*, staged in 1811, an opera which is, among other things, an attack on political corruption, the difference between these works and productions of the

Anacreon order is obvious. Moore was becoming a political commentator. The epistles, it is true, had made trenchant observations on American society, but to the British public the failures of democracy had only a faint, corroborative interest. Moore now determined to throw in his lot with the enlightened Whigs.

When Charles James Fox died of dropsy on a clear September afternoon in 1806, that best and greatest of men (in Lord Holland's opinion) took with him to the grave the parliamentary liberalism of the eighteenth century. An election the following April had gratified George III with cries of "No Popery" and other sound sentiments, after which party government degenerated into the monotonous shuffling of cabinet posts among a select group of noblemen, more or less Tory. Nothing could shake that Venetian oligarchy— neither aimless military expeditions to Buenos Aires, the Dardanelles (that grave of British reputations), Alexandria, and Walcheren, nor the spectacle of the Duke of York's cast mistress selling commissions in the army, nor the spread of the Napoleonic empire from the Niemen to the Guadalquivir. The Portland ministry sent the Duke of Richmond to govern Ireland, where he remained from the spring of 1807 to August, 1813, a man not distinguished for Catholic sentiments, whom the ministry fortified with the extraordinary powers of an Arms Act and an Insurrection Act. That much-castigated island sank into apathy, broken only by respectable petitions from the Roman Catholics for the removal of disabilities, petitions which were invariably rejected. Then in May, 1808, occurred an episode of some importance to Moore's development.

To enlightened Whigs the practical difficulty in Catholic Emancipation was the question of allegiance, especially of Irish prelates; and, observing that on the Continent bishops were often nominated by temporal governments to the Holy See, they suggested that if His Majesty's ministers were empowered to veto appointments by the Vatican to Irish bishop-

rics, the path of Emancipation would be smoother. Who
first advanced the idea is not clear. At any rate, Lord Fingal
arranged a meeting between Ponsonby, the Whig parliamentary leader, and Dr. Milner, the English agent of the
Irish prelates, in which this concordat was outlined; and the
idea further received the dubious blessing of the Prince of
Wales, upon whom, amid the splendors of Carlton House,
Lord Fingal and Lord Holland called May 25, when "His
Royal Highness spoke to us for a good hour and a half by
the French clock on the chimney-piece." [1] As the Irish
bishops had tentatively agreed to a similar scheme in 1799,
no difficulty was anticipated. But unfortunately young
Daniel O'Connell saw his opportunity and stormed up and
down the land rousing the peasantry with his silver voice as
he denounced this betrayal of the independence of the church.
The fact that the proposed plan was in line with general
European practice did not matter; the bishops, under pressure, hastily repudiated the scheme in September, and Catholic
Emancipation was again postponed.

Now Moore had returned from America a believer in government by the wise and good. "Every step I take," he had
written, "not only *reconciles*, but *endears* to me, not only
the excellencies, but even the errors of Old England." The
errors and excellencies of Old England, however, were one
thing, viewed from the wilds of Baltimore, and quite
another, seen from lodgings in Dublin. The wise and good
had let loose the North Cork Militia and the Ancient Britons
to harry the island in 1798; they had made a slaughter house
of Wexford, his mother's home, and executed Robert Emmet,
his college friend, in front of St. Catherine's Church, less than
a mile from Molesworth Street where Moore was living; they
had extinguished the Irish Parliament in a muddy rain of
bribery, and they had cynically betrayed the Catholic cause.
On the other hand, the ignorant many, roused by a demagogue, had destroyed a fair chance of settling the Catholic
question, and had so frightened the government that in 1810

it outlawed the Catholic Committee and arrested its leaders. Neither the Tories nor the Whigs seemed to know how to act. But Charles James Fox (a name "of which I can never think but with veneration and tenderness") would have known how to act; and in the hope of outlining a program of rational liberalism, Moore set himself the ambitious task of reviving the Fox tradition. His weapons were pitifully inadequate, but he did what he could.

Moore's theory was simplicity itself. If the Glorious Revolution had destroyed the prerogative of the crown, the eighteenth-century Whigs had skillfully substituted patronage, which, in the poet's opinion,

is become the vital principle of the State, whose agency, subtle and unseen, pervades every part of the Constitution, lurks under all its forms, and regulates all its movements,

as the example of Ireland under either Whig or Tory government amply proved. England had had "a Revolution without a Reform, she may now seek a Reform without a Revolution." The reform, however, was not to be brought about in O'Connell's fashion, by heady appeals to the mob. "There is no one," he wrote in his "Prefatory Letter" to the third number of the *Irish Melodies*, "who deprecates more sincerely than I do any appeal to the passions of an ignorant and angry multitude"; and he sprinkled the opening pages of the *Letter to the Roman Catholics of Dublin* with denunciations of the "misinterpretations of the ignorant, and the cold-blooded rancour of the bigoted." A sound politic must place government in the hands of the liberal and the enlightened; it must guard against the corruption of the right and the demagoguery of the left; it must appeal, not to the passions and animosities, but to the reason of mankind. It must, in short, be in the tradition of Grattan and Fox.

Bribery was the obvious point to attack; and to the castigation of public venality Moore devoted his rhymed invective, "Corruption," thirty pages of couplets in the manner of Churchill, with supporting notes in prose. He pictured prerogative metamorphosed into patronage,

> Whose silent courtship wins securer joys,
> Taints by degrees, and ruins without noise.
> While Parliaments, no more those sacred things
> Which make and rule the destiny of Kings,
> Like loaded dice by ministers are thrown,
> And each new set of sharpers cog their own!
> Hence the rich oil, that from the Treasury steals,
> And drips o'er all the Constitution's wheels,
> Giving the old machine such pliant play,
> That Court and Commons jog one joltless way,
> While wisdom trembles for the crazy car
> So gilt, so rotten, carrying fools so far!

The Whigs were not immune from the universal miasma, for, as

> bees, on flowers alighting, cease their hum,
> So, settling upon places, Whigs grow dumb;

but the Tories came in for the fiercer denunciation:

> But, oh poor Ireland! if revenge be sweet
> For centuries of wrong, for dark deceit
> And withering insult. . . .
> . . . thou *hast* that dæmon's bliss;
> For oh! 'tis more than hell's revenge to see
> That England trusts the men who've ruin'd thee!
> .   .   .   .
> All, that devoted England can oppose
> To enemies made fiends and friends made foes,
> Is the rank refuse, the despis'd remains
> Of that unpitying power, whose whips and chains
> Made Ireland first, in wild, adulterous trance,
> Turn false to England's bed and whore with France!

The attack in "Intolerance" was less effective because more vague. Moore lashed out against both Catholic and Protestant bigotry, bringing the poem to a close with the curious picture of Fox as an ideal Christian! The eighteenth-century rationalism which the poet managed to combine with his Roman Catholicism appears in his repudiation of

Bulls, Decrees, and fulminating scrolls

.   .   .   .   .   .

When Heaven was yet the Pope's exclusive trade,
And Kings were *damn'd* as fast as now they're *made.*

But a general plea for a wider diffusion of "all-atoning Love,"
whatever its moral rightness, does not create effective satire,
so that "Corruption" is distinctly the stronger of the two
poems. That the attack in some degree struck home, despite
Moore's later belief that the pamphlet did not go into a second
edition (which it did),[2] is evident from a contemporary
notice in the *Anti-Jacobin Review,* which uncharitably supposed that the satires were written by a madman and wondered that an Irish writer "should have polluted his immacu-
late Irish mind by using the English language."[3] Probably
because Moore published the pamphlet anonymously, these
satires did not receive the attention which their vigor deserved.

The Sceptic stands a little apart from the preceding poems,
an odd blend of seriousness and humor, in which Moore set
himself the difficult task of disentangling Pyrrhonism from the
odium of French Revolutionary philosophy. He repudiates
bigotry; yet he argues that a "rational and well-regulated
scepticism is the only daughter of the schools that can be
selected as a handmaid for Piety." The prose introduction
is, to tell the truth, the most interesting part of this weak
performance, which is too marked by contemporary allusions for modern comprehension, and which is both too long
and too short for its original purpose—too long because, the
theme once grasped, Moore simply revolves it through a
series of applications; too short, because he never grapples
with the real difficulties of his metaphysical position. The
poem concludes with an extraordinary *non sequitur:*

> Hail, sceptic ease! when error's waves are past,
> How sweet to reach thy tranquil port at last,
> And, gently rock'd in undulating doubt,
> Smile at the sturdy winds, which war without!

The little poem attracted small attention then or later; in view of its undistinguished verse, one finds it interesting only because it is Moore's solitary formal statement of his philosophical position.

Some of the ideas scattered through these poems Moore gathered together and focused upon the Catholic question in his admirable prose *Letter to the Roman Catholics of Dublin* in April, 1810, the occasion being a reaffirmation by the Irish clergy in March of their stand on the veto question. No other piece of prose by Moore has the large utterance of this neglected essay. Written with force and dignity, it is notable even in an age which produced the great political pamphlets of Burke and Mackintosh, Wordsworth and Shelley. If it never mounts to the passion and poetry of Shelley or Burke, it lacks the cumbrousness of Wordsworth's *Convention of Cintra;* and the simple dignity of its style shows what Moore could have accomplished in this vein. Had the subject been less local, had the veto question not sunk to a footnote in the history books, there is no reason to suppose that the *Letter* would not now be read as one of the important documents in the polemical literature of the age. Appealing from the passions of the day to the enduring wisdom of statesmanship, Moore indignantly repudiates the demagoguery of Irish politics, reaffirms his belief in the liberal mind, denies the ultramontanist position, unites Catholicism and liberty, and urges the claims of tolerance, good sense, and expediency. One can cull from the pamphlet such aphorisms as these:

The decisions of the ignorant are always violent in proportion to their erroneousness. . . .

. . . the experience both of past and present times proves, that the mixture of religion with this world's politics is as dangerous as electrical experiments upon lightning—though the flame comes from heaven, it can do much mischief upon earth.

The power connected with creeds is always much more obnoxious than their errors. . . .

The Protestants fear to entrust their constitution to you as long as you remain under the influence of the Pope; and your reason for continuing under the influence of the Pope is that you fear to entrust your Church to the Protestants.

Throughout the letter Moore insists upon the autonomy of the Irish church and urges the bishops to follow the example of the Gallican church, "so long free and so long illustrious," rather than sink "so low in ecclesiastical vassalage as to place their whole hierarchy at the disposal of the Roman Court." Whatever Catholic orthodoxy may think of these statements today, there is no denying the force and dignity of Moore's appeal.

II

Even the woes of Ireland could not, however, entirely metamorphose the butterfly into a grasshopper. The future Lady Morgan, whose memoirs begin with a fluttery "protest against DATES," to the confounding of literary historians, remembered how she was taken to Aungier Street by Sir John Stevenson one evening to hear Tommy sing; how the little poet rushed in between dining with Croker at the Provost's house and attending a "grand party" at Lady Antrim's; how he seated himself at the piano and sang "Friend of my soul" so meltingly that her sister wept, perceiving which, the gratified poet followed with "Will you come to the bower"—"a very improper song, by the bye, for young ladies to hear," says the author of *The Wild Irish Girl* with unexpected prudishness; and how he then rushed off to his second party of the evening.[4]   And there were other attractions for Moore —Arthur Clark, "a dwarf in height, a buck in dress, a wit, a musician, a man of science, a lover of quips and anecdotes, a maker of pleasant verses, an excellent table talker," who belonged to the Tom Moore "set" and who presently married Olivia Owenson because, as Lady Morgan said, he was "not only a most excellent and intelligent man in every way," but he "kept a carriage, an advantage which a woman must have lived in Dublin thoroughly to understand." There were Joe

Atkinson, and Lord Mountjoy, and James Corry, and Richard Power (no relative of the publishers); jolly dinners and song, wine and adoring women. Presently Moore was a member of the Kilkenny theatrical group, where he was to lose his heart for good and all.

The elder Owenson had built a theater in Kilkenny in 1794, which, like most enterprises undertaken by that impractical being, ended in financial disaster; but in 1802 a group of gentleman amateurs, bitten by the prevalent rage for private theatricals, took over the house. Three years later the future Sir John Carr, visiting Kilkenny, described the bustle of the dramatic "season":

At Kilkenny I found quite a jubilee-bustle in the streets, and elegant equipages driving about in all directions. The annual theatricals of this delightful little town had attracted a great number of fashionables from Dublin and the surrounding country. These dramatic amusements, varied by races, balls, and concerts, are supported by a number of gentlemen of rank and fortune, for the purpose of converting the result of a highly intellectual and social gratification into a permanent source of relief for those who are sinking under want and misery. . . . The theatricals of Kilkenny last about a month [October], and at the end generally leave a balance, after deducting the expenses of the house, dresses not included, of two hundred pounds, which is applied to charitable purposes. . . . The theatre, which is the private property of the gentlemen who perform, is small and elegant, and the whole, except the back of a gallery, is laid out into boxes, the admission to which is six shillings. Over the proscenium of the stage is written the following elegant and expressive motto, from the pen of general Taylor: "Whilst we smile, we soothe affliction." I saw Henry the Fourth performed: the principal characters were admirably supported, and the dresses were uncommonly superb. Lord Mountjoy appeared one night in a dress valued at eight thousand pounds. The female performers were engaged from the Dublin stage. The house was crowded, and enabled me to speak with confidence of the beauty and elegance of the higher orders of Irish ladies. The principal characters at these theatricals are supported by Mr. R. Power, Mr. Lyster, Mr. R. Langrishe, Lord Mountjoy, etc.[5]

There were dances, shooting parties, balls, and *fêtes champêtres;* the Countess of Ormonde opened her castle for *déjeuners* on a vast scale; and there were large public dances at the hotels. John Wilson Croker attended in 1804, acting Westmoreland in *Henry IV, Part I;* he returned in 1805 to write some bad verses:

> Here Youth and beauty, tread the maze;
> Here Age oblivious loves to gaze;
> While gleams afar, with festive blaze
>   The Castle;

and in the following year he appeared as Seyton in *Macbeth,* Jeremy in *She Stoops to Conquer,* and the Sentinel in *Pizzaro.*[6] Hither came the Blessingtons in 1807; hither came Miss Owenson in 1808; hither came Miss Edgeworth in 1810; and hither came, at one time or another, everybody of prominence in Ireland. The newspapers, dazzled by this array of wealth and talent, spoke of the performances with bated breath—all except the splenetic *Satirist,* which jeered at the desire of the "vain and gay" for fame, excused the "venal performers" (i.e., the professional actresses), who were merely earning an honest penny, and came down hard on Power and others for playing the fool in a "mouldering theatre." [7]

Tommy had already revived the habits of his youth by entering a private theatrical group in London, where, in January, 1807, at a performance of *Of Age Tomorrow* given for the benefit of the Royal Hospital by a glittering cast which included the Marquis of Tavistock, Lord William Russell, and three Lady Stanhopes, he had repeated Joe Atkinson's epilogue and had sung his songs between acts.[8] He seems to have been introduced into the Kilkenny company by Atkinson, where, on the nineteenth of October, 1808, he appeared as David in *The Rivals,* and "kept the audience in a roar by his Yorkshire dialect and rustic simplicity," and where he also appeared as Mungo in *The Padlock,* an afterpiece. On the twenty-eighth he sang the part of Spado in *The Castle of Andalusia,* and on the twenty-ninth he was Trudge in *Inkle and Yarico.* The delighted Atkinson, in his "Three Weeks at Kilkenny," could not conceal his pleasure in having secured so notable a lion:

> Then Moore came the lyre of Apollo to string,
> And give us pure draughts of the Helicon spring;
> And the banks of the Nore shall long echo the lays,
> That his melodies breathe to record Erin's praise,[9]

from which one gathers that Moore probably sang the *Irish Melodies* during the season. A later passage gives some glimpse into the reasons for Moore's popularity as an actor:

> Tho' last, not the least in our favour, I'm sure,
> Our hearts can't forget dear Anacreon Moore;
> The house loudly praised him, (and they're the best judge),
> In *David,* in *Mungo,* in *Spado* and *Trudge;*
> And they instantly caught at his saying so droll,
> 'Can such a small body contain so much soul?'
> 'Twas quite apropos, and himself to a tittle,
> For know, 'entre-nous' he's the *great Thomas* Little.

Atkinson's reference is to a line in *The Castle of Andalusia,* spoken by Spado, who also says: "Even Sanguino allows I'm a clever little fellow," a statement which Moore remembered as "always a signal for [a] sort of friendly explosion" of applause. In this character he was called upon to sing the following highly applicable verses:

> Though born to be little's my fate,
>   Yet so was the great Alexander;
> And, when I walk under a gate,
>   I've no need to stoop like a gander.
> I'm no lanky, long hoddy-doddy,
>   Whose paper kite sails in the sky;
> Though wanting two feet, in my body,
>   In soul, I am thirty feet high.[10]

This was fair enough fooling; but, in view of the Moore-Jeffrey fiasco, one wonders with what emotions Moore acted

David in *The Rivals*, whose main purpose in the plot is to stop the duel between Bob Acres and Faulkland, and into whose mouth are put such cruelly appropriate lines as: "I suppose there an't so merciless a beast in the world as your loaded pistol"; and "I'll call the mayor—alderman—*constables* —church-wardens—and beadles; we can't be too many to part them!"

In October, 1809, Moore returned to Kilkenny to speak his own prologue lamenting the death of Lyster, to repeat his Spado and Mungo, and to add to his repertoire the part of Peeping Tom in a play about Lady Godiva on the second, the part of Sadi in the *Mountaineers* on the thirteenth, and that of Risk in *Love Laughs at Locksmiths*, an afterpiece performed on the eighteenth. The *Leinster Journal* turned a shower of compliments and capital letters on the performances:

Since the establishment of the Kilkenny Theatricals there never was such an assemblage of rank and fashion as our City can boast this season. How delightful thus to behold the genius of Pleasure walking hand in hand with Charity! to see the Loves and Graces dancing in the train of humanity! to view the 'Crew of Mirth' laying their offerings at the Temple of Distress! wiping the tears of the Orphan, and pouring sympathy into the broken heart!

Among the Crew of Mirth the inspired journalist singled out the "Poet of the heart" for special laudation. As Peeping Tom, "the delight and darling of the Kilkenny audience appears to be *Anacreon Moore*," who "speaks and moves, in a way that indicates genius in every turn," and whose "presence always animates the Stage." All of which was wormwood to the embittered *Satirist:*

It was indeed 'a sorry sight,' to behold the *greatest* lyric poet in the world! the renowned, modest and unassuming M——! adorned with cap and bells, and exposed in the broad glare of theatric exhibition to the laughter of a polite mob.

The gentlemen amateurs of Kilkenny, as Carr remarked, were accustomed to engage the "female performers" from the Dublin stage. In the playbill of October 12, 1808, the name of Miss A. Dyke first appears; she played an attendant in *A Comic Ballet.* Apparently she pleased, for the next year she returned with her sisters Mary, or Mary Ann, and "Miss E. Dyke." Mary, who became the celebrated Mrs. Duff (she married John R. Duff of the Dublin Theatre in 1810), born in 1794, if her biographers are to be believed, was at the incredible age of fifteen an actress sufficiently talented to play Queen Elinor in *King John* and Isabella in *The Revenge.*[11] In all probability she was born some time between 1790 and 1792. Miss Anne, or Anne Jane, Dyke, who married William H. Murray of the Theatre Royal, Edinburgh, in 1819 and thus became the wife of a theatrical manager, took such roles as Lucius in *Julius Caesar* and Lucy in *The West Indian.* She was the youngest of the three sisters, born in 1796 or thereafter.[12] "Miss E. Dyke," an enchanting slip of a girl, was cast as Lady Godiva to Moore's Peeping Tom in the opening bill of 1809 and appeared in a small variety of minor roles as well. All three sisters were dancers, pupils of their father and of Monsieur G. D'Egville or D'Edgeville, who won some reputation as a dancing master in London. All three were pretty and attractive, the ill-natured *Satirist* remarking after the season was over that the Dyke sisters were "frivolous," "certainly pretty, and possess an unconquerable propensity to coquetry."[13] This last slur probably means no more than that they thoroughly enjoyed the admiration of the stage-struck nobility and gentry.

The origins of the Dyke sisters are veiled in that same baffling obscurity which seems to overhang everything genealogical connected with Thomas Moore. The birth certificate of Bessy Dyke shows that her parents were named Thomas and Johanna "Dikes." The only other available information comes from the prejudiced pen of Thomas Crofton

Croker, who, irritated at Lord John Russell, wrote John Wilson Croker a long letter, undated but presumably in the late summer of 1853. The relevant passages are as follows:

[The] father, old Dyke, gave me a few lessons in a Street off Patrick Street in Cork, after I left *my Bishops* dancing School in George's Street conducted by Fountaine. He (Dyke) wandered about to teach dancing at the Schools at Fermoy . . . and Middleton School, and became a great favourite by making puppet Shews for the boys. I think I have some of the Scenery of one painted by him . . . and it really is a very clever scene painting. . . . But I well remember he was a drunken fellow, who generally brought home with him a black eye or two from his weekly visits to Fermoy and Middleton, and I think my lessons in that or any piece of tuition under his instruction did not exceed half a dozen in consequence of some desperate affray in which a poker was used to the disadvantage of a very dirty wife who was cooking his dinner. It is quite clear to my mind that all the three Misses Dyke were dancers originally however afterwards they may have been promoted. . . . Mrs. Dyke, the mother died at an advanced Age in a Street off the Strand about 1840 (Howard Street, I think) and I know was buried in the Savoy.[14]

An even more ill-natured letter from Thomas Mulock to John Wilson Croker, March 14, 1854, makes it clear that Mrs. Dyke was English and "sharp." [15]

Tom was to marry "Miss E. Dyke," who became "his Bessy," but not, according to legend, until he had laid siege to the heart of Mary Ann. Her biographer, Joseph N. Ireland, says categorically that Moore "found himself passionately in love with her," and that "it is certain that she rejected his offers of marriage—a circumstance that gave rise to the composition of the celebrated song annexed:"

> Mary, I believed thee true,
>   And I was blessed in thus believing;
> And now I mourn that e'er I knew
>   A girl so fair and so deceiving,—
>   Fare thee well!

The only difficulty is that the song in question appeared in *The Poems of Thomas Little* eight years before Tom knew that the Dyke sisters existed. There is not, it may be added, a single reference to Mary Ann Dyke in the eight volumes of Moore's *Memoirs, Journal and Correspondence*, none in any of the unpublished material, and no reference to Moore in any of the available documents having to do with Mrs. Duff, so that the sources of Ireland's certainty must remain unknown! Though there is nothing inherently improbable in his story, in the absence of more credible testimony, it must be put aside.

Of "Miss E. Dyke" before her appearance at Kilkenny we know almost nothing, and it is even in dispute whether she was older or younger than Anne. Through the kindness of Cyril J. Palmer, Esq., of Plymouth, it has been possible to recover her baptismal record from the Stoke Damerel Parish Church:

> January 9, 1795, Elizabeth, daughter of Thomas and Johanna Dikes.

T. C. Croker, following some investigations of his own, says that she was born on shipboard in Plymouth Harbor, the ship having come from Ireland, but he gets the date wrong, making it November 15, 1793, and adds the surprising information that "Bessy may have altered the Certificate of her Baptism, which Mr Power several years ago procured for her from Plymouth, and in consequence defeated the object for which it was required 'Life Insurance.' " [16] The official record, however, is as Mr. Palmer has transcribed it; and in view of Croker's animus against Bessy, we need not take his information very seriously. On the other hand, it is undoubtedly true that Bessy thought her own birthday was November 15, and that she represented herself with entire innocence as being two years older than she actually was, for we read in Moore's journal that she and her husband celebrated her "twenty-fifth year" on November 15, 1818. It is not surprising, if one considers the circumstances of her birth and of her family, that she should not know when she was born, nor is it surprising her parents should represent her as older than she was, in order to secure employment for her on the stage. Any suspicion that the "Elizabeth Dikes" of the birth certificate is not the "Bessy Dyke" who married Thomas Moore disappears before an acrostic in an album belonging to Eliza Branigan, now in the National Library of Ireland, dated May 22, 1808, the initial letters of which form the name, "Eliza Dyke." The change to "Bessy" came afterwards; and the acrostic is preserved as a relic associated with Tom Moore. When it is remembered that the poet consistently got his own age wrong, we need not be troubled that the age of the obscure girl actress, born in Plymouth Harbor, was not correctly known in Ireland.

In 1809 Bessy was, when Tom first met her, about fifteen years old. She could not have had more than elementary education. Her training as a dancer must have begun when she was seven or eight—the usual age for beginners. She seems to have appeared with her sisters on the Dublin stage either just before or just after the Kilkenny season; at least T. C. Croker remembered her playing Columbine at the Crow Street Theatre sometime in 1809 when the pipes of a hydraulic temple burst and flooded the stage with water.[17] In spite of her dreary origins and lack of formal culture, she seems to have possessed instinctive good taste and was by all accounts gentle, affectionate, and retiring. No good picture of her is available; but if the two crayon sketches by G. S. Newton which open the pages of Bessy Moore's album, now preserved at Bowood, are portraits of its owner, as there is good reason to suppose, she was slight of figure, possessed the same long, oval face which appears in portraits of her sister, Mrs. Duff, had a quantity of red-gold hair, and a delicate and creamy skin. That the portraits are almost certainly of Bessy Moore is shown by a "Moore Centenary Scrapbook," now in the Royal Irish Academy, in which T. M. Ray jotted down notes describing various articles exhibited in Dublin in 1879. One of these was a miniature of Bessy, not now available, on which his comments are: "Very light brown hair in profuse broad curls at both sides of face—very handsome face—fine full blue eyes—nose longish, slight bend towards aquiline—mouth rather broad—lips handsome—neck bare—face oval but inclining to roundness." Her voice, we know, was low and pleasant. Any pretty girl would presumably have done for Lady Godiva; and as Bessy was also cast for Blanche in *King John*,[18] it is a fair assumption that she was best fitted for those minor roles which require only a pleasing personality and some stage presence.

What wooing went on by the banks of the Nore or in the Kilkenny greenroom we have no means of knowing, for Tom was curiously reticent about this phase of his life. As it is sometimes said that his song, "Fly from the world, O Bessy! to me," was written for his future wife, it should be pointed out that this lyric appears first in the *Thomas Little* volume, but it is fair conjecture that he found the poem applicable, and that the change from Elizabeth to Bessy (Betsey Dyke on the marriage license!) owes something to the song, for there exists a loose sheet at Bowood in Bessy's handwriting, without date, in which she made a pathetic attempt to write an answering lyric. So far as the confused state of the manuscript makes it legible, this runs as follows:

I'll fly from the world dearest man with thee
without thee there's no pleasure in it
thy cottage will be a Palace to me
Since thou's[t] vowed I'm to thy Bosom the dearest
no more will I tell thee with a tear or a Sigh
That I cannot consent to love thee

Dearest Moore I'll give up the world for the[e]
no more give thee pain for a minute
my lips shall meet thine with Loves willingness sweet
no longer kind Heaven forbids it
Let us fly to thy shed and there make our abode
until tyrant death does us visit

BESSY MOORE (?)

there Ill watch o er thy sleep with Affection and care
on thy Bosom Ill make Loves Soft pillow
and fondly embrace thee & thy Lullaby de[   ]
and thy Life's wheel will run rownd with Love & pleasure so
    Sweet
that the Longest Life will seem but one minute
that when Lifes Glass is quite run we will each other embrace
and thy kiss sign Betsy's Passport to Heaven

The gods had not made her poetical, but Moore probably
valued this effusion above the sonnets of Shakespeare.

Although Tom returned to Kilkenny in October, 1810,
and although Miss Dyke and Miss A. Dyke again appeared,
the playbills are silent about their sister, Mary Dyke taking
over the role of Lady Godiva on the twentieth. The reasons
for Bessy's disappearance from the scene are unknown, and
the conjecture that her canny mother withdrew her from the
advances of the poet for prudential reasons remains mere conjecture. Moore greatly increased his repertoire, appearing,
in addition to some of his former roles, as Robin Roughhead
in *Fortune's Frolics,* Sim in *The Weathercock,* La Gloire in
The Surrender of Calais, Sam in *Raising the Wind,* and
Walter in *Children of the Wood.* During the interval the
sisters had apparently been appearing in Dublin, for one finds
a Miss Smith reciting at a benefit for the Misses Dyke in Dublin Moore's *Melologue on National Music*—an unimportant
work which he published in 1811, and which he had recited
at Kilkenny October 2, 1810, amid universal applause. He
had been fairly drowned in adulation:

We hardly ever heard a more beautiful composition, and never,
perhaps, a more delightful piece of recitation. Mr. Moore's voice
is to a degree musical, his accent pure, his elocution articulate,
and his manner simple, spirited, and feeling.

On the twenty-first there was a banquet, when "the spirit of
Anacreon's self appeared to hover" over the boards since "the
sweetest of his Poets was among them"; and on the concluding night he seems to have delivered an original epilogue to

the season. And all these flattering "notices" were reprinted in the London papers! [19]

In December, 1810, Moore went briefly to London ostensibly to look after his publishing interests with James Power. Was Bessy also there? In January he was back in Dublin, "most romantically situated at the end of Dirty Lane, which leads out of Thomas Street," catching "the odoriferous breezes of a tanyard," and dining with his parents on boiled veal and Irish stew. In February he returned to London. On March 25, 1811, "Thomas Moore of the parish of St James Westminster Bachelor and Betsey Dyke of this parish spinster" were married by license in St. Martin's Church, London, the witnesses being James Power and Anne Jane Dyke. The young couple went to Brompton "about two miles from town." Moore did not inform his parents of the marriage until the following May. If Mrs. Dyke was present at the ceremony, there is no record of it; and this union between a Catholic and a Protestant, between the brilliant creator of the *Irish Melodies,* who, that very month, had dined at Lord Holland's with "Lord Lauderdale, Lord Erskine, Lord Bessborough, Lord Kinnaird, &c. &c.," and a penniless actress who had, in Stephen Gwynn's phrase, "only the intelligence of the heart," has all the appearance of a runaway match which prudence and the wisdom of the world united to condemn. Unfortunately for the credit of the wisdom of the world and fortunately for Moore, it was the beginning of forty years of perfect domestic felicity.

III

However the happy groom might poetically entreat his Bessy to "fly to his shed from a world which I know thou despisest," the awkward question of a cash income had still to be solved. Moore had been struggling with the problem since his return from Bermuda. John Wilson Croker had become Secretary to the Admiralty; and to the vast indignation of this gentleman (hotly expressed forty years later),

Moore twice wrote him in December, 1809, suggesting an arrangement not uncommon in that easy-going age:

What I wanted to know was simply this—whether if the deputy I should appoint would make it worth my while to resign in his favour (i.e., in plain placemen's language, would consent to purchase the appointment), you could have interest enough to get him nominated my successor, as by that means I should get rid of the very troublesome medium of a deputation, and have a good large sum at once in my pocket. . . .[20]

Nothing came of this extraordinary scheme, though it would appear that Sheddon was appointed deputy in Moore's place in succession to an earlier deputy about this time. What the poet's arrangements with Carpenter were is not clear, but the income from this source was small and irregular; and as for the immensely successful *Irish Melodies*, forgetting the experimental nature of the first two issues, Moore complained that he had thrown them away, though, as he wrote his mother, "little Power is of wonderful use to me, and, indeed, I may say, is the first *liberal* man I have ever had to deal with." The publication of Part Three in 1810 led to protracted negotiations between William Power in Dublin and James Power in London which did not come to a head until March, 1812, when James Power agreed to pay the poet £500 annually for seven years. In the spring of 1811 it would appear that Tommy was in the impecunious state customary among poets.

He staked his hope on an opera; and the fact that his marriage was followed by the production of *M. P., or, The Blue Stocking* at the Lyceum Theatre, London, September 9, 1811, by an excellent cast,[21] suggests that he had some notion of floating the matrimonial bark on a sea of theatrical royalties. Atkinson had encouraged him, and the producer, Samuel James Arnold, though he thought the piece too good for the audience, said it was in the best style of comedy. Moore was in such an agony of nerves that he did not attend the opening, though he went on a subsequent evening. His attitude toward the piece was oddly ambivalent: he told Mary Godfrey that he was writing down to the mob and knew it, but he was irritated because the censor cut out a few phrases.[22]   He wrote a letter to the London papers calling the piece a bagatelle and denying that it had any political application; whereupon Arnold, fearful of the effect on the box office, had to issue another letter saying that the piece was a "brilliant and unqualified success."   Yet Moore was firmly convinced that Arnold had somehow cheated him!

Both author and producer were right as to the worth of the composition. *M. P.* has small "literary" merit, and Moore was right in not reprinting it among his collected poems; but in stage terms it was an effective and amusing musical comedy, having an initial run of eleven days, and revivals in October, 1811, January and February, 1812, July and August, 1815, and October, 1816.   There were also performances in Dublin and Bath.   The plot is no more artificial than that of most musical comedies, and the characterization of certain parts— Sir Charles Canvas, the corrupt member of Parliament, Leatherhead the bookseller, and Lady Bab Blue, the bluestocking—is adroit within the conventions of the genre.   The love plot and the domestic scenes are bathed in sentimental diction—but in what musical comedy are they not?   The satire on political corruption has not lost its sting, and though the wit of the piece suffers from the persistent search for puns, beloved of that age, some of the lines and some of the songs have a Gilbertian deftness.   Sir Charles Canvas, for example, proposes to put a tax on *billets-doux:*

Mr. Chairman! I move that all love-dealings shall be transacted upon *stamps.*—Soft nonsense, Sir, upon a *one-and-sixpenny*—when the passion is to any amount, an eighteen-pen'orth more—and a proposal for marriage—No—curse it—I'll not lay any thing additional upon marriage.

Leatherhead's song is in the ancestral line of the Savoy patter-songs:

Mr. Orator Puff has two tones in his voice,
  The one squeaking *thus*, and the other down *so*,
In each sentence he utter'd he gave you your choice,
  For one half was B alt, and the rest G below.
    Oh! oh! Orator Puff,
  One voice for one orator's surely enough.

But he still talk'd away, spite of coughs and of frowns,
So distracting all ears with his *ups* and his *downs*,
That a wag once, on hearing the orator say
'My voice is for war,'—ask'd him, '*Which* of them pray?'
    Oh! oh! &c.

The piece, moreover, had an excellent press, barring the *Times* and one or two others. The *Morning Chronicle* thought that "when the stage is polluted by the lowest ribaldry," an opera by "the tender and fascinating MOORE" was an event "ardently anticipated," said that the house was crowded, liked the sentimental songs, and professed astonishment "at the flashes of satyrical merriment which the eye of the licenser (generally so jaundiced) had passed over without objection." So much for the opening night; on the second evening it found the opera improved by judicious omission, though the incense burned to the Prince Regent seemed a bit offensive still. The *Morning Post* thought it an "opera of uncommon merit" played before a "prodigiously crowded house and rapturous applause." The *Dramatic Censor*, it is true, could not forget *The Poems of Thomas Little*, and delivered a splenetic attack which was, in fact, a testimony of Moore's success.[23] But Moore was for some reason disheartened, even though late in October, 1811, he admitted that the opera had succeeded better than he had expected; and he resolved "never to let another line of mine be spoken upon the stage, as neither my talents nor my nerves are at all suited to it." It was perhaps an unfortunate decision, for it meant that he was to devote his talents to the dreary gorgeousness of *Lalla Rookh* when he might have anticipated Gilbert and Sullivan. If he had in him the potentialities for the mingled wit and lyricism of Gilbert, he suffered like Sullivan from the fixed idea that such pieces were beneath him, and strove to make his lighter talent soar to the grand style and the epic form. Fortunately the necessities of earning a living forced him to take up political satire and to continue writing songs, genres in which he was to excel his contemporaries.

Chapter VII

WHILE Moore had been penning satires in Dublin and wooing his Bessy in the brisk October at Kilkenny, the Napoleonic empire had slowly passed into its dubious afternoon. Under the far-off western horizon the indignant Americans were gradually heaping up the grievances which led to Mr. Madison's war. The Peninsula was enduring dull horrors as the half-savage soldiers of four nations were let loose on Portugal and Spain, and Viscount Wellington, released from an unprofitable interlude at Dublin Castle, doggedly pushed back the incessant advances of French armies that were beaten only to return. His elder brother, for a few brief years an ornate Secretary of State, had, at the other end of Europe, neatly detached General Bernadotte, the Swedish crown prince, from his French connections, while the Continental system slowly wrecked the clumsy economics of Bonaparte and a new emotion burned like underground fire in what was left of Prussia. Josephine was gone, but Maria Louisa adorned the Tuileries and presently gave birth to the King of Rome. Already a faint frost that was not winter was creeping out of the vast Russian plain to chill the golden bees on the imperial embroideries, while in Vienna Metternich, profoundly distrustful of his master's son-in-law, waited until the stage should be set for his ironic duplicities. In England the brief baroque comedy of turning the First Gentleman of Europe into the Prince Regent was being played against this vast background of purple and blood.

Worn out by domestic tensions and paternal grief, in the
autumn of 1810 George III sank into insanity, broken at first
by fits of playing Handel and inquiries as to the intentions of
his hated son, and then not broken at all as the poor blind
imbecile raged in his padded room or sank into the hopeless
apathy that was to endure ten years. Expectation of the
event produced whorl after whorl of palace intrigue, in
which everybody wrote notes or held conversations contra-
dicting everybody else. Expecting to be turned out, and fearful of the creation of Whig peers, the Tories nervously produced Pitt's old Regency Bill restricting the powers of the
Prince of Wales. The Prince, who disliked the measure, directed Lords Grey and Grenville to draft a protest; then,
finding the composition too weak, had Sheridan rewrite it;
then, finding his position untenable, suddenly discovered that
he was not a "party man" and dished the Whigs. The hopes
of the Catholics for Emancipation ran high until it was discovered that if, in point of canon law, Mrs. Fitzherbert's
marriage to the fat Adonis of fifty was legal, the Protestant
succession was endangered; whereupon the Prince virtuously
cut Mrs. Fitzherbert in favor of the autumnal charms of Lady
Hertford, and Catholic claims were again postponed under
Perceval, who had found time, amid his duties as First Lord
of the Treasury, to write a tract on the prophecies of Daniel.
The First Gentleman of Europe had worked out a list of
Whig ministers so complete that Moira was on the point of
starting for Dublin as Lord Lieutenant; but Grey and Grenville would not have either Sheridan or Moira, the Prince
would not suffer the dictation of the two peers, and, declaring that he would not interfere with his father's recovery by calling in the opposition, he took the oath as Regent
at a Privy Council in Carlton House under a bust of Charles
James Fox. The Queen wrote her son that "she was persuaded he would be highly gratified to hear that the King
was improved in health"; and the Prince, declaring some
lawyer had written the letter, dined out privately with Lord

Grey. In the sequel the Tories remained in office for twenty years.

Amid this political kaleidoscope the tall figure of Lord Moira seemed to loom like some dim Irish god beside that of the Prince; and in London little Tommy Moore anxiously waited for regential favor to smile upon his patron. In December "Moira is out of town" and "the King has got bad again within these two days past." A few days later, "a regency will be proceeded on immediately," and he was sure of "the introduction of Lord Moira into the cabinet." Hope fell in a later bulletin written on a dateless Wednesday: "for some time I do not think there will be any material change in the Ministry," only to rise a few days later when "the plot begins to thicken here very fast." In June the young husband attended the famous Regency Gala, which he did not leave until past six in the morning. (Bessy stayed at home.)

Nothing was ever half so magnificent; it was in *reality* all that they try to imitate in the gorgeous scenery of the theatre; and I really sat for three quarters of an hour in the Prince's room after supper, silently looking at the spectacle, and feeding my eyes with the assemblage of beauty, splendour, and profuse magnificence which it presented.

Some of this profuse magnificence probably found its way into the pages of *Lalla Rookh*. "The Prince," Moore added, "spoke to me, as he always does, with the cordial familiarity of an old acquaintance." By October Moore was hoping to get the Prince's assent to a translation of Lucien Bonaparte's poem; in January, 1812, though "there is no guessing what the Prince means to do," "Lord M. is continually at Carlton House" and he "has not, for a long time, been so attentive to me as since his last return to London."

But the virtuous constitutionalism of the Regent ended Whiggish hopes; and though an artillery officer named Blomfield was made secretary for playing the cello well, and Colonel McMahon became Paymaster of the Widows' Pensions and (for a time) Keeper of the Privy Purse, the princely

conscience was satisfied to reward Irish constancy with a
mere Garter. Moore wrote bitterly that "in Lord Moira's
exclusion from all chances of power, I see an end to the long
hope of my life," and told his mother that since his noble
patron "meant to withdraw entirely from politics," he,
Thomas Moore, "must only look to myself for my future
happiness and independence." There was a last wild flare of
hope when Moira was at length made Governor-General of
India. But Moore wrote vengefully to Hunt that Moira "had
nothing sufficiently good in his Indian patronage" and, after
one or two other sallies concerning the proconsul's lack of
statesmanship, he sensibly declined being carried off to the
Vale of Cashmere.

The friends of Fox meanwhile retreated upon Holland
House, the mistress of which remarked that Grey "betrays
much soreness," while her husband grew sarcastic over Grenville's "passion for pen and ink." There, amid brilliant conversation, they contemplated the ruin of their hopes. But if
the enemy held the field, he could at least be annoyed by
light skirmishes; and Moore, who, when in town, turned up
more and more frequently in the Gilt Room of that capitol
of Whiggery, after writing a discreet apology to Lord Holland recanting "most heartily some of the sentiments against
Whiggism"[1] he had recently expressed, threw himself with
some venom into the fray. Pique and patriotism barbed his
Parthian arrows. On February 13, 1812, the Regent produced his letter to the Duke of York unctuously explaining
that "my sense of duty to our Royal father" had decided him
to keep the Tories in; and Moore promptly composed his
"Parody of a Celebrated Letter" for private circulation among
the Holland House circle. By overtone and innuendo he
managed to combine into 128 dancing lines all the meaner inconsistencies, personal and political, of him to whom the outraged Irishman had dedicated the *Odes of Anacreon* (a dedication the Tory press never permitted the public to forget):

I am proud to declare I have no predilections,
My heart is a sieve, where some scatter'd affections
Are just danc'd about for a moment or two,
And the *finer* they are, the more sure to run through,

he represents the Regent as saying; and there were few who
would not read into these lines, not merely George's desertion of the Whigs, but his desertion of Mrs. Fitzherbert.
Moore had a lady, a religion, and a political party to avenge.

What Moore needed was an organ; and the editor of the
Morning Chronicle opened its columns to him. From February, 1812, to the spring of 1842 this paper published at inter-
mittent intervals those squibs and satires which Tommy calls
his "vollies of small shot." Most of these appear in the collected works; many of them, from accident or design, he
did not include; and some of them are not now identifiable.[2]
There was also a period when he earned £200 a year by
contributing similar squibs to the *Times*. A reading of the
Morning Chronicle reveals the fact that at a period when no
paper was employing a political cartoonist, Moore was in
truth doing the work which the newspaper caricaturist does
today; and though his verses were too topical, too starred
with contemporary allusion to have meaning for the modern
reader, they were executed with a care and a polish rare in
the history of political versifying. Their timeliness, the air
of amused detachment with which he managed to surround
them, the volleys of silvery laughter which his rhymes
showered in elfin rain upon the opposition—these qualities,
together with a lyric gift which other satirists sometimes lack,
gave him, or ought to give him, a place unique and apart in
the history of political poetry. It is as if Tennyson and
Thomas Nash had met together, as if Chesterton and Mr.
Dooley had kissed each other. And the venom of the Tory
papers in attacking Moore shows how truly his shafts went
home.

Moore's immediate target was the Prince of Wales; and
nothing that obese gentleman could do or be but the poet

turned it into ridicule. He proposed that the three heron feathers of the Prince's crest be changed for feathers from a pea-hen (the Regent), a cuckoo (the cornuted Lord Hertford), and an owl (Perceval, who was solemn), and ended this poem on the ironic note: "I SERVE." He pictured George

> as cheerful, as if, all his life,
> He had never been troubled with Friends or a Wife.

He drew him at breakfast in whiskered state—on one side, unread petitions; on the other,

> tea and toast,
> Death-warrants and *The Morning Post*.

George was "King Crack," who "took to his darling old *Idols* again"; he was caricatured wearing Lord Liverpool like a nightcap "much attach'd to the CROWN"; he was turned into a carpenter whose tools were too worn out for cabinet-making and into a legal precedent justifying adultery; he was lampooned as being too fat to pass through the mountainous defiles of Spain, though, if he could pass, the French would certainly flee when "he bore down *en masse*." [3] Why, when Hunt was jailed for saying that "this 'Adonis in loveliness' was a corpulent man of fifty," and Byron hated for eight lines beginning "Weep, daughter of a royal line," Moore was permitted week after week to produce these naughtinesses is a mystery best known to the Tory cabinet. Possibly Liverpool felt, like Pitt, that certain ideas might safely circulate among the upper classes. Possibly the Regent's lingering regard for Moira protected Moira's protégé.

II

Moore, Byron, and Hunt were the light cavalry of the Whig assault, and it is significant that Moore's friendship with both coincides with his satiric attack on the Regent and the ministry. The origin of his acquaintance with Byron is not without comedy. Smarting under the strictures of the

Edinburgh Review, that noble lord had published in March, 1809, his *English Bards and Scotch Reviewers*, during the course of which he referred to the young Catullus of the day, wrote dryly of the Jeffrey duel:

> When LITTLE's leadless pistol met his eye,
> And Bow-Street Myrmidoms [*sic*] stood laughing by,

and appended the damaging note:

> In 1806 Messrs. JEFFREY and MOORE, met at Chalk-Farm. The duel was prevented by the interference of the Magistracy; and, on examination, the balls of the pistols, like the courage of the combatants, were found to have evaporated. This incident gave occasion to much waggery in the daily prints.

A second edition in October retained the offending note; and from Dublin on New Year's Day, 1810, Moore had addressed a letter to Byron, whose name, he says, was now first associated with the poem, inquiring whether he took responsibility for the "*lie* . . . given to a public statement of mine respecting an affair with Mr. Jeffrey some years since." Byron, however, who was then contemplating the ruins of Athens, never received the epistle and had not seen Moore's letter to the newspapers. A year and a half drifted by; Moore married; and when Byron returned in July, 1811, Moore's fit of anger had cooled. But was his honor safe? The death of Mrs. Byron further postponed inquiry, but on October 22 Moore dispatched a second letter (from 27 Bury Street) saying that his feelings were still injured, but that he hoped to make Byron's acquaintance. Byron replied to this singular inquiry with remarkable tact; Moore answered Byron; but punctilios were raised. Was Byron bound to acknowledge a challenge he had never received, and was Moore obligated to resent an insult which had never been intended? Finally the ubiquitous Rogers got the two poets together at dinner, Thomas Campbell also dropping in, and the Pilgrim of Eternity gazed across his vinegar and potatoes

—all he would eat—at his future friend and amiable biographer.[4]

The date of Moore's first meeting with Leigh Hunt is uncertain,[5] but it was occasioned by a passage in the 1811 version of *The Feast of the Poets,* first published in the fourth number of *The Reflector:*

> There are very few poets, whose caps or whose curls
> Have obtain'd such a laurel by hunting the girls.
> So it gives me, dear Tom, a delight beyond measure
> To find how you've mended your notions of pleasure.

This compliment on the improvement in Tommy's morals (the phrase is Mr. Blunden's) seems to have touched the Irish heart, and Moore wrote Hunt to thank him. As Hunt was also one of the most trenchant dramatic critics in London, Moore, at work on *M. P.,* thriftily wrote again, to the effect that "writing bad jokes for the galleries of the Lyceum" made him no fit companion for the editor of the *Examiner,* complimenting Hunt on his poem—"there is nothing so delightful as those alternate sinkings & risings, both of feeling & style, which you have exhibited"—and begging him, not to praise the opera, but to say, if he sincerely could, that the paper *"expected something better."* [6] Hunt reviewed that production September 15—"an unambitious, undignified, and most unworthy union of pun, equivoque, and clap-trap!"—and suggested that a "union of fancy with ethics" was the proper way to Parnassus. Of the letters subsequently exchanged Hunt observed:

His letters were full of all that was pleasant in him. As I was a critic at that time, and in the habit of giving my opinion of his works in the *Examiner,* he would write me his *opinion* of the *opinion,* with a mixture of good humour, admission, and deprecation, so truly delightful, and a sincerity of criticism on my own writings so extraordinary for so courteous a man, though with abundance of balm and eulogy, that never any subtlety of compliment could surpass it; and with all my self-confidence I never ceased to think that the honour was on my side, and that I could only deserve such candour of intercourse by being as ingenuous as himself.

Through the cloudy syntax of this sentence it would appear that the two Whig poets got along famously. Coolness arose after Byron's death; but Hunt, the most amiable of men, drew a sympathetic portrait of Moore in *Byron and His Contemporaries*, though he enshrined in it an odd quotation from Joe Atkinson which describes Tommy "as an infant sporting on the bosom of Venus." In 1811-12, however, all was peace among the anti-ministerial bards.

III

As the Whig lampoons increased in effectiveness the placemen at Carlton House saw to it that the royal mind overlooked none of the sting. Initially, at a banquet on February 12, 1812, there was an historic explosion when the Prince Regent expressed "surprise and mortification," Lord Lauderdale brusquely announced that the whole Whig party stood behind Grey and Grenville, and the young Princess Charlotte burst into tears and was ordered to withdraw. Lord Holland, abused in *English Bards and Scotch Reviewers*, gallantly called on Byron and enlisted him for the common cause, we must suppose, for Childe Harold went spiritedly to work. On the twenty-seventh he assailed the government in the House of Lords for their bill to punish frame-breaking; on March 2 he published in the *Morning Chronicle* his bitter and anonymous "Ode to the Framers of the Frame Bill"; on the seventh he printed his notorious "Sympathetic Address to a Young Lady"; on the tenth *Childe Harold's Pilgrimage* shocked the Tories with its scathing attack on the Convention of Cintra and the cruelties of the Peninsular Campaign; on April 21 he denounced the refusal of Liverpool's administration to emancipate the Catholics; and in the course of the next few months he published "Windsor Poetics" with its cutting picture of the Regent between the coffins of Henry VIII and Charles I, delivered a third speech in the Lords, wrote "The

Devil's Drive," and suppressed *The Curse of Minerva,* but not so carefully that news of the poem did not leak out to accuse the government of "perfidious war" in the Baltic, tyranny in India, famine in Spain, and corruption at home. It was also known that Dallas had deleted even more obnoxious stanzas from *Childe Harold.*[7]

Undeterred by the constant threat of trial for libel, Hunt in the *Examiner* had satirized the Walcheren expedition and the poetry of the laureate, Pye, denounced flogging in the army, won a suit brought by the government for sedition, lampooned the Regent's Gala, and rose on March 22, 1812, to new heights of denunciatory eloquence in an article entitled "The Prince on St. Patrick's Day":

What person, unacquainted with the true state of the case, would imagine . . . that this *delightful, blissful, wise, pleasurable, honourable, virtuous, true,* and *immortal* PRINCE, was a violator of his word, a libertine over head and ears in debt and disgrace, a despiser of domestic ties, the companion of gamblers and demireps, a man who has just closed half a century without one single claim on the gratitude of his country or the respect of posterity!

The government filed suit, but since the trial was postponed, Hunt continued to excoriate the head of the nation and his ministry. On February 3, 1813, however, he and his brother John, publisher of the paper, were separately sentenced to a fine of £500 and two years in prison. Hunt turned his apartments in the Surrey Gaol into a reception room where he received poetical tributes, the admiration of the Whigs, and the calls of Moore and Byron.

Moore, if less venomous, was more skillful, and where Byron castigated and Hunt denounced, he employed the subtler weapons of ridicule. What he wrote of the Regent we have already seen. He attacked the ministers in separate poems, and in a series of burlesque translations of Horace (paralleling *Horace in London* by Horace and James Smith) which appealed especially to that classic age, reduced even his opponents to helpless laughter. The Prince of Wales was made to offer the following version of Ode XI, Book II:

> Brisk let us revel, while revel we may;
> For the gay bloom of fifty soon passes away,
>   And then people get fat,
>   And infirm, and—all that,
> And a wig (I confess it) so clumsily sits,
> That it frightens the little Loves out of their wits;

while the version of the familiar *Integer vitae scelerisque purus* attributed to Lord Eldon, that Tory of Tories, begins:

> The man who keeps his conscience pure,
>   (If not his own, at least his Prince's,)
> Through toil and danger walks secure,
>   Looks big and black, and never winces.[8]

The climax came on March 20, 1813, when "Thomas Brown, the Younger" published *Intercepted Letters, or the Twopenny Post-Bag*, which went promptly into innumerable editions, set the style for a small regiment of imitators, and became, like *Rejected Addresses*, the talk of the town. To the modern reader unversed in the minutiae of Regency politics, the "point" of many of the digs is unfortunately obscured by a cloud of unfamiliar names revealed in the consonants and hidden in the vowels, but even a superficial acquaintance with the period makes it clear that the volume is in truth one of the most brilliant bits of rollicking light satire in the history of English verse.

The fiction is that a postman has dropped a packet of letters, which has been picked up by an emissary of the Society for the Suppression of Vice (an organization for which Moore had as little use as did Sydney Smith), and taken by him to the headquarters of the society. Unluckily, as "Thomas Brown" dryly observes,

it turned out, upon examination, that the discoveries of profligacy which it enabled them to make, lay chiefly in those upper regions of society, which their well-bred regulations forbid them to molest or meddle with.

The letters were therefore sold to Mr. Brown and by him turned into rhyme. Let us examine a typical letter.

In 1812 a Mr. Gould Francis Leckie published his *Practice of the British Government,* characterized by Jeffrey in the *Edinburgh Review* as "the most direct attack . . . in English upon the free constitution of England, or rather upon political liberty in general," and therefore anathema to the Whigs. In the second letter of the *Twopenny Post-Bag* the Regent's favorite, Colonel McMahon, is represented as writing a grateful letter to the author, of which the following passages are characteristic:

> But, to your work's immortal credit,
> The Prince, good Sir, the Prince has read it
> (The only Book, himself remarks,
> Which he has read since Mrs. Clarke's).
> Last levee-morn he look'd it through,
> During that awful hour or two
> Of grave tonsorial preparation,
> Which, to a fond, admiring nation,
> Sends forth, announc'd by trump and drum,
> The best wigg'd Prince in Christendom.
>
>   .   .   .   .   .
>
> Before I send this scrawl away,
> I seize a moment, just to say,
> There's some parts of the Turkish system
> So vulgar, 'twere as well you miss'd 'em.
> For instance—in *Seraglio* matters—
> Your Turk, whom girlish fondness flatters,
> Would fill his Haram (tasteless fool!)
> With tittering, red-cheek'd things from school.
> But *here* (as in that fairy land
> Where Love and Age went hand in hand;
> Where lips, till sixty, shed no honey,
> And Grandams were worth any money,)
> *Our* Sultan has much riper notions—
> So, let your list of *she*-promotions
> Include those only, plump and sage,
> Who've reach'd the *regulation*-age;
> That is, (as near as one can fix
> From Peerage dates) full fifty-six,

which age, by a strange coincidence, was that of Lady Hertford, the Regent's plump favorite.

Walter Scott came in for a little good-natured badgering *à propos* of his latest poem, in the seventh letter:

Should you feel any touch of *poetical* glow,
We've a Scheme to suggest—Mr. Scott, as you know,
(Who, we're sorry to say it, now works for *the Row* *)
Having quitted the Borders, to seek new renown,
Is coming, by long Quarto stages, to Town;
And beginning with Rokeby (the job's sure to pay)
Means to *do* all the Gentlemen's Seats on the way.
Now, the Scheme is (though none of our hackneys can beat him)
To start a fresh Poet through Highgate to *meet* him;
Who, by means of quick proofs—no revises—long coaches—
May do a few Villas, before Scott approaches.

  * Paternoster Row.

In the appendix Moore paid sincere tribute to the brothers Hunt:

> Go to your prisons—though the air of Spring
> No mountain coolness to your cheeks shall bring;
> Though Summer flowers shall pass unseen away,
> And all your portion of the glorious day
> May be some solitary beam that falls,
> At morn or even, upon your dreary walls—
>
> .   .   .   .   .   .
>
> Yet go—for thoughts as blessed as the air
> Of Spring or Summer flowers await you there
>
> .   .   .   .   .
>
> The Pride, that suffers without vaunt or plea,
> And the fresh Spirit, that can warble free,
> Through prison-bars, its hymn to Liberty!

Such was the vogue of the *Post-Bag* that Scott told Lockhart the failure of *Rokeby* was due, among other causes, to "some sarcastic flings in Mr. Moore's 'Twopenny Post Bag,'" which "had an unfavourable influence on this occasion." For the fourteenth edition (April, 1814) Moore wrote a new preface containing the transparent statement that the author, though a Catholic, was not a Papist, and that "he has a Protestant wife and two or three little Protestant children, and that he has been seen at church every Sunday, for a whole year together, listening to the sermons of his truly reverend and amiable friend, Dr. [Parkinson], and behaving there as well and as orderly as most people." Vainly the *Anti-Jacobin Review* referred to "these splenetic effusions" generously besprinkled with the "bard's favourite sauce—*ill-nature*"; [9] the damage had been done, and our present picture of the Prince Regent is still colored by Moore's amusing satires.

IV

Meanwhile, removed from the dust and heat of the political arena, the wedded life of Thomas and Bessy flowed peacefully on amid more sylvan scenes. The marriage was shyly made known to the Moore family and to the poet's more intimate friends some months after it had taken place (there is no record of how Mrs. Dyke was informed), and Tom waited with natural anxiety the reception of the penniless actress-wife by his great friends. He was soon reassured. Mary Godfrey wrote him September 22, 1811:

Be very sure, my dear Moore, that if you have got an amiable, sensible wife, extremely attached to you, as I am certain you have, it is only in the long run of life that you can know the full value of the treasure you possess.

Rogers, with whom Moore was specially intimate during these years, lost his heart to the pretty bride, whom he called Psyche, and the conquest of other acquaintances by the gentle Bessy soon followed. The young couple, as we have seen, took lodgings in Brompton; [10] and in that leafy suburb of Regency London his first child, Anne Jane Barbara, was born February 4, 1812.

But even Brompton proved too expensive for the father of a family whose hopes of political appointment grew daily more uncertain; and Moore was presently writing his friend,

John Dalby, who lived in the village of Castle Donington, to look out "some rural retreat" for him, where, as he told Miss Godfrey, he could live "on the earnings of my brains, and . . . be as happy as love, literature, and liberty can make me." Nearness to Lord Moira's library also seemed important at the time. By May, 1812, the little family was not too comfortably ensconced in what Moore described as a barn of a house in Kegworth, a village on the River Soar, some six miles from Donington Park. The house stands on the Loughborough road, a three-storey structure with a walled garden in the rear. Rogers, who visited Moore in the autumn, was not enthusiastic. "The two windows," he wrote his sister, "belong to the kitchen, the bay window to the dining-room. Two small parlours (one of them his book-room) look into the garden behind. Their bedroom is over the dining-room, the nursery over the kitchen," and there Mrs. Moore was "sitting and peeping when I came." [11] Moore had written in June that Bessy "runs wild about the large garden," and the Moiras, when they were at Donington Park, were kind, but one gathers that a Kegworth winter proved disillusioning, and from the demands on James Power for everything from candles to cash, it would appear that housekeeping was difficult. Moreover, as Moore wrote Hunt, the society of Kegworth chiefly consisted "of manufacturers & Methodists"— no very inspiriting company for a Regency poet.

He meditated a variety of schemes to increase his income. He urged that Power take him into partnership; he suggested a subscription lecture series on poetry and music with illustrations at the pianoforte by Thomas Moore; he thought at one time of compiling a dictionary of music, at another of issuing a collection of political songs to Irish airs, and at a third of a series of "Convivial and Political Songs, to Airs original and selected by Thos. Brown the Younger." Murray approached him to accept the editorship of a new review. But none of these projects eventuated in anything tangible; and Moore therefore worked steadily at the lyrics which were finally cumulated as the first number of *Sacred Songs*, issued in 1816 (was it from a desire to overcome his repute as an immoral bard?). This series contains, among other things, such favorite hymns as "Come, ye disconsolate," "Oh fair! oh purest!" and "Awake, arise, thy light is come." The fourth number of the *Irish Melodies* was published in 1811; the fifth in 1813, and it is convenient to discuss them together.

He had never written better lyrics. The fourth number contains "By that Lake, whose gloomy shore," which Poe admired; "Lesbia hath a beaming eye"; "Avenging and bright fall the swift sword of Erin"; and, shining above the rest, the tender lyric which commemorates Sarah Curran's love for Robert Emmet:

> She is far from the land, where her young Hero sleeps,
>   And lovers are round her sighing;
> But coldly she turns from their gaze, and weeps,
>   For her heart in his grave is lying!
>
> She sings the wild song of her dear native plains,
>   Every note which he lov'd awaking.—
> Ah! little they think, who delight in her strains,
>   How the heart of the Minstrel is breaking!
>
> He had liv'd for his love, for his country he died,
>   They were all that to life had entwin'd him,—
> Nor soon shall the tears of his country be dried,
>   Nor long will his love stay behind him!
>
> Oh! make her a grave, where the sun-beams rest,
>   When they promise a glorious morrow;
> They'll shine o'er her sleep, like a smile from the West,
>   From her own loved Island of sorrow!

This lyric is remarkable, among other qualities, for the complete absence from its lines of those figures of speech with which the Regency too frequently "adorned" its verses.

Good as is the fourth number, the fifth surpassed it to such a degree that Moore never again attained the concentrated excellence of these poems, of which only one ("You remember Ellen, our hamlet's pride") is positively bad, while the rest are among his most perfect achievements in the lyric written to be sung. " 'Tis the last rose of summer" has gone round the world and scarcely needs citation; but for sheer metrical felicity two other of the poems deserve notice. The peculiarities of the tune may have forced Moore's hand in the following lyric, but the haunting music, the curious rightness of the metrical effects which this difficulty created are triumphant and quite unequaled by any other of the romanticists:

At the mid hour of night, when stars are weeping, I fly
To the lone vale we lov'd, when life shown warm in thine eye;
   And I think that, if spirits can steal from the region of air
   To revisit past scenes of delight, thou wilt come to me there,
And tell me our love is remember'd even in the sky!

Then I sing the wild song, which once 'twas rapture to hear,
When our voices both mingling breath'd like one on the ear;
   And, as Echo, far off through the vale my sad orison rolls,
   I think, oh my love! 'tis thy voice from the kingdom of souls,
Faintly answering still the notes that once were so dear.

Equally perfect, though in a different vein, is a poem in which Moore partially anticipated one of the popular lyrics of William Butler Yeats:

Oh! had we some bright little isle of our own,
In a blue summer ocean, far off and alone;
Where a leaf never dies in the still-blooming bowers,
And the bee banquets on through a whole year of flowers.
   Where the sun loves to pause
     With so fond a delay,
   That the night only draws
     A thin veil o'er the day;
Where simply to feel that we breathe, that we live,
Is worth the best joy that life elsewhere can give!

There, with souls ever ardent and pure as the clime,
We should love, as they lov'd in the first golden time;

The glow of the sunshine, the balm of the air,
Would steal to our hearts, and make all summer there!
  With affection as free
    From decline as the bowers;
  And with Hope, like the bee,
    Living always on flowers;
Our life should resemble a long day of light,
And our death come on holy and calm as the night!

But the chief occupation of the Kegworth period was the preparatory work for *Lalla Rookh*, for which Moore read, to his own detriment and that of the poem, in the library at Donington Park. The project dated back to another place and another library, for, writing from Dublin to Mary Godfrey September 11, 1811, Moore speaks of getting "among the maids of Cashmere, the sparkling springs of Rochabad, and the fragrant banquets of the Peris." I shall, he then said, "do something, I hope, that will place me above the vulgar herd both of worldlings and critics." The first draft of the poem, now in the Pierpont Morgan Library, shows that he began composition November 23, 1811. Rogers was kept *au courant* with the progress of the work, which went forward at the rate of something less than a hundred lines a week; the two poets exchanged criticisms on their manuscripts (Rogers was at work on *Columbus*); and when, in September, 1812, Rogers carried Moore off on a trip to the Lake country, Moore's manuscript was thoroughly gone over, as it was again in 1813. "Rogers's criticisms," Moore wrote Power, "have twice upset all I have done, but I have fairly told him he shall have it no more till it is finished." Although the banker-poet suggested some of the larger themes in *Lalla Rookh*, his comments ran to verbal minutiae, and it is easy to see why this habit of niggling interrupted the flow of composition.

Despite the visit from Rogers and other visits from Power and Stevenson, and despite Bessy's delight in the garden, all was not comfortable at Kegworth. Disputes between James Power in London and William Power in Dublin over the copyright of the profitable *Irish Melodies* clouded Moore's happiness, and there are traces of trouble caused by an Aunt Codd, to whom Moore applied certain short, descriptive words not printed in his *Correspondence*. His sister Kate had married a Mr. John Scully, and the coming of her first child, which lived only a short while, was awaited with considerable anxiety at Kegworth, where it preceded by a few months the birth of the poet's second daughter, Anastasia Mary, born March 16, 1813. The house was therefore abandoned the following month, Moore having accepted with regrettable heedlessness an invitation from a Mrs. Ready at Oakhanger Hall.[12] When they reached that place, Moore discovered that Mr. Ready had died two days before! Nevertheless, the family was given "a suite of delightful rooms that open into each other," a wet-nurse was procured for the baby, Mrs. Ready went off to London to prove her husband's will, and Moore followed to make one of those "annual revelations of himself" which his career as a singer of his own songs rendered absolutely necessary to their success.

As the Moiras were to remain indefinitely in India, the poet felt that he need not linger in the vicinity of Donington Park; and having visited Ashbourne with Rogers and liked the place, he removed with his family to Mayfield Cottage near that Derbyshire village late in June, 1813. "I have got," he wrote James Corry,

a pretty little stone-built cottage, in the fields by itself, about a mile and a half from the very sweetly situated town of Ashbourne, for which I am to pay twenty pounds a-year rent . . . certainly until my *Grande Opus* is finished, I could not possibly have a more rural or secluded corner to court the Muses in.

A sentimental writer in the *Lady's Magazine,* visiting Ashbourne in 1829, has left us too characteristic an "effusion" concerning Mayfield, for it to be omitted

Our desire to go over the cottage which he had inhabited was irresistible. It is neat, but very small, and remarkable for nothing except combining a most sheltered situation with the most extensive prospect. Still one had pleasure in going over it, and peeping into the little book-room, yclept the 'Poet's Den,' from which so much true poetry had issued to delight and amuse mankind. . . . [We] descend[ed] to the poet's walk in the shrubbery, where, pacing up and down the live-long morning, he composed 'Lalla Rookh.' It is a little confined gravel-walk, so narrow, that there is barely room on it for two persons to walk abreast; bounded on one side by a straggling row of stunted laurels, on the other by some old decayed wooden paling; at the end of it was a huge hay-stack. Here, without fields, flowers, or natural beauties of any description, was that most imaginative poem conceived, planned, and executed.[13]

The writer was wrong about the inception of *Lalla Rookh*, but there is no doubt about the "Poet's Den" and the gravel walk.

At Ashbourne the full, rich current of the months was to flow peacefully through one of the happiest and most productive periods of Moore's life. There were, it is true, some vexations and one profound sorrow. The vexations proved to be the repair and furnishing of Mayfield Cottage, which cost more than Tom had anticipated; the sorrow was the death of Olivia Byron Moore, born August 18, 1814, to live but a few months. For the most part, however, Moore worked steadily at songs, at review articles, and at *Lalla Rookh* in full contentment. His letters show him supervising the placing of some "very *creditable*" chairs and tables about the diminutive rooms, rolling with little Barbara in the adjacent hayfield, ordering a lobster as large as himself from London for a state dinner, and practicing country-dances with his wife "in a retired green lane" when, on arriving too soon at a neighbor's party, they had to do something with an odd half-hour.

The Grand Army melted away in the Russian snows, but Tom's imagination was too full of the Vale of Cashmere to

think of the Beresina. Even the guns of Leipzig resounded so
faintly across the rolling meadows as not to take him from
his desk. Wellington entered the passes of the Pyrenees,
drove Soult from Bayonne, and rode through the spring
weather into Paris; a glittering troupe of legitimate sovereigns
flooded London, endeavoring urbanely to overlook the fact
that the Princess of Wales was a member of the House of
Brunswick and that the Princess Charlotte refused to get out
of bed to receive the Prince of Orange. Moore, however,
contented himself with accounts of these stupendous events
in letters from Dalton, Byron, Rogers, and Lady Donegal,
though, being a good Whig, he thought "the French shabby
dogs for taking back the Bourbons." But he labored at more
Melodies and at *Lalla Rookh* and was, on the whole, content.

Another distinction came his way. For Jeffrey, whom he
had once attempted to kill, sent him word *via* Rogers that
"the brilliant success of some of Mr. Moore's late (reputed)
works" made "a person of such talents and such principles" a
proper contributor to that great Whig organ, the *Edinburgh
Review*, which he was asked to "embellish" with "a classical,
philosophical, poetical article, after the nature of that on
Aristophanes in one of the later Quarterlies" and at the rate
of twenty guineas for every sixteen pages. The Tories could
not be allowed to monopolize the ancients when a man like
Moore could combine "the purity of classic literature . . .
with the depth, boldness, and freedom of modern discussion."
This was in March, 1814. Moore, nothing loath, consented,
contributing to the issue for September, 1814, a drolly ironical review of the Tory Lord Thurlow's bad poetry, and to
the issue for November an essay on the church fathers which
astonished Jeffrey by its learning, and must have astounded
pious Catholics by its skepticism. Gibbon would have smiled
approval on such a paragraph as this:

The mischievous absurdity of some of the moral doctrines of
the Fathers, the state of apathy to which they would reduce
their Gnostic or perfect Christian, their condemnation of mar-

riage and their monkish fancies about celibacy, the extreme to which they carried their notions of patience, even to the prohibition of all resistance to aggression, though the aggressor aimed at life itself; the strange doctrine of St. Augustine, that the Saints are the only lawful proprietors of the things of this world . . . ; the indecencies in which too many of them have indulged in their writings; the profane frivolity of Tertullian, in making God himself prescribe the length and measure of women's veils, in a special revelation to some ecstatic spinster; and the moral indignation with which Clemens Alexandrinus inveighs against white bread, periwigs, coloured stuffs and lap-dogs; all these, and many more such puerile and pernicious absurdities, open a wide field of weedy fancies for ridicule to skim, and good sense to trample upon.

"I have redde thee upon the Fathers," Byron wrote him, "and it is excellent well . . . and this article has been taken for Sydney Smith's (as I heard in town), which proves not only your proficiency in parsonology, but that you have all the airs of a veteran critic . . ." Byron was right; in things theological Moore and Smith were children of this world.

Chapter VIII

IN TRUTH, the Whig had swallowed up the Irishman, and from 1813, when the fifth number of the *Irish Melodies* appeared, to 1824, when he published the *Memoirs of Captain Rock*, Moore was less the nationalist than the petted bard of upper-class liberal circles in England and on the Continent. Invited to Chatsworth in January, 1815, by the Duke of Devonshire (Bessy was too timid to go), he found himself almost the only commoner in a glittering troupe of nobility; and though the old cut of Hibernia and her harp still appeared on the covers of the *Melodies*, it is significant that he wrote to Power suggesting that either Lady Cowper or Lady Boringdon, "two very tasteful artists," might be induced to do a sketch for the sixth number of the collection. He found his titled friends enthusiastic over the "Prince's song" ("When first I met thee, warm and young"), but he could not correct the impression that the supposed speaker was not Ireland, but Mrs. Fitzherbert. Ireland had become a dim blur on the western horizon, a source of perpetual irritation, a country "ruined by a . . . bigoted, brawling, and disgusting set of demagogues" and by the Catholic faith, "which is again polluting Europe with Jesuitism and inquisitions, and which of all the humbugs that have stultified mankind is the most narrow-minded and mischievous," as he wrote Lady Donegal in April. His disgust with O'Connell was supreme.

If one cannot altogether approve Moore's attitude during these months, one can at least understand it. The poet was suffering from a variety of irritations, many of them originating from his Irish connections. For one thing, possibly because of overwork on *Lalla Rookh*, his health was bad, Bessy was thin and melancholy after the death of her third child, Anastasia was teething, and little Barbara was not strong. For another, his father had lost his post in the Irish military establishment as a consequence of economies following upon Napoleon's abdication; and though he was immediately restored to half-pay, the support of Moore's father and mother fell partially upon Tom and Bessy, and Mrs. Moore, furthermore, was not well. Moreover, despite the enthusiasm of the public and of the reviews, a considerable section of the Irish had failed to join the chorus of approbation which greeted the successive numbers of the *Melodies*. At a meeting of Bunting's friends in Belfast in 1813, Moore's name had been pointedly omitted from the list of toasts to Irish poets; reviewing the sixth number in 1816, the *Dublin Examiner*, though it liked the verses, thought it unpatriotic of Moore to say that the airs were relatively modern and declared that Stevenson's arrangements were too much like those of the second-rate composers of the day.[1] And of course Moore's success had been an invitation to rival publishers; besides Bunting's collection, Irish airs were published by Thomson (the music by Beethoven), by Holden, by Whitaker, and by Fitzsimmons. Finally, Moore was not a little perturbed by the growing antagonism between the two brothers Power, an antagonism which, though it extended over a number of years, will be clearer if it is discussed as a whole.

For, by the irony of events, though the idea of the *Irish Melodies* had originated with William Power, James Power and Moore came increasingly to regard them as their peculiar property. Naturally, with James Power prospering in London, ready and willing to send the poet on demand everything from banknotes to lobsters, and with Moore only twenty-four hours by coach from the metropolis, William Power in far-off Dublin was neglected. Letters between the two brothers became more and more acid. Thus on September 1,

1813, William sent James half a fifty-pound banknote, saying he would send the other half when he had received an acknowledgment; and on June 6, 1814, James, through his chief clerk, tartly acknowledged the fragment and declined to sign a receipt until the other half had been received. A publisher named Walker having pirated the *Melodies*, James Power sued before Lord Ellenborough on May 28, 1814, to recover damages, but could not prove that the songs were his property because William retained the original deed of sale. There were endless arguments about the indebtedness of William to James and of James to William, of Moore and Stevenson to the Power brothers jointly and severally, and of the Power brothers to the poet and the musician. When Moore visited Ireland in the summer of 1815, William received a new assignment of copyright, whether through some innocent blunder of Moore's or by agreement is not clear; but on July 16, 1816, James filed a bill in the Irish court of chancery to compel William to give him the exclusive right to sell the *Melodies* in Great Britain. "Heartily, most heartily sorry am I," Moore wrote him, "that the die is cast, and that you are indeed become 'belligerent *Powers*,' instead of keeping to that 'Holy Alliance' which Nature meant between you." There was an attempt at arbitration in December (with O'Connell as one of the arbitrators!), but James would not accept the decision. In July, 1817, William sued James in London for £5000 damages, arbitration was again invoked, and an uneasy compromise patched up. Stevenson, who was in Ireland, sided with William; Moore, though he tried to be neutral, was inclined to James. Finally, James became the exclusive publisher of the remaining four numbers of the *Melodies*, though he was supposed to send copy to William. Copy for the seventh number (1818) was sent, but not for the eighth (1821); and when William hired Stevenson to supply music for the words, James, who had secured Henry R. Bishop for the eighth, ninth, and tenth numbers, got out an injunction against William.[2]

During the period of their collaboration Stevenson alternately amused and exasperated the poet. His handwriting was illegible, his habits of workmanship slipshod and loose, his social irresponsibility stupendous. One of the more diverting episodes is described in a letter of Moore's to Lady Donegal from Ashbourne, October 31, 1814:

I have been lately very much teased, and have had my time much interrupted by a constant succession of visitors. First, I had Sir John Stevenson for near a fortnight. He came upon business that might have been done in three days, and took the whole of that time in *not* doing it. He then wrote to his son to come to him here from London, and the next night changed his mind, and set off for London himself, crossing his son, in a very national and characteristic manner, on the road; and this son has ever since remained with us here, waiting filially for the father to come back again. By way of episode, Lambart and his wife (Stevenson's daughter) who were at Lord Talbot's in this neighbourhood, must needs come over to see the young gentleman (who is just returned from America), and we have had *them* to entertain: in short, amongst them all, I have not had a minute of this whole month to myself, and the loss of so much time just now is really a most grievous calamity to me. Nor is the grievance over yet, for the son is still here, inflicting all his mess-room intelligence upon me. But I trust in providence and the mail-coach for bringing Sir John down from London tomorrow, and then the day after, if there is one principle of shame in an Irish Bosom, they shall both pack out of my house for Ireland.

The Stevensons were but following the customs of Irish hospitality, and Moore's impatience, though understandable, shows how alien Irish ways had become to him. The break with Stevenson, when it came, is, however, to be regretted; the *Melodies* were to deteriorate under the less sympathetic handling of Bishop.

Moore worked conscientiously over the sixth number, which appeared in the spring of 1815, but there is no doubt that he came to the supposed end of his task with a feeling of relief, though he cannily hinted that there might be a sequel. His motive for discontinuing the work, he said, was a fear that our treasures were beginning to be exhausted, and an unwillingness to descend to the gathering of mere seed-pearl, after the very valuable gems it has been our lot to string together.

Besides the Prince's song, the volume contained one of the most memorable of Moore's phrases:

> The light that lies
> In woman's eyes,

from "The Time I've Lost in Wooing"; two admirable lyrics,

> Come, rest in this bosom, my own stricken deer!
> Tho' the herd have fled from thee, thy home is still here;
> Here still is the smile that no cloud can o'ercast,
> And the heart and the hand all thy own to the last!

and

> I saw from the beach, when the morning was shining,
> A bark o'er the waters move gloriously on;

the song to Wellington; and two poems in which Moore expresses his feeling that the Irish cause was hopelessly lost—" 'Tis Gone, and For Ever," and "Dear Harp of my Country," in which he bade farewell to his task:

> Dear Harp of my Country! in darkness I found thee,
> The cold chain of silence had hung o'er thee long,
> When proudly, my own Island Harp! I unbound thee,
> And gave all thy chords to light, freedom, and song!
> The warm lay of love and the light note of gladness
> Have waken'd thy fondest, thy liveliest thrill;
> But so oft hast thou echoed the deep sigh of sadness,
> That ev'n in thy mirth it will steal from thee still.

More ardent patriots could not forgive this despair.

Moore had an odd pride in the lyric to Wellington, which, incongruously set to the tune of "Paddy Whack," is accompanied by a florid engraving of Clio writing in a book while Ireland looks on out of a cloud (Moore admired this sort of allegory); and when, in after years, Wellington forced Catholic Emancipation through the reluctant House of Lords, he regarded the poem as prophetic. As poetry it is worthless, but it offers an interesting pendant to the companion portrait of the Prince Regent, the acid lines of which show that Moore could neither forgive nor forget:

> Even now, tho' youth its bloom has shed,
>   No lights of age adorn thee;
> The few, who lov'd thee once, have fled,
>   And they who flatter scorn thee.
> Thy midnight cup is pledg'd to slaves,
>   No genial ties enwreath it;
> The smiling there, like light on graves,
>   Has rank, cold hearts beneath it!

By an unhappy coincidence the sixth number appeared in London the month that little Olivia died; and Moore resolved to take his sorrowful wife to Dublin for a change of scene. He could scarcely complain of his reception or that of his wife—"all Dublin is at our doors, in carriages, cars, tilburies, and jingles," he wrote Rogers in June, and he visited various country homes, but he was pettishly resolved not to be pleased. When it was proposed to give him a grand public dinner, finding too many "Catholic orators, at the bottom of the design," he refused, and afterwards somewhat unfairly satirized a public dinner to "an eminent toll-gatherer" which did take place. As for Irish patriotism,

If you can imagine groups of ragged Shanavests (as they are called) going about in noonday, armed and painted over like Catabaw Indians, to murder tithe-proctors, land-valuers, &c., you have the most stimulant specimen of the sublime that Tipperary affords. The country, indeed, is in a frightful state; and rational remedies have been delayed so long, that nothing but the sword will answer now.

He was on a vacation, but he seems to have resented the fact that "near a month's ramble through the County Kilkenny" had meant that "idleness was the order of the day"; he complained to Power that "this expedition is bleeding me most profusely," though Richard Power lent the poet his Dublin house; Bessy was taken ill at Holyhead on their return in late September; and though he wrote humorously to Joseph Strutt that we "were not shot, nor even kilt, which you know ranks lowest on the scale of personal injuries in Ireland," he confessed to James Power that "I am not only at my money's ends, but my wit's end too." [3]   He was to recover a more sympathetic attitude towards his native island, and in view of his nervous exhaustion these passages need not be taken too seriously.   In truth, *Lalla Rookh* was beginning to hang over him like a nightmare.

II

On August 31, 1815, the *Morning Chronicle* had printed Moore's squib, "Epistle from Tom Crib to Big Ben concerning some foul play in a late transaction," a rhymed letter in the language of pugilism attacking the Regent for the government's treatment of Napoleon, whom Cockburn had taken on board the *Northumberland* for St. Helena on August 7. The success of this satire in Whig circles undoubtedly helped to restore Moore's self-confidence.   But the ranks of the Whig literary warriors were shortly to suffer considerable losses—the exile of Byron and the death of Sheridan, events which again dampened the spirits of the Irish bard.

Byron's friendship for Moore was one of the most honorable events in that lonely life.   Begun in the farce-comedy of Moore's challenge, it had grown and strengthened during those sorrowful months in Byron's career which elapsed between the death of Byron's mother and the publication of *Childe Harold,* months when, as Moore wrote, "the same persons who had long been *my* intimates and friends, became his; our visits were mostly to the same places . . . in the gay round of a London spring . . ."   Moore's marriage and his retreat into the country had ended the intimacy but increased the affection, and Byron poured out his thoughts to the little Irish poet in letters which have since enriched the gaiety of nations.   He was always doing kind things.   When, alarmed at Byron's invasion of the Oriental field in *The Giaour,*

Moore had ruefully hoped their poetical plans might not con-
flict, Byron generously promised to get out of the way.   In
1814 he published *The Corsair*, dedicated to Moore in a
prefatory epistle which defiantly restated the Irish cause and
tactfully notified the public of the forthcoming splendors of
Lalla Rookh.   He stood godfather to poor little Olivia Byron
Moore; he wrote at once to inform Tommy that Anna Isabella Milbanke had accepted him; a week after the wedding
he wrote again, urging Moore to publish his poem; and he
continued to write at intervals those inimitable letters compounded of wit and nonsense, shrewdness and cynicism which
make him one of the greatest letter-writers in English.   The
two men were enlisted in a common cause, and as the slow
weeks drifted over the Ashbourne hills and the roses waxed
and waned along the Derby road, Moore came to welcome
the waggish bulletins from the great world of politics and
literature which his noble friend sent him.   Then, without
warning, Moore received under date of January 5, 1816, a
letter so unlike its predecessors as to strike him "by the tone
of melancholy that pervaded it," and wrote at once, begging
Byron to "tell me you are happier than that letter has led
me to fear."   But Anna Isabella Milbanke, after writing her
husband endearing names, retreated upon Kirkby Mallory like
Juno retiring into a cloud, and the Pilgrim of Eternity was
left exposed to the outraged denunciations of Tory domes-
ticity.   The news drifted up to Mayfield Cottage in February; Moore wrote at once with tender concern; Byron replied
as soon as he could command his feelings, and under date of
March 8, 1816, sent the Irishman one of the most honorable
of his utterances on the riddle of his married life, a letter containing the pathetic sentence: "I still, however, think that, if
I had had a fair chance, by being placed in even a tolerable
situation, I might have gone on fairly."   They were not to
meet again until Moore visited Italy in October, 1819, but all
the world knows the poem, begun at the time Byron left

England, in which he revealed the depth of his affection for his friend:

> My boat is on the shore,
>   And my bark is on the sea;
> But, before I go, Tom Moore,
>   Here's a double health to thee!
>
> Here's a sigh to those who love me,
>   And a smile to those who hate;
> And, whatever sky's above me,
>   Here's a heart for every fate.
>
> Though the ocean roar around me,
>   Yet it still shall bear me on;
> Though a desert should surround me,
>   It hath springs that may be won.
>
> Were't the last drop in the well,
>   As I gasp'd upon the brink,
> Ere my fainting spirit fell,
>   'Tis to thee that I would drink.
>
> With that water, as this wine,
>   The libation I would pour
> Should be—peace with thine and mine,
>   And a health to thee, Tom Moore.

If Byron's biographer missed being present at the dénouement of that tragicomedy, he likewise failed to witness the pitiful final curtain of Sheridan's dramatic career. Moore went to town in May, 1816 (where he saw the Princess Charlotte in all her bridal finery), and, while visiting Rogers, had been alarmed by a note from Sheridan to the banker-poet begging for £150, which would "remove all difficulty. I am absolutely alone and broken-hearted . . . They are going to put the carpets out of window, and break into Mrs. S.'s room and *take me*—for God's sake let me see you." Host and guest posted off at midnight for Saville Row, where a servant assured them that the bailiffs were not yet in the house but would be in the morning; and returned early next day with a draft sufficient to satisfy the creditors. To Moore, however, Sheridan seemed as "good-natured and cordial as ever," and Tom returned to Ashbourne, thinking this was simply another of Sherry's scrapes.   In July, however, he learned with indignation of Sheridan's death on the seventh of that month, amid circumstances which pointed to the gross neglect of his quondam adviser by the Regent; and in a fury of grief and wrath Moore published his stinging "Lines on the Death of Sheridan" in the *Morning Chronicle* of August 5:

> How proud they can press to the fun'ral array
> Of one, whom they shunn'd in his sickness and sorrow:—
> How bailiffs may seize his last blanket, to-day,
> Whose pall shall be held up by nobles to-morrow!

The verses include the famous tribute characterizing the author of *The Rivals* as one

> Whose wit, in the combat, as gentle as bright,
> Ne'er carried a heart-stain away on its blade,

and end with the vitriolic lines:

> Oh, Genius! thy patrons, more cruel than they,
> First feed on thy brains, and then leave thee to die!

The poem became one of the most notable productions in the war of the Whig poets against the Tory ascendancy.   But it was a discouraging time for the liberals—a time when, as Moore wrote to Miss Godfrey, the legitimists had the world at their feet.   "We shall see," he said savagely, "whether old women priests and fat regents, assisted by French renegades and drunken corporals, are, after all, the best agents of Providence for the welfare of mankind."   With Sheridan dead and Byron in exile; with Lord Liverpool now a kind of perpetual prime minister, of whom it has been said that "respectable in everything that he undertook, he was eminent in nothing"; with Lord Eldon in the Court of Chancery and Castlereagh in the Foreign Office; with Ireland a battle-ground between the bureaucratic Peel and O'Connell, greatest of modern demagogues, Moore might well feel that Catholic

Emancipation and general reform were a hopeless cause. Accordingly he concentrated his energies on finishing *Lalla Rookh*.

III

During the long period of its gestation and birth, Moore's friends inquired after *Lalla Rookh* as anxiously as if it were indeed a baby. Whenever Hunt wrote, he wanted to know what Moore was doing, and, shortly after settling at Ashbourne, Tom assured him that "the *genius loci* has no inconsiderable influence on my mind" and that "I am writing all the better for the select company of trees, cows and birds I have got into." "Stick to the East," Byron advised him in August, 1813, "the oracle, Staël, told me it was the only poetical policy." "Go on," he wrote four months later, "I shall really be very unhappy if I interfere with you." "When do you come out?" he demanded in January. "How proceeds the Poem?" he asked in March. "I am extremely anxious to hear of your poem," wrote Jeffrey in February, 1815, and again, over a year later: "what has become of your *opus majus* . . . I am afraid you are very idle in your retreat."

But *Lalla Rookh* was not one of those things that can be dashed off. The first draft of the poem (labeled by its creator, the "Brouillon of Lalla Rookh") shows how endlessly he worked over his materials. A second draft, also in the Pierpont Morgan Library, indicates that as late as 1815 neither the order of the parts nor their names was determined, for this manuscript lacks "The Light of the Haram"; "Paradise and the Peri" was called "The Forgiven Peri"; and "The Veiled Prophet" appears as "The Prophet of the Silver Veil" and *follows* "Paradise and the Peri." Even though a clean copy was ready for the printer in 1815, the threatening financial situation caused a delay in its publication, the postponement further increasing the rumors, until even the newspapers commenced to take notice of the impending event. Incidentally, one notes that during these months Moore very honorably offered to release the publishers from their engagement to pay him a sum for the poem which has become famous in literary history. This fact calls for some discussion of the poet's connection with the house of Longman.

As the great work drew to its close, Moore's dissatisfaction with his publisher, Carpenter, had increased. Though he had meditated a break as early as 1811, he was then unable to move because he was too deeply in Carpenter's debt. For it was Tommy's unfortunate habit to borrow against his expectations and to be surprised when the accounts fell in. He had therefore been morally obliged to give Carpenter the enormously successful *Intercepted Letters,* which, to Moore's disgust, Carpenter (who was the Prince's bookseller) had feared to publish in his own name, although, when the volume became a best-seller, the timorous publisher avowed it. Fortunately for Moore, the royalties from the *Letters* wiped out his indebtedness, and he felt free to offer *Lalla Rookh* elsewhere.

The poet's memorable connection with the firm of Longman, Hurst, Rees, Orme and Brown had its beginnings in 1811 when Moore approached Thomas N. Longman with the "determination to bind myself to your service" if a retaining fee were advanced. Nothing came of these first overtures. The continuing success of the *Irish Melodies* and the extraordinary sale of the *Intercepted Letters* had elevated Moore to the first rank of desirable authors; and Murray, that Anak of publishers, suggested to him, as we have seen, the editorship of a proposed review. As news of *Lalla Rookh* got about (and never was a poem better publicized), Murray again attempted to capture Moore in 1814 by offering him two thousand guineas for the work. Moore's Whig friends seems to have advised him not to close even for this handsome amount. Had not *Rokeby* sold for three thousand? Was a Whig poet worth only two-thirds the price of a Tory bard? There were innumerable conversations; Longman finally offered three thousand guineas for the new work, stipulating only (and it seems reasonable) that he should read the poem before publishing it; to this Moore's extraordinary response was that "Murray's two thousand *without* this distrustful stipulation is better than three with it.   I mean, in a day or two, to *turn* Carpenter's *stomach* by a communication of these proposals." In December, 1814, Longman surrendered even this one proviso, agreeing to pay Moore three thousand pounds (the guineas had become pounds) upon receiving from his hands a poem of the length of *Rokeby*—a point on which Jeffrey permitted himself dryly to observe that he hoped the two poems would have nothing else in common.   Publication was delayed, but on May 15, 1817, it was announced that *Lalla Rookh* was to appear on the twenty-second and that there were also to be obtained illustrations for the poem in quarto by R. Westall, R.A.   The book actually appeared May 27, 1817, went into a second edition in June, a third in July, and innumerable other editions thereafter.   It was the talk of the literary and fashionable worlds.

That Moore scored a dazzling immediate triumph there cannot be the slightest doubt.   Under the skillful guidance of Jeffrey, the *Edinburgh Review* discovered in the poem "the beauteous forms, the dazzling splendours, the breathing odours of the East," a region in which Moore was thoroughly at home; and if there were faults in the style, if the ornamentation was too lavish, if the characters were too far above human interest, the richness of the diction and the imagery, the tender and noble feeling of the whole, the many passages exhibiting the "very Genius of poetry" more than compensated.   *Blackwoods* felicitated Moore on emerging from his faulty youth, called him the "most ingenious, brilliant and fanciful Poet of the present age," and drowned him with rosewater in such a passage as this:

The real objects of our every-day world to his eyes glow with all the splendour of a dream, and even during the noon of manhood, he beholds, in all the works of creation, that fresh and unimpaired novelty which forms the glory, and so rarely survives the morning of life. Along with this extreme delicacy and fineness of organization, he possesses an ever-active and creative fancy, which at all times commands the whole range of his previously-acquired images, and suddenly, as at the waving of a magic-wand, calls them up into life and animation.

The *Monthly Magazine* congratulated its readers on "the rising of a sun which will never set." The *Literary Panorama,* though it found very little nature in the work and though it still complained about his sensuality, discovered some passages that were "tender and touching," some episodes that were "spirited and dramatic." The *Monthly Review* told him he had filled up a gap in English knowledge of Persian lore; the *European Magazine* congratulated him on producing a work worthy of his talents and taste.[4] It was in vain for the Tories to find fault; Moore marched victoriously on from edition to edition and from translation to translation, until at length he was turned into Persian—a compliment commemorated in the famous quatrain of Henry Luttrell:

> I'm told, dear Moore, your lays are sung,
> (Can it be true, you lucky man?)
> By moonlight, in the Persian tongue,
> Along the streets of Ispahan.

His publishers were compelled to sue the inevitable pirate; and as the poem swept over Europe, Serene Highnesses in little German courts costumed themselves as Moore's characters, various operas were made out of the poem,[5] ships were named for it, and it even received the dubious honor of forming the subject of a pageant at Astley's Circus.

The book had appeared at exactly the right time. A score of travel books had whetted the appetite of readers for the glamorous East. Napoleon's exploits in Egypt and Wellesley's in India had increased the vogue of Orientalism, as had the tales of nabobs returning from the Orient with liver complaint and riches mysteriously acquired. There were Turkish ornaments above the Ionic columns at Carlton House, Mameluke saddles and an effigy of Tippoo Sahib in the armory, and

Chinese dresses and a palanquin in another chamber; there was an Egyptian Hall at the Mansion House; the Rosetta Stone puzzled gaping visitors in the British Museum; and under the innumerable minarets of the Pavilion at Brighton Chinese mandarins stared at green and pink marble panels on the walls. The fashionable world had yawned over *Thalaba* and *The Curse of Kehama*, but *The Giaour* and *The Bride of Abydos* restored passion to the East. James Mill began his *History of British India* the year of *Lalla Rookh*, and Shelley's *Laon and Cythna*, which became *The Revolt of Islam*, was completed in September. What matter if to the general imagination India and Egypt, the Turks and the Parsees, the Bosphorus and the Vale of Cashmere were indistinguishable parts of a vague, rich universe of color and dream? "Stick to the East"—it was the only poetical policy. *Lalla Rookh* was the culminating point in poetical Orientalism.

IV

And where is *Lalla Rookh* nowadays? The title, which everybody knows; a catch phrase—"the trail of the serpent is over it all"—the origins of which nobody inquires into; a passage beginning "Oh! ever thus, from childhood's hour, I've seen my fondest hopes decay," more familiar in parody than in the original; a reference in *The Autocrat of the Breakfast Table* to the Huma, the bird that is always on the wing, which nobody recognizes; some vague recollection of the story of "Paradise and the Peri"—and that is all. Neglected by the reading public, *Lalla Rookh* is scarcely known even among literary specialists. A writer in the *Literary Gazette* for June 14, 1817, hoped that "Hibernica will lay aside Lalla Rookh and her music for tracts on political economy," and Hibernica has but too well fulfilled the desire of the commentator. The book lies stranded in the Dead Sea of literature like a lavishly decorated Oriental galley, and few there are who climb aboard and explore its faded interior.

If the poem was too extravagantly praised in Moore's life-time, history has extravagantly avenged the indiscretion.

No amount of special pleading will make *Lalla. Rookh* a great poem, and yet the laudatory adjectives were not all mistaken. It is curious to inquire into the reasons of this neglect, which are, briefly, that Moore shared the defects of his time and in this poem lacked its virtues. For the two grand faults of the romantic school were bookishness and rhetoric. The bookishness has been ignored, largely because of the false importance given by scholars to Wordsworth's theory that poetry should employ the language of common life, a theory which not even Wordsworth fully obeyed. Nevertheless, scholars tend to assume that the romantics, in turning away from eighteenth-century periphrasis, somehow achieved a new simplicity. Nothing is farther from the truth. Most of them were bookish to a remarkable degree. They all read too much and remembered too much of what they had read. Southey constructed his grandiose epics out of his library. Coleridge disappeared into a perfect fog of erudition satirized by Peacock; and even poems like "The Ancient Mariner" and "Kubla Khan" sprang rather from reading than from experience. The footnotes, prefaces, introductions, and *pièces justicatifs* printed with Scott's poems would make a respectable volume by themselves. *Childe Harold* is buoyed up on notes by Byron, Dallas, and Hobhouse, and Byron's other poems ever and again cite an "authority," while his plays come straight out of the history books. Wordsworth employs an erudite vocabulary, devotes one whole section of the *Prelude* to books, unsmilingly translates his undergraduate reading into blank verse, prefixes a Latin sentence to the "Ode to Duty" and a paragraph from Bacon to "The White Doe of Rylstone." Shelley intermixes his clouds and lightning with Greek philosophy, facts out of Herschel and Erasmus Darwin, and citations from Volney and Æschylus, Dante and William Godwin. Hunt turned Italian *novelle* into English verse, and Landor was an erudite classicist. There is not the slightest objection to a poet's finding his themes in literature, and the greater men—Keats is an excellent example—usually rose above their libraries, but the net result of this passion for reading was to clog romantic utterance with superfluous erudition.

Along with this elaborate literariness went an equally elaborate rhetoric, the canons of which, though they have not, like the canons of neo-classic rhetoric, become commonplace, are nonetheless recognizable. One such stylistic quality is best described by saying that the romantics tend to write as if they were addressing a public meeting. Byron is a notable example of this oratorical manner, but who does not recall Scott's "Breathes there a man with soul so dead?" Here is a bit out of Coleridge:

> my voice, unaltered, sang defeat
> To all that braved the tyrant-quelling lance.

Open Wordsworth at random—an anti-Napoleonic sonnet begins:

> We can endure that He should waste our lands,
> Despoil our temples, and by sword and flame
> Return us to the dust from which we came,

in the manner of the Declaration of Independence. Shelley writes like a rhyming Tom Paine:

> Thrones, altars, judgment-seats, and prisons, wherein,
> And beside which, by wretched men were borne
> Sceptres, tiaras, swords, and chains, and tomes
> Of reasoned wrong, glozed on by ignorance,

a passage from the last speech in Act III of *Prometheus Unbound*. It is true that this rolling utterance was forced on the poets by their subject matter (half their poems are political pamphlets); true also that the effects are sometimes thrilling and beautiful; true that this large discourse makes their better passages memorable; and yet the general direction of this idiom is in the direction of elaboration and periphrasis. Everybody wrote as if he were addressing a parliament of archangels.

The public quality of this vocabulary united with an Elizabethan influence; and a profusion of colored words, elaborate figures of speech, literary allusions, strange phrases, and beautiful archaeology was turned into the current of English verse. Keats is the best example of the result. He wishes in *Endymion* to indicate that love is one thing, formal history another, and so he writes:

> What care, though owl did fly
> About the great Athenian admiral's mast?
> What care, though striding Alexander past
> The Indus with his Macedonian numbers?
> Though old Ulysses tortured from his slumbers
> The glutted Cyclops, what care?—Juliet leaning
> Amid her window-flowers,—sighing,—weaning
> Tenderly her fancy from its maiden snow,
> Doth more avail than these,

to the confusion of the sense and the profit of the reference-book publishers. Beautiful as is "The Eve of St. Agnes," no one can say exactly where the events occurred, what is the occasion of the dramatic tension, or precisely what the story is. The narrative stops in order that Keats may devote rich words to the stained-glass window, the sound of Madeline's garments dropping from her body, the music which, played by trumpets, a kettle-drum and a clarionet (extraordinary orchestra!), yet yearns like a god in pain, the bowl of candy so like a confectioner's window, which, for no reason whatever, Porphyro takes out of a closet and puts by the side of the bed. In spite of this deluge of gems, the poem remains a great poem, and Keats a great poet, but that is not now the point. The total effect of this elaborate rhetoric was to create a diffuse and artificial poetical dialect from which the greater men emerged at intervals and the lesser men not at all. Unfortunately Moore was one of the lesser men.

For *Lalla Rookh* is undeniably bookish, the verse carrying a train of footnotes and an appendix of annotations as long as the countless lamps which Azim saw in the halls of the veiled prophet. Moore wishes to describe the happy valley wherein lives the beautiful Nourmahal, and the reader learns

> That one might think, who came by chance
> Into that vale this happy night,
> He saw that City of Delight
> In Fairy-land,

and an asterisk directs him to a footnote which tells him that the City of Delight is "the capital of Shadukiam," and refers him to still another footnote which in turn refers him to Sale's *Preliminary Discourse on the Koran.* Or we are in the midst of the bloody struggle which forms the climax of "The Fire-Worshippers," but we must pause to discover from the bottom of a page that "the finest ornament for the horses is made of six large flying tassels of long white hair, taken out of the tails of wild oxen, that are to be found in some places of the Indies." This is doubtless very informative.

The footnotes, however, are a venial sin; deeper lies the fatal failure of the poem imaginatively to fuse the results of all this hard reading into a credible poetic world. *Vathek* is twice as successful because it labors only half as hard. Moore's perfumed Orient discovers always a lurking odor of old leather bindings. Doubtless we have been spoiled by the racier reports of Doughty and T. E. Lawrence; doubtless it would be quite unfair to demand that Moore, like Byron, go and see for himself what the Vale of Cashmere really was. But turn to another learned poet, who got up his orientalism out of equally learned books. At the opening of the second book of *Paradise Lost* Milton casually paints in the sort of rich, exotic setting in which the events of *Lalla Rookh* are supposed to take place:

High on a throne of royal state, which far
Outshon the wealth of Ormus and of Ind,
Or where the gorgeous East with richest hand
Showers on her kings barbaric pearl and gold,
Satan exalted sat.

In "The Veiled Prophet of Khorassan" Moore attempts to describe the splendors of that Satanic being, Mokanna, as young Azim, the hero of the tale, wanders through an oriental palace:

Here, the way leads, o'er tesselated floors
Or mats of CAIRO, through long corridors,
Where, rang'd in cassolets and silver urns,
Sweet wood of aloe or of sandal burns;
And spicy rods, such as illume at night
The bowers of TIBET, send forth odorous light,
Like Peris' wands, when pointing out the road
For some pure Spirit to its blest abode!—
And here, at once, the glittering saloon
Bursts on his sight, boundless and bright as noon;
Where, in the midst, reflecting back the rays
In broken rainbows, a fresh fountain plays
High as th'enamell'd cupola, which towers
All rich with Arabesques of gold and flowers:
And the mosaic floor beneath shines through
The sprinkling of that fountain's silvery dew,
Like the wet, glistening shells, of every dye,
That on the margin of the Red Sea lie.

We are to take this as one of the

scenes past all imagining,—
More like the luxuries of that impious King,
Whom Death's dark Angel, with his lightning torch,
Struck down—

a reference to "Shedad, who made the delicious gardens of Irim, in imitation of Paradise, and was destroyed by lightning the first time he attempted to enter them," as the learned author informs us. Now this is not bad writing of a kind; it is actually cleaner and firmer than *Endymion* or "The Eve of St. Agnes," and it conveys a certain atmosphere; but the difficulty is that, unlike Milton's splendors, cannily left vague, Moore's scene is *not* past all imagining—it is, on the contrary, prophetic of Hollywood.

To point out the faults in Moore's major poem is easy; it is a more interesting critical task to dwell upon some of its merits. For one thing, though Moore occasionally falls into the parliamentary manner, as in:

> the bracing air
> Of toil,—of temperance,—of that high, rare,
> Etherial virtue, which alone can breathe
> Life, health, and lustre into Freedom's wreath!

his style is in the main pure. It may lack intensity; it may sink into bathos; its liquidity may cloy; but it is not gummy with archaic "beauties" nor clogged with superfluous ornamental rhetoric. Take, for instance, a passage describing carnage in "The Fire-Worshippers"; it is as swift and lurid as anything in Scott:

> . . . listless from each crimson hand
>   The sword hangs, clogg'd with massacre.
> Never was horde of tyrants met
> With bloodier welcome—never yet
> To patriot vengeance hath the sword
> More terrible libations pour'd!
> All up the dreary, long ravine,
> By the red, murky glimmer seen
> Of half-quench'd brands, that o'er the flood
> Lie scatter'd round and burn in blood,
> What ruin glares! what carnage swims!
> Heads, blazing turbans, quivering limbs,
> Lost swords that, dropp'd from many a hand,
> In that thick pool of slaughter stand. . . .

This, to be sure, is melodrama, but carnage is usually melodramatic, and this is melodrama in which every word tells. Yet the same work which contains these bloody horrors also contains so Shelleyan a lyric as that which begins:

> A Spirit there is, whose fragrant sigh
>   Is burning now through earth and air,
> Where cheeks are blushing, the Spirit is nigh,
>   Where lips are meeting, the Spirit is there!

as well as that more famous song in which, despite one's
knowledge that it is too facile, one somehow has a persistent,
ineradicable pleasure:

> There's a bower of roses by BENDEMEER'S stream,
>   And the nightingale sings round it all the day long;
> In the time of my childhood 'twas like a sweet dream,
>   To sit in the roses and hear the bird's song.
> That bower and its music I never forget,
>   But oft when alone, in the bloom of the year,
> I think—is the nightingale singing there yet?
> Are the roses still bright by the calm BENDEMEER?

Place this beside Shelley's "Indian Serenade," and Moore's
poem perhaps sinks to a secondary order of lyricism; and yet
who, before Moore, had wrung quite this music out of English words, or who, before him, had attained this cool, luscious
beauty?

The four tales which Feramorz tells in the course of the
work are interspersed with prose passages narrating the journey of Lalla Rookh from Delhi to Cashmere and containing
the ironical comments of the pedant Fadladeen on the various
portions of the poem. These interludes are amusing, but the
difficulty is that they are in a different key from that of the
rest of the work, and that Moore's resort to prose indicates
a poverty of poetical resource. The four tales fall into two
groups, two of them tragic and two of them, in Mr. Gwynn's
phrase, pretty examples of the Arabian Nights done into
springing, easy verse. The first of these, "Paradise and the
Peri," is an oriental fairy story with a moral, pleasant and
sugary. "The Light of the Haram" is an even more sugary
bit preparatory to the not very surprising discovery that
Feramorz is really the prince whom Lalla Rookh is journey-
ing to marry. "The Light of the Haram" soon breaks down

FIRST DRAFT OF "THERE'S A BOWER OF ROSES BY BENDEMEER'S STREAM"

into a succession of mellifluous lyrics, as if Moore at length recognized that song and not epic was his proper *métier*.

Yet the other two narratives are surprisingly masculine. "The Veiled Prophet of Khorassan" is the story of Mokanna, a religious fakir, who, by hiding his face behind a silver veil, plays on the fanaticism of certain Mohammedan tribes until they rebel against the sultan. In the course of his evil career he acquires a large and variegated harem and an enormous palace. To this harem Zelica, the heroine, is the latest recruit. She has been enamored of the hero, Azim, but, since she believes him dead, credulity has placed her in the control of the prophet. Under the impression that, like one of Shelley's young men, he is to battle for the freedom of the world, Azim enrolls under Mokanna's banner only to discover Zelica in the palace, half-crazed by the loss of her virginity. Azim swears vengeance and joins the army of the sultan, which, like a prince in heroic tragedy, he leads to victory. Trapped with a small band in his one remaining stronghold, Mokanna cynically poisons his followers at a banquet which Victor Hugo might have imagined, throws himself into a burning well, and leaves the crazed Zelica his veil. This she puts on, meets the invading army alone, and is killed by Azim before he learns her identity. He spends the remainder of his life praying at her grave.

This fable lies halfway between the Gothic romance of Mrs. Radcliffe and romantic opera, and a fable so absurd could be made believable only by the burning imagination of a Shelley. This Moore did not possess. Nevertheless the narrative does move; and as the reader makes his way through these incredibilities, he perceives that it is not the absurd events but their larger significance which is important. This tale of religious fanaticism, this story of whole peoples led astray by a cynical demagogue is recited for its modern application; and it seems clear that in "The Veiled Prophet of Khorassan" Moore intended some glancing reference to the Catholic question in Ireland. It is not that Mokanna is Daniel

O'Connell, but rather the danger inherent in a situation which allows a demagogue to play upon the religious prejudices of an ignorant people—this is what Moore has in view. In an even larger sense the poem is a product of that disillusion which the French Revolution and the Napoleonic regime produced in many sensitive minds. Mokanna's speech near the opening of the tale is singularly like something from the pen of William Godwin or the younger Shelley:

> . . . this sword must first
> The darkling prison-house of Mankind burst,
> Ere Peace can visit them, or Truth let in
> Her wakening day-light on a world of sin!
> But then, celestial warriors, then, when all
> Earth's shrines and thrones before our banner fall,
> When the glad Slave shall at these feet lay down
> His broken chain, the tyrant Lord his crown,
> The Priest his book, the Conqueror his wreath,
> And from the lips of Truth one mighty breath
> Shall, like a whirlwind, scatter in its breeze
> The whole dark pile of human mockeries;—
> Then shall the reign of Mind commence on earth,
> And starting fresh, as from a second birth,
> Man, in the sunshine of the world's new spring,
> Shall walk transparent, like some holy thing!

Aware that a Moslem fakir would not talk thus of liberty, Moore deliberately sacrificed poetical verisimilitude to press home his point in this passage which seems, as it were, to anticipate Shelley; but this dream of philosophic anarchy is wholly hypocritical, and the fact that it is put in Mokanna's mouth is but another example of Moore's Whiggish skepticism of radical reform.

"The Fire-Worshippers," much the best thing in *Lalla Rookh*, is the story of the gallant resistance by a group of Persian patriots, led by Hafed, to their Moslem tyrants, the defense of Persian religion and of Persian nationality being the "note" of that resistance. The inevitable love affair between Hafed and Hinda, daughter of the Moslem emir, mixes romantic tragedy with political struggle, and there is, among the little Persian band, a traitor who sells out to the conqueror. The overtones are unmistakably those of Irish rebellion, particularly the Robert Emmet episode. Moore hymns the doomed patriots and goes out of his way to excoriate the wretch who betrayed their cause:

> Oh, for a tongue to curse the slave,
>   Whose treason, like a deadly blight,
> Comes o'er the councils of the brave,
>   And blasts them in their hour of might!
> May Life's unblessed cup for him
> Be drugged with treacheries to the brim,—
> With hopes, that but allure to fly,
>   With joys, that vanish while he sips,
> Like Dead-Sea fruits, that tempt the eye,
>   But turn to ashes on the lips!
> His country's curse, his children's shame,
> Outcast of virtue, peace and fame,
> May he, at last, with lips of flame
> On the parch'd desert thirsting lie.

This is good Irish cursing, and the suggestion that Hafed is a Persian Robert Emmet, Hinda the unfortunate Sarah Curran, and the traitor a composite portrait of government spies, is irresistible. "The Fire-Worshippers" has a vigor rare in Moore, an energy which patriotism and the detestation of treachery have breathed into the poem; and if it be true that during these years Moore lost contact with his native country, "The Fire-Worshippers" is proof that deep below the surface there were wells of indignation not wholly dry.

Chapter IX

IN ORDER to supervise the printing of *Lalla Rookh*
Moore gave up Mayfield Cottage in the middle of March,
1817, and removed to a cottage at the foot of Muswell Hill
in Hornsey, then six miles from town. The place was rented
furnished; and though, as he disgustedly wrote his mother,
he found it full of rats, it was habitable enough. Bessy was
given a taste of the pleasures of London, where her mother
was living. No sooner had they arrived than Lady Donegal
took Mrs. Moore in her carriage to look for a new bonnet,
and we hear of visits to Drury Lane and to the Opera as well
as to various acquaintances in London, including Rogers, who
took the entire family to his hospitable mansion. Bessy seems
likewise to have sufficiently overcome her timidity to call
with Tom on Lady Bessborough, Lady Cork (the original
of Mrs. Leo Hunter in *Pickwick Papers*), and other social
lights; and, in addition, William H. Murray (who was to
marry Bessy's sister, Anne), Barbara Godfrey (the niece of
Lady Donegal) and other week-end visitors thronged the little
establishment in Hornsey. Moore's health was indifferent—
he wrote his mother that he had been "a good Catholic all
this week, not having tasted a bit of *meat*"—but the success of
Lalla Rookh set him up; Croker gave his health in a flattering speech at a dinner of Trinity College graduates in June;
and though the children were none too well, Tom felt justified in running off to Paris with Rogers in July for a well-
earned vacation. Stevenson was also in Paris, and Tom reported amusingly that "the ice is too cold for his stomach,

SLOPERTON COTTAGE

and he cannot get whisky-punch for love or money—accordingly he droops."

From this pleasant interlude the poet was called home in the middle of August by news of the fatal illness of little Barbara, who had been injured by a fall. The poor child, not yet six, died on September 18 and was buried beneath the shadow of the Norman church at Hornsey, a spot to which in after years Moore was to pay many a melancholy pilgrimage. "I can bear such things myself pretty well," Tom bravely wrote his mother, "but to see and listen to poor Bessy makes me as bad as she is." Under these circumstances Hornsey became intolerable, and the stricken family took refuge in Lady Donegal's house in Davies Street, Berkeley Square, which that kind friend graciously put at their disposal. In addition to the crushing burden of sorrow, Moore also hurt his leg, and an inflammation set in which was some weeks in curing.

Lord Lansdowne had said in the spring that "he should feel delighted if I would fix my residence near his house in the country," and now wrote that he was looking for a residence in the neighborhood for Moore. When it is remembered how dependent the poet was on a library, it is understandable that Tom should write his mother: "It would certainly be an object to be near such a man; his library, his society, all would be of use to me; not to mention the probability of his being some day or other able to do me more important services." Lady Donegal urged the change; and William Lisle Bowles, rector of Bremhill, whom Moore had previously met, wrote to suggest a house at Heddington "within a quarter of a mile of the most beautiful views in Wiltshire." But the Moores preferred "a little thatched cottage, with a pretty garden" some three miles south of Bowood and three miles southwest of "sweet Calne in Wiltshire," known as Sloperton Cottage, and in the middle of November they "were likely to be very snug" in what became their permanent home.

Sloperton Cottage stands today very much as it did at

Moore's death, save that a wall has replaced the paling which formerly sheltered it from the quiet road, the thatched roof has been changed, and the ivy, brought from Tara, which once covered the walls, has disappeared. House and barns were modest enough: Moore originally paid only £40 a year, afterwards becoming a tenant under a repairing lease at £18. There was a raised bank on one side of the kitchen garden, and on this terrace, where a convenient table was placed, Moore walked up and down, if the weather was fine, as he composed; or, if it were not, he retreated to an upstairs study where he wore holes in the carpet with his restless feet. The local legend is that he used occasionally, when outdoors, to stop, lean over a low wall, and talk to the pigs. Possibly such habits gave rise to the Wiltshire saying: "Mrs. Moore she wur a angel, but as for Mr. Moore, thur he wur no good, vor he was allus in a brown stud." The interior was comfortable rather than fine; there was a good piano and plenty of books, many of them now in the Royal Irish Academy. As Moore's fame increased, Sloperton became a shrine for sentimental pilgrims, who draped it in elegant rhyme and rhapsodic prose or drew prettified pictures of the "white-walled cot of Moore," which were published in the annuals and magazines. Thus Nicholas Michell rhymes in 1832:

> The day is sultry; rich festoons of flowers
> O'er droop the porch, the shining fishes spring
> From glassy streams, no bird disturbs the bowers,
> And hums the bee on faint and drowsy wing;
> Cool is yon dim alcove adorned with vines;
> There, fanned by perfumed airs, our bard reclines.[1]

The conduct of the fish must strike all naturalists as peculiar; and inasmuch as the rhymester pictures Moore reclining with Peris and Fairies about him, one must conclude that the description is more elegant than exact. G. F. Mulvaney was somewhat more accurate in a poem called "The Poet's Walk," which, however, he illustrated with a sketch of Cupid playing the harp:

CARICATURE OF TOM MOORE

This spot to Genius consecrate? Her shrine
Of glowing thought and Poesy divine
Whose inspiration from her aerial throne
Smiles on the Bard she proudly calls her own!
Here doth he pace—to feeling all resigned
Inhaling Nature—till the awakened mind
Culling from fancies that alighting throng,
Weaves thought and feeling in harmonious song;
Here midst the splendor of departing day
The Poet's soul feasts on the bright array
Of clouds that gather round the setting sun,
As tho' in homage ere his course be run,
And pays its homage of an ardent gaze
Till twilight closes o'er the sun's last rays.

.   .   .   .   .   .

Yes, lightly tread! nor break the stillness here
Where e'en the breeze is music to the ear—
Where in each shade some magic spirit dwells
Reigning o'er us—but subject to his spells,
A Charm unbounded own—and still to be,
Since ages yet unborn shall flock to see
Where lived the Bard of Love and Liberty!

North of the cottage, Spye Park stood (and stands) perched on a hill amid its trees. Sloperton belonged to that property; Mr. A. G. Bradley tells of knowing an old lady, who, acting as secretary to the owner of Sloperton, used to receive Moore's half-yearly rent, always accompanied by an amusing note.[2] Southeast of Sloperton, across a little valley, the steeple of Bromham Church is just visible from the cottage; there Moore attended services, and there he is buried with his wife and two of his children. The home of no English poet is more peacefully rural.

But of course the great attraction of Sloperton was Bowood, some three miles north of the cottage, set in its magnificent park, and one of the show places of Wiltshire. The tall Lord Lansdowne, only son of Lord Shelburne and his wife, Lady Louisa Fitzpatrick, was a year younger than Moore, and a friend and patron after the poet's heart. So exemplary a Whig that Lord John Russell complained: "honest as the purest virgin, Lansdowne was too yielding, too mild, and most unfit to deal with men in important political transactions," he had been a member of Parliament at 21 for the family seat of Calne, Chancellor of the Exchequer in the All-the-Talents ministry at 25, and one of the pillars of the moderate opposition thereafter. An advocate of Catholic claims, the Irish cause, and political reform, he was likewise a model landlord, a patron of art, literature, and education, and an ideal host. His wife, Louisa Emma Fox-Strangways, a daughter of the second Earl of Ilchester, was a gracious hostess; and when the family was in residence, Bowood was flooded with guests—aristocrats, artists, politicians, poets. Without the Lansdownes, said Moore, Wiltshire was a "mare mortuum."

The great house is set in a vast park having nine valleys in it; the grounds had been laid out in the last century by "Capability" Brown, who left, among other improvements, a Greek temple lifting its white columns across a shining sheet of water in the park; the house itself had been remodeled by the Adam brothers in the middle of the eighteenth century, but a three-hundred-foot wing in imitation of Diocletian's palace at Spalatro had increased the general magnificence since the first remodeling. Such splendors usually so frightened Bessy Moore that she stayed at home if there were guests at Bowood, but on social occasions Moore was accustomed to walk over to the park and join the festivities. He was at all times free to roam the library, over which Priestley had formerly presided and in a room off which he is said to have discovered oxygen; and if Tom chose to spend the night, a ground-floor chamber still known as "Mr. Moore's room" was reserved for him, a pleasant, rectangular apartment containing a small single bed under a canopy. When there were guests, Moore played and sang inimitably after dinner, stimulated by the applause of the men and the perfumed adoration of the ladies.

More to Bessy's taste were the less splendid neighbors— the Phippses at Wans House, the Houltons at Farley, the Benets at Pyt House, the Hugheses, and the rest, all of whom were kind, and who assisted her charitable work among the local poor. Napier, the historian of the Peninsular War and a friend of reform, lived two fields distant after 1819, and chapters of military history were read to the poet as the book was written. Or Tom (and more rarely Bessy) might visit Longleat, the seat of the Marquis of Bath, near Warminster, or Lacock Abbey, the home of the Talbots—Henry Talbot was to be the English discoverer of photography, and, a quarter of a century later, Moore tells of being "photogenized" at Lacock and of how the portraits were not at all "like." But the oddest of the local worthies was undeniably William Lisle Bowles.

Bowles, who was fifty-five when the Moores came to Sloperton, had been for thirteen years the vicar of Bremhill, where he had dotted the vicarage grounds with stone obelisks, trellis-work arbors, stone tables, funereal urns, and a fountain. There was also a hermitage, and Moore records that "when company is coming, he cries, 'Here, John, run with the crucifix and missal to the hermitage and set the fountain going.'" He tuned his sheep bells in thirds and fifths, repaired to Stonehenge on the fourth of June in what he conceived to be Druidical attire, and added to the terrors of the tomb by inscribing his own rhymes on the gravestones of deceased parishioners. A walk through the grounds was, in the language of the day, a "short but classical tour" queerly mingled with Gothicism, for the various inscriptions on the stone *objets d'art* were ascribed to a St. Bruno, whom Bowles invented as the *genius loci*. There were endless stories of his absentmindedness and his timidity. He is credited with once presenting a parishioner with a Bible inscribed "with the author's compliments." Julian Charles Young tells an amusing anecdote of a visit to Bowood by Bowles. On this occasion Bowles and Lady Lansdowne left the room; and when

BOWOOD

they returned, Lady Lansdowne was heard to exclaim: "Bless the dear man, there is no pleasing him." Bowles then excitedly asked Young if he were going home that night, saying: "I wish I were going home too. I shan't sleep a wink here. I was shown into a bedroom to dress in, in which I was intended to pass the night; but it was on the ground-floor, where there was nothing whatever to prevent thieves from getting in and cutting my throat! I have remonstrated with Lady Lansdowne, and the dear lady, by way of rendering me easier in my mind, has transferred me to a room so high, that, in case of fire, I shall be burnt to a cinder before I can be rescued!" But after deciding to leave, Bowles discovered that a thunderstorm was rolling up, and determined to stay, letting his wife go home alone. He went to bed only after he had been given a room adjoining Rogers's, with the door between the two chambers left open! ³

With such diversified society at hand Moore's social proclivities were not cut short by his rural existence, save in the heavy winter snows. While Bessy stayed contentedly at home, he tramped off to Bowood or Bremhill, made a trip to Bath or to some one of the Wiltshire towns, or was gone for days on one of his regular visits to London. Here, for example, is a not unusual day set down in his diary for October 18, 1818:

As the morning was fine, set out to Bowood to see Rogers; caught him in the garden, on the way to Bowles's; walked with him; talked much about Sheridan. . . . Found Bowles at home; asked him would he meet Rogers and Crowe at dinner with me on Wednesday or Thursday next. Cannot, on account of the sessions at Marlborough; wants to have a statue of Melancthon executed from a fine woodcut, to put up in his projected library; anxious to consult me about some prose he is writing. Left Bowles's at half-past two. In passing through Bowood for home I was caught by Lady Lansdowne, Lord Auckland, &c. &c. She begged me to stay for dinner; said Lady Bath (who was going next day) wished very much to know me. Consented: a man and horse sent for my things. Sat with Rogers in his room till dinner.

Told me that Beckford (*the* Beckford) is delighted with "Lalla Rookh;" heard so from Beckford himself in the spring, when I met him at Rogers's in town, and he was all raptures about it. Beckford wishes me to go to Fonthill with R. . . . Party at dinner—Lady Bath, her unmarried daughter, Lady Louisa, and the married one, Lady Elizabeth Campbell, and her husband; Lord Auckland and his two sisters; Mrs. Frankland Lewis. . . . Talked of strange names: I mentioned a little child, born in Italy of English parents, christened Allegra. . . . Some traveller in America mentions having met a man called Romulus Riggs. . . . Music in the evening. Lady Bath talked to me of her sister . . . ; said how often she spoke of me; hoped I would soon visit Longleat, &c. Rogers asked me whether the "Parody on Horace," lately in the "Chronicle," was mine; said how Luttrell was delighted with it at Ampthill . . . reading it out to Lords Jersey and Duncannon, who were also much pleased with it. Told me also that he heard the verses to Sir Hudson Lowe praised at Brookes's. It is pleasant to find that these trifles do not die unnoticed. . . . Sung a good deal by myself and one or two things with Mrs. F. Lewis. She and I, and Lady Louisa Thynne, sung "The Bird let loose," (from my "Sacred Songs"), and it went beautifully. Mrs. F. Lewis sung out of the same set, "Oh Thou who driest the Mourner's Tear." Meant to walk home, but Lady L. insisted upon my having the coachman drive me over in her little gig. Cannot sleep out while dear Bessy is so near her difficulties, and without a single male or female friend near her but myself. . . . Got home rather late.

Bessy's "difficulties," which thus oddly close this day's chronicle, mean that the Moores were expecting another child, born October 24; yet on the nineteenth Moore went to a ball in Devizes, on the twenty-first Rogers visited him, on the twenty-second he visited Rogers at Bowood and the heroic Bessy invited Crowe, Rogers, and an anonymous gentleman to dine at Sloperton, on the twenty-third Crowe also came to breakfast, and on the twenty-fourth Moore spent most of the day at Bowood! However, Moore was a fond husband and father, and from the onset of Bessy's pains at half-past eleven that night to the birth of the child at a quarter to four in the morning,

I walked about the parlour by myself, like one distracted; some-times stopping to pray, sometimes opening the door to listen; and never was gratitude more fervent than that with which I knelt down to thank God for the dear girl's safety, when all was over —(the maid, by the by, very near catching me on my knees).

He slept from six to half-past nine the next morning, and then had to walk five miles to Devizes and back to secure forty pounds—"the little prodigal is no sooner born than money is wanted for him." Unconsciously prophetic lines, for this child was Thomas Lansdowne Parr Moore, whose birth the poet greeted with "unspeakable delight," and whose wild career was destined to vex his father's later years!

II

While Moore had been moving from Mayfield to Hornsey and from Hornsey to Sloperton, preoccupied with his proofs and grief-stricken over the death of Barbara, he was not un-aware that in the great world outside, kings had crept forth again to feel the sun. The map of Europe which Pitt had rolled up in 1805 had been unrolled by Metternich in 1815 to the accompaniment of a susurrus of *clichés* like legitimacy, throne and altar, and the balance of power; and the Allied Sovereigns, having signed that singular document in which they promised to follow "the sublime truths which the Holy Religion of our Saviour teaches," proceeded to rearrange Europe according to their own convenience. The result was peace of a sort—in the words of Mr. Phil Fudge:

> Europe—thanks to royal swords
> And bay'nets, and the Duke commanding—
> Enjoys a peace which, like the Lord's,
> Passeth all human understanding.

Louis le Désiré, brought back in the baggage train of the allied armies, preferring the Tuileries to Hartwell, was cau-tiously disentangling himself from the "Ultras" to the disgust of his brother and heir, but the fact did not appease the sullen discontent of the post-war generation now approaching its majority—that generation, in de Musset's phrase, which was conceived between two battles and born to the sound of cannon. The rulers of mankind, however, pretended that nothing had happened since 1789.

In Great Britain the ending of hostilities had led to the disillusion of victory. A fall in prices threatened to ruin the agriculturalists, who had been encouraged to raise bumper crops, and to bankrupt manufacturers, who had been encouraged to maintain peak production. But the home market was glutted with goods as continental nations moved to prevent the dumping of English articles, there was a rising tide of unemployment, a crisis in finance, incessant rain, a bad harvest, riot and bloodshed. An alarmed government strove to put down discontent by the ancient methods of suppression, but the Chief Justice was irascible, the Attorney-General was deaf, and the attempt to convict the leaders of the unemployed of high treason so preposterous that juries refused to find them guilty. There were rumors of dreadful secret societies designed to overthrow Christianity by demanding universal suffrage, secret ballots, and annual parliaments; and from his secure retreat in the Lake country, Southey, who knew nothing of political economy, loudly proclaimed that "the manufacturing populace are not merely discontented with the Government, but absolutely abhor it with a deadly hatred." Somebody fired an airgun at the window of the Regent's carriage, and the ministry suspended the Habeas Corpus Act in 1817. The deaths of the Princess Charlotte and her child and of a girl-baby born dead to the Duchess of Cumberland were followed by an epidemic of virtuous matrimony among the royal princes, three old gentlemen hastily securing brides in order to be the father of the next king or queen of England as the Lord might direct; and as every wedding involved an appeal to the nation for funds, the royal family sank to new depths of unpopularity. Meanwhile, the Princess of Wales was wandering about the Mediterranean with an Italian *cavaliere sirvente* named Bergami, who slept in the same tent with her in the Holy Land; and the Regent, in whom the death of his daughter in the autumn of 1817 had crystallized a desire to get rid of his wife, sent for his legal adviser (Sir Samuel Romilly hinted that that gentleman knew a little of everything except law) and compelled the cabinet to institute a private investigation into his wife's conduct.

Protected as he had been from contact with human misery, utterly lacking in financial sense, and ignorant of the simplest principles of economics, Moore, like the other moderate Whigs, could conceive of a social crisis only in terms of politics and personalities. The old enemies, so far as he was concerned, were enemies still. It was enough that the Regent was the Regent, that Castlereagh, who had been Chief Secretary for Ireland when the Union was consummated, was now in the foreign office, that Eldon, who detested reform, was Lord Chancellor, that Sidmouth, who had worked with Pitt to construct an anti-Catholic ministry, was Home Secretary. When moderates like Canning, alarmed by the condition of the country, joined the Liverpool ministry, it was to Moore desertion of the good cause—in the phrase of the day, "ratting." He therefore paused amid his other occupations to discharge a poisoned arrow or two in the general direction of the government. The bitterest of these invectives, however, he omitted from his *Poetical Works.*[4]

In an unguarded moment during March, 1818, Canning had permitted himself to make a satiric reference to the "revered and ruptured Ogden." William Ogden was a man of seventy who had been imprisoned during the recent riots and who had, he said, been carried from Manchester to London while suffering from rupture, though as a matter of fact he had been cured of his illness at the public expense. The inhumanity of Canning's reference, however, roused all of Moore's indignation, and in the *Morning Chronicle* of March 23, 1818, he flayed the minister in thirteen quatrains which are the bitterest thing he ever wrote.   Characteristic stanzas run:

Lines on a Late Display in the —— of ——

"In jocis quoque perniciosus."
Œlius Lamprid. de Commodo.

Is *this* then an eloquence, fit for the ears
   Of the Statesmen of England, the manly, the wise?
Is *this* then the wit to awaken the cheers
   Of the men on whose counsels the world hath its eyes?

To make mirth—as the mummer's last, brutal resource—
   Out of torments, the deadliest man can sustain,
And to probe, with a ridicule, cruel and coarse
   As the knife of an Indian, the vitals of Pain!

To lay bare ev'ry pang, that, in ribaldry's dearth,
   Even ribalds themselves would have cover'd with shade,
And to mock—gracious Heav'n!—with a mountebank's mirth,
   At the quiv'ring of agony's nerve round the blade.

. . . . . .

No, still let the witling—if wit it can be,
   That forsakes its own element, freedom and right,
And, like fishes whose home, when alive, was the sea,
   To *corruption* alone owes its pestilent light

No, still let the punster, the parodist draw
   From his out-of-date libels his pittance of fame,
While he helps to halloo the kean [*sic*] beagles of Law
   At the fools, who thus sanctioned, dare venture the same;

Let him plunder with those, whom he ridicul'd then,
   Let him live by the crew that then waken'd his laughter,
Like creatures we read of, (less rank than such men)
   Who befoul first their victim and feed on it after!

. . . . . .

All this let him do—even worse let him dare—
   But never, just God, let the scoffer again
Make a jest of the ills that thy creatures must bear,
   Lest thou wither the tongue that thus sports with their pain!

In 1841 Moore spoke of the "unembittered spirit, the . . . freedom from all real malice with which, in most instances, this sort of squib-warfare has been waged by me"; and in 1853 Lord John Russell, anxious to preserve the amiable character of his friend, spoke of the "ease and playfulness" of Moore's political satires.   Playful Moore could be, but on occasions like this a frenzy of vituperation shook from his small frame a torrent of fierce Irish cursing.

Both elements appear in *The Fudge Family in Paris,* which "Thomas Brown, the Younger" published on April 20, 1818, nor do they fuse harmoniously in the work, which represents both the frivolity and the bitterness of the period.   In the letters of Phelim Connor in that book Moore presents an unregenerate Irish patriot and writes as he had done in "Corruption" and "Intolerance."   Mr. Connor, for example, is pictured as sharing the views of Byron and Hazlitt with respect to Napoleon:

> Forth from its cage that eagle burst to light,
> From steeple on to steeple wing'd its flight,
> With calm and easy grandeur, to that throne
> From which a Royal craven just had flown,

as well as the disgust of Thomas Brown for the Holy Alliance:

> What, though long years of mutual treachery
> Had peopled full your diplomatic shelves
> With ghosts of treaties, murder'd 'mong yourselves;
> Though each by turns was knave and dupe—what then?
> A Holy League would set all straight again.

The appeal of the volume does not lie in this honest indignation, but in the letters of the Fudge family themselves.   Phil Fudge, Esq., is a renegade Irishman, a political turncoat and spy devoted to Castlereagh; his daughter, Biddy, gushes over Parisian fashions, and his son Bob "goes in" for French restaurants.   For their correspondence Moore revived the verse-letter which he had used successfully in the *Twopenny Post-Bag,* writing the epistles of Bob and Biddy in the light, rollicking anapaests he managed so well, and those of the elder

Fudge in tetrameter verse more appropriate to paternal dignity. His recent visit to Paris furnished him with the social substance of the satires, and his deepening dislike of the Tories with their political points. Of all Moore's satirical collections, *The Fudge Family in Paris* is today the most readable, partly because the giddy daughter and the would-be fashionable young man are eternal types, partly because the political references are readily understandable, and partly because of the general gaiety of the verse.

The volume had a good press and occasioned innumerable parodies, piracies, and continuations. Hunt's *Yellow Dwarf* thanked God that Moore was "neither a bubble nor a cheat," and instituted unsavory comparisons with "a mouthing sycophant" named Wordsworth, "a whining monk like Mr. Southey," and "a maudlin Methodistical lay preacher, like Mr. Coleridge." The *Monthly Review* said that the reader who could not enjoy the wit and humor of the volume, whatever his own politics, was to be pitied. The *European Magazine* discovered "a fund of entertainment" in the Fudges, and the *New Monthly* thought it the "most ingenious production" of the author since *Lalla Rookh*. As for the Tories, they were furious, not only because of the Fudges, but because Moore eked out the first edition with four contributions from the *Chronicle* (adding in later editions the rebuke to Canning already quoted), and despite Moore's generous tribute to Perceval (who had committed suicide), they would not be comforted. The *British Critic* sourly observed that he who flatters the follies, prejudices, and passions of mankind is always sure of supporters. The *Literary Gazette* found him profane and vulgar:

The unmeasured abuse of princes and ministers, the pandering to the basest passions of the multitude, the irrational repetition of exploded falsehoods, and the silly, otherwise mischievous, the weak, otherwise wicked misrepresentation of Britain and British subjects, are exploits commonly within the reach of such writers as can be base enough to combine a flowing versification and a seasoning of witticisms with the defamation of statesmen, the insult of monarchs, and the calumny of country.

Blackwoods advised Moore to leave the "low raving of daily and weekly newspapers," reminded its readers of Tom's immoralities, and paid him the high tribute of saying that "his political *jeux-d'esprit* [are] very dangerous weapons in the hands of a set of stupid demagogues."

But the best evidence that Moore was regarded as the most efficient satirist the Whigs could present is found in the attempts of the Tories to retaliate his own weapons upon him. For example, there appeared from the pen of Palmerston and others in 1819 a satirical volume entitled *The New Whig Guide*, containing among other matter a series of "English Melodies," in part parodies of Moore's Irish songs. The same authors, or their friends, published next *The Fudger Fudged; or, The Devil and T***y M****e*, which contains such passages as this:

> *A BALLAD-SINGER*, who had long
> Strumm'd many a vile lascivious song,
> Such as unwary youth entice
> To follow in the paths of vice,
> Worn out and impotent become,
> Beats, as he can, sedition's drum.

"His lewd erotics all forgot," Tommy is pictured as turning

> Murder and rapine to promote.

And a little later one reads:

> And he, for slander who selects,
> All whom the nation most respects,
> Dipping his pen in putrid gall,
> Complains that laws "the press enthrall."

The reader is further informed that the devil had hired a legion of such writers, and the seventeen pages of this dull stuff conclude with the advice to go to Rome and learn penance from the Pope. Such was party rage that the

Literary Chronicle called this "smart retaliation," and the *Literary Gazette*, proclaiming that Moore had descended to "the scavenger work of party," said that the "lofty and severe" tone of *The Fudger Fudged* was justified. The *Anti-Jacobin Review* printed a parody of "They May Rail at this Life" (from the seventh number of the *Irish Melodies*) entitled "Why Rail at this Life," which is perceptibly wittier:

> You commenced your career as Anacreon Little,
> Corrupting weak females emerging from school,
> So founding your fame on grounds frail and brittle,
> You've reap'd your reward in the cap of a fool.

And according to the *Literary Gazette*, fifty copies of an "Epistle to Thomas Moore, Esq., in imitation of the thirteenth satire of Juvenal" were printed and handed about among "literary friends" attacking his integrity.[5]

Some part of the Tory venom is explained by the extraordinary enthusiasm which greeted Moore on his visit to Dublin in June, 1818. He was himself in better humor; and whatever differences of opinion had existed in Ireland regarding his work, the amazing success of *Lalla Rookh* and the notoriety of *The Fudge Family in Paris* were proof that a great Irish poet was the talk of Great Britain. Sinking all partisan differences in national pride, Dublin for the first time gave him a public welcome. Two episodes in particular were memorable. He went to the theater, and, as he wrote Rogers with innocent vanity:

> It was even better than Voltaire's [reception] at Paris, because there was more *heart* in it, and the call for me at the Theatre, and the bursts of applause when I appeared with my best bows at the front of the box (which I was obliged to repeat several times in the course of the night) were really all most overwhelmingly gratifying, and scarcely more delightful to me on my own account than as proof of the strong spirit of nationality in my countrymen.

The second occasion was the public dinner on June 7 at Morrison's Great Rooms in Dawson Street, less than a quarter of

a mile from the modest dwelling where he was born. The
chair was taken by Lord Charlemont, and among those present were Lord Cloncurry, Lord Allen, Mr. Burrowes, Sir
Capel Molyneux, Sheil, Maturin, Charles Phillips, Samuel
Lover—and Daniel O'Connell! The poet sat on one side the
chairman, his father (now 77) sat on the other to hear his
son praised by the nobility and gentry (it seems to have been
a male gathering, and the proud mother perforce stayed at
home). Charlemont, Sheil, Phillips, Lover—one by one they
rose to praise him with Irish eloquence, Lord Charlemont declaring that his character was compounded of Patriotism,
Independence, and Consistency. Moore responded in a neat
speech, beginning: "I feel this the very proudest moment of
my whole life," pledging renewed allegiance to Ireland, dep-
recating party differences, and speaking the tribute to his
father already quoted. Among the toasts of the evening was
one to the living authors of Great Britain, to which Moore
also responded, paying graceful compliments to Byron, Scott,
Campbell, Wordsworth, Crabbe, and others, not forgetting
Southey—"*not the Laureate*, but the author of Don Roderick,
one of the noblest and most eloquent poems in the language."
All in all, heady wine for the tradesman's son.[6] When he
returned home, he "found Bessy walking about the garden
. . . watching for me," and his natural egotism seems not to
have been unduly inflated.

III

Why should not the Whig satirist write the life of the
Whig statesman? Why should not the greatest living Irish
poet biographize the wittiest Irish dramatist, recently dead?
The idea of a life of Sheridan originated with Murray, for in
the postscript of a letter to Joseph Strutt, Moore's Derbyshire friend, dated approximately November, 1817, one reads:

I must tell you a little triumph I have had. Wilkie [and] Murray are about to publish an Edition of Sheridan's Works complete, and they applied to me to write a poem on his Life and

Graces to be prefixed, at the same time, sending me the first
proof-sheet as a specimen of the typography. This proof-sheet
was no less than a Dedication from the Publishers to the Prince
Regent, in pursuance as they expressed thereto, of Sheridan's
own wish. I instantly said I could have nothing to do with the
undertaking, as such a Life as I should write of Sheridan could
not possibly be placed beside a Dedication to the P.R.—In consequence of which, after a little deliberation, they sacrificed his
R.H. to me, and I am to write the Essay, for which they give
me 500 *l.* about 3 *l.* a page. This (I mean about the dedication)
is *entre nous.*[7]

The poem about the "Life and Graces" was never written,
being replaced by the idea of a biographical introduction,
into the preparation of which Moore threw himself with so
much energy as to carry him far beyond the modest limits
of a preface. The details of the subsequent negotiations are
both involved and obscure, but "the indecision of Charles
Sheridan with respect to any arrangement with the book-
sellers," the claims of Sheridan's creditors and of Charles
Sheridan on the papers of the late dramatist, and counter-
proposals from Murray delayed the appearance of the intended volumes. Finally, in 1821, Murray published a two-
volume edition of Sheridan's works, for which Moore wrote a
rather pompous and empty introduction explaining that there
was to be no biographical preface and dwelling on the difficulties of a biography. Wilkie (the bookseller) disappeared
from the picture, and in January, 1819, Murray offered
Moore a thousand pounds for a formal biography of Sheridan. When, however, Moore's exile postponed the comple-
tion of the work, Murray withdrew and Longmans took it
over.

When Tom returned from Dublin in the summer of 1818,
these perplexities were, of course, all in the future, and he
went industriously to work collecting the materials out of
which the biography eventually grew. He visited Bath to
consult Mrs. Lefanu, Sheridan's surviving sister, and to be
talked to by Dr. Parr, the famous Grecian, who loomed upon

him in full wig and apron in Mrs. Lefanu's drawingroom to tell him a little about Sheridan and a great deal about Dr. Parr. He consulted the Duke of Grafton; he bought fifty-nine volumes of the *Annual Register* for the political background; he corresponded with Linley, brother of the first Mrs. Sheridan, from whom he collected many personal anecdotes. When he went down to London he talked with the Irish actor Johnstone and with Wilkie; he buttonholed Dugald Stewart (at Bowood) and Lord Holland at Holland House; he even interviewed a pawnbroker of "great delicacy and disinterestedness" who had loaned Sheridan money on his plate and his library; and he endeavored to collect all the Sheridan manuscripts he could find. For Boswell's *Johnson* had established a new ideal in biography, and Moore determined to live up to it. Composition began immediately, so that by October he had written the story through Sheridan's marriage, and before he left for France he had completed the first four chapters. But his Parisian exile put a stop to his labors—in the orotund words of the preface, "the formal duty of extracting information by written queries" proved "a slow and meagre substitute for those oral communications in which alone details are satisfactorily brought out," and the work was not actually produced until 1825.

In October, 1818, James Power published the seventh number of the *Irish Melodies*, the last in which Moore was associated with Stevenson, and the first of the second, and inferior, series, and in 1820 William Power in Dublin published an edition of the seven numbers without the music, to which he added the "Melologue upon National Music." The preface to the seventh volume confesses that "if I had consulted only my own judgment, this Work would not have extended beyond the six Numbers already published," and alleges popular demand as the reason for going on. The sixth number had closed with Moore's farewell to his harp. The seventh opened with a graceful lyric, "My Gentle Harp," reproving those who demanded a more virile strain:

Then, who can ask for notes of pleasure,
　My drooping Harp, from chords like thine?
Alas, the lark's gay morning measure
　As ill would suit the swan's decline!
Or how shall I, who love, who bless thee,
　Invoke thy breath for Freedom's strains,
When ev'n the wreaths, in which I dress thee,
　Are sadly mix'd—half flow'rs, half chains!

—words that a sound popular instinct has transferred from their original tune to the beautiful melody indifferently known as the "Londonderry Air" and as the "Irish Love-Song." For the most part the new collection (which contained a lament for Irish heroes to the haunting air known as "The Lamentation of Aughrim") echoed the old strains, though the penultimate lyric set forth a philosophy of cheerful acceptance now characteristic of the forty-year-old poet:

They may rail at this life—from the hour I began it,
　I've found it a life full of kindness and bliss;
And until they can shew me some happier planet,
　More social and bright, I'll content me with this,—

a lyric which the friendly *Morning Chronicle* characterized as possessing "all the airiness and fancy of his most youthful muse." The resumption of the series was greeted with pleasure, the *Quarterly Musical Magazine* averring that the latest number was the best which had appeared.[8] But after the seventh number it is evident that Moore, with whom the production of singable lyrics was becoming a process of manufacture, had nothing new to present.

Moore also commenced in 1818 the issuance of another series of melodies known as the *National Airs*, of which the second number appeared in 1820, the third in 1822, the fourth in 1822, the fifth in 1826, and the sixth in 1827. The lyrics were first collected in the fourth volume of the *Poetical Works* of 1840-41. The wider range which this musical eclecticism permitted the lyrics to assume, both in form and theme, explains perhaps why, as the *Irish Melodies* diminished

in value, the *National Airs* show Moore opening up fresher
veins of song. The very first number contained such general
favorites as the much-quoted "Oft in the stilly Night" and
"Hark! the Vesper Hymn is Stealing." Besides these, the
explorer finds in this portion of Moore's work some of his best
and most moving love songs. What could be better, for example, than these words to an "Old English Air"?

> Then, fare thee well, my own dear love,
>   This world has now for us
> No greater grief, no pain above
>   The pain of parting thus,
>   Dear love!
>   The pain of parting thus.
>
> Had we but known, since first we met,
>   Some few short hours of bliss,
> We might, in numbering them, forget
>   The deep, deep pain of this,
>   Dear love!
>   The deep, deep pain of this.

Equally felicitous is the following passage from "Do not Say
that Life is Waning":

> Do not think those charms are flying,
>   Though thy roses fade and fall;
> Beauty hath a grace undying,
>   Which in thee survives them all.

Something of Dryden's "manly vigor," not to speak of his
admirable execution, is discovered in two others of this series.
Each takes its title from the first line:

> O say, thou best and brightest,
>   My first love and my last,
> When he, whom now thou slightest,
>   From life's dark scene hath past,
> Will kinder thoughts then move thee?
>   Will pity wake one thrill
> For him who lived to love thee,
>   And dying loved thee still?

———

Fear not that, while around thee
  Life's varied blessings pour,
One sigh of hers shall wound thee,
  Whose smile thou seek'st no more.
No, dead and cold for ever
  Let our past love remain;
Once gone, its spirit never
  Shall haunt thy rest again.

Not only is this impeccable writing, but here are a drive and an intensity not commonly associated with Moore. Granted that most of the *National Airs* are merely workmanlike; granted that Moore nowhere displays the curious insight into national temperaments which makes Herder's *Stimmen der Völker* memorable, it is yet true that Moore was well-nigh alone among English poets of his generation in attempting to explore the possibilities of a union of "foreign" national music with appropriate verse.

The remaining work of this period, frankly turned out for money but yet directed against the enemies of liberalism, was *Tom Crib's Memorial to Congress,* begun in November, 1818, and published the following March—an exercise in "flash" writing (one thinks of Pierce Egan) of the kind represented in Moore's earlier "Epistle from Tom Crib to Big Ben." The poet worked it up with ludicrous thoroughness, interviewing "Gentleman" Jackson, the boxing teacher celebrated by Byron, going to a boxing match between Randall and Turner at Crawley ("the thing altogether not so horrid as I expected"), and characteristically hunting out pugilistic episodes from antiquity to the present time for the inevitable footnotes. The result amused the Regency, though Tories professed to be horrified at the picture of the Prince Regent stripped to the waist, being knocked about by Czar Alexander; and the *Literary Panorama* solemnly announced that, sated with sweets and tired of the odors of Paradise, the poet now inhaled "the whiffs of a stale debauch which overpower the perfumes of the flowers of Covent Garden," while the

Literary Gazette as solemnly reminded Moore that "some trifling respect is due to Kings and Rulers." [9] But the fashionable world, which simultaneously sighed over Rosa Matilda and flocked to prize-fights fought with bare fists for thirty and forty rounds, chuckled at Crib's spoofing; and the work, which hit exactly that queer mixture of classicism and slang in which Regency dandies delighted, passed at once into a second edition, almost immediately followed by a third. Modern readers have tacitly agreed, however, that *Tom Crib* is not a comic masterpiece.

Chapter X

A SHADOW hung over the little cottage, darkened the pleasures of Bowood, and haunted Moore on his visits to London. Despite friendly warnings from Croker, Tom had permitted his Bermuda affairs to drift, happy when an occasional draft came from his deputy, and careless of his own responsibility. Now the sword of Damocles was to fall and cut in two his pleasant and industrious life. Even as *Lalla Rookh* passed into its seventh edition, Moore was writing Lady Donegal on April 2, 1818:

Within these twenty-four hours I have come to the knowledge of a circumstance which may very possibly throw me into a prison for life. You know I have a deputy at Bermuda; he is nephew to very rich and respectable merchants (now my only hope), the Sheddons of Bedford Square. I had every reason to suspect his playing me false with respect to my share of the profits during the American war, and I had written so often in vain to demand his accounts for the last year of the war, that I at last gave up the matter as hopeless. I had forgot both him and the office, when yesterday I was roused into most disagreeable remembrance of them by a monition from Doctors' Commons, calling upon me to appear there within fifteen days, in consequence of my deputy having refused to produce the proceeds of a sale of ship and cargo, which had been deposited in his hands during an appeal to the Court at home. I suppose the sum was considerable, and the fellow has absconded with it. I have no security for him, as the place was so mere a trifle at the time I appointed him, that no one would have thought it worth either asking or giving security; and, at present, I see no chance for my escape but in the forthcomingness of his uncle

Sheddon, who, as having recommended him to me, is bound, I think (at least in honour), to be answerable for the defalcation.

The amount in dispute was £6000, a sum Moore could not possibly pay. Fortunately, as it seemed, the deputy was discovered to possess some property, the length of time required to communicate with Bermuda postponed the event, and Moore's legal representative did all he could to invoke the law's delay.

Meanwhile the poet continued to live as usual, with quiet courage refusing to allow his perplexities to darken his nature or trouble his confiding wife. Anne Dyke, who had gone to the Theatre Royal, Edinburgh, in 1815, was to be married to William H. Murray in the early summer of 1819, and Tom brought Bessy, the two children, and the maid to London in the middle of May in order to send them by sea for a happy visit to Anne and Mrs. Dyke on this important occasion. He seems also to have supplied the Dyke family with sundry cash gifts. Bessy returned to London two days before the Bermuda business "came on" and was dispatched to Sloperton by coach—with characteristic impracticality Tom engaged seats in the wrong vehicle. The consequence was that he faced the catastrophe alone, a mistake on the part of his attorney in addressing a letter leading the poet to think that all was well when, as a matter of fact, all was lost. On July 10 he wrote in his journal: "the truth came upon me like a thunder-clap this morning; the cause was heard and decided against me, and in two months from last Wednesday an attachment is to be put in force against my person."

Announcement of the decision produced an extraordinary burst of activity among Moore's friends and even among persons unknown to him, who felt that, whatever his legal responsibility, he was in no way guilty of moral fault. Since one of the claims against Moore theoretically proceeded from the Crown, Sir Francis Burdett suggested an application for the Crown to relinquish its claim, but Moore replied that he would rather bear twice the calamity than suffer the least motion to be made towards asking a favor of the Regent. Leigh Hunt proposed to open a subscription and said he would sell his piano in the cause; the Longmans offered to advance a sum sufficient to compromise the issue; Rogers proffered £500; Perry of the *Chronicle* placed himself at Moore's disposal; Lord Lansdowne, Lord John Russell, and his brother, Lord Tavistock, came forward; Jeffrey wrote from Edinburgh; an unknown poetess offered her house as a place of concealment; and Lord Lansdowne and the Hollands investigated the possibility of taking refuge in Holyrood House, Edinburgh, where (such being the quirks of the law) English officers could not arrest Moore. The Sheddons were sympathetic but for the moment helpless. Rejecting these offers, Moore finally resolved to follow the familiar path of English debtors, and, making Bessy and the children as comfortable as he could, accepted the invitation of Lord John Russell to accompany him to Paris. Lord John, who was about to publish an elegant volume entitled *Essays and Sketches by a Gentleman who has left his Lodgings,* was toying with the idea of giving up politics for literature at the age of twenty-seven—a notion for which Moore scolded him in the *Morning Chronicle* a year later—and he was flattered to be able to travel with the forty-year-old author of *Lalla Rookh.* Bidding farewell to Bessy, who bravely came to London alone for the purpose, Tom set off September 4, 1819, in the noble lord's carriage for Dover. On the fifth they were in Calais; on the eighth "between two and three o'clock" they arrived in Paris, went to the Hotel Breteuil, and "took the same rooms Rogers and I were in two years ago, with the addition of another bedroom, for which, between us, we pay eight napoleons a week."

The opening days of exile were gay enough, Lord John and Moore penetrating all the fashionable *rendezvous* of the Anglo-French society which, in the capital of the Bourbons, was forgetting that there had been a war. On the eighteenth the travelers were off for Switzerland, where they saw the

THOMAS MOORE IN 1819 (?)

orthodox sights; on the twenty-eighth they were in Italy; and on the fifth of October they parted at Milan, Tom having bought a "crazy little calèche" in which to journey to Venice. At La Mira he met Byron, who had grown fat, "which spoils the picturesqueness of his head." The Pilgrim of Eternity was domestically established with La Guiccioli at La Mira and had taken up the good old gentlemanly vice of avarice, besides writing *Don Juan*—a poem which, with the persistency of genius, he insisted on prosecuting in spite of Murray, Moore, Mrs. Grundy, and his mistress. Nothing could exceed the cordiality of Byron's welcome. He turned his Venetian quarters over to Tom, kicking down the door in his impatience to install his guest; he rode in every day from La Mira to be with him; and on the last day of the visit (spent at La Mira) he made Moore the fateful present of his manuscript memoirs in a white leather bag. They parted reluctantly, Byron riding some distance with Tom, who was going to Florence and Rome. They were not to meet again.

As if there were not an absconding deputy in the world, Moore embarked on a tour of the Italian cities, pausing before waterfalls, inspecting churches, looking on relics with a skeptical eye, viewing paintings and statues and trying to make up his mind about them. "To a real lover of nature," he confided to his journal, "the sight of a pretty woman, or a fine prospect" is "beyond the best painted pictures of them in the world," but he struggled to feel appropriate emotions before the Italian masterpieces. In Florence, as soon as he was dressed, he ran to see the Medicean Venus, but "I cannot," he wrote, "say I was much struck by it," familiarity with copies having dulled the freshness of that wonder. He also looked upon Canova's Venus, which was "too long and lanky, but still very fine." As his leg was troubling him again, it is possible that lameness dulled his aesthetic sensibilities while he trudged the interminable galleries. In Rome, which was still as Piranesi had pictured it, he went off alone to the

Coliseum, the little author of the *Irish Melodies* gazing respectfully upon a ruin which he found "grand, melancholy, sublime, touching." Chantrey took his artistic education in hand, telling him what to admire and why to admire it. There he also met Canova, that characteristic genius of the age of gracility, whose "last Magdalen" seemed "divine." But all of Canova's women were divine, especially his Love and Psyche, "she holding his hand so delicately while she places a butterfly upon it." He had the pleasure of seeing that sculptor's other Venus while Canova himself held a candle and paused "with a sort of fond lingering on all the exquisite beauties of this most perfect figure." Moore also met the Princess Borghese, who had served as the model for this famous piece, whose beautiful hands he kissed several times, and whose perfect foot he was permitted to fondle. Rome was in fact an education to him—he mingled familiarly in the society of sculptors and painters like Chantrey, Canova, Thorwaldsen, Sir Thomas Lawrence, and Jackson, and impartially attended the drawingrooms of the rival queens of Anglo-Roman society, the Duchess of Devonshire and Lady Davy. At the former's house he learned that Canning had been summoned back to England—a dim rumor of ministerial changes faintly echoing across the Tyrrhenian Sea. But it was more important to look at pictures and ruins, to buy Roman pearls for Bessy and books for the library at Sloperton, which Chantrey promised to send home duty free. On the return journey Bartolini modeled his bust at Florence, and Chantrey promised to create a rival statue. Then, after seeing Lady Burghersh burn her extracts from Byron's memoirs (which Moore had incautiously lent to her), he went back to Paris, arriving on the eleventh of December to inquire "with a beating heart" for letters from Sloperton. There was one from Bessy, and also one, more ominous, from the Longmans, telling him it was not yet safe for him to come home.

II

To judge by his light-hearted Italian tour, Moore had blithely supposed that some arrangement could be patched up about the Bermuda business which would permit his speedy return to England, but the sobering truth which confronted him that rainy day when he received his mail meant that he was condemned for an indefinite period to the footless life of an exile. He hunted up an apartment in the Rue Chantereine, finding out too late that the landlady was a harridan, and, wandering disconsolately the wet December streets, discovered that to a man in his circumstances not even the *filles d'Opéra* were amusing. Christmas was gloomy, but he learned on the twenty-seventh that the gallant Bessy was coming from Wiltshire with the children to join him. He lurched for a day and two nights in the mail coach over the icy roads to Calais and stood anxiously on the pier waiting for the packet. Poor Bessy had suffered a fall from a horse, about which she had said nothing, and her beautiful nose was still swelled, but they crept thankfully back to Paris, where Bessy fell ill. Moore had been fussing about with a projected "Fudge Family in Italy," which turned eventually into the mediocre "Rhymes on the Road," chiefly memorable for having awakened the supercilious scorn of James Russell Lowell; but a piano-playing young lady on the upper floor made composition impossible, Bessy wisely urged that they should not try to enter society, and it was resolved to find more secluded quarters. By the end of January, 1820, the Moores were housed in a cottage in the Allée des Veuves, an almost rural lane running from the Avenue des Champs Elysées to the Seine. With brief intervals he was to remain in exile until late in November, 1821.

For the first time in his life Moore was brought face to face with the dull facts of domestic drudgery. As he naïvely wrote Power:

I have been in a most wretched state of distraction and *un*comfort here. Indeed it is the first time since I married that my
home has been uncomfortable; for being thrown upon external
supplies for our dinner, &c. and contriving *that* but ill and ex-
pensively (from Bessy's powers of management being completely
nullified by her ignorance of the language), and being in the
midst of the bustle of a Metropolis, struggling against its distractions and its expenses without success, my *mind* I assure you
has been kept in a continued state of fever, which was not a
little increased by the Longmans having pledged me to the public
for a work of which there are not a hundred lines written, and
the proceeds of which, you may well believe, are essentially
necessary to my existence at present.[1]

Removal to the cottage in the Allée des Veuves somewhat
improved the dinner problem. Moore was to discover that
Paris was but an indifferent place for an author in his circumstances. The book which the Longmans pledged him to the
public as being about to write was the projected "Fudge
Family in Italy," but when the work was forwarded to London late in May (at which time it seems also to have included
some of the material later printed in "Fables for the Holy
Alliance"), on the advice of Sir James Mackintosh, they
pointed out that to attack Castlereagh and his cohorts was
a very poor way to settle the Bermuda claims, and the volume
was temporarily abandoned. He was next compelled to give
up the projected life of Sheridan, since he could not possibly
refer to "all those living authorities, whom I felt the necessity
of almost at every instant consulting," and proposed that
Murray and Wilkie draw on him for the sum they had advanced—"very magnificent of me," he wrote Power, "but
how I am to *manage* the magnificence is yet in the clouds." [2]
He did succeed in turning out songs, which he could do by
"fits and starts," a second issue of the *National Airs* appearing
in 1820, and the eighth number of the *Irish Melodies* being
published in 1821. Of this latter collection it may be said that
it is the first of the series in which the melodies are definitely
superior to the words, not even Moore's tribute to Grattan

("Shall the Harp then Be Silent?") rising above mediocrity. A blast against the Neapolitans, who had tamely permitted the Austrians to conquer them, published in the *Morning Chronicle* April 9, 1821, is almost the only vigorous verse emanating from the Parisian period.[3]

The fact is, he did not know what to do with himself. Paris, he plaintively remarked, "swarms with my friends and acquaintances,"[4] and the author of *Lalla Rookh* was altogether too prominent a person to be left to his rural quietude. All kinds of persons were perpetually hunting him out, and, truth to tell, Tom was not loath to be hunted. He loved the theater, the opera, the ballet, and there were restaurants to explore, either with Bessy (she seems to have led a rather gay life in France, interrupted, it is true, by illness), with Lord John Russell, who was forever turning up, or with wandering Irishmen, literary friends, or casual acquaintances. Tom early commenced to dance attendance upon the Marquise de Souza, who was sixty and whose curious career involved a decapitated first husband, the "friendship" of Talleyrand, generally supposed to be the father of her son (the Comte de Flahaut), and another "friendship" with the Duc d'Orléans. She was now married to the Portuguese ambassador. She was bringing up her natural son's natural son, the future Duc de Morny, and she was finishing a novel, which Tom obligingly reviewed in the *Edinburgh* in November. The Moores likewise became intimate with a Spanish family by the name of Villamil, who had an estate at Sèvres, whither the Moores retired in the summer months—at La Butte de Coaslin. Bessy and Madame Villamil became great friends, Bessy rising from a sick chamber to watch over the deathbed of Madame Villamil's daughter.

Cut off from political life because he was a foreigner, Moore had only a general notion that there was an undercurrent of dissatisfaction in Bourbon France, the assassination of the Duc de Berry receiving but a line or two in his journal, and the abortive uprisings of the year being chiefly interesting as spectacles. From across the channel floated curious stories concerning the bill to divorce the Queen, but Moore, who might have turned this tragicomedy to excellent satirical verse, was perforce silent. In October, to his astonishment, Canning, who was visiting Paris, asked to be introduced to him, and Moore, struck by this magnanimity as well as by the beauty of Miss Canning, impetuously resolved never to write another line against her father. A week later he called on Wordsworth; at breakfast three days later the author of *The Excursion* majestically informed the future biographer of Byron that the whole third canto of *Childe Harold* was plagiarized from "Tintern Abbey," that Scott's novels were written in "bad vulgar English," and that Canning knew nothing of poetry. In December, however, a more companionable literary light appeared in the person of Washington Irving, "a good-looking and intelligent-mannered man," and the two representatives of literary dilettantism were presently boon companions. As Irving wrote Brevoort in the spring:

I have become very intimate with Anacreon Moore, who is living here with his family. Scarcely a day passes without our seeing each other, and he has made me acquainted with many of his friends here. He is a charming, joyous fellow; full of frank, generous, manly feeling. . . . His acquaintance is one of the most gratifying things I have met with for some time; as he takes the warm interest of an old friend in me and my concerns.[5]

Moore introduced him to all his friends, and at the tenth wedding anniversary of the Irish poet, Irving and the other guests danced so hard that the floor commenced to give way.

In the midst of these distractions Moore had taken up a new interest. On July 13, 1820, one reads that he had "purchased some books on Egypt, having again taken up the idea of making that country the scene of a poem." Apparently he had in mind following up *Lalla Rookh* with another oriental tale, but the idea became entangled in his mind with a cloudy Pythagoreanism, and the pedantic side of his nature led him on until he became something of an amateur Egyptologist, buying out-of-the-way books, and interviewing the seventy-three-year-old Denon, the great authority on the subject, who had been a friend of Voltaire and a protégé of Napoleon's. Moore wrote some hundreds of lines of a poem, which he planned to call *The Epicurean:* "if I don't make something of all this, the devil's in it," he said in his journal, but the more he read, the less he wrote. The poem finally appeared as that most unreadable of his productions, *Alciphron,* and the plot was finally served up as his solitary novel, *The Epicurean,* in 1827, respectfully received in its own day, but unread ever since. In the meantime he pottered cheerfully about with Egyptian lore, trying to persuade himself that he was actually working, though in moments of honesty he confided to his journal, or to Power, that he was really wasting his time.

As the slow months drifted by, it became more and more evident that "my distractions here, in the way of visitors, &c. . . . derange very much my progress in writing"; [6] wherefore he became increasingly dissatisfied and restless. Sloperton was to be rented to another tenant, and in July, 1821, Bessy and little Tom returned to England to look after the books and the furniture, Anastasia having been put in a Paris school. Bessy was back in September, bringing the two Miss Belchers with her as guests. Tom had learned that Trinity College had pointedly omitted his name from the list of toasts at one of their dinners and was immensely irritated, finally determining (for no good reason) to visit England and Ireland in company with Lord John, whose irresolution about starting irritated him still farther. But on the twenty-second they got off, Moore transparently disguised as "Mr. Thomas Dyke" and taking a ludicrous pair of false mustachios with him. His object—what was his object?—to see the Longmans, to make final arrangements with Murray for the sale of Byron's "Memoirs," for which Murray was to pay two thousand guineas, to look into the Bermuda business, to visit his father and mother in far-off Dublin, who were getting old. But when he saw Thomas Longman to inform him that the two thousand guineas were to be devoted to settling the Bermuda claims, that excellent gentleman hesitated and finally revealed the tremendous truth that Lord Lansdowne was arranging a settlement. "How one such action brightens the whole human race in our eyes!" wrote Moore, who departed for Woburn with a lighter heart, and then went on to Dublin, where he found his family well, and where, after cautioning the newspapers not to reveal his identity, he walked the streets, sat for his portrait, and forgot the "cowardly Scholars" of Trinity. Returning to London October 22, he was met with "the important joyful intelligence" that the aggrieved persons in the Bermuda business had accepted an offer of a thousand pounds; wherefore he "walked boldly out into the sunshine and showed myself up St. James's Street and Bond Street." But he was not yet free, another claimant showing up in February; and it was not until the end of November that the Moores were back again in Sloperton, where Bessy, who had preceded her husband, surprised and astonished him by having had his study enlarged. In the meantime he had declined an offer to write "leaders" regularly for the *Times*.

III

On May 27, 1822, Moore's journal records: "wrote my letters, and began a poem called the 'Three Angels,'—a subject on which I long ago wrote a prose story, and have ever since meditated a verse one. Lord B. has now anticipated me in his 'Deluge'; but *n'importe*, I'll try my hand." The prose tale, whatever it was, seems to have vanished; but to add to one's perplexities, the preface to the original edition of *The Loves of the Angels* informs the reader that "this Poem, somewhat different in form, and much more limited in extent, was originally designed as an episode for a work, about which I have been, at intervals, employed during the last two years." Whatever Moore's original intention may

have been, composition went forward rapidly, often at the
rate of a hundred lines a week, and by November he had
begun a "revision" of the manuscript. The announcement of
a new long poem by Moore led to a deluge of orders, some
three thousand copies being subscribed for in advance of publication, which was on December 23, 1822.

In the original, or Christian, version of *The Loves of the
Angels* three fallen seraphs meet

> when the world was in its prime,
> When the fresh stars had just begun
> Their race of glory, and young Time
> Told his first birth-days by the sun,

and under the influence of twilight and

> The silent breathing of the flowers,

each one tells the story

> of that hour unblest
> When, like a bird, from its high nest
> Won down by fascinating eyes,
> For Woman's smile he lost the skies.

The first fell in love with an ethereal creature named Lea,
whose one desire was to be translated into heaven, and who,
having won from her angelic suitor (he gets but a single kiss
out of her) the spell which permits him to reascend into the
empyrean, sprouts a pair of wings and promptly mounts to
the star

> in the blue firmament,
> To which so oft her fancy went
> In wishes and in dreams before,

leaving her lover, stained by this betrayal of a heavenly secret,
forever bound to earth. The second angel, named Rubi, formerly one of the cherubim, loves and wins Lilis, the embodi-
ment of feminine pride, who demands like Semele to see him
in his original luster; but when Rubi innocently assumes his
heavenly shape, the celestial radiance turns to mortal fire and
burns her to a crisp, though not before she has implanted a

kiss upon his brow, which becomes for him the seal of Cain.
The third angel is more domestic in his amours; at any rate he
regularly weds his lady (Moore is conveniently vague as to
how, before the creation of any church, a minister could be
found to perform the ceremony), and, as a concession to this
care for decorum, the pair are but lightly punished:

> Their only punishment (as wrong,
>   However sweet, must bear its brand)
> Their only doom was this—that, long
>   As the green earth and ocean stand,
> They both shall wander here—the same,
> Throughout all time, in heart and frame—

Somehow this seems a little unfair, but as Moore assures us in
the preface that "punishments, both from conscience and
Divine justice, with which impurity, pride, and presumptu-
ous inquiry into the awful secrets of God, are sure to be
visited," form the theme of the poem, we are not to inquire
too closely into these sublime mysteries.   It will be observed
that in this work he abandoned the pentameter couplet
(which had done for *Lalla Rookh*) as well as his characteristic anapaests, for an octosyllabic line.   The verse is woven
with a creamy consistency of texture which certainly evokes
atmosphere, but which leaves the personages and events rather
vague; and if the rococo ornamentation of *Lalla Rookh* is
happily absent, the dreamy indefiniteness of time and place,
the lack of something concrete to envision in the events make
The Loves of the Angels a weaker production.

The fancy of a union between the sons of God and the
daughters of men in the pre-Noachian period of the world
possessed a curious attraction for the romantics, Byron, Croly,
Lamartine, de Vigny, and Hugo having written poems which
touch upon some version of the theme; and when in 1838
Elizabeth Barrett pictured the seraphim as moved by human
emotions, Christian piety was prepared to accept the result.
Not so, however, in the reign of George IV.   Moore's peculiar blending of heavenly eroticism and theology shocked

some of his friends and gave a handle to his enemies. His first surprise came when, on December 27, Lady Donegal wrote him that she was both "vexed and disappointed," and that she would not permit Barbara to read it. He comforted himself with reviews in the *Literary Gazette,* the *Literary Chronicle,* and the *London Museum,* "all favourable enough," he wrote, the last "the most useful, as giving me credit for a moral design in the poem," but though the three notices spilled the usual spate of adjectives with respect to his genius, there was a curious note of reserve in each. Thus the *Literary Chronicle* pictured him soaring aloft "on eagle's wings," but it also said that he was "certainly the poet of Love," and remarked on "the equivocal title of this work"; the *Literary Gazette* rather unfortunately observed that "whether or not the earthly fires of those *Loves* with which Mr. Moore has already charmed the amorous age in poetic corruscations gave promise of celestrial purity in his description of angelical amours, it is not now incumbent on us to pronounce," even though it found its "apprehensions" groundless; and the *London Museum* spoke roundly of the "preponderance of the animal propensities over the intellectual faculties" in his genius, which was "occupied with business most congenial to her disposition, when she is the herald of seduction." [7]

During Moore's absence the notorious *John Bull,* organ of extreme Toryism, which had announced in its coronation number that "we love—ardently and devoutly love" the aging George IV, had begun a systematic attack upon the Queen and upon the Whigs who supported her cause. Moore had come in for considerable vilification, *John Bull* beginning in its twenty-seventh number a series of parodies of his poems which were harmless enough, but which were preceded by headnotes charging him with "sentimental indelicacy," "indecent allusions to a lady of high rank," "a filthy libel upon female reputation," "native licentiousness," and other variants of the same crimes. On January 5, 1823, it began a review of *The Loves of the Angels* which ran through two

issues, the opening of which was more irritating because of
its condescension than were the vituperative phrases that
followed:

There is a convivial good nature and perpetual pleasantry about
little MOORE which never fails to win those with whom he
associates; the pretty manner in which he accompanies his own
trifles on the piano forte, and the adroitness with which he man-
ages the little voice he has for the amusement of the ladies, entitle him indisputably to the pre-eminence he holds amongst the
entertaining people of the day.   These claim and attractions . . .
must not blind us to faults and follies, the exposure of which
and censure of which are but acts of friendship towards an
author, and of justice towards the public.

The friendship of Theodore Hook's paper consisted of re-
minding its readers that Tom Brown had "attacked all that
was great or good, male or female, and especially the latter,
making inroads into private life never before attempted, and
setting an example of grossness which . . . required an anti-
dote . . ."; and though it pronounced *The Loves of the
Angels.* "perfectly harmless," it found the First Angel's story
"abominable" and said that it would omit any account of the
Second Angel since the details, like the details of a trial for
seduction, were not fit for the public.[8]

An attack from *John Bull* was to be expected, but other
notices of the work, even if they praised the poet's genius,
would not permit the public to forget the "licentiousness" of
his earlier volumes and the danger of blasphemy in the present subject. *Blackwoods* found it hard not to be shocked by
Moore's unawed approach to divine matters, and said that
his "familiarities with his Maker assume the appearance of
cold, glittering conceits, and the impertinences of bad taste,"
hinting that his piety squinted in the direction of publishers'
row. It also added that the angels seemed to be Irishmen,
"for such furious love was never made out of the land of
potatoes." The *London Magazine* unfairly remarked that he
deepened the sins of his youth by the "present dangerous and

questionable tone of repentance," said his muse was a "Magdalen," and found the poem badly conceived and wretchedly
written. The *New Monthly* was tepid in its praise; the
Monthly Censor wrote that if it was a choice between
Moore's old vices and blasphemy, it preferred the vices to
this "giddy irreverence"; the *Monthly Magazine* accused him
of being perpetually on the point of falling into levity; and
the *Monthly Review* made the very simplicity of his language
a fault, though it defended him from the charge of irreverence. The bedeviled author got what satisfaction he could
out of the unqualified admiration of the *European Magazine*,
which assured him of immortality, and though it hinted that
the subject was in doubtful taste, roundly concluded that the
poem "would add lustre to the brightest name in English
literature." [9]

Overwhelmed by this barrage of piety, Moore desperately
resolved, notwithstanding Lord Lansdowne's advice to the
contrary, at least to free his work from the imputation of blasphemy. Despite the reviews, or perhaps because of them,
The Loves of the Angels continued to sell, but as early as the
middle of January, 1823, he commenced to turn over his
books with the resolve of translating the angels into Turks,
a project in which his publishers encouraged him. The fifth
edition (1823) accordingly became Mohammedan, and Moslem the poem ever after remained, God being transformed
into Allah, the preface being abandoned for a learned dis-
quisition on the mythology of the Persians, and the notes
being thoroughly orientalized. The bland naïveté of this
revision is its most engaging quality. Thus a passage in the
introduction to the poem running:

> A Spirit of light mould, that took
>   The prints of earth most yieldingly;
> Who, ev'n in heav'n, was not of those
>   Nearest the Throne, but held a place
> Far off . . .

was solemnly annotated: "The ancient Persians supposed that this Throne was placed in the Sun, and that through the stars were distributed the various classes of Angels that encircled it." The "Fire Unnam'd in heaven" became "the Fire in GEHIM'S pit," a change supported by a reference to the Koran, and Rubi was translated out of the cherubim, for which Moore had cited Dionysius and Ezekiel, into the Kerubiim "as the Mussulmans call them." There being no Mohammedan theologians in London, no one raised the question why, if picturing Christian angels in love was impious, picturing Mohammedan angels in love was not equally impious. To the contemporary reader, of course, the whole discussion has the wild irrelevance of a harmless nightmare.

IV

Moore was not out of this predicament, however, before he was plunged into another. It was decided to issue in one volume the "Fables for the Holy Alliance," "Rhymes on the Road," and a few of his miscellaneous poems; and though he had destroyed the printed sheets of "Rhymes on the Road" in Paris, he sent copy for the new volume to Longmans in March. But while he was at Holland House the following month, he received on the seventeenth a note from the publishers, whose legal adviser had told them that the "Fables" were indictable as "tending to bring monarchy into contempt." Moore promptly called, offering to meet any legal consequences himself; the publishers next consulted the famous Thomas Denman, who had served as counsel for Queen Caroline and who was one of the most brilliant of the Whig lawyers. Denman gave it as his opinion that, though he could not guarantee against the folly of people in prosecuting, he would venture to guarantee the result as:

The plaintiff will be hiss'd,
My Lords the Judges laugh, and you're dismissed.

The little volume accordingly appeared on May 7, 1823, the dedication to Byron being a tacit rebuke to those who had chosen to twist the preface to the first version of *The Loves of the Angels* into jealousy on Moore's part of Byron's successes.

The book was the production of Moore's *alter ego,* Thomas Brown, and though "Rhymes on the Road" have lost all interest today (if, indeed, these poems ever possessed much life of their own), the satires on the Europe of Metternich, with their clever rhymes, are still amusing. Nor should the artfulness of the light verse conceal Moore's serious purpose. The book was definitely a Whig production, the poet attacking kings in the name of the people as Shelley had done. Politically a child of the eighteenth century, Moore thought of the people in terms of the middle class, just as he thought of monarchy in terms of simple political oppression, though, as the newly founded *Westminster Review* reminded its readers, he seemed "ignorant of the fact that not individuals but *systems* are at fault, and that the vices will remain as long as the system does." [10] His Catholic and Irish sympathies furthermore led him, in two or three fables, to attack established churches. Once again, Moore's religious liberalism permitted him to denounce his own faith for becoming an instrument of governmental oppression in Europe.

As George IV was mainly passed over, the volume concentrating on the Continental system, Tory organs failed to fall upon it with their usual frenzy. The *Literary Gazette,* it is true, after some preliminary skirmishing about genius stirring up "lurid sparks from among the stinking ashes of its fires," found the book "discreditable and degrading," remarked that it was based on Peter Pindar, and got in a home thrust by saying that "his verse . . . leaves us in the dilemma of being dissatisfied with matters as they are, without having it clearly pointed out to us how they ought to be." The radical *Westminster,* of course, said he was not radical enough, and—a mark of the essential Puritanism of the group it represented—reproached him for defending chastity because he was, after all, Thomas Little!   On the whole the volume had only a moderate press and a moderate success.[11]   Yet it was by his own special combination of satire and fancy that he was to carry on the war against the Tories in the *Times* and the *Chronicle;* and whatever the literary weaknesses of the *Fables* may be, their importance in the life of Moore lies in the fact that they represent a coming to grips with the political realities of the nineteenth century; and that as Moore's poetical fires died down with advancing years, the kind of writing he did in this little volume was to become both a source of income and a method of warfare on behalf of liberalism and of Ireland.

Chapter XI

THE England to which the Moores returned in 1822 was a soberer country than that bright, careless, pagan world which had welcomed the young translator of Anacreon almost a quarter of a century before. Byron, pausing in Genoa in 1823 on tiptoe for his flight to Missolonghi, even at that immense distance, recognized the change:

Where is Napoleon the Grand?   God knows:
  Where little Castlereagh?   The devil can tell:
Where Grattan, Curran, Sheridan, all those
  Who bound the bar or senate in their spell?
Where is the unhappy Queen, with all her woes?
  And where the Daughter, whom the Isles loved well?
Where are those martyr'd saints the Five per Cents?
And where—oh, where the devil are the rents?

Where's Brummel?   Dish'd.   Where's Long Pole Wellesley?
  Diddled.
  Where's Whitbread?   Romilly?   Where's George the Third?
Where is his will?   (That's not so soon unriddled.)
  And where is "Fum" the Fourth, our "royal bird"?
Gone down, it seems, to Scotland, to be fiddled
  Unto by Sawney's violin, we have heard:
"Caw me, caw thee"—for six months hath been hatching
This scene of royal itch and loyal scratching.

Where is Lord This?   And where is my Lady That?
  The Honourable Mistresses and Misses?
Some laid aside like an old Opera hat,
  Married, unmarried, and remarried: (this is
An evolution oft performed of late.)
  Where are the Dublin shouts—and London hisses?

225

Where are the Grenvilles? Turn'd as usual. Where
My friends the Whigs? Exactly where they were.

George III was dead; old Queen Charlotte was dead; the
Princess Charlotte was dead, having known a few brief
months of happiness; Queen Caroline, that injured and un-
predictable female, was dead. George IV, whose dropsy was
growing more and more noticeable, having landed, drunk, on
the coasts of Ireland to receive the cheers of the mercurial
Celts, had also paid his extraordinary visit to Edinburgh stage-
managed by Sir Walter Scott, who, having begged the glass
in which his royal master drunk his cherry brandy, wrapped
it up, put it in his pocket, and absent-mindedly sat down on
it. Lady Conyngham had replaced Lady Hertford in what
was left, in that vast bulk, of the royal affections; and the
thrifty Knighton had ousted McMahon as Keeper of the
Privy Purse. By and by George was to be driven about the
grounds at Windsor in a pony phaeton, screened from the in-
curious public, and to receive his ministers, sometimes in a
dirty flannel waistcoat and cotton nightcap, and sometimes
in a silk *douillette* and a velvet headpiece. Yet the royal urge
for extravagant building was remaking London under the
classical eye of John Nash. In 1830 the First Gentleman was
dead. "Sir," it was said to him, "it is princes like you who
make democrats."

The reign of the dandies had passed into its sere and yellow
leaf. Brummell was eating his heart out in Calais, where the
King had elaborately ignored him; George Hanger, now
seventy-one, sat smoking his pipe in Tottenham Court Road;
"Cripplegate" Barrymore, who invented the "tiger," was
dead; so was "Jockey of Norfolk"; so, to all intents and purposes, was Sir Lumley Skeffington, whose "Sleeping Beauty"
was not to awaken on any stage. "Romeo" Coates was forgotten; Long Pole Wellesley was living in adulterous domes-
ticity on the Continent; and the second Marquis of Hertford
had just died. A new generation was rising, which knew not
Brummell; the empire of the neckcloth was put into com-

From the picture in the Wallace Collection—by permission

GEORGE IV

mission, pending the dazzling arrival of the Comte D'Orsay; and the wit of Alvanley, the gentler humor of Luttrell replaced the gorgeous impudence of the Regency. Trousers were definitely in; so was the waltz; and women, who had been half-naked during the Revolution and classical under the Empire, turned romantic and mysterious, as the waistline took its normal topographical position, the corset was resumed, sleeves developed Gothic eccentricities, and the skirt swelled gradually into a balloon and eventually touched the ground.

For the Duchess of Richmond's ball and the dances at the Congress of Vienna had become events which the middle-aged talked about in language unintelligible to the younger generation, who had merely read of such things in the pages of the brilliant post-war novelists. In far-off St. Helena Napoleon was, incredibly, dead; and at home Castlereagh cut his throat in August, 1822. As a consequence, Wellington set off for the Congress of Verona, there to receive from the earnest and bald-headed Canning, whom he did not like, instructions that England was to be neutral in the vast problem of an invasion of Spain, which the Duke had conquered. Great Britain, for eight years the arbiter of Europe, swung majestically into that position of splendid isolation which led its foreign minister, some years later, to call in the New World (with a little help from James Monroe) to redress the balance of the Old.

For England was concentrating on its own troubles. Around the aging veterans of the late world war, younger men, earnest, humorless, self-sufficient, were rising to demand reform. The new seriousness clouded the political skies with gray while the foremost industrial country of the world struggled to adjust its medieval government to the awkward facts of an economic revolution according to the abstract logic of Malthus, James Mill, and Ricardo. As if it were not enough to listen to Huskisson's learned exposition of free-trade doctrines, drowsy country squires were lectured by the tireless and loquacious Brougham on education, chimney-sweeps, slavery, and the iniquities of the Test Act—in short, anything that might annoy the government. In Ireland Peel had beautifully succeeded in alienating the Catholics, though he had efficiently policed that island; but now, under the adroit management of O'Connell, who hated him, the Catholic question was awaking from its long slumber. In England by 1826 there was a panic, with resulting riots all over the kingdom; Parliament dissolved, and the general election, which was to have settled the fate of the Catholics, became involved in a maze of charges and countercharges about finance and free trade—muddy waters for the Whigs to fish in. But Liverpool was put back in office, though the Irish elections proved even to those who did not wish to see that something must be done to satisfy the reformers and the Romanists. Lord Liverpool fell ill; the half-crazy King obstinately refused to have anything to do with the errors of Rome; there was a shuffling and re-shuffling of places, interests, men, and families; and finally Wellington and Peel settled doggedly upon the ministerial benches. Lord John Russell rose to introduce a bill repealing the Test and Corporation Acts (which prevented all but members of the Church of England from holding office), and this preliminary skirmish being won through the dexterity of Peel, the main problem of the day was before Parliament. Then—such are the ironies of history—Peel proposed in March, 1829, the measure for Roman Catholic Emancipation, and finally the bill received the royal assent in April—what that minister acidly referred to as its *"last* and *most difficult* stage."

Behind these parliamentary maneuvers a vast, bitter confusion filled the land. The reformers resembled those who flocked to the cave of Adullam in David's time, when everyone that was in distress, and everyone that was in debt, and everyone that was discontented gathered to oppose the king. The very variety of their demands—a reform in taxation, in the Corn Laws, in the navigation acts, in the tithe system, in the organization of the Church of England, in parliamen-

tary representation—prevented the creation of a united front
except in extreme cases and at long length, for such measures
cut across party lines and even divided the incongruous minis-
tries of the reign of George IV. The confusion among these
demands was ultimately the strength of the little band of
ultra Tories, who, if they could not defeat, could always delay legislation. Lord Eldon, who was seventy-six when he
left the cabinet in 1827, had been in office for twenty years;
as Lord Chancellor he reduced legal delay to its ultimate perfection; heroically he set his aged face against change. Of
Lord Liverpool a historian of the period remarks that "no re-
pressive law was abolished, no popular change was accomplished, at his own instance, during his long administration." [1]
The University of Oxford furnished the polemical weapons
of the ecclesiastical die-hards, and though there were a few
liberal bishops, Henry Phillpotts, Bishop of Exeter, whom
Moore was constantly to attack, was more nearly typical.
He defended the conduct of the troops in the Peterloo massa-
cre; he defended the King's attack on the Queen; he assaulted
the Roman Catholic Church; he voted against the Reform
Bill; he fought the bill for the reform of the Irish Church;
and though in private life he was an austerely just and tem-
perate man, he became for many the symbol of episcopal
obscurantism.

In Ireland, meanwhile, there was a monotonous succession
of outrages and suppressions, bitter agitation and uneasy
truce, the causes of which were at once economic, political,
and religious. The fall of agricultural prices in 1816 had been
followed by the wholesale eviction of miserable peasants from
their cottages, with the result that by 1825—let us hope the
figure is exaggerated—there were supposed to be a million
mendicants in that kingdom. In 1821-22 the southern and
western counties were disgraced by outrages committed by
followers of the mythical "Captain Rock," the ignorant and
miserable having no more effective way to protest against
their unendurable lives than the burning of landlords' houses

and sometimes the landlords' families. Naturally the Irish
government (Lord Wellesley was in office) was compelled to
act; the usual Insurrection Bill was passed; the usual suspension of habeas corpus accompanied it; and the usual consequences of military suppression followed. Lord Wellesley
was suspected of favoring the Catholics and was therefore
anathema to the Protestants, whereas Henry Goulbourn, the
Chief Secretary, was supposed to be an ardent Orangeman;
and this division but too faithfully reflected the bitter religious partisanship in the land. Famine swept the country dis-
tricts in the winter of 1822, and, followed by disease, here
and there left the peasantry too exhausted to riot, but Dublin
was so little affected that obstreperous Orangemen flung a
bottle at the Lord Lieutenant when he attended the theater
in December—an episode which, followed by a farcical trial,
failed to endear Wellesley to the Irish, or Ireland to the Lord
Lieutenant. By 1823 the southern peasantry had sufficiently
recovered their health to set fire to barns, hough cattle, and
shoot down landlords and other obnoxious persons from am-
bush. Their special grievance was the necessity of paying
tithes to support a church they despised; and a reluctant ministry finally passed a bill which changed the method of collection and somewhat lowered the monthly total of murders.
But nothing was done to end the "abominable jobs" in the
curious and futile Irish Church.

Tension between Catholic and Protestant continued to increase as, under the adroit management of O'Connell, the vast
Catholic Association overspread the land and all but assumed
the functions of government itself. The outnumbered Protestants reaffirmed their belief in the glorious and immortal
memory of King William by flocking into the Orange Association or joining the Brunswick Clubs. Grimly confronting
each other, the two bodies threatened to deluge the land with
a bitter religious war. An alarmed Parliament passed a bill
dissolving all secret societies, but O'Connell simply transformed his association into another which, in strict conform-

ity with the law, continued to agitate for Catholic Emancipation. Determined to bring matters to a dramatic issue, O'Connell next commanded his followers in 1826 to elect him to a
Parliament in which he could not sit, and easily won Water-
ford from the notorious Beresford family, who had always
considered that constituency their private possession. In 1828
he repeated this triumph at the celebrated Clare election,
where he set aside Vesey Fitzgerald, a liberal Protestant who
favored Emancipation; his election meant that O'Connell
stood, not merely for Clare, but for millions of unenfran-
chised Catholic Irish, and that he had but to nod his head
when Ireland would burst into flame. In London even Wellington could read the handwriting on the wall.

II

At Sloperton life had resumed its old pattern—incessant
labor in the little library over books and writing and a mount-
ing pile of correspondence; frequent visits by Moore to
Bowood or Bremhill to listen patiently to the eccentric
Bowles or counsel with Lord Lansdowne and itinerant celebrities, mostly Whig; journeys to Bath, where Anastasia was
in school, and where there was an occasional opera; and the
inevitable trips to town to see his publishers, secure information for the eternally harassing life of Sheridan, and keep *au
courant* with events. At Sloperton on May 24, 1823, Bessy
presented him with a second son, John Russell Moore, the
name an indication of the poet's growing intimacy with the
future hero of the Reform Bill. But six days later Moore
was off to London to sing his songs, refuse the editorship of
the *Edinburgh Review*, breakfast with Rogers and Luttrell,
and dine with Lord John, Lord Dudley, and Brougham, who
was a "vast Niagara of intellect" to Moore. He was getting
slightly bald now, but his figure was as trim, his eyes as merry,
his voice as good as ever, and his pleasure in meeting people
was as keen as always. Yet at the conclusion of this visit he
heard a religious service at Warwick Chapel, where the music

"seemed to come with more effect over me, after the restless and feverish life I have been leading," and as soon as he could, he hurried home to discover that Bessy had had another fall. He was still restless and uncertain, feeling that he must somehow canalize, not dissipate, his powers; and fortunately, as it proved, Lord and Lady Lansdowne asked him to visit them in Ireland, whither they were going. Though Bessy was "much saddened and out of sorts at my leaving her for so long a time," she was wise enough to see that he needed something— he knew not what—and he resolved to go. On July 26 he was with his parents in Dublin; on the thirtieth he was in Kilkenny with the Lansdownes, wandering the river bank where he had wooed his wife. And on the next day he had an experience which was to determine his future life.

It will be recalled that Moore had known only Dublin, and that, in the last few years, he had been increasingly out of touch with Ireland. Now for the first time he was brought face to face with the realities of the situation, and his journal is evidence that he was profoundly moved.

Saw at Collan, for the first time in my life, some real specimens of Irish misery and filth; three or four cottages together exhibiting such a naked swarm of wretchedness as never met my eyes before.

It was one thing to talk vaguely about the wrongs of Ireland or to write songs lamenting her decline; quite another thing to come face to face with wretchedness, learn of a vast secret society, or discover such

a case, which occurs often, of a man, or his wife, stealing a few potatoes from their own crop when it is under distress, being put in prison for the theft as being felony, when at the worst it is but *rescue*, and kept there till the judge arrives. . . .

The very fact that Lord Lansdowne was a good landlord but pointed the contrast between the beautiful scenery of Killarney and tenants who "under-let" their small holdings

THOMAS MOORE AT FORTY

to poor wretches, who marry upon the strength of this *pied-à-terre*, and swarm the little spot they occupy with children.

For the first time the pages of his journal begin to show traces of a genuine sociological interest. He talked with everyone who could give him information about the state of the country, bought books and pamphlets, and, dodging as many social engagements as he could (he called on Catalini, who was singing in Dublin and who admired his sister Ellen, and he could not forbear looking up an anonymous poetess who had flattered him), hurried home late in August on fire to begin. If he had found new traits in the Lansdownes to admire, he had also discovered, or rediscovered, the Irish cause.

He must have been filled with honest indignation, for he was no sooner at Sloperton than, dropping everything else, he "set about reading for the little work on Ireland, which I mean to despatch." He was determined to expose the sources of this misery, to employ all his prestige and influence in the cause—for example, when he went down to London, he implored Thomas Campbell, editor of the *New Monthly Magazine*, to give the book a lift when it came out, a bid for editorial favor he rarely made. But at Sloperton his "slow *prose* pen" could not, at first, keep up with the flow of his anger. Moreover, when he commenced to explore the causes of Irish misery, the "historical detail" proved "more troublesome than I expected." It was not until October that he found a center for his book, when the happy thought came to him of writing the satiric memoirs of the imaginary Captain Rock. This gave focus to his wrath, though he had to throw away much that he had done; he was so absorbed in the idea that for two weeks in January he ceased even to keep his diary. When, on the twenty-seventh, he went down to London, he was still adding to the manuscript; and there Sir John Newport, Lord John Russell, Lord Holland, and other liberals, learning what he was about, called with suggestions and fresh information, which must somehow be got in; and in the midst of his other difficulties, he was compelled once more to bargain with Mur-

ray and the Sheridan heirs about that uncompleted task.
Finally, on April 17, 1824, there was published the *Memoirs
of Captain Rock, the Celebrated Irish Chieftain, with some
Account of his Ancestors.* It was Moore's first important
book in prose. He wrote it in his triple capacity as a Whig,
an Irishman, and a Catholic.

Like many another meritorious book, *Captain Rock,* having
served its day, is forgotten, but it is nonetheless a superb partisan political pamphlet. Under the transparent disguise of
tracing the history of the Rock family—that is, the leaders of
popular disturbances in Ireland—Moore reviews with bitter
power the history of English misrule in his native land, writing with a blend of irony, sarcasm, wrath, and humor, which
those who know him only in his songs do not suspect that he
possessed. Special objects of his satire are the proselyting
educational system (if system it can be called) thrust on
Catholic Ireland by the Protestants, and the insanity of the
tithing system which supported the Episcopal "Church Mili-
tant, as by law (and constables) established." [2] One finds
him passing from Voltairean irony to Swiftian indignation in
such sentences as these:

The Babylonians, we are told by Herodotus, buried their dead
in honey—but it is in the very gall of the heart that the memory
of Ireland's rulers is embalmed.

The Chief Judge [of legendary Ireland], on all solemn and interesting occasions, had a kind of collar placed round his neck,
which possessed the wonderful power of contracting or relaxing,
according to the impartiality of the sentence pronounced by
him. . . . The use of this collar has been since discontinued, on
account of the risk of strangulation to which it exposed many
honourable judges. . . .

My unlucky countrymen have always had a taste for justice—a
taste as inconvenient to them, situated as they have always been,
as a fancy for horse-racing would be to a Venetian.

Our modern plan, it must be confessed, improves upon the distraction of this, for not only have we Governors of discordant

politics succeeding each other, but every new Governor is provided with a Secretary to differ with him for the time being,
and both receive their instructions from a Cabinet, not one
member of which agrees with another.

. . . if Pope had been born a Munster Papist, instead of a London one, by Act 7 William and Mary, and 2 Anne, he would
have been voted an irreclaimable brute, and hunted into the
mountains. The Penal Code, enacted at this period, will for ever
remain a monument of the atrocious perfection, to which the
art of torturing his fellow-creatures may be brought by civilized
man.

As Property and Education are the best securities against discontent and violence, the Government, in its zeal for the advancement of our family, took especial care that we should be as
little as possible encumbered with either.

With respect to the [Charter Schools], it might have been possible perhaps, to manufacture the same number of rebels and
bigots at somewhat less expense, but the perfection of their machinery for the purpose is now, I believe, acknowledged on all
sides.

The courteous address of Launcelot to the young Jewess, "Be
of good cheer, for truly I think thou art damned," seems to
have been the model upon which the Protestant Church has
founded all its conciliatory advances towards the Catholics.

Caesar is supposed to have sent a million of men out of the world,
and Caesar is therefore a hero—while, if Captain ROCK, in what
the laws have taught him to consider as fair fighting as Caesar's,
puts a merciless driver *hors de combat*, or pushes a middleman's
middleman off his step in the ascending scale of tyrants, he is
a ferocious, brutal and irreclaimable savage.[3]

But though such passages represent the tensile strength of
Moore's indignant prose, it is the cumulative effect of *Captain
Rock* that is convincing—one of the most comprehensive ar-
raignments of misgovernment published in the nineteenth century, though one review spoke oddly of the "many agreeable
lights" he had thrown on the subject, and a second doubted

if the "ironical style" was effective.[4] If to our taste the book
is marred by pedantic literary allusions, it must be remembered that he was writing for the old, unreformed Parliament, whose members knew vastly more about Ovid than
they did about Ireland.

Captain Rock created a sensation. The *Times* and the
Morning Chronicle carried long quotations on the day of
publication, and a second edition had to be printed immediately, the third following soon after. The Whigs, of course,
were jubilant, the anti-government Irish press was enthusiastic, and the poverty-stricken peasants subscribed their six-
pences and shillings to buy a copy. The *New Monthly
Magazine* said that "a more complete, lively, and feeling exposure of that system, from its very commencement, has
never been made"; the *London Magazine* declared it was "an
entertaining and melancholy volume, which Englishmen
ought to be ashamed and Irishmen afraid to read"; the *Literary Chronicle*, after some hesitation, said that he adhered
to the truth. Even the *Westminster*, after warning him
against pedantry, concluded that the amount of information
in the volume belied the notion that this amatory poet was
indolent, and added that his every work must command attention and examination. The Tory organs either ignored the
volume, or, as usual, reminded their readers that he was an
immoral poet.[5] But the final tribute was the publication of a
formal reply of 450 pages, *Captain Rock Detected . . . by a
Munster Farmer*, in reality the Rev. Mortimer O'Sullivan,[6] a
controversialist whom Moore was to toast to a turn in *The
Fudges in England:*

> He comes from Erin's speechful shore,
> Like fervid kettle, bubbling o'er
>   With hot effusions—hot and weak;
> Sound, Humbug, all your hollowest drums,
> He comes, of Erin's martyrdoms
>   To Britain's well-fed Church to speak.

.   .   .   .   .

Prepare, ye wealthier Saints, your dinners,
 Ye Spinsters, spread your tea and crumpets;
And you, ye countless Tracts for Sinners,
 Blow all your little penny trumpets.

Even more gratifying, however, was the fact that the publication of Moore's volume led to an immediate amelioration of some of the harsher features of Irish law regarding the recovery of debts.[7]

III

After sending off the revisions for the second (in fact, the third) edition of his book, Moore went on a holiday round of visits, including one to Captain Houlton at Farley Abbey, where, with Pepysian delight in experience, he relished an anecdote of an antiquarian who, having introduced a quill into the mummified body of Lady Margaret Hungerford, announced that the liquid drawn off tasted "strongly aromatic." Moore had also been working at intervals on a new number of the *Irish Melodies* (the ninth, published in 1824), and a second series of *Sacred Songs* (1824). Still in a holiday mood, he went down to London to enjoy the excitement over *Captain Rock* and to speak at the Wiltshire Anniversary Dinner and at the dinner of the Literary Fund. Among other objects, he had it in mind to redeem Byron's memoirs from John Murray by repaying the two thousand guineas which Murray had lent him, but a round of engagements led him negligently to postpone doing it. When Rees, of Longmans, asked him on May 13 whether he had called on Murray, he was compelled to say he had not. Rees advised him not to delay further, and the two went off to a party at Longman's house. The next day Moore noted that the *Morning Herald* was abusing him, and called at Colbourn's Library to secure the address of William Jerdan, editor of the *Literary Gazette*. A shopman casually informed him that Byron was dead.

The world reeled for a moment, then stood still. He hurried off to see Murray, who was not home. Thus casually fate plunged him into the most controversial episode in his career.

For the next three days the Byron circle was rocked to its foundations as events shaped themselves towards the historic destruction of the Byron manuscript in John Murray's fireplace. It was an affair in which everybody acted from the highest possible motives and the deepest possible suspicion of everybody else. Everyone lost his temper; everyone contradicted everyone else; and, at the end, nobody was satisfied. The essential facts are these: [8]

Byron had given Moore the first portion of his memoirs at La Mira in 1819, sending a second portion to him in Paris later, where Moore had had a copy of the whole transcribed. This manuscript was Moore's absolute property, subject only to the restriction that, though the memoirs might be read by a few persons at his discretion, they could not be published in Byron's lifetime. As he told Moore and wrote Murray, "when I am cold, you may do what you please." Needing money to settle his Bermuda claims in 1821, Moore agreed with Murray to sell him the memoirs for two thousand guineas (both the original and the copy), subject to the same restrictions as to publication and with the added proviso that Moore agreed with Murray to write a life of Byron, if he survived that poet. This deed of sale was signed in November, 1821, but since it required Byron's approval, it passed into the hands of Byron's legal adviser, Douglas Kinnaird. Byron informed Kinnaird that he had signed the paper without reading it, and the cautious Kinnaird refused to deliver the document to Murray. In the meantime, Moore's friends had questioned the propriety (though not the legality) of the whole transaction; and this so wrought upon Moore's sensitivity that in April, 1822, he approached Murray with a new proposal, partly of his own devising, and partly because Byron had likewise changed *his* mind. Under the terms of this second agreement Moore (or Byron) was to be permitted to redeem the manuscript by the repayment of the two thousand guineas to Murray, to whom he gave a bond for that sum. The contract was supposed by Moore to change the original deed of sale into a loan secured by Murray's possession of the manuscript. This second agreement met the approval of Hobhouse, with whom Moore talked on April 29, 1822, and was signed on May 6.

By March, 1823, Murray was beginning to worry about his bond and wondering when Moore was to repay the loan, but Moore, with unpardonable negligence, took a high tone in replying to him, and then did nothing. Getting no money from Moore, Murray next wrote him a note which Moore received April 1, 1824, asking for the original deed of sale, still in the possession of Douglas Kinnaird, since, aside from Moore's bond, Murray had nothing to show as legal security for his loan unless Kinnaird would release the original instrument. Moore secured the original deed from Kinnaird and gave it to Murray, at the same time informing him of his intention of redeeming the manuscript of the memoirs altogether by the repayment of the money. This he apparently planned to do by way of the Longmans, who were to advance him the two thousand guineas (with interest), when he would redeem the manuscript. Had he done this any time before Byron's death (April 19, 1824), Murray would have presumably delivered up the memoirs, and Moore's problem would have simplified into the question of what he proposed to do with them. But his fatal procrastination plunged him into a complication of motives and counter-motives. On May 3, 1824, he received a letter from Byron, saying that he was threatened with either epilepsy or apoplexy; on the thirteenth Rees, as we have seen, told him that Longmans had the money for him. But it was too late. The fact of Byron's death had already terminated the period during which Moore was entitled to redeem the memoirs, the legal possession of which was now vested in Murray.

With his usual business incompetency, Moore had also failed to keep a copy of the agreement with Murray, and his memory at this point betrayed him. He was firmly of the opinion that he might redeem the manuscript either during Byron's lifetime or for a period of three months thereafter, and in the light of this belief he acted. As a matter of fact, the only three-months provision in the agreement was the odd one—surely a slip—that Murray could not publish the memoirs unless he should do so within three months of Byron's death! Moore's curious, though perhaps not unnatural, delusion that until the expiration of this three-months period the memoirs were in fact his must be kept in mind in judging his conduct.

On the evening of May 14 he received a note from Kinnaird, inquiring who owned the memoirs, and saying that he was ready to advance the two thousand guineas (he wrote "pounds," and the confusion between pounds and guineas increased the general irritation) "in order to give Lady Byron and the rest of the family an opportunity of deciding whether they wished them to be published or no." Moore pointed out in good faith that the manuscript was his property; that Lady Byron was scarcely the person to have the disposing of it; but that he would submit the manuscript to a chosen number of persons and, if they said it was unfit for publication, he would burn it. From this point on, events acquire the fantastic quality of an ethical nightmare. Moore called upon Brougham, for legal, and then upon Hobhouse for ethical, counsel, and there learned that Murray had just called. Also acting in good faith and with all the points of the law on his side (as Moore did not know), Murray had consulted Wilmot Horton, a relative of Byron, offering to place the memoirs at the disposal of the Byron family and hinting that the Byron family might pay the two thousand guineas. Hobhouse held the view that the manuscript should be placed in the hands of Augusta Leigh, who would certainly pay the two thousand guineas. Murray had left before Moore called; and if only Murray had remained with Hobhouse long enough for Moore to have found them together, much of the argument and most of the comedy of the situation would not have occurred.

But the ironical gods willed otherwise. There were calls and counter-calls; Moore, who at first had agreed to leave the famous manuscript with Mrs. Leigh "to be done with exactly as she thought proper," began to have qualms about destroying it. Would it be fair to Byron? Could not the objectionable parts be excised? His communication of these doubts to Hobhouse enlivened the early hours of Monday morning, the seventeenth; and as Luttrell, whom he had consulted, professed to remember a clause in the rough draft of the agreement giving Moore three months to redeem the manuscript, Moore had grown rather determined in his views. (Kinnaird, fortunately for his peace of mind, was called to Scotland.) Hobhouse started to call on Luttrell, and met Moore; and Moore, Luttrell, and Hobhouse being gathered at Hobhouse's rooms, were called on by Murray, who, learning of Moore's change of purpose, also grew "very determined," saying that the manuscript should be burnt forthwith, and that he, the tradesman, should have the honor of making the sacrifice. This speech obviously nettled the tradesman's son, who, when Murray informed him: "you have acted anything but like a man of honour," responded briskly: "Go on, sir, you know you may say what you like." The peaceable Luttrell put in a word when he could, and eventually the foursome adjourned to Murray's house in Albemarle Street, where the *dramatis personae* were increased by Horton, who represented Lady Byron, and Colonel Doyle, who represented Augusta Leigh.

With six contestants present, the conversation grew peppery, Moore protesting against the destruction, and Hobhouse protesting against his protestation. Everyone seems to have stood finely on his honor, and the first act closed on a high point in the dialogue when Colonel Doyle said to Moore: "I understand then that you stand to your original proposal to put the MSS. at Mrs. Leigh's absolute disposal." Moore replying, "I do, but with the former protestation," the Colonel then responded dramatically: "Well then, on the part of Mrs.

Leigh I put them into the fire," which, with a little help from Horton, he succeeded in doing. When Hobhouse was cozily offered an opportunity to burn something, he loftily declined, remarking that "those only who were empowered by Mrs. Leigh should have any share in the actual destruction." With the signing of a paper by Moore that, to the best of his belief, no copy had existed except that which had been burned along with the original, and of another by Murray that no copy had been taken while the memoirs were in his possession, something like calm descended upon the argument.

But not for long. Though the property in dispute had just gone up in smoke, the debate was renewed with acrimony when it was proposed to see the loan repaid, the bond returned, and the agreement canceled. In the first place, Murray could not find the agreement; then an anonymous solicitor briefly enters the light of history long enough to lay a "foul copy" of the agreement on the table and disappear; next, like a *deus ex machina,* he returns with the proper document. The extraordinary three-months clause was read. Moore said he was not aware of any such condition being contained in the agreement. Murray said that the chance of publishing the now vanished manuscript was the only security he had had against losing two thousand guineas. Hobhouse asked how, if the motive of the agreement was "Lord Byron's and Mr. Moore's not now inclining to make the said MSS public," Moore could argue that the destruction of the memoirs injured the noble poet—which, at this distance, looks like a curious piece of reasoning. Moore said that he had never read the original indenture. Horton and Colonel Doyle said they were surprised. Then the original contract of sale was burnt, and everybody but Murray and Moore said it was too bad that Murray had not earlier produced the agreement, which "would have spared all the parties the unpleasant altercations which had attended the transaction." Moore then tried to pay Murray the money, but Murray said he would not take it, as he had only destroyed his own property "and he would not take money for that." Moore said that he had supposed it was *his* property which was being burned, and insisted that *he* ought to pay. Matters were carried on in this lofty fashion for a few minutes when Luttrell sensibly reminded Moore that he had, after all, borrowed the money, and Moore paid. The bond was canceled. That exhausted pair, Horton and Colonel Doyle, left the room, and Murray said he was sorry he had "used harsh words" to Moore. Hobhouse said he was sorry he had been obliged to tell Moore what he thought of his changing his mind. Moore said that if Hobhouse had got out of bounds, he would have stopped him (and he did, as a matter of fact, write Hobhouse a rather silly letter which the latter received at half-past six). And eventually everybody went home. There were exaggerated stories in the newspapers later, and corrections by Moore, to which Hobhouse objected, but on the whole everybody was amiable thereafter.[9]

That literature lost anything of value in this extraordinary episode has never been contended, but the solemnity with which the event has been discussed has arisen, of course, from the hope that the memoirs threw some light on the Byron "mystery." On the whole, it seems clear that they did not. Through the fog of charges and counter-charges it is evident that four or five high-strung gentlemen got themselves entangled in a problem of casuistry which an earlier resort to the documents in the case might quickly have simplified. Though Moore felt injured and hinted momentarily that the second, and crucial, agreement did not contain the terms he had intended it to contain, not the slightest suspicion has ever attached itself to Murray; nor, allowing for his unbusinesslike habits and his transitory pique, should any attach to Moore. In truth, his very quixoticism, his high Irish sensitivity was in part the cause of the wrangle. Waiving the question of his legal rights (which were entirely fictional), one sees that he had a difficult choice to make under circumstances of pressure from various sides coming upon him all at once; and one can have little regret, and no blame, that he agreed to the destruction. In the realm of practical affairs, however, the last word came from the sardonic Rogers, who told Moore that he ought to consider his wife and children, and not pay back to Murray the two thousand guineas. When Moore insisted upon the propriety of this gesture, Rogers replied: "Well, your life may be a good poem, but it is a d——d bad matter of fact." [10]

Chapter XII

For the next few days Moore's friends in London insisted upon going over and over again the casuistical problem of the Byron memoirs; the poet had also to fend off well-meant efforts of the Byron family to pay him the two thousand guineas; and he had to suffer the usual misrepresentations in the press.[1] Eventually he shook London from his weary shoulders and went home, "nervous and languid from the agitation in which I was kept." The two thousand guineas advanced him by the Longmans seem to have been secured by a life insurance policy, though the details are vague, but the debt made him face once more the realities of his financial situation. His children were growing up; he was getting older; and he needed money. There was nothing for it but to fall back on the *Sheridan*, of which he was tired, but before he got fairly down to work, Washington Irving came over from Bath to visit him—they had met again while Moore was in London. With his pleasure in the English country-side, Irving was a delight, though he was likely to fall silent at dinner parties, being, as Moore noted with grave irony, a "domestic animal." Irving read from manuscript parts of the *Tales of a Traveller*—"rather tremble for its fate," wrote Moore in his journal—but on June 18 he was gone, and the familiar pattern of life at Sloperton was resumed. But before Tom had got over the exhaustion of that scene in front of Murray's fireplace, he was called again to London to attend Byron's funeral on July 12. It affected him deeply:

When I approached the house, and saw the crowd assembled, felt a nervous trembling come over me, which lasted till the whole ceremony was over; thought I should be ill. Never was at a funeral before, but poor Curran's. The riotous curiosity of the mob, the bustle of the undertakers, &c., and all the other vulgar accompaniments of the ceremony, mixing with my recollections of him who was gone, produced a combination of disgust and sadness that was deeply painful to me. . . . Left the hearse as soon as it was off the stones, and returned home to get rid of my black clothes, and try to forget, as much as possible, the wretched feelings I had experienced in them.

Unfortunately, when he went for a walk in the park with Rogers, he met a soldier's funeral, and almost broke down. It was small comfort to breakfast next morning for the first time in the Athenaeum Club, which he had helped to found.[2] He spent some days making further researches for the Sheridan life and then returned to Wiltshire.

The nine-years task neared its end amid inevitable interruptions—a visit from Luttrell, dinners at Bowood, songs for Power, negotiations for writing a life of Byron, an attempt to compose a duel between two of his neighbors, journeys to town—all the trivial and necessary details of his busy life. But he struggled on, trying to improve his prose style by ridding it of ornamentation, trying also to tell the truth about Sheridan, about the Prince of Wales, about the Whigs. The long grind of the proofs came in the autumn, and finally, on October 13, 1825, the work for which the political and literary worlds had looked so long was published, *Memoirs of the Life of the Right Honourable Richard Brinsley Sheridan* by Thomas Moore. Of the first edition a thousand copies were sold in ten days. He braced himself for the inevitable squabbles. They soon came. As he noted in the fifth edition,

The Tory, of course, is shocked by my Whiggism;—the Whigs are rather displeased at my candour in conceding, that they have sometimes been wrong, and the Tories right; while the Radical, in his patriotic hatred of both parties, is angry with me for allowing any merit to either.[3]

And the discussion is renewed every time a new book on Sheridan appears—Mr. E. M. Butler, for example, observing in his strange volume, *Sheridan: A Ghost Story,* that Moore "has a curiously woolly mind" and that he "was more than pleased with himself" in the biography, a statement which, in view of Tom's many expressions of dissatisfaction with the work, seems a little unkind.[4]

Moore's *Sheridan,* nevertheless, is not a great biography as his *Byron* is a great biography, and it is illuminating to inquire into the reasons why it is not a better book. In the first place, while it is theoretically true that the Sheridan papers were placed at his disposal, the pages of his journal show how frequent and vexatious was the interference of the Sheridan heirs in the allocation of this material to Moore and to the publishers. In the second place, he undoubtedly labored at it so long that he grew tired of his task. One of the reasons was, of course, the interruption caused by his Paris exile, a fact which Moore's condemners have conveniently overlooked. Another was the just desire to learn the truth about Sheridan, a quest which led Moore to devote endless hours to interviewing Sherry's friends, acquaintances, and enemies, often with very little result. A third was the inevitable delay caused by the necessity of earning money while the *Sheridan* was going forward. But an even deeper cause for the dubious merits of the book lies in the fact that he had no model to go on. He was trying to depict one of the most elusive and quicksilver-like of English geniuses, and he could not invent the formula by which to do it. The repeated attempts for a hundred years since to write a life of Sheridan which will be at once lively and true indicate that where Moore did not succeed, no one since has triumphed.

When his book came out, Boswell's *Johnson,* with which modern methods in biography may be said to begin, was only thirty-four years old, but the example of Boswell had scarcely been followed, and the problems presented by Dr. Johnson's temperament were very different from those presented by Sheridan. Except as Boswell showed him the desirability of documentation and of including the little, graphic, portrait-making events of his subject's life, Boswell could not greatly assist Moore. Between Boswell and Moore English biography had to show only such books as Malone's *Dryden* (1800), an antiquarian job overshadowed by Scott's inaccurate but immensely vital life in 1808; Godwin's *Chaucer* (1803), a byword for badness; Southey's *Nelson* (1813), which was a brilliant piece of wartime propaganda; Roscoe's *Leo X* (1805), which used to repose, unread, on the shelves of gentlemen's libraries; and Southey's monumental *Wesley* (1820), which was no help to Moore. Poor Tom quite literally did not know what to do with his subject. His early chapters are a lively, and even whimsical, picture of a young scapegrace who got himself involved in incredible duels and an elopement, and are, as literature, the best part of the book; but unfortunately for the biographer, Sheridan's life did not continue on this plane—he became not only the brilliant dramatist but the parliamentary orator and the backstairs politician; the line of his life cut across gambling hells and the Regency question, arrests by bailiffs and the conduct of the Napoleonic wars. Sheridan becomes, like Cerberus, a literary gentleman with three heads, to the despair of all his biographers, none of whom has found his secret. By the end of the volume Moore had in fact given up the line of Sheridan's life to write a great political pamphlet which, despite the author's protestations of impartiality, was to justify the conduct of the old-line opposition. And Moore's self-satisfaction, so far as it existed, arose, not from the feeling that the biography was satisfactory, but from the conviction that he had done considerable damage to the Tory cause.

The style of the book is unfortunate. Moore could on occasion write a sinewy and eloquent prose which approximates the grand manner, and he could, as in the *Byron,* write a lucent, easy style through which the subject everywhere shows itself. But in the *Sheridan* he did neither. The style is conscious and mannered; it is as if he had deliberately gone back to the artificial fulsomeness of the days when Warren Hastings was being impeached, and all the orators adopted the language of the Lower Empire. He wants to tell you that, on occasion, Sheridan rivaled Burke: this becomes—"Another passage in the second day's Speech is remarkable as exhibiting a sort of tourney of intellect between Sheridan and Burke, and in that field of abstract speculation, which was the favourite of the latter." Or consider this polysyllabic elegance: "In the instructions here given by the poet to the musician, we may perceive that he somewhat apprehended, even in the tasteful hands of Mr. Linley, that predominance of harmony over melody, and of noise over both, which is so fatal to poetry and song, in their perilous alliance with an orchestra. Indeed, those elephants of old, that used to tread down the ranks they were brought to assist, were but a type of the havoc that is sometimes made both of melody and meaning by the overlaying aid of accompaniments." This, surely, is the "florid style, in which Mr. Sheridan was not very happy," as Moore gravely reminds us. Neither was Moore, who, when he wants to inform the reader that King George III was praised by "a Noble Earl" for violating the constitution, writes that "though this was the mere ebullition of an absurd individual, yet the bubble on the surface often proves the strength of the spirit underneath"; and who, when Sheridan annoys Burke, writes of "the unseasonable stimulant" to Burke's temper, and of how, "the divergence of the parties once begun, it was in vain to think of restoring their parallelism," as if politicians were propositions in Euclid. And then there are the unfortunate figures of speech. The *Westminster Review* unkindly estimated that there were 2500 similes in the book. These, it is true, are more sparsely scattered through the latter chapters, written when Moore set himself consciously to pruning his prose, but they are oddly in the way. If he wrote a book which all students of Sheridan must consult, he did not succeed in writing a biography which has lived in its own right.

Whether Moore was at all points just to Sheridan is a matter for the special student to determine. That he was jealous of Sheridan's wit cannot, however, be seriously urged. Moore had his little vanities, but the writer of the stinging lines on the death of Sheridan was not given to this kind of conceit. The argument that Moore's insistence upon Sheridan's "plagiarisms" somehow shows that he was jealous is preposterous. Sheridan's habit of borrowing his material where he found it was an open secret, which lay in the way of his biographer and had to be dealt with. Moore, who had a scholar's curiosity, naturally had to look into the problem, and the general line of his conclusions is indisputable. That, however, he understood Sheridan cannot be pretended. On the contrary, it is clear that Moore was profoundly puzzled by a temperament so mercurial and so brilliant, a mind that could act from the highest motives of patriotism and at other times indulge in petty trickery. This problem he could not solve; and it is to Moore's credit that he nowhere pretended to have solved it.

The complaint that Moore mishandled his documentary evidence is true, but it must be remembered, first, that he had to consider the susceptibilities of scores of living acquaintances of Sheridan; and, second, that editorial standards were not in our sense of the word scientific. Lockhart was not candid in his *Scott,* and in the *Byron* Moore silently suppressed or altered passages in Byron's manuscript and sometimes joined together what Byron had put asunder. In this respect, however, he simply followed the standards of the age—the same standards which caused Jared Sparks to improve the grammar and spelling of the Father of his Country. The severe methods of later German university research were as yet unknown, and the biographers of the first part of the nineteenth century can scarcely be blamed for not doing what they had never been trained to do.

No previous book of Moore's, not even *Lalla Rookh*, enjoyed a more brilliant press, for even the Tories felt that the publication of the biography was a portentous literary event. The *Westminster Review*, for example, which in general was likely to judge such a publication by far higher standards than either the Whig or Tory periodicals, felt that "no one else could have escaped entanglements any better," and that Moore's treatment was scrupulously fair, though the reviewer objected to the style and, of course, found fault with the politics. The *British Critic* was naturally hostile, and argued, as the Tory reviewers generally argued that, whatever Moore's reasons for hating the Prince of Wales, he should not have allowed them to bias the book. The *Monthly Review*, however, though it objected to the "labored flatteries" of the living Whigs, grudgingly admitted that it was "one of the most magnificent biographies" in the language. *Blackwoods* attacked the Whiggery but was unexpectedly gentle, finding the volume "not discreditable." The heavy artillery on the conservative side was discharged by the *Quarterly*, which, in a long and characteristic article, said that Moore was jealous of Dr. Watkins' (now discredited) life of the dramatist (1817), fell foul of the style, charged Moore with wholesale inaccuracies either "from ignorance or purpose," reviewed Sheridan's political career disapprovingly, and could admire only Moore's treatment of Sheridan the playwright.[5]

The stately enthusiasm of the *Edinburgh Review* covered not only the biography, but the political history. Moore was no "mere poet," but the author of the "best historical notice yet published of the events of our times," the pages of which are marked "by dispassionate truth and monitory wisdom." The *European Magazine*, which confessed to many fears, found that the book belied them all, and that there was nowhere any attempt to violate truth or make Sheridan seem what he was not, even though the volume "emanates from an avowed politician." The *Literary Chronicle* spiritedly attacked those who accused the author of libeling either Sheridan or the Prince; the *Metropolitan Quarterly Magazine* pointed out that, far from being spoiled by his aristocratic friends, Moore recognized that his true allies were the people. Said the *Literary Gazette:* "Moral right is never perverted, and one of the chief praises of Mr. Moore's work is its honest adherence to the truth in general." [6] And, in addition to these flattering notices, the volume received the best possible advertising—it was everywhere the subject of conversation and debate in the political and literary worlds. Tommy had scored a hit; and if it went a little to his head, it is not surprising.

II

Because the long labor of seeing *Sheridan* through the press had given Moore the fidgets, the wise and faithful Bessy insisted on his taking a vacation—France, Scotland, Ireland, anywhere he could "amuse himself a little." The weary biographer chose Edinburgh. Back from Ireland, where, as he wrote Moore, he had "met with everything that was kind," Scott had urged him with hearty affection to

bring wife and bairns. We have plenty of room, and plenty of oatmeal, and *entre nous* a bottle or two of good claret, to which I think you have as little objection as I have. We will talk of poor Byron, who was dear to us both. . . .

The Muse of History has a delicate sense of humor. For it is well to note that the account of the visit of the "warm-hearted minstrel of Erin," as Lockhart calls him, which appears in the life of Scott was worked up by that biographer from Moore's journal, Moore having "kindly allowed me the use" of it; that Lockhart was the author of the hostile review of the *Sheridan*, already noticed, in the *Quarterly*, despite his father-in-law's generous efforts to hold him in reason; and that he was presently to write Sir Walter, who recorded in his diary his impressions of Moore's "manly frankness . . .

perfect ease and good-breeding," that the *Sheridan* was "full
of baseness." Unconscious of these little ironies, however,
Moore arrived at Abbotsford on October 29, 1825, where the
two poets walked and talked and drove and drank together,
holding such converse about men and books and things as
forever endeared them to each other. The unpretentious
great-heartedness of the Wizard of the North completely
won the little Irishman:

Could not help thinking, during this quiet, homely visit, how
astonished some of those foreigners would be, to whom the name
of Sir Walter Scott is encircled with so much romance, to see
the plain, quiet, neighbourly manner with which he took his
seat among these old maids, and the familiar ease with which they
treated him in return; no country squire, with but half an idea
in his head, could have fallen into the gossip of a hum-drum
country visit more unassumingly.

And as for the cant interpretation that Moore "dearly loved
a lord," let the penetrating eye of Scott look upon him:

Not the least touch of the poet or the pedant. A little—a very
little man. Less, I think, than [Matthew] Lewis, and somewhat
like him in person; God knows, not in conversation, for Matt,
though a clever fellow, was a bore of the first description. . . .
Moore has none of this insignificance. His countenance is plain,
but the expression so very animated, especially in speaking or
singing, that it is far more interesting than the finest features
could have rendered it

. . . I was curious to see what there could be in common betwixt us, Moore having lived so much in the gay world, I in the
country, and with people of business, and sometimes with politicians; Moore a scholar, I none; he a democrat, I an aristocrat—
with many other points of difference; besides his being an Irishman, I a Scotchman, and both tolerably national. Yet there is
a point of resemblance, and a strong one. We are both good-
humoured fellows, who rather seek to enjoy what is going forward than to maintain our dignity as Lions; and we have both
seen the world too widely and too well not to contemn in our
souls the imaginary consequence of literary people, who walk
with their noses in the air, and remind me always of the fellow

whom Johnson met in an alehouse, and who called himself '*the great Twalmly—inventor of the flood-gate iron for smoothing linen.*'

If this self-depreciation be the humility proper to genius, it is only fair to record Moore's confession to his host that his own poetry wanted "manly training," that "the only thing, indeed, that conduced to brace and invigorate my mind was the strong political feelings that were stirring around me when I was a boy, and in which I took a deep and most ardent interest." Scott records that "it would be a delightful addition to life, if T. M. had a cottage within two miles of one," and when they visited the theater in Edinburgh, pushed Moore forward in view of the applauding pit, saying, "It is you, it is you; you must rise and make your acknowledgment." At the end of each act the house insisted on cheering, and Scott was delighted—he had been similarly welcomed in Dublin. Jeffrey was also in the box, Jeffrey whom Moore had tried to kill so many years before, and it had been pleasant to hear Jeffrey tell him that "you can think and reason solidly and manfully, and treat the gravest and most important subjects in a manner worthy of them." [7] And Moore was also charmed with the William Murrays—Anne Dyke had not, so far as he could see, altered in fourteen years. Not dreaming of the catastrophe about to overwhelm the great novelist, Moore left Edinburgh in a glow; as he told Lockhart long afterwards:

I parted from Scott with the feeling that all the world might admire him in his works, but that those only could learn to love him as he deserved who had seen him at Abbotsford. I give you *carte blanche* to say what you please of my sense of his cordial kindness and gentleness; perhaps not a very dignified phrase would express my feeling better than any fine one—it was that he was a *thorough good fellow*.[8]

But when he returned to Sloperton, calamity found him out. His sister Ellen wrote that the elder Moore was on the point of death; and Moore, doubly frightened because of the

financial panic, scarcely knew whether he could cash a bill
on Power to provide funds for the necessary journey to Dublin. He set out in a state of nervousness and depression, half-consciously noting the stagnation into which the panic had
plunged the country, rode through a storm of thunder, lightning, and hail in Wales which threatened to wreck the coach,
was deadly ill on the packet, and reached Dublin without
having eaten anything for twenty-eight hours. Bessy had
hoped he would not arrive in time to see his father die; and
the Moore family, knowing his abnormal sensitivity, protected him from the customary death watch:

It was their strong wish I should not ask to see my father, as
he was past the power of knowing me, and it would only shock
me unnecessarily. This a great relief, as I would not for worlds
have the sweet impression he left upon my mind when I last
saw him exchanged for one which would haunt me, I know,
dreadfully through the remainder of my life.

His father died on December 17, the morning after his son's
arrival; but though Moore was spared the necessity of dealing
with the undertakers of that day (one recalls Dickens's gallery of these gentry), he had, of course, to attend the funeral:

The weather was wretched, and altogether the scene shocked
and afflicted me beyond anything: the vulgar apparatus of the
ceremony seems such a profanation!

And there were harassing financial problems, for, though
Lord Wellesley generously offered to continue the father's
pension, Moore refused, fearing acceptance of this grant from
the government might be misunderstood. Back in Sloperton
Bessy was heroically trying to work out a scheme for getting
along with one servant in order that Tom might contribute to
his mother's support, but he managed to avoid this necessity;
and after calling on O'Connell, seeing his friends, and learning
at first hand something more about the agitation for Catholic
Emancipation, he re-crossed the channel in a storm of sleet
and got home again.

He could not understand where the money went to, but he buckled down to work again, first on the Egyptian story which he had begun in Paris and laid aside; next, on some songs for Power; and finally, on the project for a life of Byron. This meant, of course, that he would have to go to town and see Hobhouse and Murray, and he remembered with uneasiness the terms on which he had parted from them. His correspondence with Hobhouse proved not too encouraging, and some of his friends advised against his undertaking so difficult a task, but May found him in London, where Hobhouse proved considerate, and where he stopped Murray on the street to proffer his hand and to suggest oblivion for the past. Murray was delighted, but Moore's obligation to the Longmans had to be reckoned with. The Longmans were characteristically generous, and the agreement with Murray was made; and, what was more to the financial purpose, he concluded an arrangement with Barnes of the *Times*, to which he had been contributing satires, whereby that paper advanced him four hundred pounds in consideration of further poems. He was immensely relieved; and he could relish a breakfast at Rogers', where Sydney Smith was in his best form. When he and Smith called on Newton, the painter, who was doing a portrait of Moore, Smith said, in his gravest manner: "Couldn't you contrive to throw into his face somewhat of a stronger expression of hostility to the Church establishment?" Aside from an increasing absent-mindedness, Tom seemed to be fully himself and returned to Sloperton in better spirits than he had been.

The liberals considered him fully one of them; and the squibs he contributed to the *Times* under a transparent veil of anonymity were the talk of London. They began with the "Amatory Colloquy between Bank and Government" on February 7, 1826, and were continued at least until 1835. The earlier ones were concerned with the financial measures of the Tories, but after that they broadened to include Catholic Emancipation, the Corn Laws, slavery in the colonies, rotten boroughs, and the general iniquities of the unreformed Parliament. It requires a minute knowledge of the political life of the period fully to comprehend these glancing lines which stung the Tories into rage or reduced them to laughter, but it is still possible to see the fun and satire in some of them. "All in the Family Way" has not wholly lost its point in a world which has seen the New Deal:

> My senators vote away millions,
>   To put in Prosperity's budget;
> And though it were billions or trillions,
>   The generous rogues wouldn't grudge it.
>   .   .   .   .   .
> My labourers used to eat mutton,
>   As any great man of the State does;
> And now the poor devils are put on
>   Small rations of tea and potatoes.
> But cheer up, John, Sawney, and Paddy,
>   The King is your father, they say;
> So, ev'n if you starve for your Daddy,
>   'Tis all in the family way.
>
> My rich manufacturers tumble,
>   My poor ones have nothing to chew;
> And, even if themselves do not grumble,
>   Their stomachs undoubtedly do.
> But coolly to fast *en famille*,
>   Is as good for the soul as to pray;
> And famine itself is genteel,
>   When one starves in a family way.

The "Epitaph on a Tuft-Hunter" is one of the neatest of these effusions:

> Lament, lament, Sir Isaac Heard,
>   Put mourning round thy page, Debrett,
> For here lies one, who ne'er preferr'd
>   A Viscount to a Marquis yet.
>
> Beside him place the God of Wit,
>   Before him Beauty's rosiest girls,
> Apollo for a *star* he'd quit,
>   And Love's own sister for an Earl's.

Did niggard fate no peers afford,
　　He took, of course, to peers' relations;
And, rather than not sport a Lord,
　　Put up with even the last creations.

Even Irish names, could he but tag 'em
　　With 'Lord' and 'Duke,' were sweet to call;
And, at a pinch, Lord Ballyraggum
　　Was better than no Lord at all.

Heaven grant him now some noble nook,
　　For, rest his soul! he'd rather be
Genteelly damn'd beside a Duke,
　　Than sav'd in vulgar company.

Reactionary Anglican bishops were read a lecture in "Ode to a Hat":

That brim of brims, so sleekly good—
　　Not fiapp'd, like dull Wesleyans', down,
But looking (as all churchmen's should)
　　Devoutly upward—towards the *crown*.

Orangemen were pictured as petitioning the government:

That, forming one seventh, within a few fractions,
　　Of Ireland's seven millions of hot heads and hearts,
We hold it the basest of all base transactions
　　To keep us from murd'ring the other six parts.

Lord Eldon was roundly basted in "A Vision by the Author of Christabel"; Benthamites were impartially satirized in a succession of squibs; and fifteen scorching stanzas on the death of the Duke of York, entitled "The Slave," reminded Londoners that, though the Irish might dislike the bigotry of that nobleman, they could be generous in death to

A Prince without pride, a man without guile,
　　To the last unchanging, warm, sincere,
For Worth he had ever a hand and smile,
　　And for Misery ever his purse and tear.[9]

Some of the fiercest of these castigations he did not choose to preserve. One is a scathing attack on "Orator" Hunt:

'Tis true the Papist's sword would pass
  Through England's foes, when H-nt would quail;
But then, the Papist goes to mass,
  And H-nt goes nowhere—but to jail.

·   ·   ·   ·   ·   ·

Bad as he is, the knave we've got
  Was christen'd at the Establish'd font;—
Though "Social order" owns him not,
  "Holy Religion" claims her H-nt.

Then let's console us, as we can,
  With the sweet thought, that, though we fag hard,
'Stead of a Popish *gentleman*,
  We've H-nt, a Protestant and b——d.

A second was a satire on Lord Eldon's receiving a silver-gilt
cup from the King, which pictures the Chancellor drinking
from the goblet:

Shall we replenish with the groans
  Of ruin'd orphans, with the tears
Of helpless widows, dulcet tones
  I long have drunk in—at my ears?

That vintage now bears no increase,
  Long since that wine-press has run dry,
When hearts are broken groans must cease,
  Despair still wears a tearless eye.

My cup is fill'd with tears alone,
  Its bitterness will soon be past.
Here's to the King, in Eldon's own,
  'Tis self, all self, from first to last.[10]

He threw himself into the struggle for Catholic Emancipation with a bitter vehemence that did not spare his quondam
idol, Wellington, who had become

Ungrateful, sullen, savage, cold,
  The people's scorn, the army's hate.

When in March, 1827, the bill was again defeated, Moore's
rage boiled over in a poem which pictured Bigotry counting
the majority and seeing

by gift of second sight,
The mingling flash of pike and sword,
And the burning cottage's crimson light,
On the baleful Orange banner pour'd!

A worried government sent five million cartridges to the Irish garrisons; the embattled poet wrote his scathing parody, "A Pastoral Ballad":

I have found out a gift for my Erin,
A gift that will surely content her;—
Sweet pledge of a love so endearing!
Five millions of bullets I've sent her.

.   .   .   .   .

Even W-ll—t-n's self hath averr'd
Thou art yet but half sabred and hung,
And I lov'd him the more when I heard
Such tenderness fall from his tongue.[11]

But he could also pause to be droll, as in his picture of Lord Anglesea riding two horses (Protestant and Catholic) at once, or his "Ode to the Woods and Forests by One of the Board" (a notorious refuge for place-hunters):

Let other bards to groves repair,
Where linnets strain their tuneful throats,
Mine be the Woods and Forests, where
The Treasury pours its sweeter *notes*.

.   .   .   .   .

Long may ye flourish, sylvan haunts,
Beneath whose *'branches* of expense'
Our gracious K—g gets all he wants,—
Except a little taste and sense.

Long, in your golden shade reclin'd,
Like him of fair Armida's bowers,
May W-ll———n some *wood*-nymph find,
To cheer his dozenth lustrum's hours;

To rest from toil the Great Untaught,
And soothe the pangs his warlike brain
Must suffer, when, unus'd to thought,
It tries to think, and—tries in vain.

There were others who wondered whether the Hero of Waterloo, at the age of fifty-eight, was likely to think. When in June, 1828, Moore cumulated his satires as *Odes upon Cash, Corn, Catholics, and Other Matters*, the question, so far as Moore was concerned, was still an open one.

III

In the midst of these alarms and excursions the tireless poet continued to pour forth collections of songs—the fifth and sixth numbers of *National Airs* (1826, 1827); *Evenings in Greece* (1826); *A Set of Glees* (1827); and *Legendary Ballads* (1828), for all of which the amiable Bishop supplied music like weak tea. *Evenings in Greece*, which, capitalizing the interest in the Greek revolution, connects "a series of songs by a thread of poetical narrative," is the most pretentious of these productions, which were all respectfully received and which have been enthusiastically forgotten. To turn over their yellowing pages is to summon up the ghosts of a vanished world—when the overture to *A Midsummer Night's Dream* was new and exciting and Mendelssohn was paying the first of his ten visits to England; when Spohr conducted in London; when Mrs. Gore (Disraeli's "full-blown rose") was a fashionable novelist; when Vivian Grey was exclaiming "O London dinners! empty artificial nothings!" and his tailor was informing young Mr. Pelham that "we must live for effect in this world"; when Miss Barrett, not yet imprisoned in Wimpole Street, was studying Latin and Greek, and the young Mr. Tennysons, to their quiet astonishment, made a profit of twenty pounds from *Poems by Two Brothers;* when the future William IV was quarreling in the admiralty and the future Queen Victoria was a child of ten. Alas! it is to be feared that both words and music are the sort which especially appealed to Richard Swiveller!

> The moon is in the heavens above,
>   And the wind is on the foaming sea—
> Thus shines the star of woman's love,

we read, just as we read of "woman's blush, to woman's
look," of "violets, transform'd to eyes," which "inshrin'd a
soul within their blue." The queer combination of sentiment
and pedantry, of rhetoric and naïveté in these period pieces!

> Farewell—what a dream thy suspicion hath broken!
> Thus ever Affection's fond vision is crost;
> Dissolv'd are her spells, when a doubt is but spoken,
> And love, once distrusted, for ever is lost!

Shoals of songsters breathed out such lines over the piano; a
sigh and a smile came to whiskered lips as, leaning noncha-
lantly over the music rack, the contemporaries of Captain
Dobbin sought to catch the eye of pre-Victorian maidenhood
coyly intent on the melodies of Moore. Tommy was not a
great poet; but it is something if, nearing fifty, he could still
supply the ballads to express the vague nostalgia of love's
young dream.

And he published in 1827 that curious offering to oblivion,
his solitary novel, *The Epicurean*, a book which led the
Ladies' Monthly Museum to exclaim that he was "an acknowledged master of the passions," the beauties of which
seemed to the *Lady's Magazine* "numerous and striking," a
tale which drew a stately reproof from the *Christian Examiner*, that dull magazine discovering in it, however, a
"glimmering of a purer light." The *Westminster Review*
found it worth thirty-three solid pages of print and rebuked
him:

. . . when he steps out of his way into the garden of Epicurus,
and commits havoc among the roses . . . he must be treated like
a mischievous boy in a flower-garden, and turned back into the
fields where he has been accustomed to pick nosegays with
impunity.[12]

The mischievous boy, who was forty-eight when the book
appeared, took his drubbing calmly enough; Lord Strangford told him *The Epicurean* was "the most delicious piece
of prose that had ever been written," and Lady Lansdowne

was late in coming down to receive her guests in order to read the volume to the end. The *Westminster* article, though he seems not to have known it, was by Thomas Love Peacock and was a severe indictment of Moore's classical learning, the one dilettante informing his fellow that the author of *The Epicurean* was ignorant of the philosophy of Epicurus.

Moore's novel, which enjoyed the dignity of being illustrated by no less a personage than J. M. W. Turner in 1839, and of being re-issued in 1900, when the popularity of Rider Haggard's *She* created a controversy as to whether or not it was partly plagiarized from Moore, is an unread, but by no means unreadable, philosophic romance. As both a first draft of the book and the completed manuscript exist to prove,[13] he read enormously for the work, the inception of which goes back to his Paris days when he was dreaming of a poetical narrative, *Alciphron*, the fragments of which form the appendix to the 1839 edition of the novel.[14] A young priest or hierophant of the Epicurean sect in the third century, A.D., is told in a dream to go to Egypt, there to learn the secret of immortality. Arrived in Alexandria, he is instantly drawn to a young priestess of Egypt, Alethe, whom he follows through a series of marvelous happenings which require in the reader a willing suspension of disbelief, and which lead him into the midst of the Egyptian mysteries. They escape to the Nile together by means of a curious anticipation of a modern roller-coaster; on a boat in that river Alciphron learns that Alethe is secretly a Christian. Her he delivers to the monks of the Thebaïd, where he is himself converted to Christianity, but in the persecutions under Valerian, Alethe dies the death of a martyr. We learn in a postscript that Alciphron suffered a similar end a little later. The fragmentary poem, "Alciphron," tells the same narrative as that found in the first third of the novel; Moore added to this a letter from the high priest of Memphis exulting in the triumph of paganism and bigotry.

If the world has lost little by ignoring *The Epicurean*, critics of Moore have erred greatly by not giving serious consideration to this religious romance.   Christianity, it is true, formally triumphs, but an important section of the book is devoted to the exposure of priestly wiles, and this portion, taken together with the rhymed letter of the high priest of Memphis which Moore wrote especially for the 1839 "Alciphron," has more than antiquarian significance. When we read how

> the Priest, set aptly within reach
> Of two rich worlds, traffics for bliss with each,

and hear Orcus exclaim:

> Did I not keep still proudly in my mind
> The power this priestcraft gives me o'er mankind,—
> A lever, of more might, in skilful hand,
> To move this world, than Archimede e'er plann'd,

we are irresistibly reminded of that earlier satire, "Intolerance."   Moore was no formalist.   If he fought Protestant bigotry in the name of Catholic Emancipation, he denounced Catholic bigotry in the name of humanity.   Fascinated by his reading in neo-Platonism, his exploration of a vast literature on the religious cults of the East, he translated Catholicism into that same vague and troubling poetry which infuses the prose of Chateaubriand.   There is a touch of Voltaire in Moore; but there is more than a touch of the *Génie du christianisme*—not that Moore was directly influenced by the eloquent Frenchman, but that, like other poetical believers of his age, he took flight into verbalism and sonorous general nouns.

Chapter XIII

W HEN at length the imperturbable Wellington forced Catholic Emancipation through the reluctant House of Lords, Thomas Moore was within a few days of being fifty years old. He was already the victim of his own legend, and those who described him in this decade of his busy life were determined to see in him the epicurean and the *flâneur* and to ignore the serious writer and the student. Thus Gerald Griffin, the Irish novelist, driving through the rain to Sloperton in November, 1832, on a serious political mission, pictures "the nightingale in his cage" on the second floor of the cottage:

a table before him covered with books and papers, a drawer half opened and stuffed with letters, a piano also open at a little distance; and the thief himself, a little man, but full of spirits, with eyes, hands, feet, and frame for ever in motion, looking as if it would be a feat for him to sit for three minutes quiet in his chair . . . a neat-made little fellow, tidily buttoned up, young as fifteen at heart, though with hair that reminded me of 'Alps in the sunset;' not handsome . . . finished as an actor, but without an actor's affectation; easy as a gentleman, but without *some* gentlemen's formality . . . a hospitable, warm-hearted Irishman, as pleasant as could be himself, and disposed to make others so.

The gilded and gossipy Willis met him at Lady Blessington's in 1834, and in a report full of misinformation and zeal somehow managed to give an indelible portrait of the man:

"Mr. Moore!" cried the footman at the bottom of the staircase, "Mr. Moore!" cried the footman at the top. And with his glass

at his eye, stumbling over an ottoman between his near-sighted-
ness and the darkness of the room, enter the poet. . . . Sliding
his little feet up to Lady Blessington (of whom he was a lover
when she was sixteen, and to whom some of the sweetest of his
songs were written [!]), he made his compliments, with a gayety
and an ease combined with a kind of worshipping deference,
that was worthy of a prime-minister at the court of love. With
the gentlemen, all of whom he knew, he had the frank merry
manner of a confident favorite, and he was greeted like one.
He went from one to the other, straining back his head to look
up at them. . . .

Moore's head is distinctly before me while I write, but I shall
find it difficult to describe. His hair, which curled once all over
it in long tendrils . . . is diminished now to a few curls sprinkled with gray, and scattered in a single ring above his ears.
His forehead is wrinkled, with the exception of a most prominent development of the organ of gayety, which, singularly
enough, shines with the lustre and smooth polish of a pearl, and
is surrounded by a semicircle of lines drawn close about it, like
entrenchments against Time.* His eyes still sparkle like a cham-
paign bubble, though the invader has drawn his pencillings about
the corners; and there is a kind of wintry red, of the tinge of
an October leaf, that seems enamelled on his cheek, the eloquent
record of the claret his wit has brightened. His mouth is the
most characteristic feature of all. The lips are delicately cut,
slight and changeable as an aspen; but there is a set-up look about
the lower lip, a determination of the muscle to a particular expression. . . . It is written legibly with the imprint of habitual
success. . . . The slightly-tossed nose confirms the fun of the
expression, and altogether it is a face that sparkles, beams, radi-
ates,—everything but *feels.*

What the palpitating Willis meant by denying feeling to
Moore's mobile countenance remains an impenetrable mystery, but he adds a description of Moore at the piano which,
for all its sensibility, is a valuable record:

. . . I have no time to describe his singing. It is well known,
however, that its effect is only equalled by the beauty of his

---

* On phrenological charts the "organ of mirthfulness" is situated in the
temporal region just above, and a little back of, the eye.

own words. . . . He makes no attempt at music. It is a kind
of admirable recitative, in which every shade of thought is
syllabled and dwelt upon, and the sentiment of the song goes
through your blood, warming you to the very eyelids, and starting your tears, if you have soul or sense in you. . . . We all sat
around the piano, and after two or three songs of Lady Blessington's choice, he rambled over the keys awhile, and sang "When
first I met thee," with a pathos that beggars description. When
the last word had faltered out, he rose, and took Lady Blessington's hand, said good-night, and was gone before a word was
uttered. For a full minute after he had closed the door, no
one spoke.

They wept more readily in the tender thirties; Willis records
admiringly that women sometimes fainted when Moore sang;
but there is other testimony to the peculiar power of his performances at the piano.[1]

The Moore whom Griffin and Willis describe is, of course,
what may be called the public Moore—the legendary poet,
who would not down. He might, and did, devote the last
twenty-five years of his laborious life to exhausting work as a
biographer and a historian, but, however highly a limited
group might rate his remarkable talents as a scholar, the
world insisted on looking at him as the pet of drawingrooms,
and as (in Shelley's phrase) the sweetest singer of Ireland's
saddest wrong. The world was partly right, but the adulation which he received was the foolish product of an age of
sensibility, and when he records it in his diary, it is usually
with a canny sense of the real value of such tributes. A lady
in Birmingham wrote him that her heart was an Æolian lute
and rather hinted that he was expected to blow on it. He
shook hands with an anonymous miss one evening, who instantly wrapped her hand in a shawl, saying that no one else
should touch it that night. A Mrs. Cooper preserved the
"Pens with which Mr. Moore wrote Lalla Rookh," together
with a bit of one of his old torn gloves. A note was delivered to his hotel in Cheltenham addressed "To the immortal Thomas Moore, Esq.," upon which Moore's comment

is: "only think of an immortal *esquire;* expected to hear the chambermaids cry out 'Some hot water for the immortal gentleman in No. 18.' "

Behind the scenes, however, a rather sad little gentleman of fifty was anxiously trying to make both ends meet, worrying over the health of a family, no member of which was strong. In the midst of his incessant journeys to collect materials for the life of Byron, he was torn with anxiety over the health of Anastasia, who was fourteen in 1827, who had been away at school, and whose health, now that she was home, was giving her parents increasing concern. In June of that year the news came that Bessy's sister, Anne, was seriously ill in Edinburgh; her death on the twenty-eighth deeply affected Mrs. Moore. To the health and happiness of "dear, excellent Bessy" the devoted husband and harassed author was compelled to devote an increasing amount of time. Anastasia continued to fail, an attack of the measles in November being followed by complications; by the beginning of 1829, it was evident that she was doomed, and on Sunday, the eighth of March, she died. There are no more moving pages in Moore's journal than those which, in dramatic contrast to the glittering London records of most of the diary, tell the story of the poet's agony at the loss of his daughter:

Next morning (Sunday, 8th) I rose early, and on approaching the room, heard the dear child's voice as strong, I thought, as usual; but, on entering, I saw death plainly in her face. When I asked her how she had slept, she said, 'Pretty well,' in her usual courteous manner; but her voice had a sort of hollow and distant softness not to be described. When I took her hand on leaving her, she said (I thought significantly), 'Good bye, papa.' I will not attempt to tell what I felt at all this. I went occasionally to listen at the door of the room, but did not go in, as Bessy, knowing what an effect (through my whole future life) such a scene would have upon me, implored me not to be present at it. Thus passed the first of the morning. About eleven o'clock (as Bessy told me afterwards) the poor child, with an appearance rather of wandering in her mind, said, somewhat wildly, 'I

shall die, I shall die;' to which her mamma answered, 'We pray
to God continually for you, my dear Anastasia, and I am sure
God must love you, for you have been always a good girl.'
'Have I?' she said; 'I thought I was a very naughty girl; but I
am glad to hear *you* say that I have been good; for others would
perhaps say it out of compliment, but you know me, and must
therefore think so, or you would not say it.' 'But every body
thinks the same, my love. All your young friends love you.
Lady Lansdowne thinks you a very good girl.' 'Does she,
mummy?' said the dear child; and then added, 'Do you think I
shall go to Lady Lansdowne's party this year?' I don't know
what poor Bessy answered to this. In about three quarters of
an hour or less she called for me, and I came and took her hand
for a few seconds, during which Bessy leaned down her head
between the poor dying child and me, that I might not see her
countenance. As I left the room, too, agonised as her own mind
was, my sweet, thoughtful Bessy ran anxiously after me, and
giving me a smelling-bottle, exclaimed, 'For God's sake don't
you get ill.' In about a quarter of an hour afterwards she came
to me, and I saw that all was over. I could no longer restrain
myself; the feelings I had been so long suppressing found vent,
and a fit of loud violent sobbing seized me, in which I felt as
if my chest was coming asunder. The last words of my dear
child were 'Papa, papa.' Her mother had said, 'My dear, I think
I could place you more comfortably; shall I?' to which she
answered, 'Yes,' and Bessy placing her hand under her back,
gently raised her. That moment was her last. She exclaimed
suddenly, 'I am dying, I am dying, Papa! papa!' and expired.

The grief-stricken mother insisted on performing all the last
sad offices herself; and the last touch of pathos is added when
one reads that she found somewhere a bunch of cowslips to
place on the dead girl's breast. Moore wisely insisted that
on the morning of the funeral, a chaise should come to take
Bessy and himself out of the way of the ceremony; and the
"prime-minister at the court of love" and his beautiful wife
drove aimlessly for two dreadful hours over the rolling Wiltshire hills, green and beautiful with spring, while their
daughter was buried in Bromham churchyard. "Such," wrote
the father sadly, "such is the end of many years of fondness

and hope; and nothing is now left us but the dream . . ." If he shrank then, as always, from the physical phenomenon of death, he faced the future with calm and quiet courage.

II

It was in the midst of the long sorrow culminating in this catastrophe that he labored on his *Life of Byron.* "Biography," as he wrote Rogers, "is like dot engraving, made up of little minute points, which must all be attended to, or the effect is lost." The inception of the work was clouded with difficulties, the appearance of such books of gossip as Medwin's unreliable *Journal of the Conversations of Lord Byron* immediately after the poet's death having disgusted such staunch friends as Hobhouse; whereas Hunt's *Lord Byron and some of his Contemporaries* in 1828 disgusted Kinnaird.[2] Even after the reconciliation between Moore and Murray took place, the publisher was uncertain about his own plans, and at one time it appeared that the Longmans might bring out the book. In February, 1828, however, the last difficulties vanished; Murray agreed to pay Moore four thousand guineas for the work, and a contract was signed which permitted the anxious poet once more to juggle his debts. In the midst of everything else Tom decided to rebuild Sloperton, which meant that for the greater part of 1829 the Moores camped out in the homes which various friends placed at their disposal; and, as a matter of fact, a large portion of the first volume was written at Richmond. The poet was still in technical possession of his unlucky Bermuda post —an office which he tried vainly to get Croker to dispose of for him; and he was also contributing to the *Edinburgh Review,* as well as writing squibs for the *Times* and songs for Power. He could not go to London to look up materials without being involved in an endless social round; and he was also full of anxiety about the Reform Bill, which followed hard on the heels of Catholic Emancipation.

Moore's tact won Hobhouse over, if he did not altogether

soften Kinnaird; [3] and in search of the "little minute points which must all be attended to, or the effect is lost," he began diligent journeys about England to visit the places associated with Byron and to interview those who had known him.   Mary Shelley, with whom he sometimes breakfasted in London, proved unexpectedly helpful, giving him a great bundle of letters and entering upon a long correspondence. He went to Harrow and looked at the tomb where Byron had liked to sit, and at the books Byron had given the library. He talked to Drury, Dr. Butler, and Dr. Glennie about Byron's youth.   On his visit to Newstead, where Colonel Wildman was kind, he went out of his way to visit Donington Park and Kegworth.   Studying Byron's youth, he found the memories of his own returning upon him.   At Donington Park, everything looked so familiar—the breakfast room, the old clock, the pictures, even the letter boxes!   Thirty years had gone by since "I felt myself so grand at being the inmate of such a great house."   "*Oh curas hominum!*" he exclaimed.   "Poor Lord Hastings!"   How much *had* changed since that time!   At Kegworth he went to see the old house where he and Bessy had lived in 1812.   Then he went to Mayfield to walk in the orchard where he had "paced along" in writing *Lalla Rookh.*   He remembered the gay suppers and the play-reading, and he visited the lonely grave of his little daughter, Olivia.   It was, on the whole, a sorrowful pilgrimage; at Hucknall, where Byron was buried, as Moore stood over the vault, "the picture of what he *had* been, and what he was *now*, presented itself to me, and at once a sort of flood of melancholy feeling came over my heart, which it was with difficulty I could conceal from those around me." And once, in London, he went to his old lodgings in Bury Street, where he had been ill for eight weeks and almost died, and where the beautiful Duchess of St. Albans had amazingly visited him.   It was all so long ago!

The letters, the anecdotes, the reminiscences poured in upon him—from Mrs. Musters, who cried when he sang to her;

from "Gentleman John" Jackson, the pugilist, who proudly remembered that "nobody could be more fearless" than Byron; from Lord Sligo, who told him about *The Giaour;* from Harness, and Lord Holland, and all the rest. There was so much to tell, so much to organize; and always in the background there were the silent figure of Lady Byron and the enigmatic person of Augusta, whom he had met in 1825. It was not until November, 1827, that he resolved upon the nature of the work—"letters and journals" rather than a formal biography; not until March, 1828, that he could make his "first regular start" at composition, with poor Anastasia installed in the library. After her death he threw himself into his task to forget; though, for weeks after, when he tried to sing, either at home or in the house of a friend, he was seized with violent fits of sobbing, the reaction from which sadly interfered with his writing. His nervous habits certainly grew no less; he was unable to work in his familiar room at Bowood, because, as he wrote Lord Lansdowne, "I am in the habit of pacing about all day while at work." [4]   At Richmond he finished the manuscript of the first volume on August 14, 1829; four days later, the printer had all the copy. Through the rainy summer and disagreeable autumn he toiled over the proofs, alarmed by the illness of young Tom, who had been put in the Charterhouse School and who came home "pale as death," and distracted by the changes at Sloperton. At the close of the year he learned that his dear friend, Lady Donegal, had died. Late in December he crawled over the miserable roads to London to look at the final revises—on the return journey he almost lost his life as the coach left the road on Marlborough Downs in a blinding snowstorm—and on January 16, 1830, he received a copy of the printed volume (the book was officially issued on January 18). He was cheered during the next week by "loads of letters" and "most flaming eulogies" of what he had done.

Augusta Leigh, who, Moore wrote Murray, "*is* a very odd person," [5] was silent; but Lady Byron now informed the world in a pamphlet that "Mr. Moore has promulgated his own impressions of private events in which I was most nearly concerned, as if he possessed a competent knowledge of the subject," though how, in view of her refusal of all information, the biographer was to proceed otherwise is left for the admiration of posterity. Blandly resolved to include Lady Byron's remarks in the appendix to the second volume, Moore worked steadily on amidst the storm of discussion which the first part brought forth. To Murray's tactful censorship he submitted,[6] but nothing which appeared in the reviews seems to have materially affected part two. He refused an opportunity to write the biography of Canning, though he began his life of Lord Edward Fitzgerald before the *Byron* was complete. During the spring of 1830 he was much troubled by his private griefs—Tom's health, his mother's weakness, and Bessy's sorrowful face (she was "looking sadly ill" in April), but he labored cheerfully, fortified by the admiration of Sydney Smith among others—"the first book of mine (or indeed any one else's) I ever heard him give a good word to." When George IV died on June 26, composition was mainly concluded, so that he departed for a triumphant visit to Ireland in August—after writing a "thing" for Power called *The Summer Fête* (1831)—with a lighter heart. The concluding volume appeared early in January, 1831, and with it Moore enrolled himself among the great English biographers.

For, despite the incessant controversies of the Byron scholars, Moore's life remains one of the four or five great literary biographies in the English language. In a letter to Murray of August 6, 1830, Moore thanked that publisher for his "kindness, courtesy and tractableness," and spoke of the work as "a task trying enough to the temper & courage of us both, and surrounded both by risk & difficulty."[7] In truth, the estimate is a fair one. To have written the life of the most discussed personality in England, and to have written it so well that all subsequent biographers have had to return to its estimate; to have moved tactfully among the

thorny problems of Byron's career, among his friends with
their frequently clashing views, and among his family with
their reticences and their hostilities; to have discussed with
reasonable accuracy the political and social problems, both
national and international, which the tracing of Byron's career
involved; and to have left on the reader after almost fifteen
hundred pages of print an indelible impression of so complex a being—this, in sum, is Moore's unforgettable achievement.   The excellence of the accomplishment is curiously
proved by the remarks which Hobhouse, who never warmed
to Moore, grudgingly wrote down in his diary: "I find Moore
has managed with much adroitness to make such mention of
me as I can hardly quarrel with even, although the general
result is rather unsatisfactory than otherwise.   As to Byron's
character, he has, on the whole, portrayed it fairly."   And
again, with reference to the second volume, "it presents a
tolerably fair picture of Lord Byron's real character, and
some of Moore's observations are exceedingly just and conveyed in appropriate language."   It is true that, unlike Moore,
Hobhouse denied that the biography would raise Byron "in
public estimation as a man of talent," [8] but Hobhouse's cold
admission that Moore had fairly portrayed Byron's character
is worth more as a testimonial to the book than a dozen discussions by those who had never known Byron in the flesh.

Like other great nineteenth-century biographies—Lockhart's *Scott* and Forster's *Dickens* are cases in point—Moore's
Byron has required, and received, correction in the century
which has elapsed since it appeared.   This is inevitable; but
it does not mean that the small triumphs of subsequent in-
vestigators in pointing out Moore's errors invalidate the book
as a whole.   That he took a sympathetic view of Byron and
tended to exculpate or soften certain episodes which later
biographers have condemned is natural and necessary—had he
not been *en rapport* with his subject he would not have written a great book.   Probably the two most serious defects in
the study are Moore's failure in handling the problem of

Byron's relations to his half-sister, and his failure in what today we consider elementary editorial honesty. As to the first of these, it is to be observed that Moore had only rumor to go on and that it was wildly impossible for him to discuss what Lord Lovelace's *Astarte* did not reveal until decades later. His book would have been suppressed, had he attempted it. As to the second, there is no doubt that Moore is culpable. Lord Ernle, who, as Rowland E. Prothero, edited the *Letters and Journals* a century later, sums up the matter when he says: ". . . as Byron's letters became more bitter in tone, and his criticisms of his contemporaries more outspoken, Moore felt himself more justified in omitting passages which referred to persons who were still living in 1830. From 1816 onwards, it will be found that he has transferred passages from one letter to another, or printed two letters as one, and *vice versâ*, or made such large omissions as to shorten letters, in some instances, by a third or even a half." But, as we have already seen, there is no use in judging the editorial standards of Moore's generation by the editorial standards of our own, and Moore simply did the best he could. More regrettable is the fact that he seems to have destroyed, not only Byron's letters to Moore, but also many letters entrusted to him by others.[9] In this respect he is, judged by any standards, deeply to blame.

But when all is said, the fact remains that Byron lives and moves and has his faulty being in Moore's pages in so vivid a manner that the discussion of that fascinating personality has ever since followed the lines (in the main) which the biographer laid down. Moore's triumph is owing principally to three considerations. In the first place, it is evident that the book is written *con amore;* that Moore, though he loved Byron, was fortunately sufficiently remote from him to achieve something like objectivity, yet sufficiently close to him to write sympathetically. In the second place, Moore's prose is, for once, lucent and easy; gone are the similes, the rococo decoration, the false oratorical style; as a consequence,

we look *through* the style, and not *at* it.   And in the third
place, by adopting the "letters and journal" method Moore
sacrificed the vanity of authorship to a triumph of art.
Tommy was vain enough in small ways; but he was in this
instance wise and humble enough to realize that no one could
speak for Byron as Byron could speak for himself.   The result is that, almost everywhere in the book, we feel we are in
contact with one of the most vital and electric spirits in the
whole range of English literature.   Moore does this so easily
that we are not conscious of his extraordinary management
of the materials at his command; but to turn from Moore to
the pages of Galt or Medwin or Parry or other small fry who
were so conscious of their importance in talking to Byron
that they will not let Byron talk for himself without their
constant interference is to realize the sagacity and the ingenuity of Moore.   He could so easily have "done" Byron
as he had "done" Sheridan, and the result would have been
disaster!   But he did not, and the result was the one book
by which Moore really lives today.

III

Of the innumerable articles, most of them controversial,
occasioned by Moore's biography, it is difficult to give an
orderly account.   For one reason, some critics noticed the
first volume at length and ignored the second; and some made
the publication of the second the excuse for a long article on
Moore or Byron or both.   Some re-opened the Byron controversy; some went off on a tangent respecting Moore's
career; and the partisans of Lady Byron further confused the
simple issue of the merits of the work.   The book almost immediately took on the proportions of a national event, the
Morning Chronicle printing long extracts for three successive
days in January, 1830, and the *Times* remarking that the
fidelity and accuracy of the study "admit of no dispute."
Minor periodicals like the *Literary Gazette*, the *Lady's Magazine*, and the *Ladies' Museum* were generally fulsome, but the

major periodicals varied according to the prejudice of the writer and the policy of the magazine. The importance of Macaulay's famous essay in the *Edinburgh,* whatever its limitations, is twofold: it represented the judgment of the rising generation, and it stuck to the point of estimating the work as a literary production. *Blackwoods,* oddly enough, was rather lyrical. The *Monthly Review* paid tribute to the "independent and historical spirit" of the biographer. An early notice in the *Monthly Magazine* found the book "amusing" and said that, except for the "one grand merit of impartiality, the biographer may claim universal praise. He let out the *facts,* be they what they will, and run a muck at whom they may." [10]

The *Westminster Review,* on the other hand, read Moore a lesson in university education *à propos* of Byron's career at Cambridge, told him never to philosophize, and was sanctimonious about religion. It then descended from this lofty point to charge that Moore had scraped an acquaintance with Byron, said that he was hiding behind the curtains of the *Edinburgh Review,* remarked the "farcical nature" of his politics, and charged him with being unable to produce a figure of speech that would "stand analysis." The virtuous glow with which the article concludes illustrates Macaulay's phrase about seven-year fits of morality: it was, it seems, the duty of this magazine to show the

real scope and purpose of a series of shallow sophisms and false assumptions wrapped up in bundles of metaphors, put forth with a specious semblance of reason and liberality, and directed to the single end of upholding all abuses and delusions by which the aristocracy profit.

With the snarling remark that it was impossible for Moore to do justice to either the dead or the living, this precious piece of criticism closed. [11]

Even more extraordinary was the performance of Thomas Campbell in the *New Monthly Magazine.* He had had a letter from Lady Byron, a woman unfortunate in her de-

fenders; and in an enormous spate of words he informed the
astonished public that she was a much injured woman (which
she undoubtedly was); he published her letter (which he had
no authority to do); and he got himself into a hopeless tangle
between saying that Mr. Moore was his friend, a gentleman
of the highest delicacy, and thanking heaven that *he* did not
have to answer for "the tact of Mr. Moore's conduct in this
affair"—such as "dishing up the inconsistencies of Lord
Byron" on the subject of his wife and showing a "gallant indifference" to Lady Byron's acquittal. The general tone of
his article was that he could tell more if he chose (which he
could not), and that Moore had known more than he had said
(which it is doubtful that he did). This was in Volume
XXVIII. But in Volume XXX the magazine returned to the
biography in a short article which remarked that half a dozen
sentences would scarcely do to express its admiration of
Byron's genius and its warm feeling for the "brilliant talents
of his no less distinguished friend," and which concluded with
a letter from Campbell to Moore expressing the warmest
affection for both Moore and Byron. "Ah! my dear Moore,
if we had him but back again, how easily could we settle
these matters!" This strange epistle is dated February 18,
1830! [12] But in 1831, reviewing the second volume, the *New
Monthly* left poor Tommy with scarcely a rag to cover his
nakedness. He had "belied . . . the great expectation of his
work"; by including Byron's petulant expressions and degrading acts, his sneers and his intrigues, he had roused resent-
ment; and "if we wish to array every moral principle of the
reader against a hero, what better method of doing it, than
by dwelling upon his most vicious actions? and assuming that
pseudo-tone of apology, which only revolts the sense of right
it affects to blind?" "Who cares," it inquires with an air of
learning, "when Byron took salts?" It charged that all this
was a mask Moore put on "to hide his envy" and his fear and
dislike of Byron. What is so shameful, it said, as the semblance of friendship and the reality of hate? The article con-

cludes in a growing crescendo of hatred for Moore unexampled in reviews of his work:

We would ask Mr. Moore what is the perfidy, what the effrontery of that man, who, even while he is bartering for gold the confidential letters of his deceased friend [i.e., letters not intended for the public] yet dares to withhold the MS. entrusted to his charge for the sole and positive purpose of being laid open to the world?

The review represents the burning of the memoirs as malicious chicanery, talks of Moore's "invidious and masked battery," represents Byron as uniformly generous and Moore as uniformly deceitful, and comes down heavily on "the base spirit which, for grain or for grudge, violates the confidence and degrades the memory of the dead." [13] Small wonder that Moore wrote Murray: "if there should be any very choice *praise* of us, I should like to have it—but the abuse may always stay where it is." [14]

That queer publication, the *National Omnibus,* saluted the second volume with an amusing parody of "John Gilpin," the best stanzas of which run:

> I really am not worth a damn,
>   As all the world doth know,
> But if Lord Byron says I am,
>   Why, then, it must be so
>
>   .   .   .   .   .   .
>
> Tom Little shook him by the hand,
>   O'erjoyed was he to find,
> That when he went, he meant to leave
>   His manuscript behind.
>
> The morning came—the Poet went,
>   And when his life was o'er,
> The tale of all his wicked loves
>   Was left with Thommy More.

The *Critic* said it had not often read a book "so unworthy of public patronage," and remarked that Moore being the son of a tradesman, "for sharpness in business, and extract-

ing emolument for a good-for-nothing work does honour to
his birth." But the *Quarterly* was unexpectedly amiable,
finding the work superior to *Sheridan* and paying tribute to
Moore's "modesty, candour, and manliness." It could not,
however, forego the pleasure of an ironic dig at its great
rival:

Mr. Moore 'walks delicately,' like Agag, when the course of his
narrative brings him to the truculent critique on these boyish
essays which appeared in the *Edinburgh Review*. Himself a distinguished victim and prop of that journal, he writes elegantly
and eloquently on the subject, and contrives to drop no hint of
what every human being felt at the time to be the simple truth
of the whole matter—to wit, that out of the thousand and one
volumes of indifferent verse . . . printed . . . in 1807, only one
bore a noble name on the title-page.[15]

Such was literary criticism when William IV was king.
Moore's mild revenge was to send a squib to Murray on the
faithlessness of editorial friends:

> No—editors don't care a button
>   What false and faithless things they do;
> They'll let you come and cut their mutton,
>   And then they'll have a *cut* at *you*.
> With Barnes I oft my dinner took,
>   Nay, met ev'n Horace Twiss, to please him!
> Yet, Mister Barnes traduc'd my Book,
>   For which may his own devils seize him!
> With Doctor Bowring I drank tea,
>   Nor of his cakes consum'd a particle,
> And yet, th' ungrateful L.L.D.
>   Let fly at me, next week, an article!
> To sup with Wilson was my lot,
>   Mong bards of fame, like Hogg and Packwood;
> A dose of black-strap then I got,
>   And next a dose, still worse, of Blackwood.[16]

·   ·   ·   ·   ·   ·   ·

IV

He was not quite through with Byron, however, for
Murray entered into correspondence and argument with him

to edit Byron's works. The edition in seventeen little pocket
volumes, published from 1832 to 1833/34, which may still
be picked up in second-hand bookstores, and which is often
referred to as Moore's edition, is the one in question; but,
though the biography occupies the first six volumes of the
set, Moore declined to be responsible for the rest. There
was not a little wounded vanity in his refusal:

The fact is, I have been able to trace the progress of his [Mur-
ray's] mind all along through the changes of his advertisements.
Somebody having, most likely, told him (for he is always the
slave of his last adviser) that the "Life" was the most ticklish
part of the whole undertaking . . . he gave as little prominence
to this part of the book as possible; putting the "Works of Lord
Byron" in capitals at the head, and omitting my name in the
advertisements altogether: gradually, however, I saw the "Life"
and name taking a respectable station in the announcement; at
least my name was rather barefacedly put forward, as if I was
the editor of the whole; and latterly the heading of "Works of
Lord Byron" has been exchanged in some advertisements for
"Life, &c. &c., by Thomas Moore."

Having experienced "several kindnesses" at Murray's hands,
however, Moore sensibly declined in "a civil and indeed
friendly letter to him." [17]

In the meantime, Moore had involved himself in his third,
and last, biography, *The Life and Death of Lord Edward
Fitzgerald*, which the Longmans published in two volumes in
1831. In April, 1830, Henry de Ros had given Moore certain family papers, consisting, among other material, of some
interesting letters relating to the last moments of the unhappy
and star-crossed Irishman. Moore's fancy kindled; and with
the encouragement of Lord Holland and others he impetuously resolved to write the story of that short, romantic life.
He collected further materials in the summer; and on his trip
to Ireland late in August he interviewed those who had
known the rebellion of '98, including Major Sirr and the
Duke of Leinster. The latter, though the Major had killed

his uncle thirty-four years before, referred to that aging officer as "a good sort of man." Returning to Sloperton in
October, Moore began composition. A second trip to Dublin
brought him more material; and despite his complaint of his
own slowness, the writing proceeded with such rapidity that,
somewhat to the alarm of Lord Lansdowne and Lord John
Russell, to whom the prospect of an Irish work by their Irish
friend was, in the political situation of the day, alarming, the
work appeared in September.

Overshadowed as it was by the *Byron*, the *Life of Fitzgerald* attracted only a moderate degree of attention, though
it has remained the standard life of a minor figure. *Blackwoods* oddly complained that the volume lacked the "warmth
of the voluptuary, the pungency of the satirist, the fierceness
of sedition [and] the sting of treason," and charged Moore
with the crime of growing old without repentance. The
Quarterly more kindly said that the biographer had done
justice to Fitzgerald's "more agreeable side," but of course
complained that Moore seemed to defend rebellion. The un-
predictable *Westminster* liked the book—"the water-colour
and tinted hue of portraiture, which distinguishes the biographical efforts of Mr. Moore"—and thought the time had
come for old rancors to disappear. Most of the reviews accepted the work as interesting but not important.[18]

Moore's last biography is a clear, well-documented, and
straightforward account of a rash and high-minded youth,
full of the ardors of the French Revolution, who engaged in
an enterprise foredoomed to failure, and whose life, even
badly told, must awaken pity. He had to deal with a personality that was frank and simple; and, after the success of his
method in the *Byron*, he depended for a large measure of his
effect upon the presentation of letters and the accounts of
eye-witnesses. Besides being a biography, the work is a
political history of the years of Moore's own young manhood; the tone is everywhere dignified and sympathetic; and

the preface, in particular, pleads for a settlement of Irish wrongs by some more modern method than that of violence. It marks a revival of Moore's interest in the problem of reform in both kingdoms; and to this phase of his life it is now time to turn.

Chapter XIV

O_{N THE} night of June 25, 1830, the unlamented George IV went to his dubious reward, and early next morning Sir Henry Halford clattered on horseback through the empty streets of Windsor to inform the Duke of Clarence, otherwise known as "Silly Billy," that he was king. The new Queen burst into tears; the new King opened seven years of momentous change, sounding the note of low comedy which was to characterize his reign, by remarking, as he signed the declarations: "This is a damned bad pen you have given me." The next day being Sunday, the royal pair attended divine service, where they were preached at by the Rev. Augustus Fitzclarence, one of the ten left-hand offspring with whom Mrs. Jordan had blessed the sailor monarch. The sermon is darkly described as "suitable to the occasion."

In October the Iron Duke, on whom neither time nor change had the slightest perceptible effect, informed the gratified House of Lords that "if at the present moment I had imposed upon me the duty of forming a Legislature for any country . . . I do not mean to assert that I could form such a Legislature as we possess now, for the nature of man is incapable of reaching such excellence at once," and in November he resigned. The King shed tears; the patient and weary Grey, oddly compared by Lady Granville to "a spring morning," assumed office; British patriots threw stones at the Queen's carriage to indicate their approbation of reform; barns were burned in the midland counties and machinery destroyed in the factories; cholera and fear of a French war loomed large across the narrow seas in one direction, and O'Connell loomed quite as menacingly in the other. On the first of March Lord John Russell brought forth the Reform Bill in the Commons, and the long struggle was on, marked by such striking episodes as the breaking of Wellington's window-panes, the burning of Nottingham Castle in fact and of bishops in effigy, the complete rout of the Tories, and the final triumph of the bill. It was characteristic of the general confusion of everything that the Princess Victoria was conspicuously absent from the coronation, and that the King obstinately refused to live in the cold discomfort of Buckingham Palace, which stood, empty and new, Cipriani's painted ceiling looking down on nothing at all. When, in October, 1834, Parliament House burned to the ground, the new age was definitely severed from the old.

For Moore the Reform Bill was a leap into the dark which at once frightened and fascinated him. He saw that a change was inevitable, but "we are," he wrote, "hastening to the brink with a rapidity which, croaker as I have always been, I certainly did not anticipate." He thought the "cause of liberty" lost rather than gained under a Whig administration. Had reform come under the Tories,

it would have been dealt out with a reluctant hand, which would not have let it run so rapidly through the fingers as it is doing at present, when the government and the people are both on one side.

On the other hand, if he distrusted the reformers, he had faith in Lord Grey, Lord Lansdowne, and Lord John Russell. They were his friends—even Lord Grey, who had got young Tom into the Charterhouse School, and because of whom Moore refused to write the life of Canning. Canning had opposed Grey; and Moore could not reconcile "my high opinion of him, and my gratitude to him for much kindness" with a job of that sort. As for Lord Lansdowne and Lord John—what had they not done for him? They recognized his importance to them, as the fear they expressed that the publication of *Lord Edward Fitzgerald* might jeopardize reform by seeming to encourage Irish rebellion, exists to prove. And his power of ridicule was recognized by their enemies—"if the Tories had such a person as you on their side," a great lady told him, "we should be made to feel the difference."

But reform meant change in the old, comfortable world to which he clung more closely in proportion as it crumbled around him. Like Washington Irving, of whom he was seeing a good deal in these months, Moore was essentially an eighteenth-century gentleman; and he beheld the last remnants of the eighteenth century dissolving around him with infinite regret. "I agreed with the Whigs in the *principles* of the measure," he told Lord Lansdowne. "I also agreed with the Tories in their opinion as to its consequence." It was the dilemma of eighteenth-century liberalism. Once in the spring of 1831, dining with Rogers, he dogmatically expressed the opinion that "after all, it was in high life one met the best society"; to his amazement Rogers took the democratic view; but a year later Moore told Van Buren, the American minister, very much the same thing, two little gentlemen lamenting change together. Van Buren expressed "strong disgust at the perpetual struggle towards this higher region that was visible in those below it"; Moore argued that the "absence of this sort of ambitious effort . . . gave the upper classes so much more repose of manner, and made them accordingly so much better company." It was in this sense that he dearly loved a lord; it was also in this sense that he bitterly castigated those lords, spiritual and temporal, who were not worthy of their high station. If reform was to come, let it be given graciously. It was a mistake, he thought, for the high Tories to risk revolution rather than give up their rotten boroughs.

So he joined somewhat tepidly in the fight, preferring to attack the unworthy aristocrat rather than to support the aspiring bourgeoisie. He was merciless on Wellington, of whom he said: ". . . *all* Englishmen are Turks in grain, and the Duke of Wellington [is] the worst Turk of all." The Duke had opposed Catholic Emancipation and was now opposing Lord John Russell:

> Missing or lost, last Sunday night,
>   A Waterloo coin, whereon was trac'd
> The inscription, 'Courage!' in letters bright,
>   Though a little by rust of years defac'd,

he wrote when the Duke advised his majesty not to dine with the Lord Mayor for fear of the people. When a few of the great lords threatened to migrate to Paris if the bill was passed, he wrote a mock letter "From the Hon. Henry ——, to Lady Emma ——":

>   though you think, I dare say,
>   That 'tis debt or the Cholera drives me away,
>   'Pon honour you're wrong;—such a mere bagatelle
>   As a pestilence, nobody, now-a-days, fears;
>   And the fact is, my love, I'm thus bolting, pell-mell,
>   To get out of the way of these horrid new Peers;
>   This deluge of coronets, frightful to think of,
>   Which England is now, for her sins, on the brink of.[1]

If he knew the value of society, he knew also its shams, and sang them in *The Summer Fête* of 1831:

> That Fête to which the cull, the flower
> Of England's beauty, rank and power,
> From the young spinster just come *out*,
>   To the old Premier, too long *in*—
> From legs of far-descended gout,
>   To the last new-mustachio'd chin—
> All were convoked by Fashion's spells
> To the small circle where she dwells.

He could satirize the unintelligent reactionary who refused to light Grosvenor Square by gas:

That last impregnable redoubt,
   Where, guarded with Patrician care,
   Primeval Error still holds out—
Where never gleam of gas must dare
   'Gainst ancient Darkness to revolt,
Nor smooth Macadam hope to spare
   The dowagers one single jolt;—
Where, far too stately and sublime
To profit by the lights of time,
Let Intellect march how it will,
They stick to oil and watchmen still.

And he could also ridicule the unintelligent reactionary who
would not yield to any political reform whatsoever:

I pledge myself through thick and thin,
   To labour still, with zeal devout,
To get the Outs, poor devils, in,
   And turn the Ins, the wretches, out.

I pledge myself, though much bereft
   Of ways and means of ruling ill,
To make the most of what are left,
   And stick to all that's rotten still.

Though gone the days of place and pelf,
   And drones no more take all the honey,
I pledge myself to cram myself
   With all I can of public money;

To quarter on that social purse
   My nephews, nieces, sisters, brothers,
Nor, so *we* prosper, care a curse
   How much 'tis at the' expense of others.

I pledge myself, whenever Right
   And Might on any point divide,
Not to ask which is black or white,
   But take, at once, the strongest side.
   .   .   .   .   .

Betwixt the Corn-Lords and the Poor
   I've not the slightest hesitation,—
The people *must* be starv'd t'insure
   The Land its due remuneration.

I pledge myself to be no more
  With Ireland's wrongs bepros'd or shamm'd,—
I vote her grievances a *bore*,
  So she may suffer, and be d——d.

Or if she kick, let it console us,
  We still have plenty of red coats,
To cram the Church, that general bolus,
  Down any giv'n amount of throats.

.   .   .   .   .   .

So here's, with three times three hurrahs,
  A toast, of which you'll not complain,
'Long life to jobbing; may the days
  Of Peculation shine again!'

Such men it was who kept up the

                        puppet-show, call'd Parliament,
  Perform'd by wooden Ciceros,
  As large as life, who rose to prose,
  While, hid behind them, lords and squires,
  Who own'd the puppets, pull'd the wires;
  And thought it the very best device
  Of that most prosperous Paradise,
  To make the vulgar pay through the nose
  For them and their wooden Ciceros.[2]

He had not lost his old skill at trenchant satire.

II

His real interest, however, was not in rotten boroughs but
in Ireland. He wrote Lord Lansdowne as early as December,
1830:

As to my poor practical politics they are the same, God help
them, as they have been ever since I can remember them. At
the time of our Catholic triumph, I thought their task, like that
of the 'tricksy Ariel' was done & that I should have no more
occasion for them. These late events, however, in the world
have affected me, as they have other people, and have given a
new shake to the bottle which has brought up all the Irish spirit
(or sediment, if you please) again into ferment. The author of
the Green Flag & Captain Rock would prove himself to have

been but a firebrand of the moment *then* if he did not go on
burning a little *now*. The Union I always detested the very
thought of, and though I lament most deeply the introduction
of the question now, & under auspices that would disgrace a
far better cause, I never could bring myself so far to sanction
the principle, origin or mode of carrying that measure as to
oppose myself to any steps taken for its Repeal.[3]

It will be observed that Moore really disassociates himself
from any immediate measure advocating the repeal of the
legislative Union between Great Britain and Ireland, but to
understand the significance of his letter, as well as the drift
of his political satires in this decade of his life, it is necessary
to understand the political confusion of the times.

For the Reform Bill, instead of settling everything, seemed
to settle nothing; and under a king whose penchant for
rambling speeches drove his ministers frantic, the parties of
the old regime rocked back and forth in a haze so confusing
that Tory ministers brought in Whiggish bills, and Whig
majorities went to pieces over their own measures. Old alle-
giances were crumbling, new parties were being born, and
on the ministerial benches Melbourne and Grey, Peel and
Melbourne succeeded each other like figures in some insane
political kaleidoscope. Lord John made speeches; the Duke
briefly occupied the foreign office; young Mr. Disraeli, who
was not quite sure whether he was a Radical or a Tory, was
four times enthusiastically rejected by the reformed electorate
of various boroughs; and grave young Mr. Gladstone of the
"pale, expressive, intellectual face" entered Parliament as a
Tory, and presently devoted his serious leisure to studying
the lamentable state of the Church. Everything needed re-
forming, but nothing must be radically altered; and, whatever
measure was up—the emancipation of blacks in the colonies
or the remarkable inability of the poor to appreciate political
economy, the admission of Quakers to Parliament or the re-
distribution of episcopal revenues—the Irish problem, vague
and ominous, a cloud from which Daniel O'Connell dimly

thundered like a Celtic Jupiter, frightened the timid and appalled the brave. The Irish problem was, as usual, multiform, but its principal branches in King William's reign seemed to be two: O'Connell's vague threats to dissolve the legislative union, which took definite and disastrous form in the early forties, and the patent absurdity of the Irish Established Church. That remarkable monstrosity lived on tithes which were seldom paid for the benefit of congregations which, for the most part, did not exist; and it presently seemed quite clear to almost everybody except Bishop Phillpotts and his kind that it was no good taxing Irish Catholics, who refused to pay, for the benefit of a church they were doggedly determined to destroy.

Unfortunately for harmony, to strike at the revenues of the Church in Ireland was to call attention to the scandals of the Church in England, an organization chiefly remarkable for its ability to support an indefinite number of younger sons and its inability to do anything very helpful in the way of spiritual consolation. "The Church," as Dr. Arnold gravely remarked at Rugby, "the Church as it now stands no human power can save." He overlooked, however, the potentialities of Oxford, where Mr. Keble preached on national apostasy *à propos* of a bill to abolish certain useless Irish dioceses, and young Mr. Newman unprophetically set foot on the road which, as the slow years drifted by, was to lead to Rome. The Oxford movement began by denying the right of the government to abolish any diocese whatever, which added strength to those who opposed the reformation of the Irish Church; and it ended by an alarming drift to Catholicism, which led pious Protestants into violent denunciations of the Pope. The excitement mounted in 1837 to such a degree that the cry of "the Church in danger" shook the land. Not for two centuries had religious controversy been so venomous or so entangled in politics.

Next to Daniel O'Connell Moore was possibly the best known and most popular figure in Ireland, as that uncrowned king found it tactful to recognize at a meeting of the Dublin Political Union on November 24, 1832, when he said:

I attribute much of the present state of feeling, and the desire for liberty in Ireland to the works of that immortal man—he has brought patriotism into the private circles of domestic life.[4]

Enthusiasts like John Henry Keane spilled the lavender water of rhetoric over their pages in mentioning his name:

[Ireland] dwells with natural tenderness on [the name] of her poet; of him who sings so sweetly of her former glories, who decks her out in all the luxuriance of a fond imagination, and who shows her to her sons as she was and as she ought to be; she blesses his glories, she acknowledges his worth; from the dawn of day to its close her golden harp swells with his thrilling lays, from all sides she hears them repeated by her sons, her soul melts with the continued melody until in the midst of his inspired enthusiasm she invokes a blessing upon "her own sweet poet!"—upon "Erin's bard!"   Let any Irish child as soon as he can lisp out the name of his parents upon Earth and a prayer to his parent in heaven be taught the Melodies of his own native isle. . . .[5]

Which means that the *Irish Melodies* were widely sung, and the concluding number (1834) was greeted with regret.   In the words of the *Dublin Evening Mail:* "The music of Ireland like the music of Greece may be forgotten, but the poetry of the Irish Anacreon is imperishable while there exists a heart to beat with love, or pant with patriotism"; and for a time even those who thought Moore's treatment of the songs was not essentially national differed with him most respectfully, like the correspondent of the *Dublin Penny Journal,* who, though he took exception to the music, declared

that next to the honour of being a native of the country where first such exquisite music was breathed, do I estimate the pride of being born in the same isle with our talented and accomplished bard.[6]

Whenever the aging poet visited his native kingdom, popular enthusiasm was in striking contrast to the dubious attitude of the "monks of Trinity" thirty years before. When he and Bessy came to Dublin in 1830 (they made a pilgrimage to Kilkenny, where the theater had been turned into a horse bazaar) and Moore addressed a meeting called to celebrate the advent of Louis Philippe, his reception was "almost astoundingly enthusiastic"; leaving the meeting, he and Bessy

found outside a large concourse of people to receive us, who hurrahed, shook hands, &c.; and when we got into the carriage, insisted upon taking the horses off, and drawing us home. When we had proceeded half up the quay, however, I prevailed upon them to put the horses to again, and having provided myself with a pound's worth of silver, scattered it all for a scramble among my escorters. . . .

What a triumph for the son of the provision merchant!

A visit of 1831, occasioned by the serious illness of his mother, who, however, lingered on until May 8, 1832, was naturally no occasion for popular rejoicing; but in August, 1835, being in Dublin while the British Association for the Advancement of Science was meeting, he received the curious honor of being proposed for membership "without the usual formalities or fees" and was voted in by acclamation.[7] When he attended the theater on the evening of August 15, he was almost mobbed. Compelled to leave his box by shouts of "Come, show your Irish face, Tom; you needn't be ashamed of it!" he and sister Ellen descended to the pit.

Then came, indeed, the real thunder of the gods. The people in the pit stood up and hurrahed; and many of them threw up their hats, trusting to Providence for their ever returning to them again.

He was called upon for a speech while the actors were left standing idly on the stage, and was afterwards really imperiled by those who wanted to shake his hand, but he escaped—an odd and characteristic combination—to go to supper at the Lord Lieutenant's.

Even more extraordinary was his reception ten days later when he went to visit Wexford and Bannow in company with a Mr. Boyse. At Wexford some old women ran before him to a wretched house, exclaiming: "Here, Sir, this is the very house where your grandmother lived. Lord be merciful to her!" and after the poet had contemplated this dwelling, he and Boyse entered a carriage and four, the horses with rosettes at their ears, and the hats of the drivers being decorated with cockades. The farmhands cheered; a procession of horsemen bearing green banners, and surrounded by people on foot, came out to meet them, and escorted them to the bridge of Kiltra, which was crowned with a triumphal arch. The Nine Muses in the persons of some "remarkably pretty girls" advanced and crowned his bald head with myrtle and laurel. Moore was requested to enter a decorated car, which he did after inviting three of the Muses to ride with him. The car was drawn by two rows of young men in procession following the "Slaney Amateurs," a band of musicians in blue jackets, caps, and white trousers; and whenever the procession came to another arch, it stopped while the band played one of the *Irish Melodies*. An enthusiastic Muse wished that the route "was more than three hundred miles," but they got him instead to the lower gate of Boyse's house, The Grange, where there was a final arch inscribed: "Welcome to Bannow —Welcome Tom Moore." Boyse made a speech praising Moore as a poet, and Moore made a speech praising Boyse as a landlord; the crowd rushed forward to seize the poet's hand, and the exhausted bard was at length permitted to retreat to his host's bedroom. During the night there were bonfires, the next day there were dancing on the green and a balloon ascension, visiting delegations, and more speeches; and during his visit he laid a cornerstone, wrote his autograph for two "very nice Quaker young women," flattered the superior of a convent, visited all the pretty girls, danced with the most beautiful of the Nine Muses, planted a myrtle tree for the nuns, and eventually returned to Dublin, exhausted and happy, with "a very pretty young girl" and her "musical aunt" for companions in the coach.[8] And in September,

1838, he was again welcomed at the Theatre Royal, Dublin, with what "seemed madness of joy."

Despite this popular acclaim, however, Moore's course was not plain sailing. He liked Lord Grey, but Lord Grey supported the inevitable Irish Coercion Bills. He admired Lord John Russell, but Lord John was opposed to Repeal. He owed everything to Lord Lansdowne, but when that nobleman was debating the propriety of becoming Lord Lieutenant of Ireland, he pointed out to Moore the impossibility of abolishing the Irish Church, "which had grown up under the auspices of England"; and reduced Moore to a feeling of the "hopelessness, utter hopelessness" of any permanent cure for "Ireland's miseries." Chiefly, however, he was suspicious of O'Connell. He recognized the great value of that agitator's services to the Irish cause, but he was forever talking with his friends about O'Connell's deficiencies. O'Connell, on the other hand, though he praised Moore in public, was ever and again flaring up at some fancied insult from the poet. As early as July, 1832, there was a move to return Moore to Parliament from Limerick—it was, indeed, to urge him to this step that Gerald Griffin and his brother drove through the November rain to Sloperton—but one of the conditions was that he should oppose the insufficient Irish Tithe Bill; he was publicly advertised as an unqualified Repealer, which he was not; and he was informed that Lord Lansdowne's support would be detrimental. At this slur upon his independence, all Moore's pugnacity flared up, and he wrote spiritedly to Moran in July that he would not enter Parliament except as "an unfettered and independent Irishman," and denied that his aristocratic friends "have ever interfered for a moment or *can* interfere with either my right of thinking for myself or of speaking with perfect freedom what I think." Which meant that he would not be merely a member of O'Connell's "Irish phalanx." Finally, in November, he declined the perilous honor on the ground that his literary labors and the support of his family required all his time. O'Connell read his answer

to a political meeting in Dublin, remarking with suspicious
enthusiasm that the "sentiment" was "becoming of him who is
equally great in his writing as he is delightful in private life."
Was the great Dan perhaps relieved that he would not have
an independent member to cajole?   There seems little doubt
that Moore could have been returned from Limerick, had he
wished to be.[9]

In truth, so long as he remained in England as an independent Whig, he could perform services to the Irish cause
which nobody else could render.   He believed in the two-
party system; he did not believe in the validity of pressure
groups, such as was represented by O'Connell; he regarded
himself as a regularly enlisted member of the English liberal
group which respected the right of private political judgment.
Perhaps the clearest expression of his political philosophy is
contained in the speech he delivered at Bristol, November 10,
1835, at a dinner given to Lord John Russell, when he said:

. . . I was myself one of the victims of that old, penal system,
which my noble friend, your guest, has so truly and eloquently
remarked upon. . . . Neither do I regret that such was my
destiny; as I verily believe that the being born a slave has but
given me a keener sense and relish of the inestimable blessings
of freedom, and a more enlarged sympathy with all those—whatsoever may be their race or creed, and whether they be blacks
or whites—who, with even a glimmering sense of what they seek,
are contending for those just rights and privileges of civilized
man, without which, civilization itself in its truest sense, cannot
exist.   But while I thus welcome and hail with joyfulness every
new example . . . of men boldly and successfully working out
their own political salvation, I can also understand and make due
allowance for all those who, like a large and powerful party in
this country, view with distrust and alarm the great movement
of the popular mind that is now in progress, and . . . oppose
themselves to the current. So far am I from feeling out of
humour with these our opponents that I seriously look to them
as assisting parties in that wholesome process of action and coun-
teraction, by which alone the grand struggle between the two
principles now going on can be brought to a safe, well-sifted,

and satisfactory result. . . . I will beg leave to repeat that to the energies of our adversaries, as well as to our own, to the force of the *check*, as well as of *impulse*, I look for the attainment of that due balance in our political institutions, that *safe* as well as *free* working of the machinery of the State, which is all that any of us here, of whatever shades of liberalism, can desire.

On the same occasion he had the courage to defend the aristocracy, saying, with cutting sarcasm, that "I shall be facetiously described as having kindly taken the nobility under my protection and patronized the peerage," but also saying that if, after due trial of the Reform Bill, it be found that progressive legislation

is likely to be embarrassed and even stopped . . . by frequent collision with an irremovable and irresponsible body [the House of Lords], it will then certainly become a question whether there exists any thing in the legislation of the *past*, so inviolably sacred as to entitle it to interfere with the pressing interests of the *present*.

And he hinted that, under such circumstances, the House of Lords, that "overgrown and encumbering branch," should be lopped off rather than that "the sturdy trunk of your liberties, should be exhausted of its sap, or stunted in its growth . . ." [10] He was faithful, in short, to the liberal eighteenth-century idols of his youth; he would not swerve from his belief in the general rationality of mankind.

III

Moore's speech took the more courage because, at the suggestion of Lord Lansdowne, the Melbourne ministry granted him late in August a pension of £300, an incident which was received with yells of execration by his enemies. A Tory Irish member, Mr. Bateman, arose in his place later on to ask whether the pension was granted "for making luscious ballads for love-sick maidens, or for writing lampoons upon George IV, of blessed memory," and was spiritedly rebuked by Mr.

Spring Rice, who pointed out that the Tory Southey also
enjoyed a pension, and that both had "added to the literary
pleasures and instruction of their age and country." [11]   (This
was, however, in November, 1837.)   In 1835 the newspapers
avidly discussed the propriety of Melbourne's grant, the *Age*
declaring that Tommy had for years libeled the brother of
William IV, polluted the land with sentimental indecency,
and disseminated treason and sedition throughout the empire,
and the *Dublin Evening Mail* complaining of Moore's un-
mitigated and scurrilous abuse of Protestantism.   Whig and
liberal papers naturally congratulated the government.   The
battle was fought all over again after the parliamentary discussion of 1837.[12]

Meanwhile the serious thirties darkened into the hungry
forties; Mrs. Fitzherbert approached the end at Brighton, as
King William died, weary of speeches, and a slim girl at
Kensington Palace prepared to be Queen of England.   One
by one the lights of the Regency were extinguished.   A little
wearily, Moore clung to his trenches and continued the light
artillery fire which had helped to make him famous.   The
infamous Irish tithe system and the absurd Irish Church drew
from him satiric pictures of Ireland as a barnyard where
"decimate ducks" and "chosen chicks" were

> Doom'd by the Church's dispensation
> To suffer eternal decimation.

Or he compared the Irish to Strassburg geese, fattened to
make *pâté de foie gras* for the bishops, or penned ironical
resolutions in rhyme for ecclesiastical adoption:

> Resolved—such liberal souls are we—
> Though hating Nonconformity,
> We yet believe the cash no worse is
> That comes from Nonconformist churches.

He suggested that automata would do quite as well in Irish
benefices, and sketched a ludicrous picture of an episcopal
quadrille,

> Bristol capering up to Derry,
> And Cork with London making merry,
> While huge Llandaff, with a See, so, so,
> Was to dear old Dublin pointing his toe,

when the sudden abolition of ten Irish bishoprics threw the dance into wild disorder. Or he fancied a scientist in the year 2836 unearthing the bones of an extinct animal, Episcopus Vorax:

> And Tomkins, on searching its stomach, found there
> Large lumps, such as no modern stomach could bear,
> Of a substance call'd Tithe, upon which, as 'tis said,
> The whole Genus Clericum formerly fed.[13]

He did not scruple to name names. He pictured Bishop Phillpotts of Exeter being burned by imps, riding a runaway horse, inventing a new catechism:

> What's the Church?—A large money-establishment, giv'n
> To pamper up priests, for the honour of heav'n;
> And inspiring a zeal in each reverend man,
> Just proportion'd to what he gets *by* it per ann.

In fact, some of his attacks on this embattled curate were so venomous that Moore omitted them from his *Poetical Works,* as in "A Dream on Friday Night, June 14," where Phillpotts appears
> all in a shovel hat—
> Looking exceedingly sleek and fat,

or in a squib occasioned by a letter of Lord Lansdowne to that reverend prelate:

> If the devil had meant the world to see
> What a noisome thing a priest may be,
> And how a religion of love and light
> May be turned to shame and scorn and spite;
> Had he wished to show what hate and pride
> And bitterness sleeves of lawn may hide,
> And exhibit to modern days and climes
> The vilest spirit of vilest times—
> How well had P——s served his plan:
> He had only to say—"Behold the man!"

> . . . never was truth so sorely shamed,
> And never was charity so defamed,
> And never the Church was so traduced,
> And never the Bible so abused,
> By scribbling wit or by sceptic peer
> As now—by the B——p of E——r.

It was but the first of a series of such attacks in 1839-42, which must have made the prelate wince.[14]

Orangemen and Robert Southey, the latter

> First, into Whig Pindarics rambling,
> Then in low Tory doggrel scrambling;
> Now *love* his theme, now *Church* his glory
> (At once both Tory and ama-tory);

the *Quarterly Review*, and the Irish Chief Secretaries—he took them all on. Especially savage was his treatment of "Scorpion" Stanley, who owed the nickname to O'Connell, and who, as Chief Secretary in 1830, as Colonial Secretary in 1833, and as a Tory member of the House of Lords, though he did much for Irish education, consistently opposed every measure of political and ecclesiastical reform. Moore dubbed him "the boy statesman"—

> For you pray'd for a boy, and you now have a boy,
> Who'll continue a boy to the end of his life.

He pictured him as a thief arrested for passing false coins; he put a poem into his mouth called "Thoughts on Mischief," in which Stanley was made to boast of

> Mischief, combining boyhood's tricks
> With age's sourest politics;
> The urchin's freaks, the veteran's gall.

He pictured him at war with all mankind; he dreamed of him
> sitting with air so jaunty
> Astride his piebald Rosinante,

"old Mother Church—the Hibernian She" mounted behind him until they both rolled in the ditch; and in "The Retreat

of the Scorpion" he rejoiced at his defeat. He included in the
Poetical Works the Drydenesque "Portrait of Lord Stanley,"
the title being softened into "A Character," which begins:

> Half Whig, half Tory, like those midway things,
> 'Twixt bird and beast, that by mistake have wings;
> A mongrel statesman, 'twixt two factions nurst,
> Who, of the faults of each, combines the worst—
> The Tory's loftiness, the Whigling's sneer,
> The leveller's rashness, and the bigot's fear,

but he omitted the equally severe "Farewell to Lord Stanley,"
which he printed in the *Chronicle* in 1836:

> Oh! it grieves us to think—self-destroy'd as thou art—
> What a frailty of temper thy spirit betrays!
> How a mountebank head and a renegade heart,
> Have their victim diverted from liberty's ways! [15]

And during the anti-Corn Law agitation of the early forties,
he denounced those who would let Irishmen (and Englishmen) starve rather than give up their profits.[16]

IV

But he did not confine himself to the newspapers—the
Times up to 1836, the *Chronicle* thereafter, with occasional
pot-shots in the *Examiner*. Late in November, 1831, we read
that "ever since I got rid of my 'Lord Edward,' have been
reading hard at theology for a work I have now in hand,
'Travels of an Irish Gentleman in search of a Religion.'"
He undertook a preliminary skirmish with German rationalism in an article for the *Edinburgh Review* in September,
1831, and toiled with his usual scholarly thoroughness over
his self-appointed task, interrupted though it was by a bout
of writing for the *Metropolitan Magazine* in 1832. His early
reading in the church fathers stood him in good stead, and he
explored religious controversy from the beginning of the
Christian era for his two volumes, issued by the Longmans in
1833, a work which like almost everything else he wrote in
prose started a violent controversy. "This defence of their

ancient, national faith," runs the dedication, "is inscribed to the people of Ireland."

In the first volume we are introduced to a student sitting alone in his chambers, up two pair of stairs in Trinity College, on the evening of April 16, 1829, when the news that the royal assent had been given to the Catholic Emancipation Bill has just reached Dublin. Freed of the penalties which had attached to being a Catholic, but hitherto debarred by honor from being anything else, the young man exclaims: "Thank God! I may now, if I like, turn Protestant." The Protestants, he says, were "a set of gentlemanlike heretics, somewhat scanty in creed, but in all things else rich and prosperous, and governing Ireland, according to their will and pleasure, by right of some certain Thirty-nine Articles, of which I had not yet clearly ascertained whether they were Articles of War or of Religion." As the Protestants argued that they had restored primitive Christian faith, Moore ironically pretends that his Trinity student now searches the church fathers to ascertain how the corruptions of Catholicism had crept in; but the more he reads, the more he finds that the antiquity of his own church is confirmed.

In the second volume the sister of the agent of an absentee landlord hints that our young student might have the rich living at the disposal of her brother, if he but turn Protestant and look kindly upon her. "I saw the power of presentation in her eyes; felt the soft pressure of induction in her hand," Moore writes dryly. The young student goes to Germany as the principal source of Protestantism and of rational theology. Moore retorts upon the Protestants the charges of ignorantly accepting miracles, dwells upon the inconsistencies of the Protestant sects, and carries German rationalism to its logical conclusion, the destruction of Christian faith. He also thriftily uses in this book some verse translations which are apparently from his unpublished book on pious women. Were the tone of irony found in the opening chapters of each volume sustained throughout, he would have constructed a masterpiece, but he could not carry it through; and while one must admire the command of abstruse theological information and the lucidity with which it is presented, Moore's characteristic fault of pedantry loads his pages with unnecessary learning.

On the whole, the book was scarcely a success. The Protestant magazines said what might be expected of them, and the Tory reviewers applied the usual adjectives. "The trifler of the green-room—the companion of sceptics and profligates," whose "prurient writings" had corrupted the moral sense of the daughters of Britain was not expected to know anything about theology. Of all "the impudent productions" he had written, this was the worst. He had

spent the talent of his youth in effusions calculated to debauch and to destroy the human soul; and now he has employed the labours of his declining years in attempting to pour the poison of infidelity and superstition, into the only fountain of mercy, that heaven has given. . . .

It was impossible to divine the object of his book. It was really comic to see "Mr. Thomas Little actually metamorphosed into a controversial divine." Or else it was really to be hoped that he was not the author.[17] It was not, however, so absurd that it did not call forth long and grave replies— Moore's old adversary, the Rev. Mortimer O'Sullivan publishing *A Guide to an Irish Gentleman in his Search for a Religion* in 347 mortal pages, and that strange genius, Joseph Blanco White, favoring the world with the *Second Travels of an Irish Gentleman in Search of a Religion* in two volumes, both books appearing in 1833. The Rev. Mortimer spoke pleasantly of the "hypocrisy" of Moore's nature. The Rev. Blanco White hinted that Moore did not believe any form of Christianity to be true.[18] One of the ablest of these performances is the anonymous *Letter from Ignoramus, to the Irish Gentleman* . . . published in London in 1834.

The Rev. Mortimer O'Sullivan annoyed the poet a good deal, and in *The Fudges in England*, published in 1835,

Moore etched his portrait as the Rev. Mortimer O'Mulligan and hung it up for the admiration of posterity. Truth to tell, the satiric account of this convert is the liveliest thing in a volume in which the Fudge family has grown old and lost something of its sprightliness; nor does the inclusion of a number of Moore's newspaper squibs save the work from a sense of being labored. Larry O'Branigan, who writes his letters in dialect, is amusing, it is true; and there are good things scattered here and there in the pages, but on the whole the book is not a success, partly, it would appear, because of the weight of theological controversy which the lines are made to bear. The reception of the book was mixed. The *Times* and the *Literary Gazette*, for example, thought it lacked pungency; the *Courier*, however, referred flatteringly to the "ingenious and admirable Mr. Brown," the *Dublin Freemans Journal* thought it an "admirable exposé of the spiritual but Quixotic proceedings" of the Protestants, and the *Court Journal*, though it regretted the partisan gall of its pages, liked the fun, as did the *Mirror*. More solemn articles made the book a peg on which to hang long disquisitions about ecclesiastical strife. The *Westminster Review* hailed him as "the poetical scourge of saint-craft and priest-craft" who "walks in the path of Swift," and flatteringly placed him, if not by the side of the author of the Drapier's letters, in "a niche at least directly under." The excessively Protestant *Dublin University Magazine* naturally viewed him with alarm. It was a sight both

extremely ludicrous and extremely *pitiable*, to contemplate this elderly gentleman so sadly regardless of the external decorums of even poetical license of character, as still to be found in clumsy dalliance awkwardly trifling with the toys which became his youth so gracefully, now frolicking in pun, now foaming in politics; half freak, half frenzy; and in the desperate consciousness of declining fame determined to mistake the rotten breath of the filthiest faction that ever befouled the annals of any country for the incense which virtue and feeling gratefully offer to their interpreter and guardian.

They took their poetry seriously in 1835.[19]   And as for the
Rev. Mortimer O'Sullivan, he declared pleasantly in a public
address in September, 1835, that Moore

wrote as one who glories in the dark murders which disgrace his
country—he wrote as one who teaches murderers to think lightly
of crimes which he, their favoured poet, commemorates as if
they were matters for sport and levity (hear, hear). . . . Safe
from danger—affluent in all the enjoyments of domestic life, of
public favour, of powerful friends—thus he writes of the afflic-
tions and wrongs of a class of men like the Protestant clergy of
the south and west of Ireland—thus he writes of men surrounded
by brutal and pampered tormentors—thus he writes, whose words
have, as he well knows, power to exasperate those remorseless
enemies, and to point their fell passions towards unprotected victims (hear, hear).

Reporting this speech, the *Morning Herald* spent a column
discussing the "bigotry and venom" of the poet, and, after
the manner of the *Eatanswill Gazette*, concluded that it
could not discuss this "disgusting subject," but would

leave Mr. MOORE to enjoy what the debasement of his poetic
genius has earned for him, the reprobation of all generous minds,
and a Whig pension.[20]

About this time the affluent Mr. Moore had received a letter
from his poor Bessy, beginning: "My dearest Tom,—Can it
be *really* true that you have a pension of 300*l*. a year? . . .
I have my fears that it is only a castle in the air. I am sure I
shall dream of it; and so I will get to bed, that I may have this
pleasure *at least;* for I expect the morning will throw down
my castle."

Chapter XV

HE HAD done much for Ireland, but he was to do more—he was to kill himself in her service as truly as did Emmet or Fitzgerald, except that death was merciful to them and came quickly, whereas in Moore's case it was to be protracted over interminable years. As early as February, 1829, the Longmans had approached him with a proposal that he write a history of Ireland in one volume. This was to be part of a popular series of instructive books, known as the Cabinet Cyclopaedia, edited by a serious-minded and prolific gentleman named the Rev. Dionysius Lardner, whose services in the cause of learning were registered by a long string of initials after his name. The proposed book was intended for popular consumption; and the series had resulted from that drive for general education which had led Brougham to found the "Society for the Diffusion of Useful Knowledge" and to launch the *Penny Magazine* and the *Penny Cyclopaedia.* Moore's book was to parallel a one-volume history of Scotland by Sir Walter Scott, and a more pretentious work on England by Sir James Mackintosh. As Lord John Russell remarks, if Moore had kept within the restriction of one volume, the result might have been an easy, agreeable, and readable work. The publishers expected nothing more from him, and they turned to him as having some knowledge of Irish history and as being the most prominent Irish writer before the public.

Everything surrounding the enterprise has its faint note of disaster. Sir James Mackintosh died shortly after completing

his work, which, unfortunately for Moore, set a standard for
the series which it was relatively easy for the trained historical writer to achieve, but which plunged Moore into innumerable difficulties. Sir Walter Scott's book ran to two
volumes, part of that immense labor which brought on a
paralytic stroke in February, 1830. When Moore dined with
him for the last time at Lockhart's in London in October,
1831, he wrote in his diary: "On looking over at Scott once
or twice, was painfully struck by the utter vacancy of his
look. How dreadful if he should live to survive that mighty
mind of his!" But no angel twitched the Irishman's ear to
tell him that in this sentence he had written his own doom.
On the contrary, he took the contract; and in February, 1832,
we find the Longmans writing to him to know when they
might expect the manuscript. But he was busy with other
matters; and unfortunately resolving to begin at the beginning and do a thorough job of it, he plunged into reading the
ancient Greek and Latin authorities (he knew no Gaelic),
and the more he read, the more the work swelled under his
hand. He offered to turn the job over to somebody else,
but the Longmans had advertised the book as coming from
his hand; and the result was, as he wrote, "for the first time
in my literary life" I "feel myself a thorough *hack*." A first
volume finally appeared in April, 1835, but it brought the
story down only to the seventh century. Two years later,
amidst increasing difficulties, he brought out the second
volume, and was not yet through the Middle Ages. Still
laboring drearily on, he published a third volume in 1840,
and a fourth, the production of his exhausted old age, in
1846. There is a pathetic passage in the broken fragments
of his later diary expressive of his failing powers and his tired
disgust with the whole enterprise:

Though I had delivered, as I hoped and thought, the last pages
of my weary work (the History of Ireland) to the Printer, there
still remained enough of my task to worry and delay me; and,
worst of all, was the supposed necessity of my prefixing some

sort of Preface to the Volume. In vain did I try for two or three days to satisfy myself with a few prefatory sentences, but they would not come as I wished; and at last, in utter despair, I left to the Longmans to finish the abortive Preface.

It is probable that no living person has read through this dull work, a task utterly unfitted to its author and wholly without standing as an authoritative treatise. The first volume, appearing as it did in the midst of the spirited controversy over the Irish Church, received a tolerable amount of attention in the reviews, but, on the whole, as the work progressed, the successive volumes sank, unnoticed, into the sea of oblivion. Fanatic Irishmen resented his dismissal of the Milesian stories as so much fable, and embattled Protestants were on the lookout for papistical heresies. The *Christian Examiner* snarled that there was no reason why Moore should not fill his purse and occupy his mind with a *"thing called an Irish history,"* and used the first volume as an excuse to justify English rule. The *Westminster Review* paid it what compliments it could. The *British Magazine and Monthly Register* found fault with his authorities; *Tait's Edinburgh Magazine* rallied him on his credulity; the *Spectator* thought that, for an Irishman, he displayed impartiality. As for the Irish periodicals, the intransigent *Dublin University Magazine* said that a history of Ireland was still to be written, the *Dublin Penny Journal* found fault with his inability to get at original materials, the *Belfast News Letter* said he had "forgotten the duties of the historian amidst the partialities of the controversialist," and only the extreme Catholic press really rallied to the book.[1] It was among these tepidities that he was required to drive drearily on through the centuries. Was everything that he wrote, even in his old age, to be clouded with controversy? His study was "overloaded with learned rubbish, of various kinds"; he tried vainly to reassure himself that "as long as I have health" I do not desire "any thing better."

His painful labors were, however, pleasantly diversified by

the publication of his *Poetical Works* in 1840-41 in nine volumes, a tenth, containing *The Epicurean*, being added by Longmans apparently in 1848. For this he went through all his writings, sometimes revising the texts; and for this he wrote individual prefaces to the several volumes in that familiar, autobiographical style in which one wishes he had written more. How much he had accomplished! Eighty or ninety thousand lines of verse! He reviewed his performances with pardonable pride, noting, for example, that *Lalla Rookh* was founded "on a long and laborious collection of facts," from whence "arises that matter-of-fact adherence to Orientalism" for which the experts gave him credit. He took the public into his confidence, telling them of his early struggles, his journey to America, his indebtedness to Bunting's *Airs*, without which "the greater part of our musical treasures would probably have been lost to the world," how he wrote *Lalla Rookh*, and how good his friends had been to him. He was not above dressing up his own legend a little—his squibs, for example, had never hurt anybody (which was scarcely true), since he was "by nature so little prone to spleen and bitterness." He was, as a matter of fact, a little proud of them: "their ridicule, thanks to the undying nature of human absurdity, appears to have lost, as yet, but little of the original freshness of its first application." But, discovering that so much of his verse had been satiric, he was put to it to explain why so amiable a person as himself had become so ironic, and he thought that he had showered "ridicule on a political adversary, without allowing a single feeling of real bitterness to mix itself with the operation." It is to be doubted whether Bishop Phillpotts and the Rev. Mortimer O'Sullivan, Lord Stanley and Lord Eldon, the Duke of Wellington and the Prince Regent would have entirely subscribed to this pleasing theory. However that may be, the edition was gracefully dedicated to Lord Lansdowne, "in grateful remembrance of nearly forty years of mutual acquaintance and friendship."

The publication of the *Poetical Works* gave rise to an

enormous number of critical articles in which the Victorian reviewers tried to estimate the enduring worth of the Regency poet. Scores of newspapers reprinted parts of the prefaces, especially that to the first volume. The *Monthly Chronicle* thought that "perhaps no man was ever more endeared by his social and intellectual powers," and called him "one of the few poets of all times who have not disappointed in private the ideals formed of them from their works." The *Literary Gazette*, the *Glasgow Mail and Argus*, the *Spectator*, the *United Service Gazette*, the *Observer*, the *Tablet*, and other papers congratulated him on omitting or modifying the "prurient poems" of his youth. The edition was, said one editor, "the consummation of his glorious and unequalled career," but others were more cautious, the *Times* remarking his "cold and glittering conceits" and "overwrought elegancies of phrase and figure." Once more, however, the question of morality was debated. Said the *Spectator*:

. . . the principle that present enjoyment is the end of life, and should be pursued without regard to moral duties or future consequences, and a sort of refined but lascivious sensuality, are too deeply seated in the poems to be easily eradicated.

And the old charge of his being full of spleen reappeared: "if there ever was, *par excellence*, a personal libeller, Mr. Moore is the man." There was general agreement, however, that the *Irish Melodies* formed the most important part of his work, so far had *Lalla Rookh* already faded. The *Morning Post*, of course, could not forgive him his "ill-natured squibs, full of personal scurrility . . . upon the Prince Regent's amours or his whiskers," and advised persons "who feel scrupulous as to the decent and honourable character of the books they admit into their houses" not to buy the third volume, which contained these things. The reviews make an interesting cross-section of average Victorian opinion; on the whole they indicate that the publication of the *Poetical Works* put a seal on Moore's career.[2]

II

On a Saturday late in October, 1830, Tom had driven
down to Earlstoke Park in Wiltshire with Watson Taylor,
where he had been "rather amused with being behind the
scenes to see the fuss of preparation for a royal reception,"
the Duchess of Kent and the Princess Victoria arriving at
half-past five. There had been music in the evening, when
he had listened respectfully while royal throats warbled a
duet, and music on the following Monday when he had
joined these exalted personages in song, but there had been
no music on Sunday, the Duchess "very prudently" protesting against it. It was in such faint premonitory ways that
the Victorian era announced its triumph. Now it was 1840,
and the little Princess, clad all "in articles of British manufacture" and grown taller, was marrying that strangest of Baron
Stockmar's intellectual inventions, Prince Albert of Saxe-
Coburg-Gotha. The Queen had liked to dance all night and
then watch the sun rise over St. Paul's in the morning; presently she sat listening over her embroidery while Albert the
Good read aloud from Hallam's *Constitutional History of*
England. As the nation entered the hungry forties, German
philoprogenitiveness saw to it that maternal cares divided the
burdens of empire in the royal mind. In 1841 that last relic
of the eighteenth century, Lord Melbourne, finally went out,
and that descendant of a calico printer, Robert Peel, again
came in. In June, 1842, the Queen ventured to travel by rail
from Windsor to Paddington, her coachman obstinately riding in the engine cab, where his scarlet livery became exceedingly dirty.

There were new voices in the magazines, new volumes on
the book-stalls. In 1840 *Pickwick* was three years old, *Sartor
Resartus* was a perplexing book, and *Sordello* an even more
perplexing poem. Down in Dorsetshire a Mrs. Hardy was
contemplating with maternal satisfaction a small mite of humanity christened Thomas, and up in Northumbria the three-

year-old son of Admiral Swinburne was exciting the admiration of cooing ladies. The Tennysons had just moved to Tunbridge Wells, where Alfred, still hoping that he might marry, was repolishing the poems which were to delight the world in 1842. In 1840 Macaulay, back from India where he had attempted to introduce the natives to the blessings of a free press, was again astonishing the drawingrooms with brilliant intervals of silence; in another year, Tract Ninety was to alarm all sound Protestants; in three more, readers of *Punch* were to weep over "The Song of the Shirt"; in four more, *Vestiges of Creation* was to announce the advent of Darwin. The world which had known Robert Emmet and *Anacreon* was half a century away. How remote seemed Grattan and Dr. Duigenan, Sheridan and Beau Brummell, the scandals of Brighton and the long heroism of the Napoleonic wars!

Moore shrank from this unfamiliar, industrialized England, swamped with labor troubles and loud with the agitation of the chartists. About the youngest literary generation he knew and cared little; such new friends as he made were among the transition group—men like Macaulay, who was "wonderful; never, perhaps, was there combined so much talent with so marvellous a memory"; or Sergeant Noon Talfourd, "radiant with . . . recent fame"; or Henry Taylor, author of *Philip van Artevelde;* or Dean Milman, the future editor of Gibbon. His visits to London became more and more infrequent; when he went down, he clung to Lord John Russell, who was never too busy to see him, or dined with Samuel Rogers, who was to outlive him, lean and sardonic to the end, or chatted at Holland House—but Lord Holland died in 1840, Lady Holland in 1845. He was still a popular idol—in 1839 there was produced a play, *Tim Moore*, built around Moore's own life, which he attended incognito, and which kept him in a state between laughing and crying the whole time. Once, waiting in the rain for a cab with Irving "like a pair of male caryatides," he was accosted by a loiterer who

said, "Shall I get you a cab, Mr. Moore? Sure, ain't *I* the
man that patronizes your Melodies?" and who refused a tip.
Another time, when he was reading in the British Museum, a
poor Irish laborer engaged in repair work offered a pot of ale
to a fellow workman to point out the defender of Ireland,
and was so pleased to have seen the poet that he doubled the
pot of ale. Another time, when he was returning from Dublin, a bevy of young ladies invaded his cabin in the packet and
demanded to be kissed all round; an older and apparently unattractive female, not willing to be omitted, knocked at his
door after they left and demanded to be kissed also, which he
did amid the first twinges of seasickness. It was pleasant to be
loved by the people, but literature was passing him by.

As the slow years drifted over the little cottage at Sloperton
with its trellised doorway and its shrubbery, the poet's circle
grew smaller and smaller. There were always the Lansdownes, and there was Bowles, who had grown quite deaf
and used an ear-trumpet to hear himself talk but sometimes
forgot to raise it to his ears when other persons talked to him.
But there were many gaps in the neighborhood, and, as he
thought about his old friends, he could have exclaimed with
Wordsworth,

> How fast has brother followed brother,
> From sunshine to the sunless land!

Lady Donegal, Joe Atkinson, Byron, his parents, his sister-in-
law, Mrs. Murray, his sister Kate, dead in 1834, Mrs. Dyke,
Stevenson, his daughters, Rees, the kindly partner of Longman—they were all gone. Thomas Norton Longman followed Rees in 1842. Presently Sydney Smith died—that ecclesiastical Yorick who had so often set the table in a roar.
Moore's sister Ellen came often to Sloperton to visit him, but
in 1846 she passed away in Dublin. And he clung to his
friends with the closer attachment as, one by one, they left
him. He had long since made up with Hume, his second in
the ludicrous duel with Jeffrey. In June, 1841, he wrote

Leigh Hunt, begging him to forget their quarrel over Byron. In October, 1845, he accepted a dinner invitation from Thomas Campbell, at which young Crabbe and Samuel Rogers were the only other guests, and that bitterness was healed. He even clung to Wordsworth, whose greatness he was beginning to understand. But as troubles and sadness thickened around him, he felt his powers fail. The death of Ellen was a shock from which, it is said, he never recovered. More and more, he lived the life of a recluse.

III

There was, of course, the eternal money problem; and he who had supported so many people—his mother-in-law, his father, his mother, his sisters, his sister-in-law Mrs. Murray (the remaining Dyke sister, as Mrs. Duff, was pursuing a somewhat eccentric career in far-off America)—he was scarcely able to support himself, his wife, and his sons. As early as 1832-33, his accounting with Power, too long postponed, revealed a tangle so complex as to require arbitration before it was settled; and though Power spoke of Moore as one of the few honest men he had dealt with, the settlement of these accounts left both poet and publisher, friends for so many years, a little sore in spirit. Ever and again Moore was surprised to discover that his balance at the Longmans was not inexhaustible, was on the contrary against him, though that kind and friendly firm never pressed him for cash, merely begging for another poem which, one conjectures, he knew he would never write. And as late as 1840 he was still in debt to Carpenter. These were the vexations of his later years, but they were merely vexations. There were longer sorrows to come—the careers of his remaining children.

Thomas Lansdowne Parr Moore, who was born in 1818, and John Russell Moore, who was born in 1823, had each been entered at the Charterhouse School, the one through the kindness of Lord Grey, the other at the nomination of Sir

Robert Peel. Moore was continually surprised to find out how much it cost to keep two young gentlemen, but especially Tom, in funds. Temperamentally, Russell resembled his mother; his brother was a wild, harum-scarum, heedless youth, on whom the delicate responsibility of being the eldest son of a genius did not sit with grace. He was always in trouble, but his father and mother were always hoping for the best. Too late they recognized that he had been spoiled.

Young Tom thirsted for a life of action. To satisfy him, his father finally purchased an ensigncy in the Twenty-second Foot at a price he could ill afford; and with some vague notion of preparing him for a military life, the poet removed him from the Charterhouse School and put him in a French *pension* at Caen—where Moore dined sorrowfully with Beau Brummell, old, forgotten, and forgetful. Young Tom entered the service in March, 1838, joining his regiment in Cork. In May he was shifted to Dublin, though the new Ensign seems also to have been in Belfast during the spring. What happened there is not clear, but he was supposed to have insulted a young woman on the street. One account is that the girl's mother appealed to the colonel of the regiment; another account is that young Moore was actually ill in bed at the time of the supposed encounter. This episode called the poet to Dublin, where young Tom tramped up to his bedroom, "looking very pale and ill." A few days later, on September 19, 1838, Ensign Moore published a spirited note in the *United Service Gazette* denying the truth of the story in the newspapers.[3]

Young Tom remained an officer, but in 1840 he was sick again. Moore's old friend, Dr. Crampton, reported, however, that his convulsive seizures were caused by the tight collar of the hideous uniform of the day. Ill or not, he drew bills on his father which the poor poet was scarcely able to meet, though again this may have been due to the approaching departure of the regiment for India, for we find Ensign Moore

garrisoned in Lower Scinde in November, 1841, ill, disconsolate, and wrathful. The next thing the anxious father knew
was that young Tom had sold the commission purchased with
such hope, and was loose on the world.

In the meantime, Russell Moore, happier in temperament
and weaker in physique, likewise resolved on colonial adventure, had removed from the Charterhouse School to a Dr.
Firminger's at Edmonton that he might be prepared for a
cadetship in the Indian service. The news that a son of the
poet was coming out was flatteringly received in Bombay,
where the paper said:

A writership for [Moore's] son would, we should have thought,
have been within the reach of one who has so steadily adhered
to his political party . . . but we believe the young man has a
military penchant and preferred the charms of the cantonment
to the luxury of the cutcherry. On the arrival of Tom Moore's
son, India will be able to boast that she has provided for the
progeny of four of the first poets of Great Britain—Burns, Walter
Scott, Allan Cunningham, and the author of Lalla Rookh.[4]

With this flattering future before him, young Russell Moore
sailed from the East India Docks in April, 1840, his father
and mother going down for the painful parting, when,

as long as the vessel continued in sight my poor Bessy remained
at the window with a telescope, watching for a glimpse of her
dear boy, and telling me all she saw, or *thought* she saw, him
doing.

He was appointed to a post in Bengal; but he had scarcely
landed when he fell ill. Though Lord Auckland, the Governor-General, and his daughter, Emily Eden, the future author
of *The Semi-Attached Couple*, were immensely kind, Indian
medical service could not check tuberculosis; and young Russell had to be invalided home, arriving at Sloperton in April,
1842. From the first his case was hopeless. He lingered until
November 23, when there was another painful funeral in
Bromham churchyard.

Half-crazed with grief, the distracted parents had still to solve the problem of their elder son. There was a vain attempt to restore him to his regiment, but partly from a romantic love of adventure, partly from a feeling of rebellion and disgrace, that young gentleman resolved to enter the French army. The poet, who had known the family of Louis Philippe in their adversity, now appealed to them in their prosperity, with the result that the young scapegrace was appointed *sous-lieutenant* in the Foreign Legion serving in Algiers. But the real reason why young Tom was eager to enlist is unexpectedly revealed in an unpublished letter from his father to Mrs. Villamil, now in the Lord John Russell papers in the Public Records Office:

> Sloperton, Chippenham
> October 24, 1842

My dear M^rs. Villamil. You see I address you by your old English title—it was that by which I first knew you and I cling to it fondly. The intelligence, my dear friend, your letter conveys, would have been hailed by me with the sincerest delight, if so many difficulties do not stand in the way of such a union as my poor sanguine boy proposes. To Tom himself an alliance with your family and with such a young person as I am quite sure a daughter of yours must be would be absolute salvation. For Tom wants steadying, and the gentle control of an affectionate and sensible wife would be the best as well as most agreeable sort of discipline for him. But, alas, my dear friend, *money* is, in this strange world the thing upon which every thing turns, and my son, so far from being able to support *others* has thrown away the only chance I was able to give him of supporting himself. However, as the very prospect of such a union may stimulate him to try and *deserve* it, I say "yes" to the proposed marriage most willingly; and, though I have already made myself bankrupt for him no effort shall be wanting to further so desirable an object.

You ask me in confidence about his temper. Owing to the absurd practice in England of sending Boys away from home at so early an age, Fathers and Mothers are in general those who know least about their own children. But, I should say, from

all I *do* know, that Tom's is, on the whole, a very good temper.
I happened to be from home when your letter arrived which
must account for the few days delay of my answer.

With kindest regards to my excellent friend Villamil I am ever
your's most truly

THOMAS MOORE.

With the idea of making a career in the French service so
that he might marry his sweetheart, young Tom refused to
come home where his brother lay dying; and on the very
last day of that disastrous year informed his parents that he
would not see them before sailing for Africa. In Algeria,
however, he found himself "twenty times worse off than he
was in India"; and presently wrote his father for fifty pounds
to keep him out of prison. His father did not have fifty
pounds to send him. This was in December, 1843.

Under these accumulating griefs the health of both parents
gave way, though Bessy rallied as Tom did not. In September, 1845, they learned that their remaining child was
dangerously ill with fever in Africa. For a time it seemed
that he might recover, but the gods willed otherwise. In
February, 1846, Bessy had the desperate task of telling her
bewildered husband that his sister Ellen had died; in March,
that their son was dead in a distant land. "Why," she had
written him, "why do people sigh for children? They know
not what sorrow will come with them." "The last of our
five children is now gone," he wrote in his diary, "and we
are left desolate and alone. Not a single relative have I now
left in the world!" It was small comfort to learn that at the
end, young Tom, worn out by the horrors of warfare with
the Arabs, had exhibited "a manly and cheerful spirit."

The night was gathering fast. In 1838, and again in 1842,
while Moore was singing at the piano for a dinner-party, a fit
of hysterical weeping had compelled him to leave the room.
His absent-mindedness increased—Sydney Smith once wrote
him an amusing letter detailing a list of articles Moore had left

THOMAS MOORE IN 1842

behind on a visit—and everyone was worried. He dined out at the wrong houses, or forgot engagements. At Lady Minto's he could not associate names and faces, enthusiastically wringing the hand of a woman who was a total stranger to him, under the impression she was an old friend. In 1842, having dined out in London, he could not, when entering the event in his journal, remember the name or face of a single guest. He gave up a project to write the life of Sydney Smith. The mere keeping of his journal became a burden which he was more and more loath to assume. Small wonder that the broken old man who had been the poet of all circles and the idol of his own could not, when the time came, finish the preface to the last volume of the fatal *History of Ireland.* In a letter to Rogers, written June 23, 1847, saying he hoped to have "a few more breakfasts with you (to say nothing of dinners) before 'time and the hour has quite run out our day,' " he added the ominous postscript: "I am sinking here into a mere vegetable."

Sometime in 1847 he was unable to sign his name. In 1848, while Lord Lansdowne and Lord John Russell were sitting with him, he suddenly collapsed, sinking into senile dementia, which, with only brief flashes of reason, was to last four years. Sometimes he could recognize his faithful Bessy, who nursed him to the end, and who would permit no one else to see him in this state. When he was rational, he wanted the Bible read to him, or asked Bessy to sing a favorite hymn, "Come to Jesus," the poor, quavering voice that had once brought so many to tears, joining uncertainly in the refrain. From those deep wells of courage which had sustained her all her life, Bessy drew an endless fortitude, never admitting to her friends that her beloved Tom would never be himself again. "My mind," she wrote Rogers,

is full of fears, but God gives me the great comfort of nursing him; he knows me, talks of you and other friends, his evanescent temper is now a blessing to himself and me. . . .

He grew fond of a certain kind of biscuit, which Mrs. S. C. Hall could supply; and Bessy, writing that lady, displayed an unshakable optimism:

He is now sitting up with the window open, and the sun shining on him. I can hardly believe that I write the truth. His sleep is excellent, and in all ways he improves daily. I am not at all well, and begin to feel I require rest, which I will take if I can. But he is yet too feeble to be left, and I do not like to bring a stranger about him.

Yours affect^{ly}
BM.

He is sitting close by me, and is anxious to walk.[5]

In 1851 she took him to Bath in the hope of amendment, but he displayed no consciousness of where he was or who were around him. On February 26, 1852, Mrs. Starkey wrote Rogers

to inform him that Mr. Moore has been gradually sinking the last few days, and yesterday evening, at six o'clock, he breathed his last, with the utmost calmness and apparently without pain.[6]

On March 3, 1852, "the remains of our amiable and highly gifted neighbour, Mr. Thomas Moore, were . . . interred in the churchyard of Bromham." The hearse was followed by but a single coach in which rode Thomas Longman the younger, Dr. Brabant, Mr. Kerry of Melksham, the medical adviser, and the Rev. Mr. Drury of Bremhill, successor to Bowles, who had died in 1850. Lord John Russell and Lord Lansdowne could not attend. The fashionable world, which had sung his music and admired his epigrams, sighed over his lyrics and hung on his anecdotes, had forgotten him, or, if it remembered, did not bestir itself to come up to an obscure Wiltshire church on a raw March day to attend the funeral of a poet they no longer cared for. If there were no bellowing crinolines or Prince Albert coats in the churchyard, the common people had not forgotten him, for the little enclosure was filled with a quiet and respectful group, the greater number attired in mourning. There had been a request to bury him in Ireland, which Bessy had denied, that he might lie in the same vault with two of his children.[7]

IV

Alone in her little cottage save for the servants, Bessy had but one hope and one delusion—that young Tom was not dead, that he would return to her, that some beloved voice would speak to her out of the appalling silence. In the great world of the Crystal Palace and the foreign policy of Palmerston, the world where Disraeli and Gladstone thundered nightly at each other, and people asked anxiously what the new Emperor of the French was going to do, she had no interest and no curiosity. Lord Lansdowne was not a great Whig peer, who, like herself, was more or less belated in a hurrying world, he was her neighbor. Lord John Russell for her was not the distinguished Prime Minister, he was simply one of Tom's kind and trusted friends. She had very little to live on—a small pension which was granted her after her husband's death, and such income as remained from her husband's writings, now, alas! outmoded in the Victorian age. Consequently, when Thomas Longman came to her rescue with an offer of £3000 for Moore's journal and correspondence, provided Lord John would edit the material, she saw no reason why it should not be done. When Lord John consented to undertake a task he had neither time nor equipment to carry through, she was simply, utterly grateful. "Words cannot express my deep feeling of gratitude to you," she wrote him in her awkward, illegible penmanship, "for consenting to immortalize his name and serve me so essentially."[8] She wore her eyes out over Tom's minute scrawl, arranging (and confusing) his papers, and sending them down in batches to London or to Lord John's country home.

Lord John was fighting for his political life. Out of office in February, 1852, he was busy under Lord Aberdeen's administration as Foreign Secretary (1853) and as President of

the Council (1854); busy again over an abortive reform bill
in 1854, and out of office in 1855. Next he went off to
Vienna, and then he became Colonial Secretary in May, only
to retire in July, still the stormy petrel of politics. He could
not devote much time to the remains of his literary friend, but
he managed to get out eight ugly volumes entitled *Memoirs,
Journal, and Correspondence of Thomas Moore* from 1853 to
1856—an awkward and incompetent editorial job, as his enemies gleefully pointed out. For the old animosities were not
dead. John Wilson Croker, who was old and sick and on the
edge of the grave, conceiving himself aggrieved by certain
passages in the journal, printed in the *Times* (and later in
pamphlet form) a set of letters to Russell, together with the
latter's replies, in which, among other things, he said that
Moore had possessed an animus against him since 1820, when
Mrs. Croker had failed to be "nice" to Mrs. Moore in Paris.
To this charge the harassed statesman could only reply by
denying the animus, and asking the aged Tory:

. . . were you justified in embittering the last years of the widow
of Moore, sneering at his domestic affections, and loading his
memory with reproach, on account of the few depreciatory
phrases to which you refer?

"What a bitter unfeeling man he is!" wrote Bessy to the
statesman, but otherwise she kept her hurts to herself.[9]

The *Memoirs, Journal, and Correspondence* formed Moore's
last communication with a world which had forgotten him as
a man, and remembered him only as a fading literary ornament of a former age. The magazines seized upon that awkward publication as an excuse for damning Lord John and
for balancing the defects and virtues of Thomas Moore, sum-
moning for the purpose that air of mortuary righteousness
with which each literary generation sits in judgment upon the
work of its predecessor. Unable to see, or uninterested in
seeing, the bright pageantry of Regency society pass through
its crowded pages, they damned his diary for being trivial and

heavily went over all the old arguments again—his lusciousness, his triviality, his personal charm, his vanity, his music,
his supposed love for lords and ladies, his outmoded poetic
style.   The Irish reviews, it is true, paid tribute to his devotion to the Irish cause, but almost no one saw the significance
of his long warfare for tolerance and liberalism, or if anyone
did, the tribute was wrapped in an elegant rhetoric that
rivaled his own.[10]

Bessy suffered in silence.   The Russells and the Lansdownes were very kind, Lord John providing a safe pony for
her to drive about the neighborhood, and Lady Lansdowne
taking an interest in Bessy's poor pensioners.   Her life cen-
tered in the cottage where she had spent so many happy years,
wrapped in the worship of the man she had idolized.   Her
pleasures were few—to attend to the wants of the poor and to
talk with her rare visitors about the charm and wonder of her
husband.   Every morning she rose at half-past five, when, if it
was summer, she gave directions to the gardener; after breakfast, she went upstairs to sit in Tom's old room, to be alone
with her memories.   She grew feeble from some internal complaint which the reticence of the age does not particularize,
suffering greatly in her last years, scarcely able to walk, yet
insistent to the end that the terrace where Tom had paced up
and down composing his immortal lines should be kept free of
weeds, that the ivy brought from Tara should be cared for.
She lingered until the autumn of 1865, almost forgotten save
by a few friends.   On September 8 the vault in Bromham
churchyard was again opened, and "the last rose of the poet's
glorious summer" lay beside her husband.   Her only surviving relative, William Murray, the son of her sister Anne, in-
herited the little estate.[11]

When queer little twisted Lady Morgan had read of
Moore's death in the *Times*, she had burst into tears—"I did
not think," she wrote, "I should ever shed tears again."   In
March, 1852, she wrote to a Mr. M'Garel in Dublin, suggest-

ing that "some monumental testimony to Moore, Ireland's greatest poet, should be raised in St. Patrick's cathedral." In the outburst of regret at the poet's death, a public subscription was raised for a monument to the author of the *Irish Melodies*, but the resultant statue pleased neither Lady Morgan then nor anyone interested in the poet since. For the fund, with characteristic Irish improvidence, was never completed, and the statue, cast in inferior metal, has turned rusty in the Irish rains. It was placed in front of Trinity College in Dublin, and dedicated in October, 1857. There was an immense crowd, the tops of the houses, the roofs of the Bank of Ireland and of the college buildings, and the very lampposts being filled with spectators; there was oratory from Lord Charlemont and Lord Carlisle, not to speak of a speech by Mr. O'Hagan, "an immense flow of *words* of the best *language*." Then the Lord Mayor spoke his bit, and the statue was unveiled—to Lady Morgan's understandable disappointment, for "it was almost *grotesque*, and might be anyone else than little Moore." [12] Cruelly bald-headed, the little poet stands there today, wrapped in an immense college gown, a pencil in one hand, a pad of paper in the other, in an attitude of gazing expectantly at the Bank of Ireland across the way. If the sculptor supposed that he was representing the bard in a moment of inspiration, the look of anxious longing he directs towards the bank is too characteristic of his troubled financial career for idealization; if he is supposed to be writing that favorite song, "The Meeting of the Waters," visitors to the Irish capital discover that the statue is oddly placed.

In Bromham churchyard he is more worthily commemorated. There a richly ornamented Irish cross, cut in stone, watches over the untrimmed grass of the churchyard, the dandelions sprouting at its foot, the lichen-covered gravestone at its base. On it the casual tourist may read in Gaelic lettering:

Dear harp of my country! in darkness I found thee
The cold chain of silence had hung o'er thee long
When proudly, my own island harp! I unbound thee
And gave all thy chords to light, freedom and song.

The poet of all circles and the idol of his own.
Byron.

The gravestone records the names of Anastasia and Russell Moore, of "their father Thomas Moore tenderly beloved by all who knew the goodness of his heart," and of the faithful Bessy; there is also a half-obliterated line on it, which reads: "in the memory of their dear son, Thomas Lansdowne Parr Moore." Inside the slumbering church, a large stained-glass window, somewhat inappropriately picturing the last judgment, commemorates the poet, and a window at the other end of the little edifice remembers Bessy. The quiet of the Wiltshire countryside lies all around. Across the little valley Sloperton Cottage stands as it did when the hearse and one carriage of mourners came to the graveyard; stately Bowood rises in dignity amid its ancient trees; and not far away at Bremhill Bowles's monuments and inscriptions slowly crumble beneath the lichens and the rain. To the grave of the Catholic buried in a Protestant churchyard, of the Irishman at rest in Wiltshire, of the genius once thought to be immortal and now no longer read, almost no one comes.

Notes to Chapter I

1. From files of these papers in the National Library, Dublin.
2. The best source of information about upper-class life in eighteenth-century Dublin is *The Georgian Society: Records of Eighteenth Century Domestic Architecture and Decoration in Dublin*, 5 vols. (Dublin: Dublin University Press, 1909-13). Vol. V is concerned only with county houses. This was edited by Walter G. Strickland and a committee which included the Rev. J. P. Mahaffy and R. C. Orpen. See also Richard Twiss, *A Tour in Ireland in 1775* (London, 1776); J. T. Gilbert, *History of the City of Dublin* (London, 1859); *The Picture of Dublin* (Dublin, 1811); J. Warburton, J. Whitelaw and R. Walsh, *History of Dublin*, 2 vols. (London, 1818).
3. Warburton-Whitelaw-Walsh, *op. cit.*, Vol. I, pp. vii-viii, 444-56.
4. M. A. Hickson, "Old Kerry Records: The Moores of Kerry," originally published May 31, 1882, and reprinted in *The Kerry Evening Post*, October 23, 1909. Mr. Seamus MacCall adopts Mr. Hickson's theory in his recent *Thomas Moore* (London and Dublin, 1935), pp. 9-11.
5. *The Kerry Evening Post*, October 18, 1913.
6. *County Kerry Past and Present* (Dublin, 1931), pp. 239-40.
7. "Memoirs of Myself, begun many Years since, but never, I fear, to be completed.—T. M. (1833)," published in the first volume of Lord John Russell, *Memoirs, Journal, and Correspondence of Thomas Moore*, pp. 1-76. Inaccurate though this is, it remains the chief source of information concerning Moore's formative years. The substance of the "Memoirs" also appears in the prefaces to the *Poetical Works* of 1840-41.
8. S. C. Hall, *A Memory of Thomas Moore* (London and Dublin, 1879). This pamphlet of 32 pages was issued to raise money for the memorial window at Bromham. The substance of it first appeared in the *Art Journal*, January, 1865, and afterwards in *A Book of Memories of Great Men and Women* (London, 1871). Bessy Moore read the proofs, as is noted in the pamphlet.
9. Printed by Russell, I: 130-32. The catalogue of the sale of the Moore-Power correspondence (1853) lists two notes from John Moore to Power, but beyond this John Moore's correspondence is not available. According to *Lady Morgan's Memoirs*, 2 vols. (2d ed., London, 1863, Vol. I, p. 82), John Moore took over his provision shop from the brother of Oliver Goldsmith.
10. As indicated in the text, Miss Browne kindly secured for me an official transcript of the birth and baptismal certificate of Anastatia [*sic*]

Codd from the Wexford Parochial Register. This certified copy is dated "23-4-36."—The letters of T. C. Croker to J. W. Croker are to be found in the William L. Clements Library, Ann Arbor, Michigan. The fragment quoted in the text is undated, but belongs with other correspondence of 1851-53. On June 1, 1853, T. C. Croker repeats the statement, and adds that he has secured information about Moore's "fourteen Maternal Uncles and Aunts," from the "Register in the possession of the Parish Priest of Wexford."—Regarding the Codd family the curious may consult an article contributed in 1864 by Herbert F. Hore to *The Journal of the Kilkenny and South-East of Ireland Archaeological Society* (Vol. IV, New Series, 1862-63), Dublin, 1864, pp. 38-84, in which he established to his own satisfaction that Anastasia Codd was descended from one "Squire Cod" of Castletown, a prominent Protestant in the time of Charles II. Anastasia was, of course, a devout Catholic. The *History of Wexford* abounds with legal documents, petitions, and the like, in which the name "Codd" or "Cod" appears. According to R. R. Madden (*Literary Life and Correspondence of Lady Blessington*, 3 vols., London, 1855, Vol. III, pp. 59-60), the elder Codd owned a slaughter house.

11. *Evening Freeman*, May 10, 1832; *Dublin University Magazine* (April, 1852), Vol. XXXIX, pp. 477-96. The writer seems to have been very well informed.

12. It used to be thought that Catholic births could not be registered under the law existing in 1779, but this is not correct. Under date of January 21, 1854, T. C. Croker sent J. W. Croker a copy of an attested extract from the parish records of the Church of St. Andrew, Westland Row, Dublin, giving the baptismal record of Thomas Moore. He was baptized May 30, 1779, the sponsors being James Dowling and Margaret Lynch. A copy of this certificate is also printed in the *Irish Quarterly Review*, Vol. III, pp. 151 ff.; and in John P. Gunning, *Moore: Poet and Patriot* (Dublin, 1900), p. 2. A long letter of May 30, 1853, in the Croker papers says, among other things, that "the mode . . . of recording occurrences by engraving the dates upon Crown and half Crown pieces and in some instances upon pence and half pence was a very common practice both in England and Ireland"; and T. C. Croker reproduces two, one recording a duel his father fought, and the other being a "medal" given him as a schoolboy in Cork "for Superior Merit" in 1810. The Moore "medal" is now in the British Museum.

13. James D. Herbert, *Irish Varieties* (London, 1836).

14. There is a vast fund of information about musical life in Dublin. See, *inter alia*, W. H. Grattan Flood, *A History of Irish Music* (Dublin, 1905); J. C. Walker, *Historical Memoirs of Irish Bards* (Dublin, 1786); Michael Conron, *The National Music of Ireland* (Dublin, 1846); *Journal of the Irish Folk Song Society;* John S. Bumpus, *Sir John Stevenson: A Biographical Sketch* (London, 1893); *The Reminiscences of Michael Kelly* (London, 1826); S. M. Ellis, *The Life of Michael Kelly, Musician, Actor, and Bon Viveur, 1762-1826* (London, 1930).

15. Moore's own copy of *The Sentimental and Masonic Magazine*, 6 vols., 1792-95, is now among his books in the Royal Irish Academy, Dublin. A note in the poet's hand on the fly-leaf of Vol. I confirms the statement in the "Memoirs" about the refusal of his mother to permit the

publication of her son's picture. It is a mark of the liberal temper of the Moore family that they did not forbid Tom this periodical which frankly propagandizes the principles of Masonry. It also fully reported the trials of A. H. Rowan, Horne Tooke, and others, for sedition.

16. This silver medal was exhibited at the Moore Centenary Celebration in Dublin in 1879 and is described in the *Catalogue of the Loan Collection of Relics* compiled by Thomas Sexton, a copy of which may be found in the National Library of Ireland.

17. A so-called "second edition" of Whyte's *Art of Speaking* appeared in Dublin in 1763. The suppressed essay, first printed in 1761, may be found, however, in the second part of *Miscellanea Nova* (Dublin, 1800). What led Whyte to suppress the essay is not clear. The quoted paragraph is from the 1800 edition.

18. This certificate is now in the possession of Thomas Conolly, Esq., of Chicago.

19. The abridgment of Richardson was exhibited at the Moore Centenary Celebration. The accompanying certificate had a characteristic scroll representing the emblems of literature and music, with a figure blowing a trumpet at the summit of a temple on a seaside cliff. Whyte's letter to John Moore is in Lord Lansdowne's collection at Bowood.

20. On the Mary Doyle episode see Madden, *op. cit.*, Vol. III, pp. 59-60.

21. Other early poems of Moore's appear in the *Sentimental and Masonic Magazine*, Vol. VI, as follows: July, 1795: "Anacreontique, To a Bee"; August, "Myrtilla, to the Unfortunate Maria, A Pastoral Ballad" and "The Shepherd's Farewell, A Pastoral Ballad," as well as "Friendship." Moore preserved none of them in the *Poetical Works*.

Notes to Chapter II

1. I have depended largely on W. E. H. Lecky, *History of England in the Eighteenth Century*, especially Vols. VII and VIII.

2. Lecky (Vol. VI, chap. xxv) discusses the growth of deism. Thomas Addis Emmet's testimony is reprinted in the very unsatisfactory *Life of Robert Emmett* by John W. Burke, Charleston, 1852. See especially pp. 245-60.

3. For discussions of Moore's religion from the Catholic point of view, see an article by Dr. Daniel Ambrose, M.P., in the *Irish Ecclesiastical Record* for January, 1895; and a second, by John Canon O'Hanlon, *ibid.*, March, 1895.

4. *Irish Quarterly Review*, Vol. XV, pp. 502 ff. See also Herbert's *Irish Varieties*, pp. 47-53. The catalogue of the Moore Centenary Celebration

describes a silver medal given Moore by the Historical Society in February, 1798, for "distinguished merit in composition."

5. T. C. Croker to J. W. Croker, June 24, 1853, in the William L. Clements Library. T. C. Croker at one time thought of writing Moore's biography. The confusion of Willis and Ellis in the name of the secretary is perhaps a natural calligraphic error.

6. Henry Grattan, *Memoirs of the Life and Times of the Rt. Hon. Henry Grattan* (London, 1842), Vol. IV, p. 223. Grattan delivered a noncommittal reply, for which see p. 224.

7. Moore's own copy of *Extracts from the Press: A Newspaper published in the Capital of Ireland, during part of the years 1797 and 1798. Including Numbers Sixty-Eight and Sixty-Nine, which were suppressed* (Philadelphia, 1802) is in the Royal Irish Academy and contains annotations in his hand. Against the Ossian fragment he has written: "Mine."

8. The histories of Trinity College by Stubbs and Dixon both depend upon Moore's account. An independent statement, purporting to be from the "posthumous ms" of an anonymous writer is printed in the *Dublin University Magazine* (May, 1846), pp. 549-59, which adds certain details. See also Herbert, *loc. cit.*

9. There is much futile discussion over the tune in question. Moore says he was playing "Let Erin remember the Day" i.e., "Let Erin remember the days of old," the air of which is founded on "The Little Red Fox." But this air was not generally available until it appeared in Holden's *Collection of Old Established Irish Slow and Quick Tunes* (1806), when Emmet had been dead three years. A. P. Graves (*Irish Literary and Musical Studies*, p. 194) and others propose to substitute "The Fox's Sleep," which was printed by Bunting in 1796, to which Moore later wrote the words of "When he who adores thee," but this air is scarcely martial.

10. T. C. Croker to J. W. Croker, February 19, 1851, and May 30, 1853.

11. Identified through the reference in Herbert's *Irish Varieties*. A prose travesty of Mrs. Radcliffe, which dates from Moore's college days, entitled "The Lamp of St. Agatha," may be read in R. H. Shepherd, *Prose and Verse by Thomas Moore* (London, 1878), pp. 6-8.

12. Discrepancies in accounts of the date when Moore was graduated are quickly ended by consulting the *Catalogue of Graduates Who Have Proceeded to Degrees in the University of Dublin* (Dublin, 1869), p. 410: "Moore (Thomas), B.A. *Vern.* 1799." Burston took his degree at the Summer Commencement. See p. 81. I see no reason to doubt, as some have done, the fact of Moore's taking a degree.

Notes to Chapter III

1. The necessity for caution on the part of an Irishman is confirmed by a sentence in Moore's letter to his mother of April 5, 1799, in which, after saying that to secure a seat in the coach he took the name of another passenger, he adds: "Mr. Patrickson represented to me strongly the danger of such counterfeiting in times like the present, which you may be sure prevented me from much sleep that night, but in the morning I contrived to have my proper name inserted" (Russell, I:83).

2. Two sketches of Atkinson containing interesting personal details may be found in the *Dublin Inquisitor*, Vol. I, pp. 19-25 (January, 1821), and *The Thespian Dictionary* (London, 1802).

3. From a biographical sketch of Moira in *Public Characters of 1798-9*, 3d ed. (London, 1801).

4. T. M. Ray's annotated copy of the catalogue of the Moore Centenary scrapbook (now in the Royal Irish Academy) describes a miniature of the poet by Comerford which I have not seen, painted when he was about 25; and also a sketch in pencil by Edwin Hayes from 1815. I have compounded my description from these passages and from the much later account in the *Dublin University Magazine*, Vol. XXXIX, pp. 477-96 (April, 1852). The latter is an especially interesting portrait of Moore in 1830: "No two faces could be more different than Moore's in repose or in action. The features drooped, the eye was dimmed, or seemed to gaze into remotest space, when Moore was silent or reflective: the up-drawn brow gave an anxious expression to the countenance, whilst the dilating nostril alone gave animation to it. Curiously enough, even when the whole countenance was lighted up, the eye had often the same dimness, which gave a look of absence. . . . It might be, perhaps, in some degree accounted for by his being near-sighted."

5. See John S. Bumpus, *Sir John Stevenson: A Biographical Sketch* (London, 1893).

6. Dr. Lawrence's Greek ode apparently gave place to the one by Moore himself which prefaces the *Anacreon* volume.

7. Modern Anacreontic scholarship is summarized in W. Schmid and O. Stählin, *Geschichte der griechischen Literatur*, Vol. I, pp. 430-41; and O. Crusius's article in the Pauly-Wissowa *Realencyklopädie*, Vol. I, pp. 2045 ff. The fragments of the real Anacreon with a translation may be conveniently found in J. M. Edmonds, *Lyra Graeca*, Vol. II, pp. 120-221 (Loeb Classical Library). Recent verse translations include S. C. Irving, *Odes of Anacreon* (Evanston, 1902); J. F. Davidson, *The Anacreontea* (London and New York, 1915); and E. Richardson, *The Odes of Anacreon* (New Haven,

1928). This last may be profitably compared with Moore's elaborate paraphrases.

8. *Select Odes of Anacreon, with Critical Annotations. To which are added Translations and Imitations of other Ancient Authors* (London, 1802). This duodecimo of 167 pages is by a graduate of Trinity who took his degree in the spring of 1743. It is dedicated to the Earl of Moira by the editor, Robert Drought, another Trinity graduate, who is either the Robert Drought of 1779 or a man of the same name in the class of 1795.

9. Sir Jonah Barrington, *Personal Sketches of His Own Times*, 3 vols. (London, 1827-32), Vol. II, pp. 163 ff.; William Jerdan, *Autobiography* (London, 1852), Vol. IV, pp. 90-93; from the *Remains of Rev. Edmund D. Griffin*, quoted in *Blackwoods*, Vol. XXXII, pp. 110-11.

10. All that apparently remains of *The Gypsy Prince* is the musical score, of which there is a copy in the British Museum: *The Gypsy Prince, A Comic Opera in Two Acts, Now Performing with universal applause at the Theatre Royal, Haymarket, Compos'd and Selected by Michael Kelly.* This is a music folio of 67 pages. Some of the airs were taken from Paisiello, but Moore seems to have supplied the tune for "I have roamed through many a weary round," sung by Kelly. As Kelly quotes this poem entire, calling it "very pretty," in his *Reminiscences*, Vol. II, pp. 162-63, the absence of Moore's name from the title page need not be construed as an intentional slight. The plot of the play is given in *Walker's Hibernian Magazine*, August, 1801, and runs as follows: The scene is Spain. The opera opens with a view of a camp of gypsies, whose prince humanely rescues an old Jew from the Alguazils, who were hurrying him off to appear before the Grand Inquisitor. This seriously imperils the life of the prince, and in attempting to elude the Inquisition, he wanders into the garden of one of the Inquisitors. There he chances upon Antonia, the niece of the Inquisitor. They fall in love. The girl strives to conceal the prince, who is, however, discovered and haled before the Inquisitors, one of whom recognizes in him a long-lost nephew. He is pardoned and marries the girl of his choice. The account further says that though the piece was not very interesting as drama, it served as a vehicle for some pleasing music; and that the humor depended chiefly upon Fawcett, who acted Rincon. *The Monthly Mirror* (July, 1801), then edited by Edward Dubois, printed a full review typical of contemporary "notices," finding the piece flimsy and uninteresting, but praising the creditable taste and "scientific arrangement" of the music. In his *Account of the English Stage*, Vol. VII, p. 522, Genest says it was acted about ten times and quotes the opinion of the *Dramatic Censor* that it was a very poor piece.

11. Moore mentions this larger dramatic piece in a letter to his mother dated March 28, 1801 (Russell, I:112). There is in the British Museum (Add. MSS. 25,926) part of a ballad opera attributed to Moore, in the George Patmore collection. This is written on paper watermarked 1795, and begins "As the bird with trembling pinion." The *dramatis personae* include Justice Homespun, Mr. Worry, Captain O'Shannon, etc. There is of course the possibility that this is a lost opera of Moore's, but in the absence of any reference by him to any other opera than *The Gypsy Prince* and *M.P.*, and since none of the songs in the manuscript appears in

Moore's collected poems, the attribution seems doubtful. Moore did, however, compose an operatic squib, "Apollo at Oxford," the manuscript of which is in the British Museum.

12. What this periodical work was, is not clear. Two volumes of a weekly magazine called *The Pic-Nic* were issued in 1803, the outgrowth of a private club and theatrical society organized by Col. Henry Greville. *Walker's Hibernian Magazine* (November, 1806, pp. 673-76) prints the prospectus of a weekly periodical called "The Picnic," and says that "from various circumstances, it never having appeared according to its original designation, this production is now presented to our readers." The essay has all the appearance of being Moore's, and furthermore opens with a quotation from Catullus, *Carmina*, xiii, which is identical with the motto of the first number of Greville's *The Pic-Nic* under date of January 8, 1803. The actual magazine, however, does not seem to follow the lines of the prospectus. It is of course possible that Moore wrote a prospectus for Greville in good faith and that, owing to the attacks on the Pic-Nic Society said to have been instigated by Sheridan, who feared competition with Drury Lane, he withdrew from the project.

In this connection one may as well dispose of *The World at Westminster*, a periodical attributed to Moore even by the careful W. J. Mac-Manus in his valuable *Bibliographical Hand-List of the First Editions of Thomas Moore* (Dublin, 1934). The two bound volumes of this magazine, edited by "Thomas Brown the Younger" are dated 1816 (not 1818, as Mr. MacManus has it) and comprise thirty papers dealing with life in Westminster School from November 28, 1815, to May 16, 1816. Neither in subject nor in style do they suggest Moore; and several of the essays discuss internal affairs at the school which he could not possibly have known. The poet first signed himself "Thomas Brown the Younger" when he pubished *Intercepted Letters* in 1813. I suggest that a bright undergraduate "borrowed" the cognomen.

13. Mrs. Tighe is thus described in Alfred Webb, *A Compendium of Irish Biography* (Dublin, 1878). According to the Moran MSS. in the British Museum (Vol. II, Eg. 2150), Moore's lyric, "I saw thy form in youthful prime," refers to her unhappy matrimonial life.

14. For "The Invisible Girl" see *Notes and Queries,* 6th Series, September 6, 1884, p. 196. The original "Invisible Girl" was a mechanical illusion described in the *Poetical Register* for 1802 (pp. 195-97) and in Dennie's *Port Folio* (Vol. IV, p. 191) as follows: "From a glass globe, suspended in the midst of a room, and having no apparent communication with any thing else, a female conversed with the spectators in four different languages, and played upon the piano forte: her breath might even be felt." The illusion was first exhibited in Leicester Fields.

Notes to Chapter IV

1. On Colonel Hamilton see Hugh Edward Egerton, *The Royal Commission on the Losses and Services of American Loyalists 1783 to 1785* . . . (Oxford: Printed for Presentation to the Members of The Roxburghe Club, 1915), p. 185. A memorial by Hamilton says he was born in Ireland, came to America in 1767, settled in New York in 1774, and later removed to Charleston, where he managed the affairs of W. Clarkson and became a merchant on his own account. He was for six weeks a member of the American forces, apparently under compulsion. After the siege of Charleston he saw active service with the British, was taken prisoner at the capture of Ninety Six, and was later exchanged. See also Lorenzo Sabine, *Biographical Sketches of Loyalists of the American Revolution* (Boston, 1864), Vol. I, pp. 511-12; and *Travels through the United States of North America . . . in the Years 1795, 1796, and 1797* by the Duke de la Rochefoucault-Liancourt (London, 1800, 2d ed.), Vol. III, pp. 4 ff., for Hamilton's later life. Further details about Norfolk can be gleaned from Isaac Weld, Jr., *Travels through the States of North America . . .* (London, 1799, 2d ed.), Vol. I, pp. 169 ff.; and Thomas J. Wertenbaker, *Norfolk: Historic Southern Port* (Durham, 1931), especially chaps. iii and iv. No city suffered more severely in the Revolution, and in few were antagonisms so fierce.

2. G. P. R. James, who was later British consul at Norfolk, collected a number of anecdotes of Moore's sojourns in Virginia, which he told to B. J. Lossing. See "Tom Moore in America," *Harper's New Monthly Magazine*, Vol. LV, pp. 537-41 (September, 1877).

3. According to the *Bermuda Gazette* of January 14, 1804, the *Driver* arrived the previous Saturday and, after a week in port, sailed in company with the *Boston*.

4. Moore to Douglas, Maggs Bros. Sale Catalogue, June, 1912. His second letter to that officer, quoted in the text, is from a catalogue of March, 1912.

5. On Moore's adventures among the Bermudian ladies see J. C. L. Clark, *Tom Moore in Bermuda. A Bit of Literary Gossip* (Boston, 1909, 2d ed.); and the excellent Rider-Cooper *Bermuda: A Guide Book for Travelers* (New York, 1924), especially pp. 91, 106-7. According to Dennie's *Port Folio*, Vol. IV, p. 223 (July 14, 1804) Moore's "The Wedding Ring" (which became "The Ring: To . . ." in the collected edition) "was written while the author was at Bermuda. . . . Mr. Moore being in company with a lady of the place, she playfully proffered him a *ring*. He gallantly replied in the following gallant verses." It may or may not be significant

that the two concluding stanzas disappeared from later versions of the poem:

> While thus to mine thy bosom lies,
>   While thus our breaths commingling glow,
> 'Twere more than woman to be wise,
> 'Twere more than man to wish thee so.

> Did we not love so true, so dear,
>   This lapse could never be forgiven . . .
> But . . . hearts so fond! and lips so near!
>   *Give* me the ring, and now . . . O Heaven!

I quote the *Port Folio.*

6. In his pamphlet attacking Moore's memory, published in 1853, John Wilson Croker points out that there were two deputies in succession who filled the poet's post in Bermuda after his departure. He writes that "in the autumn of 1809—Moore got into some difficulty by the incompetence or misconduct of his deputy in the Admiralty Court of Bermuda," and appends the footnote that: "This was not the affair that produced his great embarrassment—which occurred from a different deputy in 1818" (p. 23). This second deputy was named Sheddon (Russell, II:133). A letter in the Croker papers from Croker to Moore, dated December 25, 1826, which Croker does not mention in his pamphlet, seems to indicate that Sheddon was appointed by the Governor of Bermuda, and advises the poet to retain the post if it is likely to be profitable: "You do not tell me what the office now produces—I conclude next to nothing; but if it pays its own expenses you may look upon it as a lottery ticket in your drawer, which may turn up, one day or other, a £20,000 prize. If the profits be little, I conclude the risk cannot be great; and as the Governor has appt. the deputy, and that you have, as I presume from your letter, not confirmed by any formal act, that appointment, I doubt whether in want of any loss you could be held personally responsible." The letter offers to "recommend you some man in the Naval Department who would undertake it for you." Inasmuch as in the pamphlet Croker pretends to be shocked at Moore's proposal in 1809 to resign in favor of someone who would pay him for the appointment, the letter of 1826 is of considerable interest.

7. The *Bermuda Gazette* for Saturday, April 28, says that the *Leander, Cambrian,* and *Boston* departed the preceding Wednesday.

8. Quoted in Wandell and Minnigerode, *Aaron Burr* (New York, 1925), Vol. II, p. 182.

9. This poem was first published, with a facsimile, by James G. Johnson in *The Bookman,* Vol. VII, pp. 386-87 (July, 1898). Mr. Johnson says he got it from a grandchild of Mr. William Wischam, Moore's host in Richmond. But Moore speaks only of "Mr. Wickham, one of their celebrated legal characters, . . . a gentleman, whose manners and mode of life would do honour to the most cultivated societies," and I know of no William Wischam who acted as host to Moore. See *Epistles, Odes, and Other Poems,* p. 151.

10. Jefferson's letter is printed in the *American Historical Review,* Vol. 33, pp. 832-35 (July, 1928). For the authoritative account of Merry's

social difficulties see Henry Adams, *History of the United States during the Administration of Thomas Jefferson*, Bk. II, chap. xvii.

11. From Moore's commonplace book now in the Pierpont Morgan Library.

12. For Moore's experiences in Philadelphia see Harold M. Ellis, *Joseph Dennie and His Circle* (Austin, Texas, 1915); Albert H. Smyth, *The Philadelphia Magazines and their Contributors* (Philadelphia, 1892); Ellis P. Oberholtzer, *The Literary History of Philadelphia* (Philadelphia, 1906).

13. The two letters of Moore to Dennie which I have quoted were first printed in *The Critic*, n.s., Vol. IX, p. 270 (June 2, 1888). For the conversation with Vaux and the two letters to Hall, one written from Ashbourne June, 1816, and one from Devizes July 12, 1818, see *The Collector*, Vol. IX, pp. 66-67 (February, 1896).

14. On Moore's "Canadian Boat-Song" see Ernest Gagnon, *Chansons populaires du Canada* under the title: "J'ai trop grand' peur des loups."

15. Apparently Douglas suggested Moore's visit to Niagara: "Indeed, indeed, my dearest friend, I never can sufficiently thank you for having persuaded and facilitated my visit to this very wonderful place." The letter is printed in the sales catalogue of Maggs Brothers (No. 291) for June, 1912.

Notes to Chapter V

1. See P. W. Clayden, *Rogers and His Contemporaries* (London, 1889), Vol. I, p. 24.

2. A small notebook of 36 pages in the Henry E. Huntington Library contains a clean draft of 15 of the poems, and the library also possesses manuscript versions of a number of others. After the publication of *Epistles, Odes, and Other Poems* (from which I have consistently quoted in Chapter IV), Moore subjected the contents of that volume to considerable stylistic revision, so that the final form of the poems in the Oxford edition—today the most convenient collection of Moore's verse—sometimes differs importantly from the first versions. The changes are usually in the direction of euphony.

3. *Monthly Review*, Vol. XXXV, pp. 404-9; *British Critic*, Vol. XX, pp. 27-32; *Monthly Magazine*, Vol. XII, pp. 106-7; *British Critic*, Vol. XVIII, pp. 540-41; *Monthly Review*, Vol. XXXIX, pp. 174-79; *Edinburgh Review*, Vol. II, pp. 462-76.

4. Moore's account of the duel, written as a continuation of the "Memoirs of Myself" in 1833, may be found in Russell, I:199-214. Rogers' account, which corrects Moore's in certain small particulars, is in *Recollections of the Table-Talk of Samuel Rogers* (New York, 1856), pp. 276-78. Jeffrey's side is briefly set forth in Lord Cockburn's *Life of Lord Jeffrey*

(Edinburgh, 1852), Vol. I, pp. 171-74. On August 22, 1806, Jeffrey wrote George J. Bell that he had explained to Moore: "I considered myself merely as the censor of the morality of his book, and . . . intended to assert nothing as to the personal motives or personal character of the author, of whom I had no knowledge at the time." Moore "has professed his penitence for what he has written, and declared that he will never again apply any little talent he may possess, to such purpose . . . He has behaved with great spirit throughout this business."

The foregoing passage is of some importance as a possible clue to a suppressed book by Moore, of which only a single copy, now in the London office of Longmans, is known to exist. This consists of folded sheets ready for binding, and runs to eight pages of introduction and 104 of text. The work is entitled *Sketches of Pious Women;* the introduction, signed "P. P.," says that the articles are taken from a *Dictionary of Female Biography* begun some years before. Mr. MacManus has identified this latter as a work by Mary Hays, published in London in six volumes in 1803. There are 22 sketches in Moore's work, the characters running from Mary Magdalen to Pope Joan [!], and each is like a *chante-fable—* i.e., prose, followed by verse, the verse usually translated or paraphrased from the Greek or Latin of a church father. The prose oscillates between a learned pruriency and a sort of amorous reverence. This curious relic is enclosed in an envelope on which is written: "Printed sheets of a poem printed by Carpenter, never published/ Thomas Moore/ to the care of/ Messrs. Longman/ left by Mr. Moore with Longman and Co Apr 27/41/ Mr. Moore paid £100 to Carpenter for the suppression of the enclosed." The date, of course, is the date of the leaving the package with Longman, with whom Moore had no connection in 1806. The manuscript of part of the work is now in the Pierpont Morgan Library. It is written on paper watermarked 1802. In the same library a letter from Moore to Carpenter, dated September 5, 1814, asks Carpenter to send him the "pious women." Moore further says he will make good any "pilferings" from the manuscript.

On August 29, 1806, Moore wrote Lady Donegal that he was about to go bury himself "among my St Chrysostoms and Origens" in Marsh's Library in Dublin, so that he was reading, or about to read, the church fathers in the summer of 1806. The versification in *Sketches of Pious Women* is of the general order of Moore's early amatory poems. This suggests that Moore may have planned the volume, worked it up, and then, as a consequence of the attack on his morals, and perhaps also because of his statement to Jeffrey, abandoned the project sometime in 1806 or 1807.

5. *Monthly Review*, Vol. LI, pp. 59-70; *Eclectic Magazine*, Vol. II, Pt. 2, pp. 811-15; *Annual Review and History of Literature*, Vol. V, pp. 498-99; *Critical Review*, Vol. IX, pp. 113-25; *Beau Monde*, Vol. I, pp. 37-41; *Anti-Jacobin Review*, Vol. XXIV, pp. 263-71, and Vol. XXVI, p. 125; *La Belle Assemblée*, Vol. I, Pt. ii, pp. 344-49; *British Critic*, Vol. XXIX, p. 700.

6. For a discussion of the Murphy Sallust see "The First Edition of Arthur Murphy's *Sallust*" by J. Homer Caskey, *Philological Quarterly*, Vol. XIII, pp. 404-8. According to Allibone's *Dictionary of Authors*, Vol. II, p. 1389 (quoted by Mr. Caskey), the translation was completed by

Moore, but like Mr. Caskey I am unable to discover any authority for this assertion except a statement in the *Repository of Arts, Literature, Commerce,* etc., Vol. III, pp. 316-19, which in turn quotes the *Biographical Dictionary of Living Authors.*

7. On the musical taste of the period consult Henry Davey, *History of English Music* (London, 1921, 2d ed.), especially chaps. viii and ix; John Ashton, *Social England under the Regency* (London, 1890, 2 vols.); also his *When William IV was King* (London, 1896); Kelly's *Reminiscences* already cited, and Ellis's *Life of Michael Kelly* (London, 1930); the appropriate sections of *Grove's Dictionary of Music and Musicians;* and biographies of the singers and performers of the period.

8. On the Celtic revival see Edward D. Snyder, *The Celtic Revival in English Literature, 1760-1800* (Cambridge, Mass., 1923).

9. Moore's letters to Thomson are in the British Museum, Add. MSS. 35, 263, folios 265, 267, 274-75.

10. The dating of this letter to Stevenson as "Feb. 1807" threw the bibliography of the *Irish Melodies* into confusion for some years. See Stephen Gwynn, *Thomas Moore* (New York, 1905), pp. 43-44, 193 ff.; and the fuller discussion by Percy H. Muir, "Thomas Moore's Irish Melodies 1808-1834" in *The Colophon,* Part xv (September, 1933), which in turn corrects certain particulars in the Gwynn discussion.

11. The *Notes from the Letters of Thomas Moore to his Music Publisher . . . with an introductory letter from Thomas Crofton Croker* (New York, [1854]) gives a very prejudiced account of Moore's relations to James Power. This publication was instigated by T. C. Croker, who hoped to bring it out in London, but who was prevented by an injunction granted Longman. A fairer account of Moore's relations with both the Powers is James Dowling's *Moore's Melodies: The Original Publishers, and their Lawsuits . . .* (Dublin, 1863).

12. There is a vast literature on the relation of the *Irish Melodies* to their originals, most of it in the *Journal of the Irish Folk Song Society.* Partisans of Bunting have been especially bitter in their comments on Moore and Stevenson. One of the fairest estimates, however, is that of Charles Villiers Stanford, *The Irish Melodies of Thomas Moore* (London and New York, 1895), though even Stanford does not sufficiently allow for the conditions of the problem set before poet and composer. See also Michael Conran, *The National Music of Ireland* (Dublin, 1846); Alfred Moffat, *The Minstrelsy of Ireland* (London, 1897); Charles Villiers Stanford (ed.), *The Complete Collection of Irish Music as noted by George Petrie* (London, 1903); James E. Culwick, *Distinctive Characteristics of Ancient Irish Melody* (Dublin, 1897).

Notes to Chapter VI

1. Lord Holland, *Memoirs of the Whig Party During my Time* (London, 1854), Vol. II, p. 249.

2. In his preface to the third volume of the *Poetical Works* of 1840-41 Moore says, half apologetically, that the ideas in "Corruption" were "caught up from Bolingbroke, Sir William Wyndham, and other statesmen of that factious period," and adds that these satires "met with but little success,— never having attained, I believe, even the honours of a second edition." A second edition was, however, published in 1809.

3. The *Anti-Jacobin Review*, Vol. XXXI, pp. 308-9 (1808). A more favorable notice may be found in *Beau Monde*, Vol. IV, pp. 119-20 (1808), though the review remarks that the whole pamphlet was a peg to hang votes on. The *Monthly Review* for April, 1809, was laudatory.

4. *Lady Morgan's Memoirs: Autobiography, Diaries and Correspondence* (London, 1862), Vol. I, pp. 180-83. If the passage refers to an earlier visit by Moore, its spirit is as true of the later one.

5. John Carr, *The Stranger in Ireland: or, A Tour in the Southern and Western Parts of that Country, in the Year 1805*, Philadelphia, 1806, pp. 267-69. The chief source of information on the Kilkenny theatricals is the privately printed *The Private Theatre of Kilkenny, with Introductory Observations on other Private Theatres in Ireland, before it was opened*, 1825. Moore's own article, "Private Theatricals," in the *Edinburgh Review*, October, 1827, is a flourish of erudition about the history of private theatricals since the Greeks.

6. Letter from T. C. Croker to J. W. Croker, May 2, 1853, in the W. L. Clements Library.

7. The *Dublin Satirist*, November, 1809, pp. 51-52. This vituperative periodical, which ran for two years, attacked Moore as "The Egotist" in a series called "Characteristics of Notorious Individuals in Dublin," and was answered by *The Satirist Satirized, or the Junto Unmasked*, Dublin, 1809.

8. The authority for this hitherto unsuspected performance is a clipping from the London *British Press* in the Moran MSS. Vol. IV (Eg. 2152 B.M.). The clipping, dated January 27, 1807, announces that on Monday a select party of one hundred witnessed the performance. The Marquis of Tavistock and Henry Stanhope performed the quarrel of Brutus and Cassius, and Moore's future biographer, Lord John Russell, then fifteen, delivered a "very neat Epilogue of his own composition." The *Leinster Journal*, as quoted in *The Private Theatre of Kilkenny*, p. 38, was therefore in error in speaking of Moore's appearance in the role of David as "the

first appearance of this Gentleman on any Stage," a statement which has naturally misled Moore's biographers.

9. Atkinson's poetical epistle is printed in the *Cyclopaedian Magazine*, Vol. II, pp. 688 ff., December, 1808. In October (p. 588) this periodical had objected to the "inflated puffings—the bombastic daubings which characterize the critiques that have appeared in our prints relative to Kilkenny theatricals," but admitted that "they have gained a vast accession of interest in Anacreon Moore."

10. See Moore's preface to Vol. VII of the *Poetical Works*, pp. xxi-xxii.

11. See the life of Mary Ann Dyke Duff by Muriel Shaver in the *Dictionary of American Biography*. Joseph N. Ireland, *Mrs. Duff* (Boston, 1882), gives a fuller account but throws little light on Mrs. Duff's sisters.

12. On Anne Dyke see *Notes and Queries*, 8th Series, Vol. II, pp. 427, 472, 510; and Vol. III, p. 135.

13. *The Dublin Satirist*, December, 1809, p. 109.

14. In the W. L. Clements Library.

15. Also in the Croker collection of the W. L. Clements Library. Mulock says: "By the way I knew Bessy (Dyke) before Moore was acquainted with her—and my clear opinion was that Moore wished to have her on other than conjugal terms—which however her sharp, English Mother prevented by forbidding his further visits until a formal proposal was made—This fell within my own knowledge." An undated letter in the Lockhart papers in the same library, addressed to J. W. Croker, then engaged on his review of the Russell *Memoirs* for the *Quarterly*, says: "I recollect that when Moore married there was a rumour of Murray's (i.e., William H. Murray) having discovered an intrigue and used rough arguments with the Poet: but I think Scott had never given any credit to that story & now after reading the volumes pubd I feel that it cd not be true." Aside from the extreme improbability that either Mulock or Lockhart could have had first-hand information on a subject of this nature, Lockhart's story falls to the ground on a comparison of dates. Murray did not meet his future wife until 1815, when she joined the Edinburgh company (J. C. Dibdin, *Annals of the Edinburgh Stage*, Edinburgh, 1888, p. 498). He could not therefore have used "rough arguments" with Moore in 1811 concerning a girl of whose existence he was utterly ignorant.

16. T. C. Croker to J. W. Croker, in a letter dated "Saturday," apparently written in May or June, 1853.

17. T. C. Croker to J. W. Croker, January 19, 1854. In a letter of July 4, 1853, T. C. Croker says that he danced with the "youngest Miss Dyke" in 1806; that the Dykes lived in "a wretched dirty ruinous house" "on the opposite side of Patrick Street from my Grandmother's in a Street called Bowlinggreen Street," and that his partner, who was much taller than he was, blacked the eye of Spencer Vassall and kicked him downstairs. Young Vassall was ten, Croker was eight, and "Miss Dyke," by whom he apparently means Anne Dyke, was eleven or twelve when this children's party took place.

18. Bessy also appeared as Mrs. Bruin in *The Mayor of Garret*.

19. The London clippings are preserved in the Moran MSS., Vol. IV (Eg. 2152, B.M.).

20. Croker prints this letter in his pamphlet containing his correspondence with Lord John Russell about the *Memoirs.*

21. The cast was as follows: Sir Charles Canvas, Mr. Oxberry; Captain Canvas, Mr. Horn; Henry de Rosier, Mr. Phillips; Mr. Hartington, Mr. Raymond; Leatherhead, Mr. Lovegrove; Davy, Mr. Knight; La Fosse, Mr. Wemitzer; Lady Bab Blue, Mrs. Sparks; Madame de Rosier, Mrs. Hamilton; Miss Selwyn, Mrs. Mountain; Miss Hartington, Miss Kelly; Susan, Mrs. Bland. Students of the period will recognize the ability of these actor-singers, Oxberry, Phillips, Mrs. Mountain, and Miss Kelly being at the very top of the profession.

22. In a letter to Miss Godfrey, September 11, 1811 (erroneously dated by Russell (VIII:91-93) from Dublin, though London is clearly meant), Moore says that "I had a long struggle with [the] licenser for the retention of several most ticklish passages about bribery." A letter to Leigh Hunt now in the British Museum (Add. MSS. 37,210), without date but written in 1811, adds that "the opera underwent a very severe cutting from the Licenser for a very opposite quality to Courtiership" and re-affirms Moore's determination not to write more for the stage. The original manuscript of *M.P.* is in the Larpent collection in the Henry E. Huntington Library, and shows that the omissions required by the licenser were trifling. There are a number of variants between the manuscript and the printed version which probably represent changes introduced during the run of the piece. It is of course possible that the Larpent manuscript is a revision submitted after the licenser had cut up a previous version, but this seems unlikely.

23. The *Morning Chronicle* reviewed the opera September 10, 1811, and again, September 11; the quotation from the *Morning Post* is from the issue of September 11; the quotation from the *Dramatic Censor* is from the issue of September 9, and was probably written up from the dress rehearsal.

Notes to Chapter VII

1. Moore's letter to Lord Holland, dated only 1812, is among the manuscripts in the smoking room at Holland House printed in *Holland House* by the Princess Marie of Liechtenstein (London, 1874), Vol. II, pp. 84-85. Although the work is inaccurate in some particulars, there seems to be no reason to doubt the validity of her transcript.

2. The problem of identifying Moore's contributions both to the *Morning Chronicle* and to the London *Times* is a vexing one. Some are unsigned, but of course may be identified because they are printed in the *Poetical Works.* Others appear under a variety of signatures. Two epigrams in the *Chronicle,* April 14, 1812, are signed "R," one of them being in the

Poetical Works, a fact which serves to establish this signature provisionally, though a second contributor to this paper used the same letter, and a third signs himself "Tower . . . R." "The Insurrection of the Papers" is signed "O." The burlesque odes of Horace, which begin September 8, 1812, are signed "Bibliopola Tryphon," which, by the time of the appearance of the "Lines on the Death of Sheridan" August 5, 1816, is shortened and re-versed to "T. B." (Thomas Brown). These poems also appear in part in an edition of Moore's works published at Leipzig by Ernest Fleischer in 1833, to which the highly inaccurate "Biographical and Critical Sketch of Thomas Moore" by J. W. Lake, dated 1827, serves as an introduction. The letter of November 2, 1818, protesting against Blackwood's misrepre-sentation of "The Legacy" (see Russell, II:208) is signed "J. P." from Croydon, but "So may my Lady's prayer prevail" (September 22, 1818) is signed "Brunetto," and "Go, Brothers in Wisdom" (August 18, 1818) is signed "P. F." Later contributions to the *Chronicle* in the thirties and forties are either unsigned or attributed to "B." I have examined the files of this paper from 1812 to 1852 with the exception of the years 1832-35. The quotations in the text are from the original newspaper versions. In the *Times,* to which Moore began contributing in January, 1826, he usually signed himself either "S" or "E" or used no signature. Unsigned poems, of which one can only say "aut Morus aut Diabolus," can sometimes be identified by Moore's habit of using footnotes, even in his newspaper verse.

3. The various passages on the Prince Regent may be found in the order in which they appear in the text, as follows: "To a Plumassier," *Morning Chronicle,* March 16, 1812; "Extracts from the Diary of a Fashionable Politician," *M.C.,* March 30, 1812; "The Insurrection of the Papers," *M.C.,* April 23, 1812—the version in the *Poetical Works* does not contain the stanza likening Liverpool to a nightcap; "The Sale of the Tools," *M.C.,* December 21, 1812; "Correspondence between a Lady and a Gentle-man," *M.C.,* January 6, 1813; "Reinforcements for Lord Wellington," *M.C.,* August 27, 1813.

4. Moore's first letter to Byron appears in his *Life of Byron,* where Byron's several replies are also printed, but Moore's other notes are now in the possession of Sir John Murray at his historic London office.

5. On the relations of Moore and Hunt see Edmund Blunden, *Leigh Hunt and His Circle* (New York and London, 1930); and his *Leigh Hunt's "Examiner" Examined* (New York and London, 1928). Hunt's own ac-count may be read in *The Autobiography of Leigh Hunt with Reminis-cences of Friends and Contemporaries, and with Thornton Hunt's Intro-duction and Postscript,* newly edited by Roger Ingpen, 2 vols. (West-minster, 1903). See especially Vol. II, pp. 85 ff.

6. Hunt's letters to Moore are in the British Museum, Add. MSS. 37,210. These were published in *Prose and Verse Humorous, Satirical, and Senti-mental by Thomas Moore.* Russell (VIII:120-23) prints a letter from Hunt to Moore as of September 12, 1812, which should *follow* those in Shepherd.

7. See Dora Neill Raymond, *The Political Career of Lord Byron* (New York, 1924).

8. Moore did not collect all of the "Horace" series in the *Poetical Works*. The two quoted in the text appeared September 8 and 16, 1812, in the *Morning Chronicle*. A third, attributed to the much hated Duigenan, was printed October 6. The version of Ode XXXVIII, Lib. I ("Persicos odi, puer, adparatus") in the *Poetical Works* lacks a stanza animadverting on the Regent. This poem appeared in the *Chronicle* October 19, 1812.

9. *Anti-Jacobin Review*, Vol. XLIV, pp. 266-68; from a notice of the twelfth edition.

10. Mr. Stephen Gwynn (p. 53) says "the two lived together, in Bury Street, for a year, till after the birth of their first child." But Moore speaks explicitly of Brompton.

11. P. W. Clayden, *Rogers and His Contemporaries*, Vol. II, p. 104.

12. In describing this episode Russell (VIII:141-43) leaves the name blank, but it is supplied in a letter from T. C. Croker to J. W. Croker in the W. L. Clements Library, dated June 23, 1853, which adds other details.

13. "Anecdotes of a Celebrated Poet," *Lady's Magazine*, n.s., Vol. X, pp. 88-90. This is one of a series of such gushing personalia in the magazine.

Notes to Chapter VIII

1. *Dublin Examiner*, Vol. I, pp. 241 ff., August, 1816. Other reviews and notices in this publication had been in the main laudatory.

2. This running account of the legal battles of the Power brothers is largely based on the pamphlet by James Dowling already cited. The quotation from Moore's letter to James Power is from an excerpt of Moore's letter of July 31(?), 1816, which may be found in *Notes from the Letters of Thomas Moore to his Music Publisher, James Power . . .* New York, n.d. The value of this book is unfortunately lowered by the arbitrary character of the extracts printed.

3. From the same book, letters written in June and July, 1815, and again in September and October. The quotation from the letter to Strutt, however, is taken from the letters printed by J. Charles Cox in his "Some Unpublished Letters of Tom Moore's," which may be read in *Littell's Living Age*, Vol. 241, pp. 437-42, April, 1904. The other passages are from Russell.

4. *Edinburgh Review*, Vol. XXIX, pp. 1-34, November, 1817; *Blackwoods Magazine*, Vol. I, pp. 279-88, June, 1817, and again pp. 503-10; the *Monthly Magazine*, Vol. XLIII, pp. 450-51; the *Literary Panorama*, n.s., Vol. VI, pp. 897-914; the *European Magazine*, Vol. 72, pp. 55-58. The quotation from the *Monthly Review* is taken from a reprint of the article

in the *Lady's Magazine*, Vol. XLVIII, which extends over a number of pages (343 ff.; 387-89; 435 ff.; 531 ff.). The Tory *British Review*, Vol. X, pp. 30-54, severely attacked the poem, which it found imitative of Byron, and wanted to know why poets could not content themselves with English themes. The *Literary Gazette*, May 31, 1817, also said Moore was imitating Byron, but concluded an eight-column review with the theory that "there is no diminution of Mr. Moore's genius." The *British Lady's Magazine*, Vol. I, n.s., pp. 180-81, called the poem "a chaos of Eastern Rhapsodies" concealing immorality, impiety, and voluptuous vice, a calamity for literature and an obstacle to the advance of human refinement. The *Critical Review*, 5th series, Vol. V, pp. 560-81, published one of the shrewdest of the unfavorable notices.

5. A "German" opera, *Lalla Rook*, the music by C. E. Horn, was produced in Dublin in 1820, and failed. David's *Lalla-Roukh*, opera in two acts, was produced in Paris in 1862. Anton Rubenstein's *Lalla-Roukh*, "German" opera in two acts, was produced in Dresden in March, 1863, and afterwards, recast as *Feramors* in three acts, produced at Vienna in 1872. There also exists a *Lalla Roukh. Divertissement mêlé de chants et de danses*, as staged at the "château royal, Berlin" in 1822. As for the piracy, according to the *Observer*, November 5, 1837, Longmans compelled Raymond Perceval and Charles Smith, proprietors of the weekly *Ladies Newspaper*, publicly to advertise their piracy of "Paradise and the Peri."

Notes to Chapter IX

1. Nicholas Michell, *Living Poets and Poetesses: A Biographical and Critical Poem* (London, 1832). The description of Moore occupies pp. 79-82. Hall's *A Memory of Thomas Moore*, already cited, contains the best description of Sloperton. Mulvaney's poem is found in a blank book in the British Museum, Add. MSS. 41,260.

2. A. G. Bradley, *Round About Wiltshire* (New York and London, 1907), pp. 161-78, describes the neighborhood and records some local legends.

3. On Bowles see Garland Greever's rather unsatisfactory *A Wiltshire Parson and His Friends* (London, 1926). Bremhill is interestingly described in *The Gentleman's Magazine Library: English Topography*, Part XIII (ed. F. A. Milne, London, 1901), pp. 211-15. The vicarage and the church are little changed, though some of the inscriptions have disappeared. I owe to the courtesy of the Rev. Arthur E. G. Peters the pleasure of inspecting both the house and the church, as well as the reference to the *Memoir of Charles Mayne Young, Tragedian, with extracts from his son's*

Journal, by *Julian Charles Young* (London and New York, 1871), from which the anecdote of Bowles at Bowood is taken (pp. 225-26).

4. "Lines on a Late Display in the —— of ——" appeared, as later indicated in the text, in *The Fudge Family in Paris*, but was not collected into Moore's *Poetical Works*. In the same volume Moore reprinted some, but not all, of his *Chronicle* contributions. The "Epistle from Tom Crib to Big Ben" was printed in the *Chronicle* August 31, 1815, and is an assault on the Regent for not giving Napoleon sanctuary in England. "Fum and Hum, the Two Birds of Royalty" appeared February 8, 1816, and "To Sir Hudson Lowe" October 3, 1818. Moore was one of the earliest to attack the governor of St. Helena:

> Sir Hudson Lowe, Sir Hudson *Low*,
> (By name, and ah! by nature so).

5. The *Yellow Dwarf*, April 25, 1818, p. 132 (the review may be Hazlitt's); the *Monthly Review*, Vol. LXXXV, pp. 426-32; the *European Magazine*, Vol. LXXIII, pp. 516-19; the *New Monthly Magazine*, Vol. XLV, pp. 342-44; the *British Critic*, 2d series, Vol. IX, pp. 496-500; the *Literary Gazette*, April 20, 1818, December 5, 1818, and September 11, 1819; *Blackwoods Magazine*, Vol. III, pp. 129-36. The *New Whig Guide* shows the desire of the Tories to retaliate in the lighter forms of satire. The quotation from the *Literary Chronicle* is from the issue of August 14, 1819, pp. 199 ff. Among other replies and parodies may be listed *The Cheltenham Mail Bag; or, Letters from Gloucestershire, edited by Peter Quince, the Younger* (London, 1820); *Fudge in Ireland* (London, 1822), and *Bath* (a "satirical novel") by Thomas Brown, the Elder (London, 1818). The later quotation from the *Anti-Jacobin Review*, Vol. LV, pp. 270-71, is but one of many; see, for example, Vol. LVIII *passim*; on pp. 313 ff. the *Irish Melodies* are characterized as "strains of sedition and bigotry." The Rev. John Graham produced a poem, "God's Revenge against Rebellion," in the same magazine (pp. 231-34) attacking Moore for his "licentious song," which, it appears, Irish peasants sing "in midnight orgies over Freedom's Grave." The reference to the *Literary Gazette* is to the issue for September 4, 1819, p. 570.

6. There is a detailed account of the banquet in James Burke, *The Life of Thomas Moore* (Dublin, 1852).

7. From the article by Charles Cox in the *Athenaeum* already cited.

8. *Morning Chronicle*, October 5, 1818; *Quarterly Musical Magazine and Review*, Vol. I, pp. 264-67. See also the *Monthly Review*, Vol. LXXXVII, pp. 419-33.

9. *Literary Panorama*, n.s., Vol. IX, pp. 686-88; *Literary Gazette*, March 13, 1819.

Notes to Chapter X

1. *Moore's Letters to Power*, p. 77.

2. *Ibid.*, p. 82.

3. On February 27, 1821, the *Morning Chronicle* had printed some "Stanzas to Naples" signed "T. B.," which, however, are apparently not Moore's.

4. *Moore's Letters to Power*, p. 83. He makes the same complaint repeatedly in other letters to Power.

5. On Irving's relation to, and opinions of, Moore, see Pierre M. Irving, *Life and Letters of Washington Irving*, 4 vols. (New York, 1862-64); and Stanley T. Williams, *The Life of Washington Irving*, 2 vols. (New York and London, 1935), index *sub* Moore in each case.

6. *Moore's Letters to Power*, p. 83.

7. The *Literary Chronicle*, December 28, 1822, pp. 817-19; the *Literary Gazette*, December 28, 1822, pp. 815 ff.; the *London Museum*, December 28, 1822, Vol. I, pp. 561-62.

8. *John Bull*, June 27, July 22, September 30, November 18, November 25, 1821; January 6, 13, 20, February 3, 1822. The review of *Loves of the Angels* appears in the issues of January 5 and 12, 1823. *The Loves of the Angels*, a "Romantic mythological and musical drama," by the way, was produced in London in 1835.

9. *Blackwoods Magazine*, Vol. III, pp. 63-71; *London Magazine*, Vol. VII, pp. 212-15; *New Monthly Magazine*, Vol. IX, n.s., pp. 74-75; the *Monthly Censor*, Vol. II, pp. 335-41; the *Monthly Magazine*, Vol. LV, pp. 35-39; the *Monthly Review*, Vol. C, pp. 79-95; the *European Magazine*, Vol. 83, pp. 256-59. The *British Critic*, Vol. XIX, 2d s., pp. 636-46, reviewed the *Fables for the Holy Alliance* and *The Loves of the Angels* together unfavorably. There were other reviews, but these are representative.

10. *Westminster Review*, Vol. I, pp. 18-26. This review is important as marking the tone of the rising generation, full of "new seriousness," towards so characteristic a Regency figure as Moore.

11. *Literary Gazette*, May 10, 23, pp. 289 ff. See also the *Literary Chronicle*, May 10, 1823, pp. 289 ff.; *Blackwoods*, Vol. XIII, pp. 574-79; and the *Ladies Monthly Museum*, Vol. XVIII, pp. 101-2, for representative notices.

Notes to Chapter XI

1. Spencer Walpole, *A History of England from the Conclusion of the Great War in 1815* (London, 1890), Vol. I, p. 294.

2. *Memoirs of Captain Rock*, p. 19. Moore says the volume was published April 9, 1824, but the newspaper notices show it was published on April 17.

3. *Ibid.*, pp. viii, 4, 20, 32-33, 121-22, 141, 161, 165, 250-51. As the volume is rare, it may not be amiss to quote Moore's tribute to the idols of his youth: "When I [i.e., Captain Rock] contemplated such a man as the venerable Charlemont, whose nobility was to the people, like a fort over a valley—elevated above them solely for their defence; who introduced the polish of the courtier into the camp of the freeman, and served his country with all that pure, Platonic devotion, which a true knight in the times of chivalry proffered to his mistress;—when I listened to the eloquence of Grattan, the very music of Freedom—her first, fresh matin song, after a long night of slavery, degradation and sorrow;—when I saw the bright offerings which he brought to the shrine of his country, wisdom, genius, courage, and patience, invigorated and embellished by all those social and domestic virtues, without which the loftiest talents stand isolated in the moral waste around them, like the pillars of Palmyra towering in a wilderness;—when I reflected on all this, it not only disheartened me for the mission of discord which I had undertaken, but made me secretly hope that it might be rendered unnecessary; and that a country, which could produce such men and achieve such a revolution, might yet, in spite of the joint efforts of the Government and my family, take her rank in the scale of nations, and be happy!" (pp. 236-37.) It will, of course, be remembered that the Rock family are ironically pictured as thriving only in times of discord.

4. *Westminster Review*, Vol. I, pp. 492-504; *Metropolitan Literary Journal*, Vol. I, pp. 145-48.

5. The *New Monthly Magazine*, Vol. XII, n.s., p. 216; *London Magazine*, Vol. IX, pp. 583-98; the *Literary Chronicle*, April 17, 1824, pp. 241-44. The *Westminster* review has been noted above. Typical of the hostile reviews are the *British Review*, Vol. XXII, pp. 419 ff., which, though it called him "deservedly eminent on account of the genius, talents, and literary accomplishments" he had, said the tendency of his writing was corrupting; and the *British Critic*, Vol. XXI, 2d s., pp. 421-33, which, in an amusing review, accused him of plagiarizing from his own poetry, said the style was "precisely that of a leader of rebel banditti," and characterized the substance of the book as filled with self-contradictions, inconsistencies, savage malevolence, disgraceful ignorance, and willful falsehoods.

A notice marked at once by critical penetration and naïveté appeared in *The Man of Letters*, April 17, 1824, pp. 33-36, which said that the little-ness of the man led the public to expect little books from him, remarked the polish of his prose, and on the one hand paid tribute to the knowledge and warmth of the volume, and on the other, thought its tendency was damaging. There were other reviews, as Moore notes in his journal, but these are representative.

6. *Captain Rock Detected* appeared from the house of Cadell in 1824 and is an able volume. Moore and O'Sullivan crossed swords a number of times thereafter, and since O'Sullivan was a convert from Catholicism to Protestantism, this fact may have given venom to some of Moore's retorts. There is a biographical sketch of O'Sullivan in the *Dictionary of National Biography*. Reviewing O'Sullivan's publication, the *British Critic* (Vol. XXII, 2d s., pp. 317-33) pretended that Moore was too honest to have written the original *Captain Rock*, but presently abandoned this attitude, and concluded: "So much for Thomas Moore! Lord Byron himself never made him appear so ridiculous, and if the Munster Farmer does not suffer the quondam fate of Mr. Jeffery [*sic*] the valour of the 'little lion' must be of the coolest and most gentlemanlike character. We hate personali-ties, but no writer of the day has been so offensively personal as Mr. Moore . . ."

In this connection it may be noted that a periodical, *Captain Rock in London, or, the Chieftain's Gazette*, began publication in London March 5, 1825, and apparently died December 16, 1826.

7. After Moore's death the *Dublin University Magazine* (Vol. XLI, pp. 632 ff.) said in 1853 that some of Moore's information came from John Scully, Moore's brother-in-law, who had been nearly killed by miscreants in Tipperary, and from Joseph Abbott, an Irish barrister of note; that in consequence of the publicity given the practice of Irish sheriffs in recover-ing debts, Mr. Abbott was summoned before committees of Parliament in 1824, and that the law was changed. On Moore's intimacy with Abbott, consult the index to the *Memoirs, Journal, and Correspondence*.

8. The primary sources of information for the story of the burning of Byron's memoirs are Moore's *Memoirs, Journal, and Correspondence*, espe-cially Vol. IV, pp. 186 ff. (Lord John Russell unfortunately "omitted . . . a long account" of the destruction, but apparently did not tamper with the journal entries); Moore's *Life of Byron*, the concluding pages; "Narra-tive of Events connected with the destruction of Lord Byron's Memoirs" in John Cam Hobhouse (Lord Broughton), *Recollections of a Long Life* (London, 1910), Vol. III, pp. 327-62; Samuel Smiles, *A Publisher and His Friends: Memoir and Correspondence of the late John Murray* (London, 1891), Vol. I, chapter xvii; and Murray's letter to Horton, May 19, 1824, in the appendix to the English translation of Elze's *Life of Byron* (London, 1872), reprinted from the *Quarterly Review*, Vol. XCIII, pp. 311-14. I have principally followed Hobhouse and have considerably simplified the narrative, I hope without essential injustice to the actors. The best modern account is probably that of Ethel Colburn Mayne, *Byron* (London, 1912, 1924), Vol. II, Appendix ii. It may be true, as Miss Mayne remarks, that Moore's assumption of an "attitude of magnanimity and sacrifice . . . was wholly unsanctioned by the facts"; yet, had he desired, he could have

created an embarrassing situation for the Byron family. It is unfortunate that Moore permitted himself such expressions as: "were I again placed in the same circumstances, I would—even at ten times the pecuniary sacrifice . . . again act precisely in the same manner," since his actual pecuniary sacrifice was small.

9. My attention has been called to a curious little puzzle in connection with the Byron memoirs, which involves Washington Irving. The manuscript and the copy were, as we have seen, destroyed on May 17, 1824. On June 17, 1824, Irving was visiting Moore at Sloperton and says that he sat up late reading Byron's memoirs! (*Journal* for this date; and see Stanley Williams, *The Life of Washington Irving*, New York and London, 1935, Vol. I, p. 260.) As there is no reason for questioning Moore's good faith in his signed statement that no copy of the memoirs survived, I assume that what Irving read was Byron's "Journal," which Moore published in the *Life*. Irving's reference to "memoirs" may easily be a slip for "journal."

10. Clayden, *Rogers and His Contemporaries*, p. 378.

Notes to Chapter XII

1. Typical of the unkinder cuts was the treatment Moore received from the notorious *John Bull*. On May 23, 1824, this paper published an account of the destruction of the memoirs which said that Murray's conduct was honorable, that Moore had kept the money, and that two or three copies of the memoirs were still at large. On May 30 it printed Moore's explanatory letter to the newspapers, but added that Mrs. Leigh had forced him to surrender the work and that "high and grand as Mr. MOORE'S feelings may be represented by himself, there can be no doubt but that his regret at losing the two thousand pounds is not diminished." As part of its general campaign this paper also published on September 12 an article accusing Moore of having plagiarized *Anacreon* from a number of sources, including a translation by George Ogle, which, as a matter of fact, Moore had never seen.

2. Croker was instrumental in enlisting Moore's aid in the founding of the Athenaeum. He wrote him December 13, 1823, enclosing a prospectus and suggesting Lord Lansdowne as a member. Ten days later he wrote, throwing an amusing light on the project: "Our Club must consist of individual bores—no doubt—that is as generic a designation of individual men as homo—but we hope that by *mingling the bores*, we may, like the chemists and painters [,] produce from separate acids shades or harshnesses, an agreeable result." The letter concludes: "For myself I have no object but to afford an Asylum to those whom the new fashioned Clubs

have left upon the Town in a very different situation from that in which men of letters and artists were ten years ago." From the Croker papers in the William L. Clements Library.

3. For the fifth edition, in two volumes, published in 1827, Moore wrote a preface defending himself against three specific charges of inaccuracy.

4. London, 1931, p. 8. I find it difficult to follow Mr. Butler in such reckless statements as that Moore's "treacherous attitude . . . is apparent throughout the book" (p. 11) and that "Moore had furnished a specimen of the subtle treachery of his race . . ." (p. 18). The curious may consult the opinions of other biographers of Sheridan, which vary from Mrs. Oliphant's uncritical praise to the complaint of the Marquess of Dufferin and Ava (Sheridan's great-grandson) that Moore is "somewhat ungenerous and subacid." Inevitably, modern research has corrected a number of errors of omission and commission in Moore, but it is noticeable that every subsequent biographer depends to a greater or less degree upon this much abused life.

5. *Westminster Review*, Vol. IV, pp. 371-407; *British Critic*, 3d s., Vol. I, pp. 436-52; *Monthly Review*, Vol. CVIII, pp. 149-62; *Blackwoods Magazine*, Vol. XIX, pp. 113-30; *Quarterly Review*, Vol. XXXIII, pp. 561-93. The last two notices did not appear until 1826.

6. *Edinburgh Review*, Vol. LXXXIX, pp. 1-48 (December, 1826!); *European Magazine*, n.s., Vol. I, pp. 295-300 (this review, which is signed "G.," is very able); *Literary Chronicle*, October 8, 1825, pp. 641-50; *Metropolitan Quarterly Magazine*, Vol. I, pp. 203-55; *Literary Gazette*, October 8, 1825, pp. 641 ff. There were other reviews.

7. Scott's letter to Moore may be found in Lockhart's *Memoirs of the Life of Sir Walter Scott, Bart.* (Edinburgh and London, 1837), Vol. VI, pp. 73-74. For Lockhart's account of the visit, containing the phrases quoted in the text, see pp. 90-95. For the Scott-Lockhart correspondence about Lockhart's review see the *Private Letter-Books of Sir Walter Scott*, pp. 144, 146-47. Sir Walter's opinion of Moore may be read in his diary in Lockhart, pp. 128-29.

8. Lockhart, p. 95.

9. Moore's contributions to the *Times* were either unsigned or have the signatures "S" (sometimes a Greek sigma) or (very rarely) "B." The poems quoted in the text appeared as follows: "All in the Family Way," April 14, 1826; "Epitaph on a Tuft-Hunter," August 17, 1826; "Ode to a Hat," August 21, 1826; "The Petition of the Orangemen of Ireland," August 24, 1826; "A Vision by the Author of Christabel," August 29, 1826, reprinted in the *Morning Chronicle* August 30; "The Slave" (retitled in the collected poems, "The Irish Slave"), January 11, 1827.

10. The poem on Hunt, entitled "Ode to Sir T—S L-THB—GE," (Sir Thomas Lethbridge) was printed in the *Times* June 26, 1826, and is the poem referred to in Russell, V:87. "Lord Eldon," which can only be by Moore, was printed May 9, 1827.

11. The first two lines on Wellington are from a poem, or rather series of satiric portraits, entitled "Sortes Virgilianæ," printed in the *Times* April 17, 1827, which I attribute to Moore, though they are not in his usual style. The second is from a similarly uncollected poem, "The Witch's Sabbath—a Fragment," published March 13, 1827, which is almost

certainly his. One must, however, recognize the danger of too casual attribution; the "Soliloquy of a Decorous and Very Pure Statesman," a droll piece of irony at the expense of Peel, which concludes with a bitter reference to Croker, I thought to be Moore's until his express disclaimer of the poem (Russell, V:162-63) undeceived me. As Lady Jersey wrote him: "what other living poet could have written them?"

12. *Ladies Monthly Museum*, Vol. XXVI, pp. 107-8; *Lady's Magazine*, n.s., Vol. VIII, pp. 381-85; *Christian Examiner*, February, 1828, pp. 108 ff.; *Westminster Review*, Vol. VIII, pp. 351-84. This was Peacock's first full-dress attack on Moore. For an interesting discussion of Peacock's criticisms of the poet see Jean-Jacques Mayoux, *Un Epicurean Anglais: Thomas Love Peacock* (Paris, 1933). There were, of course, many other reviews, some of which Moore notes in his journal. See also *Literary Chronicle*, August 4, 1827, pp. 484-85; *Repository of Arts, Literature*, etc., Vol. X, p. 166; *Blackwoods Magazine*, Vol. XXII, pp. 374-402 (*Blackwoods* found the work dull); *Arliss' Pocket Magazine*, n.s., Vol. VII, pp. 157-65; *Ladies Monthly Museum* (second notice), imp. series, Vol. XXVII, pp. 242-44; *The Citizen* (Dublin), Vol. I, pp. 84 ff., etc., etc.

13. The Huntington Library possesses (1) a notebook of 63 sheets and, of course, the two inside covers, labeled "Epicurean," in which Moore assembled notes from his reading and drafts of his manuscript. He carried the story forward on the recto of sheets 4-30, and the verso of these pages is given over to corrections and to notes from his reading. The narrative picks up again on sheets 32-49; then on sheets 51-54; after which it is necessary to turn the book upside down and read backward to 63. It also possesses (2) a manuscript of 255 faded blue pages, which are a fair copy of part of the novel. In the Pierpont Morgan Library there is (3) a manuscript of 104 pages, consisting of notes, memoranda, and an original draft of a small portion of *The Epicurean*.

14. On the bibliographical puzzle presented by "Alciphron" in relation to *The Epicurean*, see the MacManus bibliography already cited. The 1900 re-issue of *The Epicurean* was published in London by Greening and Company, illustrated by Will Smart, with an introduction by Justin Hannaford. There was also an American edition, New York, 1875.

Notes to Chapter XIII

1. Griffin's account is reprinted in Russell, I:xxxii-xxxiv, with which Moore's own account may be compared in Russell, VI:301 ff. Russell also incorrectly extracts Willis' account, which follows his version of Griffin's visit. The original may be seen in *Pencillings by the Way* (Auburn and Rochester, 1854), pp. 510-13, 517-26. Willis' accuracy may be gauged

from the fact that he makes Moore an official in Jamaica, and calls him a lover of Lady Blessington when she was sixteen. There is no record of any amatory passage between Moore and this lady, who, at sixteen, had just entered upon the first year of her unhappy marriage with Captain Farmer. As for the account Willis gives of Moore's conversation, it is expressly contradicted by the latter in Russell, VII:130-31.

2. Kinnaird to Moore, February 28, 1828: I "am not aware that I could in any manner render you service in your undertaking. You have correctly divin'd the view I take of what is call'd for on the part of Byron's friends in consequence of the use to which all sorts of persons have turn'd the intercourse they may have had with him . . . If on the one hand Mr. Hunt's evident motives disqualify him from being a competent authority to judge of Lord B's character, the pen of a friend must be supposed to lie under an equal disqualification for fixing public opinion." British Museum, Add. MSS. 36,464, folio 260 (Hobhouse papers). Moore's disgust with Hunt was so great as to lead him to publish in the *Times* his "The 'Living Dog' and 'The Dead Lion'" after reading Hunt's book. This severe castigation of Moore's former friend (which may be read in the *Poetical Works*) was rather feebly answered by Hunt, or one of his friends, in "The Giant and the Dwarf," which may be found in Prothero's *Letters and Journals* of Byron, Vol. II (London, 1898), pp. 461-62. The latter poem is full of inaccuracies.

3. Kinnaird, of course, died before Moore's *Byron* appeared.

4. Moore to Lord Lansdowne, August 14, 1829. The letter is in the Bowood collection.

5. Moore to Murray, March 20, 1829. The letter is in Sir John Murray's collection.

6. Moore's letters to Murray, which have been curiously neglected in discussions of the biography and which are preserved in Sir John Murray's collection, throw considerable light upon the character of Moore's suppressions and Murray's editorial principles. Moore writes on December 8, 1829: "I am getting on very well, having satisfied myself with respect to the Italian Loves, by omitting the whole of the letter about Angelica (making a love the less) and transferring the long account of Margarita from the place of its date (where it jars with our Guiccioli Romance) to an earlier period where it chimes in with his dissolute course of life, and thus keeps the character of each epoch more consistently." On December 17 Moore acknowledges a letter from Murray in which the latter had apparently raised some objection to what Moore calls the plenitude of the abomination of Byron's verses to Lady Jersey, which accordingly came out. On January 24, 1830, Moore writes that "some of my qualms respecting those plaguey Italian loves have returned," and suggests a conference among Lockhart, Murray, and himself, and the next day is of opinion that "the suppression of some of the details in his long letter about the Fornarina" will suffice. On April 14 he writes agreeing to most of Murray's deletions in the proof except about La Guiccioli, and imploring Murray not to spare surplusage and dullness, for, says Moore, I am "too superstitiously fond of every line of his to do justice in this way."

7. Moore to Murray, August 6, 1830. In Sir John Murray's collection.

8. Lord Broughton, *Recollections of a Long Life* (London, 1910), Vol.

IV, under date of January 15, 1830, and January 31, 1831. Hobhouse remarked that Moore was most at fault in attributing Byron's "singularities" to his college days, and says that he had "nothing to learn" after Harrow and "his Southwell recreations," but as he prides himself on not having contributed to the work, Moore can scarcely be blamed for not including what Hobhouse did not tell him. The second entry concludes with a sneer at Moore for putting thirty-five hundred pounds in his pocket as profits from the book. On May 27, 1831, Moore wrote Murray that "all I have heard and read upon the subject (receiving letters as I do from all quarters—almost of the globe—about it) convinces me that the result of the work has been to raise considerably the average estimate of our friend's personal character."

9. For Prothero's discussion of Moore as an editor see the prefaces to Vols. I and II of the *Letters and Journals*.

10. The *Morning Chronicle* published extracts from Vol. I on January 14, 15, 16 before the official date of the appearance of the book; on March 22 it printed Lady Byron's letter to Moore; and on April 1 it printed almost two columns from Campbell's review in the *New Monthly* (see note 12). The *Times* also noticed the book at length. For the other reviews mentioned in this paragraph of the text see the *Literary Gazette*, January 1, 1830, pp. 33-40; the *Lady's Magazine*, imp. ser., Vol. I, pp. 20-25; the *Ladies Museum*, Vol. I, pp. 107-10; *Blackwoods Magazine*, Vol. XXVII, pp. 389-420, and (Part 2), pp. 420-54 (largely a summary of Byron's life); the *Monthly Review*, n.s., Vol. XIII, pp. 217-37; the *Monthly Magazine*, n.s., Vol. IX, pp. 183-97. This magazine noticed the second volume (n.s., Vol. XI, pp. 145-59) less favorably. A review in the *Dublin Literary Gazette*, January 23, 1830, pp. 51 ff., interesting as reflecting Irish opinion, is highly laudatory. Macaulay's essay is readily available.

11. *Westminster Review*, Vol. XII, pp. 269-304.

12. *New Monthly Magazine*, Vol. XXVIII, pp. 377-82; Vol. XXX, pp. 94-95. On Lady Byron and Campbell see Ethel Colburn Mayne, *The Life and Letters of Anne Isabella, Lady Noel Byron* (London, 1929), pp. 319 ff. Moore says (Russell, VI:113) that on April 1, 1830, Lord Melbourne showed him a letter of Lady Byron's expressing regret at Campbell's "injudiciousness." His relations with Campbell continued to be friendly: in June, 1832, declining the editorship of the *Metropolitan*, he wrote Marryat that "though I should consider it an honour to *succeed* Campbell, I could not possibly think of *supplanting* him" (Russell, VI:275). See in this connection William Beattie, *Life and Letters of Thomas Campbell*, 3 vols. (London, 1849), especially Vol. II.

13. *New Monthly Magazine*, Vol. XXXI, pp. 159-64. This is apparently not by Campbell.

14. Moore to Murray, January 15, 1830, in Sir John Murray's collection.

15. *National Omnibus*, January 1, 1831, p. 5. But this periodical was highly favorable to Moore's edition of Byron (January 6, June 8, 1832). The *Critic*, April, 1832, pp. 49 ff.; and May, 1832, pp. 177 ff.; *Quarterly Review*, Vol. XLIV, pp. 168-226.

16. Moore to Murray, October 25, 1831, in Sir John Murray's collection. See also Russell, VI:234.

17. Moore's relations with Murray may be studied from the side of the

publisher in Smiles, *A Publisher and His Friends,* Vol. II, chap. xxx. It was
at Murray's request that Lawrence painted his portrait of Moore.

18. *Blackwoods,* Vol. XXX, pp. 631-46; *Quarterly Review,* Vol. XLVI,
pp. 213-63; *Westminster Review,* Vol. XVI, pp. 110-21. Other characteristic notices may be found in the *Mirror,* Vol. XVIII, pp. 122-26; and
the *Literary Gazette,* July 30, 1831, pp. 481 ff.

Notes to Chapter XIV

1. The stanza on Wellington is from "Advertisement," printed in the
Times November 15, 1830. Moore's statement about Wellington's being a
Turk appears in a letter to the Rev. John Guthrie, October 18, 1828, in
the Lord John Russell papers, Public Records Office. "From the Hon.
Henry ——, to Lady Emma ——" appeared in the *Times* April 9, 1832.

2. The first two quotations are from *The Summer Fête;* the third is
from "Tory Pledges" (*Times,* August 30, 1832); the fourth, from "Fools'
Paradise" (*Times,* May 8, 1832).

3. Moore to Lansdowne, December 7, 1830. In the Bowood collection.

4. Edward Raleigh Moran, whose intimacy with Moore begins about
1830, collected five volumes of clippings and manuscripts towards a life of
Moore which was never written. These are now in the British Museum.
They are especially valuable for the study of Moore's reputation in the
thirties. The quotation from O'Connell is from Vol. I of these manuscripts.

5. From *An Address to the Young Men of Ireland* (London, 1835), p.
26. In the Moran MSS.

6. *Dublin Evening Mail,* May 24, 1837, from a clipping in the Moran
MSS.; *Dublin Penny Journal,* Vol. I, p. 42, April 13, 1833. An unidentifiable clipping in the Moran MSS. (Vol. III, 2151) says that the ninth
number of the *Melodies* is "the most Irish part of that national work,"
and finds a correlation between nine of the songs and Moore's visit to
Ireland. The *Dublin University Magazine,* reviewing Hardiman's *Irish
Minstrelsy* in August, 1834 (p. 153), thought that Moore combined the
most delightful attributes of the music of a rude age and of the poetry
of a refined one.

7. *Dublin Evening Post,* August 11, 1835. From a clipping in the Moran
MSS.; and see Russell, VII:98-99.

8. I have compounded this description of Moore's visit to Bannow from
his own detailed account (Russell, VII:109-20) and a clipping from the
Wexford Independent, preserved in the Moran MSS. Russell persistently
refers to Mr. Boyse's house as "Graigue House," but the *Independent*
prints "Grange." There is also an account of his 1838 reception in the

Moran MSS., but see Russell, VII:233-35. He was selected by the manager of the theater as the official patron of a performance of "The Man about Town," "Charles the Twelfth," and "Robert Macaire."

9. Moore's correspondence can be followed in the Moran MSS., which also contain the summary of O'Connell's remarks, already quoted.

10. Moore's speech, as corrected from proof and sent to Moran, is in the Moran MSS., and should be studied at length for an understanding of his politics.

11. The *Times,* November 24, 1837. Similar accounts in other London papers may be found in the Moran MSS.

12. Clippings from the newspapers of August-September, 1835, and November-December, 1837, show how widespread and virulent was the discussion of Moore's pension.

13. The poems from which these quotations are taken are in the *Poetical Works* and appeared as follows: "Song of the Departing Spirit of Tithe," *Metropolitan Magazine,* September, 1832, reprinted in the *Times,* August 31, 1832; "Resolutions Passed at a Late Meeting of Reverends and Right Reverends," *Times,* February 24, 1834; "The Dance of Bishops," *Times,* July 18, 1833 (wrongly dated 1838 in the *Poetical Works*); "Anticipated Meeting of the British Association in the Year 2836," *Morning Chronicle,* September 8, 1836.

14. The first quotation in this paragraph is from an uncollected poem, "Some Account of a New Genus of Churchman Called the Phill-pot," *Morning Chronicle,* October 26, 1838; the second appeared in the same paper June 19, 1839; the third, untitled and signed "B," Moore's usual signature in the *Chronicle,* appeared December 3, 1839. It opened a series of vituperative attacks, all signed "B": "The Dream Explained," December 12, 1839; "An Episcopal Address on Socialism," January 28, 1840; "Another Speech from Henry of Exter," February 13, 1840; an untitled poem occasioned by a gift of a Bible to the bishop, February 18, 1840; "The Bishop and the Bible," February 24, 1840; "Mother Church and Mother Kirk," April 17, 1840. Each is signed "B" and is certainly Moore's. "An Episcopal Address on Socialism" is worth quotation:

> He wished of his task he could be rid,
> For he felt a horror—indeed he did—
> Yet had seen and heard with profound disgust
> The deeds of shame and the words of lust;
> And was able to tell them all, he said,
> The nauseous tale, from A to Z.
> And he thought the Marquess of Normanby
> Might relish the tale as well as he.
>   The Socialists were the vilest race
> That ever on earth or hell had place!
> He would not prejudge them—no! not he!
> For his soul overflowed with charity.
> Incarnate fiends! he would not condemn—
> No! God forbid he should slander them!
> Foul swine! their lordships must confess
> He judged them with Christian gentleness!

He hated all show of persecution—
Why were they not sent to execution?
To hasty censures he objected—
(But was not Lord Normanby suspected?).
He never believed a rash report—
(But who took Robert Owen to court?).
He would not call Owen a bloody man—
(But he wrote in words of blood his plan).
He would not offend, but would fain be knowing
If Normanby was not as loose as Owen?
And would ask—nought meaning by the hint—
Did he believe in God?—for Owen didn't.

15. The poem on Southey, "Announcement of a New Thalaba," appeared in the *Morning Chronicle*, October 22, 1836; "The Boy Statesman," July 16, 1836; the poem in which Stanley is pictured as a thief is "Police Reports," *Chronicle*, March 8, 1836; "Thoughts on Mischief," May 2, 1840. These are in the *Poetical Works*, as is "A Character," which was first printed as "Portrait of Lord Stanley" in the *Times* June 24, 1834, and reprinted in the *Chronicle* twice—February 11, 1836, and May 25, 1840. The uncollected poems in which Stanley is caricatured are "A Dream on Friday Night, June 14," already quoted, from the *Chronicle*, June 19, 1839, in which Stanley wars on all mankind; the "Rosinante" poem, "Account of an Extraordinary Dream," June 5, 1840; "The Retreat of the Scorpion," July 16, 1840; and "The Farewell to Lord Stanley," July 18, 1836. None of these is signed, but they are indubitably Moore's. The manuscripts of the "Account of an Extraordinary Dream" and of "A Threnody on the Approaching Demise of Old Mother Corn-Law," mentioned below, are now in the Huntington Library.

16. In addition to the satires on the Corn Laws which may be read in the *Poetical Works*, Moore published a string of uncollected poems in the *Chronicle:* "The Reign of the Wrongheads—A Dream," August 4, 1841; "Corn-Law Visions," November 2, 1841, and a sequel by the same title, December 2, 1841; "A Threnody on the Approaching Demise of Old Mother Corn-Law," February 23, 1842. These by no means conclude the number of his uncollected satires.

17. For characteristic reviews of the *Travels of an Irish Gentleman* see *Christian Examiner*, Vol. II, pp. 364-69, 420-33, 495 ff., 571 ff., 936 ff., *Dublin University Magazine*, Vol. II, pp. 101 ff.; *Westminster Review*, Vol. XXV (volume three of the *London and Westminster Review*), pp. 425-49; *British Magazine and Monthly Register*, Vol. III, pp. 690-91. There is an interesting review in an unidentifiable clipping in the Moran MSS., Vol. V.

18. O'Sullivan's attack on Moore's hypocrisy may be found on p. 272 of his work. White's may be found on pages six and seven of his first volume. There were other replies; for example, six letters addressed to the editor of the *British Magazine*, reviewed in the *British Magazine and Monthly Register*, Vol. V, p. 328.

19. The *Times*, August 7, 1835; the *Literary Gazette*, August 8, 1835; the *Courier*, August 7, 1835; the *Dublin Freeman's Journal*, August 10, 1835;

the *Court Journal*, August 8, 1835; the *Mirror*, Vol. XXVI, pp. 126-28; the *Westminster Review*, Vol. XXIV, pp. 79-92; the *Dublin University Magazine*, Vol. VI, pp. 297-305. This last is one of the most vicious personal attacks made on Moore. A dispatch to the *Calcutta Literary Gazette*, dated from London, February 7, 1836, and found in the Moran MSS., says that O'Sullivan made use of information which he had gained in private intercourse with Moore's family for his attack on the poet in his *Guide to an Irish Gentleman*, and that Moore despised him not merely for being a renegade Catholic, but also for this reason.

20. O'Sullivan's speech as reported in the *Standard* may be found in a clipping in the Moran MSS., which also contain the editorial from the *Morning Herald* of September 18, 1835.

Notes to Chapter XV

1. *Christian Examiner*, Vol. IV, pp. 381 ff., and 483 ff.; *London and Westminster Review*, Vol. XXV, p. 240; *British Magazine and Monthly Register*, Vol. VIII, pp. 651-53 (Vol. IX contains some letters from correspondents complaining of Dr. Lardner for letting Moore's "lucubrations go forth under the name of 'history'"); *Tait's Edinburgh Magazine*, May, 1835 (clipping in the Moran MSS.); *Spectator*, Vol. I, May 20, 1837; *Dublin University Magazine*, Vol. V, pp. 613-29; *Dublin Penny Journal*, Vol. IV, pp. 2-4; *Belfast News Letter* (clipping in the Moran MSS.). There are a number of other reviews among the Moran MSS.

2. Moran collected a great mass of clippings of reviews of the *Poetical Works* from which I quote, but it would be merely tedious to list the publications in question here. The passage from the *Monthly Chronicle* may be found in Vol. VI, p. 503.

3. Young Moore's difficulties in Belfast may be traced in clippings in the Moran MSS. The *Northern Whig* denied that the young officer had insulted anybody.

4. From an unidentifiable Bombay paper, May(?) 22, 1840, in the Moran MSS.

5. T. C. Croker to J. W. Croker, May 30, 1853; Clayden, *Rogers and His Contemporaries*, p. 403; Bessy Moore to Mrs. Hall, in S. C. Hall, *A Memory of Thomas Moore*.

6. *Morning Chronicle*, February 28, 1852; Clayden, *loc. cit.*

7. *Devizes and Wiltshire Gazette*, March 4, 1852; *The Wiltshire Independent*, March 4, 1852.

8. Bessy Moore to Lord John Russell, no date, from the collection of letters kindly loaned to me by Bertrand Russell. Others of Bessy Moore's

letters are among the Lord John Russell papers in the Public Records Office.

9. The Croker-Russell correspondence is among the Lord John Russell papers in the Public Records Office. Croker's pamphlet is entitled: *Correspondence between the Right Hon. J. W. Croker and the Right Hon. Lord John Russell on Some Passages of "Moore's Diary"* (London, John Murray, 1854). Croker's review is in the *Quarterly*, Vol. XCIII, pp. 239-310. This produced the anonymous pamphlet, *Remarks on the Right Hon. J. W. Croker's Review* . . . (London, 1855).

10. Characteristic reviews of part or all of the *Memoirs, Journal, and Correspondence* may be found in the *Westminster Review*, n.s., Vol. IV, pp. 165-77; the *Dublin Review*, Vol. XXXIV, pp. 104-39; *New Quarterly Review*, Vol. II, pp. 7-10, and pp. 321-25; Vol. III, pp. 153-59; Vol. V, pp. 298-306; *Dublin University Magazine*, Vol. XLI, pp. 95-111 *et passim; Blackwoods Magazine*, Vol. LXXIII, pp. 97-100, and LXXIV, pp. 519-20; *Literary Gazette*, 1852, 1853, and 1856 *passim; Irish Quarterly Review*, Vol. III, pp. 151 ff.

11. This paragraph is based on Bessy Moore's letters; on the pamphlet by S. C. Hall; and on the *Devizes and Wiltshire Gazette*, September 14, 1865.

12. *Lady Morgan's Memoirs: Autobiography, Diaries and Correspondence*, second edition, revised, 2 vols. (London, 1863), Vol. II, pp. 517, 538-40.

Index